The Translator

MICHAEL PALMA is the recipient of the Italo Calvino Award for his translation of *My Name on the Wind: Selected Poems of Diego Valeri* and of the Raiziss/de Palchi Translation Award from the American Academy of American Poets for his translation of *The Man I Pretend to Be: "The Colloquies" and Selected Poems of Guido Gozzano.* A poet in his own right, Palma has published three collections of verse, and his poetry has been anthologized in, among other publications, Penguin's *Unsettling America: An Anthology of Contemporary Multicultural Poetry.*

The Editor

GIUSEPPE MAZZOTTA is Sterling Professor of the Humanities for Italian at Yale University. He is president of the Dante Society of America (2003–09). He is the author of *Dante, Poet of the Desert: History and Allegory in the Divine Comedy* and *Dante's Vision and the Circle of Knowledge.*

A NORTON CRITICAL EDITION

Dante Alighieri
INFERNO

A NEW VERSE TRANSLATION
BACKGROUNDS AND CONTEXTS
CRITICISM

Translated by
MICHAEL PALMA

Edited by
GIUSEPPE MAZZOTTA
YALE UNIVERSITY

W. W. NORTON & COMPANY • *New York* • *London*

W. W. Norton & Company has been independent since its founding in 1923, when William Warder Norton and Mary D. Herter Norton first published lectures delivered at the People's Institute, the adult education division of New York City's Cooper Union. The Nortons soon expanded their program beyond the Institute, publishing books by celebrated academics from America and abroad. By mid-century, the two major pillars of Norton's publishing program—trade books and college texts—were firmly established. In the 1950s, the Norton family transferred control of the company to its employees, and today—with a staff of four hundred and a comparable number of trade, college, and professional titles published each year—W. W. Norton & Company stands as the largest and oldest publishing house owned wholly by its employees.

The text of this book is composed in Fairfield Medium
with the display set in Bernhard Modern.
Composition by Binghamton Valley Composition.
Drawn art by ElectraGraphics, Inc.
Manufacturing by the Maple-Vail Book Group, Binghamton.
Production manager: Benjamin Reynolds.

Library of Congress Cataloging-in-Publication Data

Dante Alighieri, 1265–1321.
[Inferno. English]
Inferno : a new verse translation, backgrounds and contexts, criticism / Dante Alighieri ; translated by Michael Palma ; edited by Giuseppe Mazzotta.
p. cm. — (A Norton critical edition)
Include bibliographical references.

ISBN-13: 978-0-393-97796-7 (pbk.)
ISBN-10: 0-393-97796-X (pbk.)

I. Palma, Michael, 1945– II. Mazzotta, Giuseppe, 1942– III. Title.

PQ4315.2.P27 2007
851'.1—dc22
2006046957

W. W. Norton & Company, Inc., 500 Fifth Avenue,
New York, N.Y. 10110-0017
www.wwnorton.com

W. W. Norton & Company Ltd., Castle House,
75/76 Wells Street, London W1T 3QT

3 4 5 6 7 8 9 0

Contents

Introduction

On March 10, 1302, the thirty-seven-year-old Dante, who while in Siena a few weeks earlier had been sentenced to exile, was permanently banished from his native Florence under pain of death. The exile, which lasted until he died in 1321, completely changed Dante's life and was the experience that turned Dante from a major Italian poet—the author of the autobiographical amorous-poetic *Vita nova* and a number of philosophical songs—into the major poet of the western tradition.

But in 1302 Dante probably did not understand exile as the spiritual, providential itinerary it became when he sat down to write *Inferno*. At that time it simply meant the loss of family, status, and security. Nothing was left to him and he could do nothing but begin walking the narrow and uncertain path—under the threat of getting lost—that would take him from one court of Northern Italy to another. He had at his disposal neither maps nor supplies, no guide or guideline to lead him, no fig-tree in the shade of which he could rest. What exactly caused his life to turn upside down?

The reversal of his fortune found Dante unprepared, but it was not sudden. Indeed, he had not lived a quiet, sheltered existence in his homeland before the bitter news of exile and threat of death hit him. The storm that caught him in the winter of 1302, while on an embassy to the pope on behalf of Florence, surprised him. Yet premonitions of danger had been everywhere. Since entering public life in 1295, he passed a harsh judgment against Pope Boniface VIII's political-financial interferences in Tuscany; he had spoken fiercely against the French king's connivance with the pope; he had denounced the ruthless political theater of Guelphs and Ghibellines (largely scheming bankers vying for control of the Church's money) that would on a daily basis and under any flimsy pretext plunge the city into anarchy; and he had no compunction, while serving as an executive officer of the city, to exile some of its prominent members, including even his friend and poet/philosopher Guido Cavalcanti.

The crossing of local and Church politics may account for the interruption of Dante's political plans and grand ambitions. Before that, the defining experience of his youth, was his childhood encounter with Beatrice, a Florentine girl who later married the wealthy banker Simone de' Bardi. When he saw her a second time, he had turned eighteen, and in his imagination she became the very incarnation of love and a sign of Providence. Even after her premature death in 1290 he cast her as star whose glow would not allow him to lose himself, and eventually she would play the role of a spirit-angel keeping watch over him. This love story is told in the *Vita nova*, the autobiographical story of Dante's double apprenticeship: in both poetry and love for Beatrice. These poems worked toward the poetic mode that would later be known as the *Sweet New Style*, a style that is adequate to Dante's refined love for Beatrice and records his inner life as well as his visionary experiences. By adopting the styles of the Provençal poets, of the Sicilian poets, of Guido Guinizelli and Guido Cavalcanti, he came to understand Beatrice as a unique, irreplaceable figure of love.

Beatrice's death brought some changes in his intellectual orientations. Till that point Dante had been schooled in the classics and in political rhetoric by Brunetto Latini, a cosmopolitan man of letters and statesman who had taken part in Florence's political life, had traveled through France, and was familiar with the philosophical debates unfolding in Europe. After 1290 Dante broadened his focus as he began his philosophical studies with the Franciscans and Dominicans. From the Dominicans, such as Remigio de' Girolami (who had been Thomas Aquinas's student in Paris) and who were housed in Santa Maria Novella, he learned the philosophical theology constructed by Aristotelian scholastics. Questions of ethics, politics, as well as larger issues, such as the legitimacy and limits of philosophy, and the necessity of theology figured in their training. And in the same Dominican circles he became familiar with the writings of the Averroists, radical Aristotelians who, like natural philosophers, denied the immortality of the soul and upheld the theory of the "double truth," the truth of faith and the truth of reason. On the other hand, from the Franciscans, such as Pierre Olivi, who had Joachistic leanings and who for a few years both gave homilies and taught in the Church of Santa Croce, he learned the theological basis for a critique of the Church, such as the one launched by the Franciscan "spirituals" (Ubertino da Casale). These ideas—the rhetorical Roman humanism of Brunetto Latini; the philosophical rigor of the Dominicans; and the moral-religious fervor and sense of reform of the Franciscans—shaped and brought complexity to Dante's later political vision. They also help explain why his political career would collide with the stubborn *real-politik* of his time, and why his public and private life floundered in 1302. The tragic contrast between the pure Franciscan sense of poverty and a cult of naked power will be memorably dramatized in *Inferno* XXVII where Dante represents the power of the pope's manipulation of a Franciscan friar.

At the beginning of his exile and for a few years (roughly between 1303–07), he devoted himself to writing a treatise on language, *De vulgari eloquentia* (*Of the Vulgar Language*) and a philosophical tract, *Convivio* (the *Banquet*). Neither of them was ever completed. In the first book of *De vulgari eloquentia*, Dante theorizes about the origin of language (which is not human, but a gift of God), as well as the historical alterations to which language is subjected, and he describes the traits of the Romance languages and, above all, of Italian. The purpose of his original investigation of language's history is clear: he is bent on forging a vulgar language, born of the Latin vernacular, which would serve the poetic, political, legal, and courtly needs of Italy. In the second book, he theorizes about poetics. Thus, he discusses the poetic forms developed by the Provençal poets (such as Bertran de Born), sentence constructions, the learned and elegant varieties of style, its degrees (lofty or tragic, middle or elegiac, and low or comical), and he cites the poetry of his contemporaries (Guinizelli, Cavalcanti, Cino da Pistoia) as well as his own.

In *Convivio*, Dante turns to pondering questions of philosophy (as ethics) and of authority (political and philosophical). These philosophical investigations, taken by themselves, signal the restlessness of his mind, his inability to remain confined within the perimeter of one discipline or the straits of received opinions. Yet he never straggles. From the standpoint of this treatise, the world of the *Sweet New Style* appears as a world apart, a distant aristocratic game of the passions, a chapter of one's youth now secluded from the turmoil of history. *Convivio*, as a matter of fact, comes through as nothing less than an epitaph of the *Sweet New Style*: in the second book (chapter twelve), Dante tells how, seeking consolation for the death of Beatrice, he read St. Augustine's *Confessions*, Boethius's *Consolation of Philosophy*, and Cicero's *Laelius (De amicitia)* (*On Friendship*). And if the *Vita nova* had given an Italian voice to the European lyrical dramatization of the subject and of love (or the desiring self), *Convivio* made the Italian vernacular the language of philosophy. Something of the ideals shaping *De vulgari eloquentia* plainly remains in the new text. But the differences between them are sharp. By writing a commentary on his own doctrinal-philosophical songs, Dante sought to provide a doctrine of the good earthly life, as such a life was led by men who are noble not by virtue of blood but by spiritual election. Around this ethical core he aimed at writing fourteen books that would prove the nature of the virtues and of rational activity, of human acts, their intentions and executions, and of the will as intellective appetite in its bearing on things of the mind.

Dante interrupted writing the *Convivio* to begin writing *Inferno*, which he completed in 1314. No doubt, the material genesis of this first canticle is to be found in the personal, moral, political, and spiritual disarray of his life. It can be called a transfigured summary of his multifaceted past experiences. A number of themes, like musical motifs, run through this first canticle of the *Divine Comedy* and they can be conveniently extrapolated: the challenges of autobiographical writing and the voice of the poet, his authority and doubts; the nature of lyrical poetry, such as the one written by the love poets of the *Sweet New Style* and by Dante himself in his *Vita nova*; the moral demands implicit in the writing of poetry; the authority of the past and the limits of the classical tradition (Virgil and the Greek hero Ulysses); the question of poetic representation and poetic language; civil wars and the lawlessness of Italian cities; the peculiar responsibilities of counselors and advisers of kings and popes (see, for instance, Pier delle Vigne in Canto XIII and Guido da Montefeltro in Canto XXVII); the modalities of prophetic language; the nature of the moral life; the pilgrim's own spiritual apprenticeship; and the dangers of reading literature and deciphering the language of others. Dante does not present these specific themes in an isolated fashion. Rather, he shows how each implicates the others and is entangled with the others, so that *Inferno* comes through as a vast poetic, political, moral, and religious phantasmagoria.

In a real way, *Inferno* recounts how the poet is capable of writing only by returning to the path of his childhood, to the memory of his love for Beatrice, who appears at the start of the poem to beg that Virgil help her friend lost in the wilderness. If this is the autobiographical impulse triggering the dramatic action of the poem, *Inferno*'s opening canto focuses on other spiritual-poetic questions. Properly speaking, it begins by featuring two journeys: the protagonist's effort to escape from the dark woods by following the direction of the sunlight as well as his actual descent into Hell. His first, attempted journey, which can be understood as a neo-Platonic effort at transcendence, ends in failure. The pilgrim cannot escape from his quandary by taking only a philosophical route. In fact, he has to learn that he can ascend to the sunlit plain of truth only by first descending into humility: in a Christian conversion, which he experiences, the way up is down into the depths of Hell as a precondition for ascending into Purgatory and Paradise. The way down—which is the journey the pilgrim will undertake—will occur under the guidance of Virgil, the author of the *Aeneid*, the poem of Rome and of history. Virgil will lead his disciple through the circles of incontinence, violence, and fraud which constitute the topography of Hell. The moral structure of Hell is figured through Aristotle's moral philosophy (and Aquinas's commentary) available in the *Nichomachean Ethics*.

The choice of Virgil (and of the *Aeneid* as the poem of Rome) is crucial to grasping the poetic-political discussion of *Inferno*. Dante was certainly aware of St. Augustine's critique of the Empire and of Virgil available in the *City of God*. Augustine, arguably the greatest Roman philosopher, had understood the originality and morality of the Roman ideas of freedom as a form of political foundation. Yet, he still objected to the imperial ideology of Rome put forth in the *Aeneid*. The Roman Empire, so he argued, far from being a providential institution, was another tragic episode in history's succession of violence. Dante provides a radical reversal of Augustine's theory of history. The Roman Empire—as he eventually will argue in *Monarchia* (written in 1317)—is willed by God as a way of healing the unspeakable violence triggered by the civil war, which for him is the metaphor of all historical reality, wherein one's neighbor is one's enemy.

Dante's pervasive consciousness of the divisions brought in by the civil war invests all forms of representation in *Inferno*. One steady rhetorical feature of this canticle can be called the "polemical," whereby characters are presented as if they were at odds with each other: they oppose each other and display unabashedly their partisan passions, as well as their penchant to think against each other. Dante's own voice belongs to this climate of partisanship and divisions: he takes sides, condemns, and passes judgments. In effect, he stages the violence of the city while he confesses the violence lodged in him. But a subtle distinction is needed. For Dante, thinking is more than a contrarian's act, it is a form of an encounter. And so, more than opposing St. Augustine's rejection of the Roman Empire, Dante figures a crossroads where Virgil's celebration of the Empire and Augustine's doubts about it converge.

Accordingly, *Inferno*'s most political cantos (VI, X, XIII, XV, XVI, XXXIII) focus not on the empire, which, as a matter of fact, is a distant and almost absent model, but on the sinister reciprocity of violence, on violence as the only form of reciprocity. In *Inferno* X, the canto where the Epicureans, the philosophers, such as his friend Guido Cavalcanti, do not believe in the immortality of the soul, Dante re-enacts the commonplace, unchanging quarrels joining and dividing Guelphs and Ghibellines in the city of Florence. The city, which for Plato is the soul writ larger, is soulless for Dante and it is tragically split into unrelated parts. In *Inferno* XV, the canto where his teacher Brunetto Latini dwells, Dante stages the sparks of violence (disguised as educational projects) that dismantle the very foundations of Florence. By the same token, *Inferno* XIX, the canto where simony (or commerce of sacred things) is punished, shows the impure mixture of the sacred and the secular, which is crystallized by the Donation of Constantine, the "gift" the emperor made to the

Church and by which the Church has historically contaminated her spiritual essence. The memorable spectacle of the popes' corruption gives rise to the poet's prophetic stance.

No doubt, through these sinners (not to mention Paolo and Francesca, who, in *Inferno* V, endlessly whirl around the circle of the lustful, seduced into sin by the reading of love-poetry and the French romance of *Lancelot*, or Ulysses, Guido da Montefeltro, Pier delle Vigne, and Ugolino), Dante unveils two insights constitutive of the moral experience: the human refusal to take guilt upon oneself and the desire to cling to familiar habits (which lies at the heart of one's surrendering to the world and eternalizing the past). These moral traits derive from Aristotle's classical moral philosophy and from St. Thomas Aquinas's commentary on the *Ethics*. For Dante, they are not abstractions available in manuals for the good life. They invest, rather, all the sinners who abide in the crater of the nine circles of Hell—those who have sinned from incontinence (lust, gluttony, prodigality and avarice, sloth and anger), those who dwell within the walled city of Dis (heretics), and the violent and deceivers (procurers, flatterers, simonists, fortune-tellers, swindlers, hypocrites, thieves, evil counselors, trouble-makers, forgers, and the traitors).

In a way, Dante responds to the philosophical musings of Aristotle and Virgil by posing the question of how man's wounded will, which is the locus of sin, can be healed. The sinners' self-deceptions and willful blindness to their own existential-moral reality is at one with their habit of sin. To break this habit, so the poetry of *Inferno* tells us and the pilgrim's dramatic experience shows, we must journey out of our familiar world and, to put it simply in Dante's own metaphor, just out of the world. By contrast, all the sinners in Hell believed that the world—this world—is the source of their beings and their values. Therefore, they were unwilling to estrange themselves from it. They would surrender and cling to its lure, even after death, in the unalterable conviction that only the world could give them a sense of their importance and value.

One can find in *Inferno* some different forms of the sinners' distorted self-understanding. Ulysses, for instance, takes a journey away from the familiar world: he leaves behind his father Laertes, his wife Penelope, and his son Telemachus as he travels into the unknown. So powerful and seductive was his adventure that the ancient neo-Platonists interpreted it allegorically in the *Odyssey* as the flight of the soul. It was an audacious venture, conducted without any guidance other than the light of his own reason, cutting through all boundaries between earth and sky. For Dante the Greek hero's quest as transgression—as evidenced in *Purgatorio* and *Paradiso*—bears an uncanny affinity to his own quest as the Christian pilgrim-poet.

But there is a radical difference between them. Ulysses ends up in a catastrophe: he plunges into the abyss as his gaze rends the night of the world. Unlike the Greek hero, Dante will manage to gather the fire of the sky and see God face-to-face.

What is the reason that would make the difference between these two heroes possible and plausible? The answer is clear. Dante differs from Ulysses because he understands the power of the "beginning" as the only way of breaking the habit. *Inferno* begins literally, "midway through the journey of our life." Dante begins his poem "midway" because, in a sense, present things, such as the crisis enveloping the pilgrim in the woods, are not the real beginnings. The present is rooted in distant origins and causes. Thus, very soon in the first canto of *Inferno*, Dante goes on to evoke the luminous puzzle of the "beginning." As the pilgrim, who had tried to climb the hill, is driven back, again and again, into the dark valley by three beasts, the poet describes the time of the day, the hour of morning, when the sun was in the constellation of Aries: "Temp'era dal principio del mattino / e 'l sol montava 'n sù con quelle stelle / ch'eran con lui quando l'amor divino / mosse di prima quelle cose belle; . ." (*Inf.* I, 37–40) (. . . It was the break of day, / the sun was mounting in the morning sky / with the same stars as when that whole array / of lovely things was first given movement by / divine love).

Ulysses, like the pilgrim in *Inferno* I, follows the sun and its repetitive cycles: like Ulysses, the pilgrim returns, over and over again, to the same place and with the same results. They get nowhere. Unlike Ulysses and unlike his own prior experience as a lost wayfarer, Dante grasps the fact that to escape his spiritual impasse, he, the poet of the first things, must look at the "principio," which is the beginning and a break with the past. He must look for what makes things new. And what makes things new and sets them in motion, to put it in St. Augustine's terminology, is the idea of the beginning of the world, which the biblical Genesis calls creation and the Romans call foundation. In short, Dante knows, in a way that Ulysses did not, that what makes things new is Love, of which *Inferno* gives merely the feeblest of glows, but which he could find as an awe-struck young man in the streets of Florence and, later, midway through the journey of his life, he could recall at the bleakest hour of his exile.

Giuseppe Mazzotta
Yale University

Translator's Note

Dante's *Inferno* is, without a doubt, the most frequently translated work of our time. Over the last decade or so, new versions have appeared in the United States at the rate of about one every year. Why are there so many? It is possible to produce a definitive translation of a novel, even a great novel, but poetry, with its rich and complex use of language and its tight interweaving of form and content, is a very different matter. One can easily imagine five or even ten translations of a single Rilke sonnet, all of them good in their own way, all of them reasonable approximations of at least some aspects of the original, and all of them substantially different from one another. With the *Inferno*, we are dealing not with a mere fourteen lines but with forty-seven hundred, with a book-length poem that not only tells a vivid and intricate story but also engages dimensions of religion, morality, history, politics, myth, philosophy, psychology, and the author-protagonist's personal experiences. In addition to all this, it is a work in which matters of tone and diction, and of form and structure, are of critical importance. A work of such stunning artistry and complexity creates space enough not only for the translations already in the field, but for undreamt-of others as well.

The often striking differences among Dante translations can be explained by an awareness of the different aspects of the original that they emphasize and the different audiences for which they are intended. Translations by scholars, conceived for a readership of scholars and students, are principally concerned to render the paraphrasable content of the text as accurately and precisely as possible. Other versions, aimed at a youthful or a broad general audience, seek to capture the poem's plot and its striking characterizations as directly, and often as simply, as they can. In both such instances, there is little if any concern with the poetic dimensions of the text, and the translations are usually either in prose or in a line-by-line rendering that makes no attempt to reproduce the rhythmic and tonal effects of the original.

As a poet myself, I have sought to re-create the poetry of the *Inferno*, as I see it on the page and hear it my head when I read the original. To me, a large and necessary part of what this means is an attempt to re-create the *terza rima* structure that Dante devised for the *Divine Comedy*. But it does not mean that I am less interested in the narrative or in any of the other aspects of the poem mentioned above, since, as I have said, the best poetry (and Dante's poetry fits that description as well as anyone's) is an interplay of form and content in which, ideally, neither element is made to suffer at the expense of the other. So far as I am aware, no other American translator of the past seventy-five years has attempted a fully rhymed version of the *Inferno*. Modern American translators of the poem, even those who are poets writing for an audience of poetry lovers, have, like most modern translators in general, chosen not to strictly reproduce the rhyme scheme of the original text. Some have abandoned rhyme (and some, even meter) altogether, while others have attempted to at least suggest the nature of Dante's practice by a more sparing use of rhyme or by the use of off-rhymes.

An ideal translation, which is of course impossible, would say everything that Dante says exactly as he says it, in exactly the same form that he employs. In attempting to approach that ideal as closely as possible, I have always translated poetry in the same way that I have always written poetry, striving to achieve the blend of form and content that I spoke of earlier. To abandon or severely compromise the poem's form in the hope of thereby honoring its content is, to my way of thinking, to destroy the balance necessary to achieve that blend. Thus, rather than begin with a hierarchy of values which dictates that some of the elements of the original must be downplayed, or even eliminated, at the expense of others, I hope to salvage as high a percentage as I can of all the elements of the poem.

In practical terms, this means that every problem of translation must be solved not by the unflinching imposition of some abstract theory or principle, but by the immediate needs, in context, of that particular moment of the poem. Sometimes that requires as literal an approximation of Dante's statement as possible; sometimes it demands the reproduction of a rhetorical figure or structure; and so on. Some compromises are, of course, inevitable: the occasional resort to inexact rhymes; the compression or expansion of content to fit the metrical pattern; and—again—so on. But while all of this was taking place, I always kept in mind the harmony, integration, and clarity of the original in order to create as harmonious, integrated, and clear an approximation as I could. The beauty of the *Inferno* lies in its tiniest details and in its grand design, and in seeking to attend to both the details and the design, I hope that I have managed to convey something of that beauty to the readers of this translation.

Michael Palma

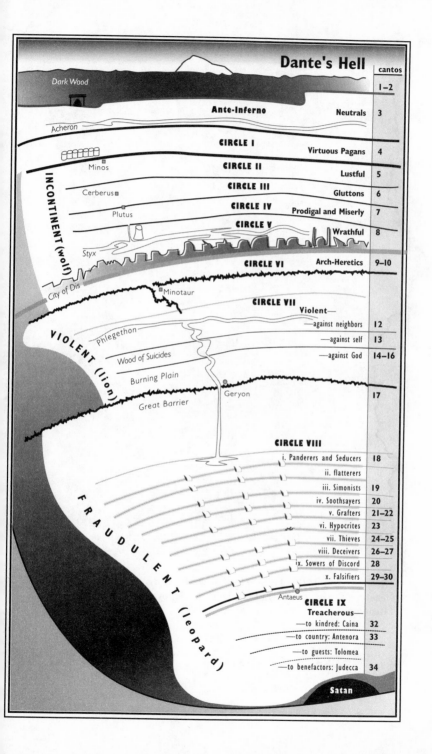

Dante's Hell

	cantos
Dark Wood	1–2
Ante-Inferno Neutrals	3
Acheron	
CIRCLE I Virtuous Pagans	4
Minos	
CIRCLE II Lustful	5
Cerberus **CIRCLE III** Gluttons	6
Plutus **CIRCLE IV** Prodigal and Miserly	7
CIRCLE V Wrathful	8
Styx	
CIRCLE VI Arch-Heretics	9–10
City of Dis	
Minotaur	
CIRCLE VII Violent—	
Phlegethon —against neighbors	12
—against self	13
Wood of Suicides —against God	14–16
Burning Plain	
Geryon	
Great Barrier	17

INCONTINENT (wolf)

VIOLENT (lion)

CIRCLE VIII

	cantos
i. Panderers and Seducers	18
ii. flatterers	
iii. Simonists	19
iv. Soothsayers	20
v. Grafters	21–22
vi. Hypocrites	23
vii. Thieves	24–25
viii. Deceivers	26–27
ix. Sowers of Discord	28
x. Falsifiers	29–30

F R A U D U L E N T (leopard)

Antaeus

CIRCLE IX
Treacherous—

	cantos
—to kindred: Caina	32
—to country: Antenora	33
—to guests: Tolomea	
—to benefactors: Judecca	34

Satan

Italy, around 1300. From *The Divine Comedy of Dante Alighieri: Inferno*, ed. and trans. Robert Durling. Copyright © 1996 by Robert Turner.

The Text of
INFERNO

Canto 1

The Dark Wood; The Three Beasts; Virgil's Appearance;
The Prophecy of the Greyhound

Midway through the journey of our life,[1] I found
    myself in a dark wood, for I had strayed
3   from the straight pathway to this tangled ground.
How hard it is to tell of, overlaid
    with harsh and savage growth, so wild and raw
6   the thought of it still makes me feel afraid.
Death scarce could be more bitter. But to draw
    the lessons of the good that came my way,
9   I will describe the other things I saw.
Just how I entered there I cannot say,
    so full of sleep when I began to veer
12   that I did not see that I had gone astray
from the one true path. But once I had drawn near
    the bottom of a hill at the far remove
15   of the valley that had pierced my heart with fear,
I saw its shoulders mantled from above
    by the warm rays of the planet that gives light
18   to guide our steps, wherever we may rove.[2]
At last I felt some calming of the fright
    that had allowed the lake of my heart no rest
21   while I endured the long and piteous night.
And as a drowning man with heaving chest
    escapes the current and, once safe on shore,
24   turns back to see the dangers he has passed,
so too my mind, still lost in flight, once more
    turned back to see the passage that had never
27   let anyone escape alive before.
I paused to let my weary limbs recover,
    and then began to climb the lone hillside,
30   my fixed foot always lower than the other.[3]
But I had hardly started when I spied
    a leopard in my pathway, lithe and fleet,
33   all covered with a sleek and spotted hide.

---

1. The poem is set in 1300, when Dante was thirty-five, halfway through his biblically allotted threescore years and ten.
2. The planet is the sun, which in Ptolemaic, pre-Copernican cosmology was believed to revolve around the earth, the fixed center of the universe.
3. This line is commonly given an allegorical as well as a physical interpretation. The feet are understood to be the limbs of the soul. The fixed foot is the left, representing will, which lags behind the right one, intellect. The fullest discussion of the line is John Freccero's "The Firm Foot on a Journey Without a Guide," in his *Dante: The Poetics of Conversion* (Harvard, 1986).

3

direct confrontation

And as I faced it, it would not retreat,
  but paced before me and so blocked my way *guard*
36 that more than once I had to turn my feet
to retrace my steps. It was the break of day,[4]
  the sun was mounting in the morning sky
39 with the same stars as when that whole array
of lovely things was first given movement by
  divine love. The sweet season of the year
42 and the hour made me think that I might try
to evade that bright-skinned beast as it came near,
  but then I felt my good hopes quickly fade
45 and in an instant I was numbed with fear
to see a lion in my path that made
  straight for me, head held high and ravenous,
48 and seemed to make the very air afraid.
And a she-wolf too, that in its leanness was
  laden with every craving. Those who seek
51 fulfillment there find only wretchedness.
The sight of this one made me feel so weak,
  so overcome with dread, that instantly
54 I lost all hope of climbing to the peak.
As a man is eager in prosperity
  but when time brings him losses can be found
57 giving way to weeping and to misery,
so did I feel as the she-wolf pressed me round
  so relentlessly that bit by bit I stepped
60 back where the sun is mute on the low ground.[5]
And as I drove myself into the depth,
  a shape was offered to my vision, wan
63 as if from a long silence it had kept.
Seeing him in that great desert, I began
  to call out. "*Miserere*—on me," I cried,
66 "whatever you are, a shade or a solid man!"
"Not man, although I was a man," he replied.
  "My parents were both Mantuans. I descend
69 from those of Lombardy on either side.

4. It is the morning of Good Friday. The sun is in Aries, as it was believed to have been at the time of creation.
5. The encounter with the three beasts is one of the most frequently and variously interpreted passages of the poem. Traditionally, the leopard, the lion, and the she-wolf have been understood to represent lust, pride, and avarice, respectively—or, in some interpretations, envy, pride, and avarice, the qualities ascribed to the Florentines by Ciacco in Canto VI (line 75) and Brunetto Latini in Canto XV (line 67). They have also been associated with incontinence, violence, and fraud, the three categories of sin described by Virgil in Canto XI. Some feel that the leopard must represent fraud, given Dante's reference to the belt with which he had hoped to snare that beast (Canto XVI, lines 106–8); there Geryon, who also has a spotted hide, is clearly linked to fraud. If this view is accepted, then the she-wolf represents lust or, more broadly, incontinence. Thus, the she-wolf gives Dante the most trouble because, while incontinence is the least grievous category of sin, it is the one to which he is most susceptible.

I was born *sub Julio,* at the latter end.[6]
    Under the good Augustus I lived in Rome
72   in the days when false and lying gods still reigned.
I was a poet, and I sang of him,
    Anchises' righteous son, who sailed from Troy
75   after the burning of proud Ilium.[7]
But why do you turn back toward trouble? Why
    do you not ascend the delectable mount instead,
78   the origin and cause of every joy?"
"Are you that Virgil then, that fountainhead
    that spills such a mighty stream of eloquence?"
81   I said this with a shame-filled brow, and said:
"Light and glory of all poets, may my intense
    love and long study of your poetry
84   avail me now for my deliverance.
You are my master, my authority,
    for it is from you alone that I learned to write
87   in the noble style that has so honored me.
You see why I have turned back from the height.
    Illustrious sage, please help me to confound
90   this beast that makes my pulses shake with fright."
"It were best to go another way around,"
    he answered, seeing tears start from my eyes,
93   "if your hope is to escape this savage ground,
because this creature that provokes your cries
    allows no man to get the best of her,
96   but blocks each one, attacking till he dies.
Of such a vile and vicious character
    and greedy appetite, she is never sated,
99   and when she has fed is even hungrier.
Many the animals with whom she has mated.
    Her couplings—till her painful deathblow is dealt
102   by the greyhound—will continue unabated.
This greyhound will not feed on land or wealth,
    but on virtue, love, and wisdom. He will be
105   born in the region between felt and felt.[8]

---

6. Virgil (Publius Vergilius Maro, 70–19 B.C.E.) was born before the reign of Julius Caesar. He was in his mid-twenties when Caesar was assassinated.
7. The Trojan prince Aeneas, son of Anchises and the goddess Venus, sailed to Italy after the fall of Troy (Ilium) and became the legendary founder of Rome.
8. This is one of the most obscure and hotly debated passages in the poem. The greyhound has been identified with various historical and religious figures, and has even been taken to signify the second coming of Christ. The most frequently proposed candidate is Cangrande della Scala, who ruled Verona from 1308 to 1329; his name suggests "great dog," and his native city, Verona, lies between the towns of Feltre and Montefeltro. The "felt" reference has also been interpreted astrologically (the Gemini, Castor and Pollux, were commonly depicted as wearing felt caps), spiritually (an allusion to the Franciscan and Dominican orders), and sociologically (suggestive of humble birth).

He will restore low-lying Italy,
for which Euryalus, Turnus, the maid Camilla,
108   and Nisus gave their life's blood.[9] Tirelessly
he will track the beast through every town until
he comes at last to drive her back into
111   that hell from which she sprang at Envy's will.
Therefore I think it would be best for you
to follow me. I will be your guide, and I
114   will lead you out of here and take you through
an eternal place where you will be greeted by
the shriekings of despair and you will see
117   ancient tormented spirits as they cry
aloud at the second death. Then you will be
with those who are content within the fire,
120   for they hope to join the blest eventually.
You will see those blest, if that is your desire,
with a worthier soul than I.[1] Into her hands
123   I will entrust you when I can go no higher.
That emperor who presides above commands,
since I did not heed his law, that none may gain
126   entrance through me to where his city stands.[2]
His rule is everywhere. There is his reign,
his city, and his throne! Happy are they
129   whom he chooses to inhabit that domain!"
"Poet," I said to him, "so that I may
escape this harm and worse that may await,
132   in the name of that God you never knew, I pray
you lead me out to see Saint Peter's gate[3]
and all those souls that you have told me of,
135   who must endure their miserable state."
I followed him as he began to move.

---

9. Nisus and Euralyus were young Trojan soldiers. Turnus, king of the Rutulians, and
Camilla, daughter of the king of the Volscians, were leaders of the indigenous Italian peo-
ples who resisted the Trojan invasion. Enemies in life, they are joined here as patriots and
as participants in the events that would lead to the founding of Rome.

1. The worthier spirit is Beatrice, whose name signifies "one who makes blessed." Associated
with Dante's neighbor Beatrice Portinari (1266–1290), she appears as a living person in
his *La Vita Nuova*, where she is celebrated for both her beauty and her spiritual example.

2. As one who lived before Christ, Virgil did not accept Christ as his savior and consequently
cannot enter heaven (see Canto IV, lines 31–42). This change of guides midway through
the journey suggests that salvation can be achieved only through divine grace, not by rea-
son and virtue alone.

3. Like other details in this canto, St. Peter's gate has inspired controversy, some maintain-
ing that it alludes to the traditional gate of heaven, which does not appear in *The Divine
Comedy*, others that it refers to the gate of purgatory, which does.

Canto II

*The Evening of Good Friday, April the 8th; The Doubts of the
Pilgrim; The Journeys of St. Paul and Aeneas; Beatrice Summons
Virgil; The Beginning of the Pilgrim's Descent*

The day was waning, and the darkening sky
    called all the creatures of the earth to rest
    after the long day's labors. Only I
3
was preparing all alone to endure the test
    of the journey and the pity of what I would see,
    as unerring memory will now attest.
6
Muses, high genius, aid me! Memory,
    that recorded what I saw among the dead,
    here you will show your true integrity.[1]
9
"O poet, you who are my guide," I said,
    "weigh whether I am fit for what lies in wait
    before you entrust me to the path ahead.
12
Of Silvius's father[2] you narrate
    how he saw the immortal world with his mortal sense
    while still immured in our corrupted state.
15
That evil's foe showed him such preference,
    aware of the result that it would bring,
    of who and what would come as consequence—
18
to a thoughtful mind this seems a proper thing.
    Empyrean heaven in her high decrees
    chose him to be the father of fostering
21
Rome and her empire. Truly, both of these
    were founded to be the holy ground whereon
    the successor to great Peter keeps the keys.
24
On his journey which you celebrate, he was shown
    and told of things that served as the foundation
    of his victory and of the papal throne.
27
The Chosen Vessel then brought confirmation,
    by journeying there, of the true faith that must be
    the beginning of the path to our salvation.[3]
30

---

1. The invocation of the muse, a traditional component of epic poetry. Canto I may be regarded as a proem to the entire *Comedy*, leaving 33 cantos for the journey through hell. Both the *Purgatorio* and the *Paradiso*, which also begin with such invocations, contain 33 cantos, making the complete work exactly 100 cantos long.
2. In the *Aeneid*, Silvius is the son of Aeneas and his second wife, Lavinia, daughter of King Latinus of Latium. In Book VI, Aeneas makes the epic hero's ritual journey to the underworld, where his father's shade reveals to him the coming glories of Rome.
3. The Chosen Vessel, so described in Acts 9.15, is Saint Paul. In 2 Corinthians 12.1–7, Paul speaks of having been raised to the "third heaven" and alludes to its secret messages. In the *Visio Sancti Pauli*, an early medieval text, there is a description of his journey to hell.

But why must I? On whose authority?
 I am not Aeneas, not Paul. Why should I seek
33 what neither I nor anyone thinks me
worthy to do? Why start upon a bleak
 and, I fear, foolish journey? You are filled
36 with wisdom, and hear more clearly than I speak."
Like someone who unwills what he has willed,
 and with new thoughts sees his resolve go by,
39 letting what was begun go unfulfilled,
so, standing on that shadowy slope, was I.
 Rethinking what with such impulsiveness
42 I had begun, I let my impulse die.
"If I have rightly comprehended this,"
 the shade of that magnanimous soul replied,
45 "your spirit has been seized by cowardice,
which has often harried men and nullified
 many a worthy enterprise, as when
48 a beast will see a shadow and turn aside.
To free you from this fear, let me explain
 why I have come, and tell you of the request
51 that first made me take pity on your pain.
I was among the suspended ones when a blest
 and lovely lady called me. So fair was she,
54 I begged that I might serve at her behest.
Brighter than stars, her eyes shone brilliantly,
 and in a tone so sweet and soft and pure,
57 with an angel's voice, I heard her say to me:
'O gentle Mantuan soul, with fame secure
 in the world above, whose name will still resound
60 as long as the world continues to endure,
my friend, who is not fortune's friend, has found
 so many obstacles upon his way
63 up the desert slope that fear has turned him round.
I fear, from all that I have heard them say
 in heaven, that I have made too late a start,
66 that already he has gone too far astray.
Go now and, with the words of your high art
 and the skill to rescue him from this distress,
69 assist him and bring solace to my heart.
I who now send you forth am Beatrice.
 I have come from a place I long to see again.
72 Love prompted me. Love makes me ask you this.
How often I will speak to praise you when
 I stand before my Lord upon his throne.'
75 She said no more, and I responded then:
'O lady of virtue, through whose power alone

humanity is able to rise higher
78   than all within the least-circling heaven's zone,[4]
I am so pleased to do what you desire
that were it already done, it would be late.
81   All you need do is say what you require.
But how is it that you did not hesitate
to leave that longed-for spacious place on high
84   and descend into this center where we wait?'
'Since you have such deep desire to know why
I am not at all afraid to venture here,'
87   she told me, 'I will briefly clarify.
The only things that should inspire fear
are those that can inflict an injury.
90   The rest need not oppress us, it is clear.
God's grace has made me so I cannot be
moved in my heart by all your suffering
93   or touched by all the flames surrounding me.
In heaven a noble lady,[5] pitying
that great distress I send you to repair,
96   has made a breech in the strict reckoning
that rules above. She summoned Lucia[6] there,
and said:—Your follower, who is faithful still,
99   needs you, and I commend him to your care.—
Lucia, who is the enemy of all
cruelty, came immediately to the place
102   where I was sitting with the venerable
Rachel,[7] and said:—Beatrice, God's true praise,
why do you not help him who loved you so
105   that he forsook the crowd and its crass ways?
Do you not hear him crying out below?
Do you not see Death battle him by that flood
108   the mighty ocean cannot overthrow?—
Never on earth did any seize his good
or flee his harm as quickly as I flew,
111   once I had heard such words and understood,
leaving my heavenly seat to come to you,
trusting your words of such nobility
114   that they honor you and all who hear them too.'

4. In Ptolemaic cosmology, the "heaven," or planet, with the "least-circling zone," or smallest orbit, is the moon. Within that zone—the center of the physical universe—is the earth.
5. The Virgin Mary. Her name, like that of Jesus Christ, is never spoken aloud in hell.
6. Saint Lucy of Syracuse, a third-century virgin martyr, patroness of those with vision problems and a symbol of illuminating grace.
7. In Genesis, the wife of Jacob. She is usually taken to be a symbol of the contemplative life and is mentioned again in Canto IV, line 60.

She turned when she had spoken. I could see
    tears shining in her eyes, making me still
117   more eager to fulfill her charge to me.
So I have come to you, as was her will,
    saving you from the beast that blocked your way
120   along the short path up the lovely hill.
What is this, then? Why, why do you delay,
    why does your heart make room for cowardice,
123   why not be bold and resolute, when they,
those three great ladies of high blessedness
    in heaven's court, are keeping you in sight,
126   when I promise you great good to come of this?"
As flowers droop and close in the chill of night,
    then stand and open out upon the stem
129   when the sun returns and touches them with light,
so my exhausted strength revived like them
    and, feeling courage rush into my heart,
132   like one who has been set free I said to him:
"How compassionate she was, who took my part!
    How courteous you were, who quickly went
135   in response to her true plea. Now let us start,
for the forcefulness of what you say has sent
    my heart new eagerness to go with you,
138   reawakening my original intent.
Lead on. There is one will between us two.
    You are my guide, my lord and master." Thus
141   I spoke. And when he moved, I entered too
the pathway through the savage wilderness.

Canto III

The Gate of Hell; The Neutral Angels; Charon; Dante faints

THROUGH ME THE WAY TO THE CITY OF DESOLATION,
    THROUGH ME THE WAY TO EVERLASTING PAIN,
3   THROUGH ME THE WAY TO SOULS IN ABOMINATION.
JUSTICE MOVED MY GREAT MAKER IN MY DESIGN.
    I WAS CREATED BY THE PRIMAL LOVE,
6   WISDOM SUPREME AND POTENCY DIVINE.
BEFORE ME NOTHING WAS CREATED SAVE
    THE ETERNAL, AND I ENDURE ETERNALLY.
9   ALL YOU WHO ENTER, LET NO HOPE SURVIVE.
In darkly colored letters I could see
    these words inscribed on a portal overhead.
12   "Master," I said, "this saying is hard for me."

Like one who knows and understands, he said:
"Here all your doubt is to be left behind,
15   here all your cowardice is to fall dead.
Now we are in the place where you will find
the ones I told you of, the wretched race
18   of those who have lost the good use of the mind."
And then, with his hand on mine, and on his face
a cheerful look that helped to calm my fears,
21   he led me down into that secret place.
Sighs and laments and loud wails filled my ears.
Those cries resounding through the starless air
24   so moved me at first that I burst into tears.
A babble of tongues, harsh outcries of despair,
noises of rage and grief, the beating of hands,
27   and shrill and raucous voices everywhere
all made a mad uproar that never ends,
revolving in that timeless darkened breeze
30   the way a whirlwind whips the desert sands.
"Master, what do I hear? And who are these,"
I cried, as the horror swirled around my head,[1]
33   "who seem so shattered by their agonies?"
"This is the miserable estate," he said,
"of the sorry souls of those who lived and died
36   winning neither praise nor blame for the lives they'd led.[2]
They are mixed with the base angels who stood aside,
who neither hastened to their Lord's defense
39   nor rose against him in rebellious pride.
Heaven repels them lest its magnificence
be tarnished, and they are turned away by hell
42   lest sinners exalt themselves at their expense."
"Master," I said, "why do they thrash and yell?
What is the fate that makes them carry on?"
45   He answered: "I will very briefly tell.
They have no hope of death's oblivion.
Because theirs is a life so blind and low,
48   they are envious of every other one.
Mercy and justice scorn them. The world lets no
report of them remain, not even a trace.
51   Let us not speak of them, but look and go."
Looking again, I saw a banner race,

---

1. Here I have departed from Petrocchi's edition of the text, which gives *error* for the more frequently preferred *orror*. Those who accept the latter reading often cite the *Aeneid*, Book II, line 559: "At me tum primum saevus circumstetit horror" ("For the first time a savage horror surrounded me").
2. These souls chose neither good nor evil, the lukewarm scorned by Christ. Rudyard Kipling treats this theme delightfully in his poem "Tomlinson."

whirling about so madly that it seemed
54   unfit to make a stand in one fixed place.   *crowds of ppl?*
Following it a line of people streamed,
        an endless line as far as I could see.   *scale/magn*
57   That death had undone so many, I had not dreamed. *tude*
There were some among them who were known to me,
        and I saw the shade of him whose cowardice
60   made him make the great refusal.[3] Instantly
I understood beyond a doubt that this
        was that craven company whom all despise,
63   that God and his enemies find odious.
Those souls who had never lived, whose lives were lies,
        were naked, and were harried through their paces
66   by swarms of stinging wasps and biting flies.
Blood mingling with their tears ran down their faces
        and splashed the earth around them, where it fed
69   disgusting worms that wriggled in their traces.
Then I saw a crowd of people up ahead
        on the bank of a broad river. "What do I see,
72   Master, who are those people there," I said,
"what compulsion makes them wait so eagerly
        for the chance to cross the river and be gone—
75   or so in this dim light it seems to me."
And he replied: "These things will be made known
        when we must still our steps a while before
78   we go across the somber Acheron."
Afraid I might offend, I said no more,
        but walked with eyes downcast, and shame-filled too,
81   until we found ourselves upon the shore.
An old man white with age in a boat that drew
        toward where we all were gathered gave a cry:
84   "Woe unto you, you miserable crew
of sinners! Put all hope of heaven by!
        I take you to the other shore, to the land
87   of heat and cold, where darkness cannot die.
And you there, you who are still living, stand
        aside from all those others who are dead."
90   But when I did not follow his command,
"By another way, by other ports," he said,
        "not here, you will be brought across to shore.
93   A lighter craft will carry you instead."

3. This passage has been taken to refer to Esau, to Pontius Pilate, and to several others. One of
the earliest identifications, and certainly the most common, is that of Celestine V, whose ab-
dication of the papacy in 1294 led to the ascension of the corrupt Boniface VIII (Boniface,
who was still pope in 1300, when the *Inferno* is set, is the object of Dante's scorn at several
places in the poem; see note 4 to Canto XIX). Opposition to this assumption is founded in
part on Celestine's canonization in 1313, while Dante was still alive.

My leader told him, "Charon,[4] no need to roar.
　　Thus it is willed where there is power to do
96　　what has been willed, so question it no more."
This stopped the grizzled chops of the boatman who
　　ferried the dead across the marshy river.
99　　Around his eyes two flaming circles flew.
But those weary, naked souls began to shiver,
　　teeth gnashing, color gone from every face,
102　　at the harsh tirade that they'd heard him deliver.
They blasphemed God, they cursed the human race,
　　their parents, the father's seed, the mother's womb,
105　　their birth, and even its very time and place.
Then they all drew together in the gloom,
　　and weeping loudly they began to go
108　　to the evil shore that waits for all to whom
the fear of God means nothing. Eyes aglow
　　like live coals, demon Charon herds them now
111　　and with his oar beats those who are too slow.
As one by one the leaves drop from the bough
　　when autumn comes, and branches watch them fall
114　　till the earth has all their treasures, that is how
it was with Adam's evil seed. They all,
　　one at a time, when signaled, left the shore,
117　　just as a bird will answer to its call.
So they cross the murky water, and before
　　they have even landed on the other side,
120　　a new crowd gathers on this bank once more.
"My son," said my courteous master, "those who have died
　　in the wrath of God all come together here
123　　from every country, eager now to ride
across the river as their time draws near.
　　As God's own justice works upon them, they
126　　begin to feel desire in place of fear.
No worthy spirit ever comes this way,
　　so if Charon complained about you, it should be
129　　clear to you now just what his words convey."
And then the dark plain shook so violently
　　that I start to bathe in sweat all over again
132　　reliving the terror in my memory.
Up from the tear-soaked ground a great wind ran,
　　flashing a bright red light out of its swell
135　　that blasted all my senses, and like a man
that sleep has overtaken, down I fell.

---

4. Among the rivers of the underworld, Charon is traditionally represented as the ferryman of the Styx, not the Acheron. He appears in Aristophanes' *The Clouds* and in Book VI of the *Aeneid*, where Virgil's physical description of him furnishes Dante with several details.

Canto IV

*The First Circle; The Virtuous Heathen; Christ's Harrowing of
Hell; Meeting with the Poets of Classical Antiquity; Limbo*

A crashing thunderclap made me awaken,
    putting the thick sleep in my head to rout.
3   I started up like someone roughly shaken
out of a slumber. Standing, I looked about,
    gazing and turning my rested eyes around
6   in every direction, trying to make out
just where I was. The truth is, I soon found
    I was standing on the edge of the abyss
9   of pain, where roars of endless woe resound.
It was so dark and deep, so nebulous,
    I could see nothing in the depths although
12   I stared intently from the precipice.
"Now let us descend into the blind world below,"
    the poet said, appearing pale and drawn.
15   "I will be first, you second, as we go."
Seeing his pallor, I said: "I lean upon
    your strength when I falter, when I am afraid.
18   If you are frightened, how shall I go on?"
"The anguish of the people here," he said,
    "colors my face in ways you read amiss,
21   thinking the pity that I feel is dread.
But let us go. The long road beckons us."
    And so he went, and had me follow, where
24   the first circle runs, surrounding the abyss.
I heard no wails of lamentation there,
    no loud complaints, only the sound of sighs
27   that agitated the eternal air.
From a sadness without torments rose the cries
    of children and of women and of men.
30   Many and vast were the crowds before my eyes.
"Do you not ask," said my good master then,
    "what spirits these may be that fill this place?
33   I will have you know, before we walk again,
they did not sin. But their merit won no grace
    because they lacked baptism, which must be
36   the gateway to the faith that you embrace.
Those who preceded Christianity
    did not worship God according to his law,
39   and I myself am of this company.
For this defect, and for no other flaw,
    we are lost, with this one punishment laid on,
42   that without hope we feel desire gnaw."

Great sadness gripped my heart when he had done.
　　Among those suspended in that limbo were
45　　　　many a worthy, honorable one.
"Tell me, my master," I said then, "tell me, sir,"
　　feeling a need to be assured anew
48　　　　of the faith that conquers all ideas that err,
"did any ever leave here for heaven, through
　　their own or another's merit?" And he said,
51　　　　seeing what my covert words were leading to:
"When I was newly placed among these dead,
　　a mighty one came among us, whom I saw
54　　　　wearing the sign of victory on his head.
He took the shade of our first progenitor,
　　Abel his son, and Noah, and God-honoring
57　　　　Moses who was the giver of the law,
patriarch Abraham and David the king,
　　Israel with his father and his sons
60　　　　and Rachel, for whom he did much laboring.[1]
He blessed all these and other paragons.
　　And I would have you know that till that day
63　　　　no souls were saved. They were the earliest ones."[2]
We did not stop, but went along our way
　　while he was speaking, passing now through some
66　　　　thick woods—not woods made out of trees, I say,
but of crowding spirits. We were not far from
　　the place where I had slept so deeply, when
69　　　　I saw a dark hemisphere that was overcome
by a fiery light. Though still a bit distant then,
　　we were close enough that I could see in part
72　　　　that the ground was held by honorable men.
I said: "O you who honor science and art,
　　who are those men who even in this place
75　　　　possess such honor that sets them apart?"
And he: "Their fame, which time does not erase,
　　still resounding in your world this very day,
78　　　　allows them to advance through heaven's grace."
Meanwhile I heard a voice before me say:
　　"Hail to the highest poet! His honorable
81　　　　shade has returned to us, which had gone away."

[handwritten margin note: worthy of salvation]

[handwritten margin note: immaterial woods]

---

1. Israel, meaning "soldier of God," was a name given to Jacob after he wrestled with the angel. His father was Isaac, son of Abraham. Rachel was Jacob's wife. His twelve sons were the founders of the twelve tribes of Israel.
2. Lines 52–63 refer to the legendary harrowing of hell. The "mighty one" of line 53 is Christ. Salvation was impossible until he had redeemed by his crucifixion the taint of original sin. At his death, which occurred roughly fifty years after Virgil's, Christ descended to the underworld to effect the salvation of many worthies who had believed in the prophecies of his coming.

Then when the voice had finished and was still,
    I saw four noble shades all moving forward,
84   their faces neither glad nor sorrowful.
Said my master: "See the one who bears the sword,
    the one who walks before the other three
87   acknowledged as their leader and their lord.
Homer the sovereign of all bards is he.[3]
    Horace the satirist is the second one.[4]
90   Ovid comes third, and Lucan finally.[5]
Because, along with me, they all have won
    the name by which I was just now addressed,
93   they do me honor, and it is well done."
Assembled there before me were the best
    of poets, the school of that sweet lord of style
96   who like an eagle soars above the rest.
When they had talked together for a while,
    they turned to me with a nod of salutation,
99   at which I saw my master broadly smile.
And then they made far greater demonstration
    of honor, bringing me up to their height,
102   making me sixth in their wisdom's congregation.[6]
So we walked onward, moving toward the light,
    and the things that were said among us it is good
105   not to say here, as to say them there was right.
We came to where a noble castle stood
    circled by seven high walls. All around
108   that citadel a lovely streamlet flowed.
We crossed the stream as though on solid ground.
    Through seven gates those sages passed with me.
111   We came to a fresh green meadow, where we found
people with looks of great authority,
    whose eyes moved slowly and were serious,
114   who spoke in quiet tones, infrequently.

---

3. Virgil's description of Homer as "the sovereign of all bards" acknowledges the *Aeneid's* heavy borrowings from the *Iliad* and *Odyssey* (Dante, who did not read Greek, knew Homer only indirectly).

4. Horace (Quintus Horatius Flaccus, 65–8 B.C.E.), who was known in the Middle Ages more for his satires than for his odes, describes himself as a satirist in the *Ars poetica*.

5. Lucan (Marcus Annaeus Lucanus, 39–65 C.E.) is the author of *Pharsalia*, an epic concerning the conflict between Caesar and Pompey. The *Metamorphoses* of Ovid (Publius Ovidius Naso, 43 B.C.E.–c. 17 C.E.) provided Dante with his chief source for classical myth.

6. This apparent nomination of himself as one of the six greatest poets of all time seems at first to be an act of breathtaking hubris on Dante's part. But Dante would have regarded his poetic talent as a God-given attribute, not a personal attainment worthy of boast, and in a poem describing the horrific fates of those who misused their God-given gifts, he can legitimately claim to be employing his, like the poets named here, for the highest ends—a claim that Milton would more overtly make for his own intentions at the beginning of *Paradise Lost* (see also Canto XXVI, lines 19–24).

Then we moved off to one side, where there was
        a luminous broad hillside that would yield
117   a view of the whole gathering to us.
Before me on that green enameled field
        such glorious spirits appeared that I still prize
120   within my soul the sights that were revealed.
I saw Electra, and could recognize
        Aeneas and Hector[7] among those with her,
123   and armored Caesar with his hawklike eyes.
I saw Camilla and Penthesilea[8] there,
        and I saw King Latinus sitting in
126   another place, with his daughter Lavinia[9] near.
I saw that Brutus who overthrew Tarquin.
        Lucretia, Cornelia, Julia, and with these three
129   was Marcia. Alone, apart, was Saladin.[1]
And lifting my eyes higher, I could see,
        seated, the master of all those who know, *Aristotle?*
132   amid his philosophic family.
All of them gaze upon him, all of them show
        all honor to him. Plato and Socrates
135   stand closest to him. I saw row on row,
Anaxagoras, Thales, and Diogenes,
        Heraclitus, Zeno, and Democritus
138   who imputes the world to chance, Empedocles,[2]
Dioscorides[3] who collected things' essences,
        Hippocrates, Galen,[4] the moral philosopher
141   Seneca, Cicero, Linus, and Orpheus,[5]

7. The Electra named here is not the daughter of Agamemnon and Clytemnestra about whom Sophocles and Euripides wrote tragedies, but the daughter of Atlas and mother of Dardanus, the founder of Troy. Aeneas and Hector, leader of the Trojan forces in the *Iliad*, are her descendants.

8. The queen of the Amazons, fought for Troy and was killed by Achilles. For Camilla, see note 9 to Canto I.

9. For Latinus and Lavinia, see note 2 to Canto II.

1. Became sultan of Egypt in 1174 and won some victories against the Crusaders before his defeat by Richard Coeur de Lion. Despite his resistance to the Christian invaders of the Holy Land, Saladin was highly regarded in medieval Europe for his piety, justice, and nobility of spirit. Tarquin was the last of the legendary Roman kings; the rape of Lucretia by his son led to his expulsion by Lucius Junius Brutus, brother of Lucretia and nephew of Tarquin, and thus the establishment of the republic. Brutus is not to be confused with Caesar's assassin Marcus Junius Brutus. Julia was the daughter of Caesar and wife of Pompey. Cornelia was the daughter of Scipio Africanus and mother of the Gracchi, the tribunes Caius and Tiberius. Marcia was the wife of Cato the Younger.

2. Aristotle (line 131) was translated into Latin in the twelfth and thirteenth centuries and was quickly established as the principal classical philosopher, in large part through Thomas Aquinas's incorporation of his work into a Christian context. The others named here were predecessors or contemporaries of Socrates and Plato; they are all presented as stages along the way to the culmination of thought in "the master of those who know."

3. Pedanius Dioscorides, a first-century Greek physician and author of *De materia medica*, catalogued the properties of plants.

4. Hippocrates (fifth century B.C.E.) and Galen (second century C.E.) were Greek physicians.

5. The mythical Greek poets Linus and Orpheus are grouped with the Roman moralists Cicero (Marcus Tullius Cicero, 106–43 B.C.E.) and Seneca (Lucius Annaeus Seneca, 4 B.C.E.–65 C.E.), suggesting an association of poetry with wisdom and moral values.

Ptolemy, Euclid the geometer,[6]
    Avicenna, and Averroës[7] whose monument
144   is the great commentary. So many of them there were,
I cannot describe them to the full extent,
    for often, with my long theme to set the pace,
147   the telling must fall short of the event.
We six become two. Out of the quiet space,
    through another route into the trembling air,
150   now my wise guide has led me to a place
where there is nothing shining anywhere.

Canto V

The Second Circle; Minos, Judge of the Dead; The Lustful; Francesca da Rimini and Paolo Malatesta

Thus I went down from where the first circle lies
    into the second, which surrounds less space
3   but much more pain, provoking wails and cries.
There Minos[1] stands with his horrid snarling face.
    He examines the sinners at the entranceway.
6   Entwining, he assigns each one its place.
Each misbegotten soul, that is to say,
    confesses all as it faces him, and so
9   that connoisseur of sinfulness can weigh
how far each spirit will be sent below.
    Each time his tail coils round him indicates
12   another level that the soul must go.
Always a swarming multitude awaits.
    They tell, they hear, they are hurled into the air,
15   flung one by one to their eternal fates.
Minos addressed me when he saw me there,
    halting the meting out of punishments:
18   "O you who come to this house of pain, beware

---

6. Euclid (third century B.C.E.) wrote the *Elements* of geometry. Ptolemy (Claudius Ptolemaeus, c. 90–168) was the Egyptian astronomer whose *Almagest* outlines his system.
7. Ibn Rushd Averroës (1126–1198), Spanish Islamic philosopher, wrote the most important medieval commentary on Aristotle. The Arabic philosopher Avicenna (ibn Sina, 980–1037) was the author of a standard medical textbook. Their inclusion, with that of Saladin, might be seen as a partial mitigation of Dante's hostility to Islam as a schism, as shown by the mosques of the city of Dis (Canto VIII, lines 70–72) and the damnation of Mohammed (Canto XXVIII, line 22ff.).
1. The son of Zeus and Europa, king of Crete. Virgil describes him and his brother Rhadamanthus as judges of souls in the underworld (*Aeneid*, Book VI).

how you enter and where you place your confidence.
Do not let yourself be fooled by the wide door!"
21   And my leader: "Why do you too take offense?
Do not obstruct the path he is fated for.
Thus it is willed where there is power to do
24   what has been willed, so question it no more."
Now all the mournful sounds are starting to
surround and overwhelm me. Now I arrive
27   where the roar of lamentation runs me through.
Here the light is mute and the atmosphere alive
with the noise of constant howling, like the sea
30   under assault by violent gusts that strive
with one another. The hellish wind blows free,
sweeping the spirits headlong through the air.
33   It whirls and pounds and mauls them endlessly.
It carries them back before the ruin,[2] where
they shriek and moan and utter their laments
36   and curse the almighty power that sent them there.
The souls condemned to bear these punishments,
I learned, are the carnal sinners, of lust so strong
39   that they let it master reason and good sense.
As large, dense flocks of starlings are borne along
by their wings in the cold season of the year,
42   just so that blast propels the sinful throng,
drives them now up, now down, now there, now here.
No hope consoles them, whether for repose
45   or even for their pain to be less severe.
As it may happen that we see long rows
of cranes above us as they chant their lay,
48   so I saw spirits crying out their woes
as the wild windstorm carried them our way,
till I said: "Master, all these souls I see
51   lashed onward by the black air, who are they?"
"The first of those," my master said to me,
"of whom you wish to hear was an empress
54   over many languages in antiquity.
She was so enslaved by lust, so lecherous,
that to keep the blame for her misdeeds at bay
57   her laws gave license to licentiousness.
She is Semíramis, who, as histories say,
succeeded her husband Ninus as ruler of
60   all of the lands where the sultan reigns today.[3]

---

2. For the explanation of the "ruin" so casually mentioned here, see Canto XII, lines 32–45.
3. Semiramis, legendary queen of Assyria, was reputed to have legalized incest to exculpate her sexual relationship with her son.

Next is the one who killed herself for love
    and betrayed Sichaeus's ashes.[4] Here the bold
63   Cleopatra comes, whom wanton passions drove.[5]
See Helen, for whom such dreadful years unrolled.
    See the great Achilles. In the end he came
66   to battle love.[6] Behold Paris, and behold
Tristan[7]—" More than a thousand, and all the same—
    love took them from our life. And one and all
69   he showed to me and told me each one's name.
And as I listened to my teacher call
    the list of each high lady and grand knight,
72   I was overwhelmed, and I felt my senses fall
to pity. "Poet," I told him, "if I might,
    I willingly would speak now to those two
75   who are paired. Upon the wind they seem so light."
"The wind will bring them into closer view,"
    he said, "and you must call them, when it does,
78   by the love that leads them. They will come to you."
When the wind had turned them near to where I was,
    "O weary spirits," I began to cry,
81   "if another does not forbid, come speak with us!"
As doves with wings held steady and raised high
    are called by desire back to the sweet nest
84   and carried by their will across the sky,
so from the flock of Dido and the rest
    they came through the evil air to where we stood,
87   through the power of my compassionate request.
"O living creature, gracious and so good
    that through this black air you have dared to go
90   to visit us who stained the world with blood,
if the king of the universe were not our foe,
    then we would surely pray to him to fill
93   your heart with peace for pitying our woe.
We will speak and hear of whatever it is your will
    to speak and hear of, while the wind will permit,
96   as it is doing now, by keeping still.

4. Dido, widow of King Sichaeus of Tyre, was queen of Tyre and then of Carthage. By her affair with Aeneas, she broke her vow to remain faithful to her husband's memory; his abandonment of her led to her suicide. The story of Dido and Aeneas is told in Book IV of the *Aeneid*, the best-known and most celebrated part of the epic.
5. Cleopatra, queen of Egypt, was the mistress of Julius Caesar and of Mark Antony.
6. Helen was the wife of Menelaus, king of Sparta; her abduction by Paris, son of King Priam of Troy, caused the Trojan War. According to a medieval legend not found in Homer, Achilles fell in love with Priam's daughter Polyxena and, in hope of an assignation with her, was lured into a fatal ambush by Paris.
7. The lover of Iseult, who was the wife of his uncle, King Mark of Cornwall. Their tragic affair is told in a number of medieval romances.

The place where I was born[8] is the city set
    along the shore where the Po descends to be
99   at peace at last with those that follow it.
Love, which in gentle hearts flares rapidly,
    seized this one for my lovely body—how
102   it was violently stripped away still injures me.
Love, which, when one is loved, does not allow
    that it be refused, seized me with joy in him,
105   which, as you see, is with me even now.
Love led us to a single death. The grim
    Caïna waits to claim our murderer."[9]
108   These words were borne across to us from them.
When I had heard those afflicted souls, there were
    long minutes while I stood and bowed my head,
111   until the poet's question made me stir:
"What are you thinking?" When I spoke, I said:
    "How strong desires and thoughts of sweet allure
114   have brought them to this grievous pass instead!"

contrast

And then I turned to face those souls once more:
    "Stinging tears of pain and pity fill my eyes,
117   Francesca, for the torments you endure.
But tell me how you came to recognize
    those dubious desires. How did love show
120   its purpose in the hour of sweet sighs?"

true love?
how good does
Dante think
this is?

And she replied: "There is no greater woe
    than looking back on happiness in days
123   of misery. Your guide can tell you so.
But if you are so eager to retrace
    our love's first root, then I will make it known
126   as one who speaks with tears upon her face.
In reading how Lancelot had been overthrown
    by love,[1] we chanced to pass the time one day.
129   We sat, suspecting nothing, all alone.
Some of the things we read made our eyes stray
    to one another's and the color flee
132   our faces, but one point swept us away.

---

8. Ravenna, the city where Dante died in exile and is buried, was the birthplace of Francesca da Rimini, whom Dante calls by name at line 117. Around 1275, a marriage was arranged between her and the physically deformed Gianciotto Malatesta; according to Boccaccio, she was tricked into believing that his handsome younger brother Paolo was her prospective husband. Sometime between 1283 and 1286, Gianciotto found his wife and brother in an adulterous liaison and killed them both. Omitted in Francesca's highly self-serving account are the facts that Paolo was also married and that both he and Francesca had children.
9. Caïna, described in Canto XXXII, is the first round of Cocytus, the ninth and last circle of hell; named for Cain, it punishes sinners who betrayed family. Caïna "awaits" Gianciotto because his death did not occur until 1304.
1. In the Old French romance *Lancelot du Lac*, Lancelot, one of the knights of the Round Table, fell in love with Guinevere, wife of King Arthur. He lost his purity through their ensuing affair and thus became incapable of discovering the Holy Grail.

We read how that smile desired so ardently
    was kissed by such a lover, one so fine,
135   and this one, who will never part from me,
trembling all over pressed his mouth on mine.
    The book was a Gallehault,[2] the author as well.
138   That day we did not read another line."
And while she told the tale she had to tell,
    the other wept. I fainted where I stood
141   out of pity, as if dying, and I fell
down on the ground the way a dead man would.

as opposed to sleep in 3rd canto

Canto VI

The Third Circle: The Gluttonous; Cerberus; Ciacco; Civil War in Florence

With my sense restored, which had deserted me
    at the pitiful condition of that pair
3   of kinsfolk, stunned by their sad history,
I start to see new torments everywhere
    and new tormented souls, wherever I range
6   or turn myself, wherever I may stare.
I have come to the third circle, where the strange
    damned freezing rainfall endlessly pours down,
9   whose quality and measure never change.

how is Dante affected?

A mass of hail and snow and filthy brown
    water comes streaming through the murky air,
12   and as it lands it putrefies the ground.
The weird and savage Cerberus[1] is there,
    his three throats barking doglike at the dead
15   who lie submerged and sodden everywhere.
With a black and greasy beard, eyes burning red,
    gross belly and huge clawlike hands, he flogs
18   and flays and quarters and rips them all to shreds.
The constant rainfall makes them howl like dogs.
    One side provides the other one's defense
21   as the wretches twist and turn inside their bogs.
The great worm Cerberus saw us and at once

no one has full humanity

---

2. Because Gallehault, Lancelot's friend and fellow knight, acted as go-between for Lancelot and Guinevere, his name had come to signify "panderer."
1. In classical mythology, Cerberus, the fierce three-headed dog, guards the entrance to Hades. In Book VI of the *Aeneid*, the Sybil distracts him with honeyed cake, allowing the living Aeneas to elude his vigilance. The mixture of human attributes with canine ones is Dante's invention.

bared the fangs of his three mouths, and never ceased
24   moving his limbs, all quivering and tense.
My master stretched his open hands and seized
            great clumps of earth, and quickly flung the foul
27   gobbets right down the throats of the greedy beast.
Just as a hungry hound begins to howl
            and then grows quiet when his food is thrown
30   to him, and strains at it with a low growl,
so too the demon Cerberus's own
            smeared faces hushed, that otherwise would roar
33   to make the dead wish they were deaf as stone.
Where shades were flattened by the hard downpour,
            we set our steps upon the emptiness
36   that still looked like the men they'd been before.
All of the shapes were lying in the mess,
            except for one that lifted up its head
39   and sat itself upright to watch us pass.
"O you who are being led through hell," he said,
            "come close to me and name me if you can,
42   for you were made before I was unmade."
"It may be that your suffering," I began,
            "has driven you from my memory, because
45   you seem to me to be an unknown man.
But tell me who you are, set in such loss
            and desolation that, although there might   *as in disgusting?*
48   be greater torments, none could be more gross."
He said: "Your native city, stuffed so tight
            with envy that the sack has overflowed,
51   contained me too, back in the days of light.
Ciacco's the name you citizens bestowed
            on me.[2] For my damned sin of gluttony   *contrapasso?*
54   I'm pounded by the rainfall's filthy load.
Nor am I the only one. These that you see
            pay the same price for the same sin, one and all
57   forever." And he said no more to me.
"Ciacco," I said, "your miseries appall,
            stirring my heart till I could weep for pity.
60   But tell me, if you know, what will befall
the citizens of our divided city,
            and if there be one just man, and why the knife
63   of discord has so rent its soul already."

2. Attempts have been made to identify this character with a poet called Ciacco dell'Anguil-
laia, but there is nothing to support the connection beyond the coincidence of names. The
text suggests that Ciacco was a nickname, one he did not especially enjoy. Since *ciacco*
connotes "pig" or "hog," it is tempting to assume that he was so called because of his glut-
tony, but it is not clear whether the word had this meaning before Dante's use of it.

He answered: "Blood will follow after strife,
      the rustic sect will drive the other one
66   out of the city, with much loss of life.
Before the third full circle of the sun
      the vanquished will turn vanquishers. Through dint
69   of one upon the fence, this will be done.
Their standard will be long in the ascent.
      They'll oppress the others, who will not be freed
72   however much they bristle and lament.
Two men are just, but no one pays them heed.
      Those people's hearts are set aflame by three
75   sparks only—envy, arrogance, and greed."[3]
Thus far he spoke his doleful prophecy.
      I told him: "I would hear more. Once again
78   with the great gift of your words enlighten me.
Of Tegghiaio and Farinata, worthy men,
      Arrigo, Mosca, Rusticucci, as well
81   as many another benevolent citizen,
I want to hear whatever you can tell,
      for I truly wish to discover if they share
84   the honey of heaven or taste the venom of hell."
"Their separate sins," he said, "have dragged them where
      some of the very blackest spirits stay.
87   Keep going down and you will see them there."[4]
But when you see the sweet world again, I pray
      that you bring me to men's memory once more.
90   Nothing else will I answer, nothing will I say."
His eyes, that had looked so steadily, now wore
      a squint. He stared at me, then bent his head
93   and lay down with the other blind ones as before.
"He will not stir again," my leader said,
      "until the angelic trump, when he will see
96   that angry power that all the wicked dread.

---

3. This is the first of the prophecies made by condemned souls at various points in the
   poem. Ciacco predicts events that were still in the future in April 1300, but that oc-
   curred, of course, before the writing of the *Inferno*. After driving the Ghibellines out of
   Florence in 1289, the Guelph party had split into rival factions, the White ("the rustic
   sect," to which Dante belonged, so called because its leaders, the Cerchi family, were
   from outside the city) and the Black ("the other one"); their rivalry flared into open war-
   fare on May 1, 1300, and the Blacks were expelled the following year. The temporizer of
   line 69 is almost certainly the reviled Pope Boniface VIII, whose support of the Blacks en-
   abled them to retake the city in 1302, sending the Whites into exile—an exile which for
   Dante would prove permanent. The identities of the two just men, who are in any event
   insufficient for the city's salvation, have not been positively established.
4. As Ciacco suggests he will, Dante subsequently encounters Farinata degli Uberti (Canto
   X, line 32), Tegghiaio Aldobrandi and Jacopo Rusticucci (Canto XVI, lines 40–45), and
   Mosca dei Lamberti (Canto XXVIII, line 106). Oddly, Arrigo, who has never been posi-
   tively identified, makes no appearance in the *Inferno* and is not mentioned again.

Each will return to his sad tomb to be
  united with his substance and his form
99   and hear the sounding of eternity."
Thus we moved slowly through the sodden scum,
  the filthy mix of spirits and of rain,
102   talking a little of the life to come.
I asked him: "Master, will this burning pain
  be even greater come the judgment day,   *ur philosophy*
105   or stay just as it is, or will it wane?"
And he replied: "What does your science say?[5]   *they keep*
  The more a thing approaches to perfection,   *moving*
108   more pleasure or more pain will come its way. *toward*
Because these people suffer God's rejection,   *lesser*
  they never can be perfect, but are meant   *perfection*
111   in future to be moved in that direction."
Along the circle of the path we went,
  speaking of more than I repeat, till we
114   arrived at where it started its descent.
There we met Plutus, the great enemy.[6]

Canto VII

The Fourth Circle: Misers and Spendthrifts;
The Wheel of Fortune; The Fifth Circle:
The Wrathful and Slothful

"*Pape Satàn, pape Satàn aleppe!*"[1]
  Plutus began to cry with a harsh cluck.
3   That gentle and all-knowing sage then kept me
from losing heart: "Do not let terror block
  your purpose. Whatever power he has, he will
6   never prevent our climbing down this rock."
And then he said: "Accurséd wolf, be still!"
  as he turned to face that bloated countenance.
9   "Aim your rage inward and eat up your fill.

---

5. The science in question is the philosophy of Aristotle, in his *De anima*, and the commentary on it by Thomas Aquinas in the *Summa theologica*.
6. The reference is either to Pluto, the god of the underworld (also known as Hades), or to Plutus, the god of wealth—or possibly to both, since even in classical times they were often thought of in terms of one another. Obviously, in Dantean terms either one would qualify as a "great enemy" of humanity.
1. Discussion of the meaning of this line has been extensive and wide ranging. Some claim that it is mere gibberish, but that interpretation seems implausible: the third line suggests that Virgil understands what Plutus is saying, and the terms Plutus uses do resemble recognizable words. The most common interpretation is that Plutus is invoking Satan as father or pope. With *aleppe*, which suggests the Hebrew *aleph*, he might be either claiming the primacy of Satan or crying out a variation on *alas*.

Not without reason do we now advance
    to the depths. It is willed on high, in the lofty skies
12   where Michael avenged the arrogant offense."[2]
As sails that are swollen when the winds arise
    collapse into a heap when the mast is cracked,
15   so the cruel beast collapsed before our eyes.

(handwritten margin note: bloated; full of air)

Going down to the fourth hollow now, we tracked
    further along that mournful shore where all
18   the evil of the universe is sacked.
Justice of God above! Who stuffs it full
    with these new pains and punishments? How can
21   we let guilt waste us so? As with the pull
of waves that swirl above Charybdis,[3] when
    they crash with counterwaves, forevermore
24   these souls must dance their turn and turn again.
Now greater than what I had seen before
    were the numbers of the damned on either side,
27   chests straining to push great weights, with a mighty roar.
They all would come together and collide,
    then each wheeled round and rolled his weight along.
30   "Why pinch it?" and "Why throw it away?" they cried.
Around the somber circle moved the throng
    till their previous positions were reversed,
33   rebuking each other with their scornful song.
When each arrived where he had been at first,
    he retraced his semicircle to joust again.
36   Feeling as if my heart were about to burst,
"Master, who are these people?" I said then.
    "The tonsured ones amassed on our left side,[4]
39   is it possible they all were clergymen?"
"When they were in the first life," he replied,
    "because they all had squinting intellects,
42   in money matters moderation died.
Their howling clearly shows you the effects,
    when they come to the two points of the circle where
45   their opposite sins divide them into sects.
The ones with heads that lack a hood of hair
    were priests and cardinals and popes. With ease
48   avarice finds its full expression there."

2. Lucifer's rebellion against God led to the expulsion of the rebel angels from heaven by the
   archangel Michael.
3. In Book XII of the *Odyssey*, Odysseus must navigate around the whirlpool Charybdis,
   located in the Strait of Messina. Dante would have been more familiar with Charybdis through
   references in Ovid, Lucan, and the *Aeneid*.
4. The placement of the avaricious on the left side suggests that their sin is worse than that
   of their opposites, the spendthrifts.

"Master," I said, "among such souls as these
    must be a few that I would recognize,
51   who were all polluted by this same disease."
And he: "It would be an empty enterprise.
    The filthy, undiscerning life they led
54   makes their features indiscernible to our eyes.
Forever they will collide and crash. These dead
    will leave the grave with fists squeezed rigidly,
57   and each of those will rise with a close-cropped head.
Wasting and hoarding, they lost eternity
    in the lovely world for this scuffle and this strife.
60   This picture needs no prettied words from me.
Here you see, my son, the brief ridiculous life
    of those goods in Fortune's keeping, for which the race
63   of men compete and squabble and connive.
Not all the gold beneath the moon's bright face,
    or that ever was, could bring rest to as much as
66   one of the weary spirits in this place."
"Of this Fortune, upon whom your discourse touches,
    Master, please tell me more" was my response.
69   "Who is she, who has the world's goods in her clutches?"
"O foolish creatures, what vast ignorance
    oppresses you," he said. "Let me impart
72   my judgment, so you may take it in at once.
He whose wisdom transcends all, at the very start
    made the heavens and gave guides to lead them right,
75   so that every part would shine to every part,
thus equally distributing the light.
    For worldly splendors he likewise put in place
78   a general guide and minister who might
transfer those empty goods through time and place,
    beyond all human wit to intervene,
81   from blood to blood, from one to another race.
One state grows fat with power, another grows lean,
    according to her judgments as she deigns,
84   which like a snake in the grass cannot be seen.
Your knowledge cannot counter her. She reigns,
    providing, judging, making calculations,
87   as do the other gods in their domains.
No truce may interrupt her permutations.
    Necessity demands that she not pause.
90   Man's lot is one of constant variations.
And this is she whom men put on the cross.
    Even the ones who ought to hold her dear
93   revile her name and blame her without cause.
  But she is blesséd and she does not hear.

With the other primal creatures happily
96   she rejoices in her bliss and turns her sphere.
Now we go down to greater misery.
The stars that rose when I set out for you
99   have now begun to sink,[5] and by decree
we must not tarry." We crossed the circle to
the other shore, above a boiling spring
102   that spilled into a ditch it had cut through.
Darker than perse was the water. Following
the downward track where the black current went,
105   we found a strange road for our journeying.
When this sad stream completes its long descent
at the base of the malign gray slopes, its path
108   ends in the Stygian marsh, where I stared, intent,
at the scene before me. In that filthy bath
was a crowd of muddy people, filling it,
111   all naked, all with faces full of wrath.
They hit each other with their fists, and hit
each other with both feet, and chest, and head,
114   and chewed each other to pieces bit by bit.
"My son, you see now," my good master said,
"the souls that anger overwhelmed, and I
117   would have you know for certain that more dead
are down there, underwater, where they sigh
and make the surface bubble with their breath,
120   as you can tell wherever you turn your eye.
Set in the slime, they say: 'We were sullen, with
no pleasure in the sweet, sun-gladdened air,   ⎞ contra-
123   carrying in our souls the fumes of sloth.   ⎟ passo
Now we are sullen in this black ooze'—where   ⎠
they hymn this in their throats with a gurgling sound
126   because they cannot form the words down there."
Between the marsh and dry shore, we walked round
the scummy pool, with our eyes turned toward the place
where the souls were gulping mud, and crossed the ground
129   till we arrived at a tall tower's base.

5. Virgil's words indicate that it is now past midnight.

Canto VIII

Phlegyas; Crossing the Styx; Filippo Argenti; The Gate of Dis

I say, continuing, before our stop
    at the base of that tall tower, our eyes were turned
3   to something gleaming at its very top.[1]
There at the summit two small fires burned
    and another signaled back from far away,
6   so distant it could barely be discerned.
I turned to the sea of all wisdom: "What does it say,
    that flame? And what is meant by the answering light?
9   And the ones who lit these fires, who are they?"
He said: "What they await is heading right
    across the foul waves already, as you can see
12   unless the marsh's fumes hide it from sight."
Never did arrow move so rapidly,
    shot whistling through the air from a bowman's string,
15   as did a boat that I saw suddenly,
coming straight toward where we waited, hastening
    with only a lone rower at the oar,
18   who called: "I have you now, accursèd thing!"
"Phlegyas, Phlegyas,[2] I fear this time you roar
    for nothing," my master said. "You have us as long
21   as it will take to reach the other shore."
Like someone who has heard that a great wrong
    was done to him, and smolders helplessly,
24   so Phlegyas glared at us, with all his strong
anger held back. My leader instructed me
    to follow him in the boat, and I complied.
27   Only when I was aboard did it seem to be
carrying weight. When we were both inside,
    the ancient prow moved forward, cutting through
30   the water more deeply than when others ride.

---

1. From Boccaccio in the fourteenth century to Giorgio Padoan (*Il lungo cammino del "Poema sacro": studi danteschi*, Florence) in 1993, the opening of this canto has led commentators to speculate that some time elapsed between the writing of the first seven cantos and a resumption at this point; such arguments have not drawn much support. Dante does, however, pursue an unusual narrative strategy here, an extended flashback until line 80, when Virgil and Dante arrive at the tower mentioned in the last line of Canto VII.
2. Here, the boatman of the river Styx. In classical mythology, he was the son of the war god Ares and a human mother, and was the father of Coronis, who was seduced by Apollo. To avenge his daughter, Phlegyas burned the temple of Apollo at Delphi, for which the god killed him and condemned him to punishment in the underworld. As a shade, he appears briefly in Book VI of the *Aeneid*, warning others against such rashness toward the gods. John Ciardi notes: "Dante's choice of a ferryman is especially apt. Phlegyas is the link between the Wrathful (to whom his paternity relates him) and the Rebellious Angels who menaced God (as he menaced Apollo)" (*The Inferno*, Rutgers, 1954).

We slipped through that dead channel. "Who are you,"
    cried a muddy shape that lifted up its head,
33   "who come down here before your time is due?"
"If I come, it is not to stay here with the dead.
    But who are you, so covered with this mess?"
36   "You see that I am one who weeps," he said.
And I: "In weeping and in wretchedness
    may you remain, damned soul, for even when
39   you are bathed in filth, I know you nonetheless."
He stretched his two hands toward the boat just then,
    but my wary master gave him a sharp thrust,
42   saying: "Back down with the other dogs again!"
Then he put his arms around my neck and kissed
    my face. "Indignant soul," he said to me,
45   "the mother who carried you is truly blest!
In the world he was arrogant. To his memory
    not a scrap of goodness clings, so his spirit stays
48   down in the mire seething furiously.
How many who think themselves great kings these days
    will lie like pigs in the muck here, and they will
51   leave behind names of horrible dispraise."
"Master," I said to him, "while we are still
    on the lake, it would please me greatly if I might
54   see him dipped down once more into the swill."
And he: "Before the shore has come in sight,
    you will have satisfaction straightaway.
57   To grant a wish like that is only right."
And soon the muddy mob began to flay
    the shade so wildly that for what I saw
60   I still give thanks and praise God to this day.
"Let's get Filippo Argenti!"[3] came the raw
    cry of the crowd, and the raging Florentine
63   turned his teeth upon himself and began to gnaw.
Enough of him. He was no longer seen.
    But my ears were hit with a wave of lamentation
66   and I strained my eyes to see what it might mean.
Said my guide: "My son, we are nearing the location
    of the city whose name is Dis, inhabited
69   by a huge brigade and a somber population."[4]

---

3. Filippo de Cavicciuoli was a member of the Adimari family, who were of the Black faction of the Guelphs (see note 3 to Canto VI). Of great wealth and short temper, he was supposedly called "Argenti" because he had his horse shod with silver. According to early accounts, his brother came into possession of some of Dante's property after the poet's exile from Florence.

4. Dis was another name for Pluto, the Roman god of the underworld, equivalent to the Greek Hades, and by further equivalence another name for Lucifer or Satan. The "huge brigade" are the angels who followed Lucifer in his rebellion against God and were "cast out / and rained from heaven" (lines 82–83).

"Now, master, I can clearly see," I said,
    "there in the valley, all its mosques aglow[5]
72   as if taken from the furnace, fiery red." *satanic?*
And he: "They look that way because they show
    the flame that burns inside them eternally
75   here in the part of hell that lies below."
We had reached the deep moats on the periphery
    of that disconsolate city with its immense
78   walls made of iron, as it seemed to me.
When we had sailed a broad circumference,
    we came to a place where I heard the boatman shout:
81   "Here's the gate! Get out!" Before the battlements
more than a thousand of those who had been cast out
    and rained from heaven, looked at us and cried:
84   "Who is this man who dares to traipse about
through the kingdom of the dead without having died?"
    And my wise master made a sign to say
87   that it was his wish to speak with them aside.
They tempered their scorn a bit: "Well, come you may,
    but come alone. As for him who has the face
90   to breach this kingdom, let him go away.
All alone, if he can do it, let him retrace
    his fool's road. You'll stay here, you who have been
93   his guide on his dark pathway to this place."
Reader, decide for yourself if I did not then
    lose heart at what those demons shouted, for
96   I thought I would never come back here[6] again.
"O my dear leader, seven times and more,"
    I said, "you have restored my confidence
99   and drawn me back from danger. I implore
that you not leave me here with no defense.
    And if our going forward is denied,
102   then side by side let us go back at once."
The lord who had brought me to that place replied:
    "Do not be afraid. No one can interfere
105   with our progress, when its warrant is supplied
by such a one. You will await me here.
    Let your weary soul be comforted and fed
108   with hope. I will not leave you, never fear,

wasn't this also asked of Aeneas travelling to underworld?

on what? no hope there!

---

5. The mosques suggest the medieval Christian view of Islam as a heresy, a rebellion against God. Also, as Bernard Lewis says of medieval and Renaissance references to Islam: "In poetry and polemic, in history and literature, they reflect the consciousness of a Christian Europe besieged and threatened by a mighty and expanding Islamic world, a Europe that in a sense was defined and delimited by the frontiers of Muslim power in the east, the southeast, and the south" (*Cultures in Conflict*, Oxford, 1995).

6. The earth, where Dante is writing his account.

        alone in the low world." So the sweet father said,
           and I remained in doubt while he walked away,
111   with yes and no contending in my head.
        I could not overhear what he had to say,
           but only a moment seemed to pass before
114   they were fighting to get back inside, where they,
        our enemies, immediately shut the door
           against my master, slamming it in his face.
117   Then with slow steps he walked toward me once more.
        He sighed, with eyes cast down, with every trace
           of self-assertion shriveled from his brow:
120   "Who dares deny me sorrow's dwelling place?"
        And to me: "Though I am vexed, do not allow
           your soul to falter, for I shall win through,
123   however they may plot to stop us now.
        This arrogance of theirs is nothing new.
           It was flaunted once at a less secret gate,[7]
126   unbolted despite all that they could do.
        You read its deadly inscription.[8] Coming straight
           past it and through the circles without a guide,
129   there is one who is on his way to where we wait,
        by whom the city will be opened wide."

Canto IX

The Furies; The Threat of Medusa; The Angel; Opening of the Gate; The Sixth Circle: The Heretics

        Seeing the color cowardice gave to me,
           painting my face when I saw my guide turn back,
3   he repressed his own new color instantly.
        He stood like someone listening, for lack
           of light enough to let his vision cross
6   the thick fog and the air that was nearly black.
        "Still, we were meant to be victorious,
           or else . . . ," he said. "She promised us such aid!
9   How long it seems till someone comes to us."
        I clearly saw how his last words overlaid
           the first part of his speech, how their intent
12   reversed the first impression he had made.

---

7. The entrance to hell described at the beginning of Canto III. Christ forced open the outer portal in his harrowing of hell (see note 2 to Canto IV, p. 15), despite the opposition of Satan and his followers.
8. Lines 1–9 of Canto III.

But the phrase that he had left unfinished sent
　　　a new fear through me as my mind supplied
15　　　more dire conclusions than he might have meant.
"Does anyone ever come down," I inquired,
　　　"to this dismal pit from the first circle, where
18　　　the only punishment is hope denied?"
"Indeed," he said, "the instances are rare
　　　that a journey like this one of mine has been
21　　　taken by anyone who dwells up there.
I myself have come here once before. It was when
　　　I was conjured by cruel Erichtho,[1] who designed
24　　　to join souls to their bodies once again.
When newly stripped of my flesh, I was assigned
　　　at her command to breach that wall and bring
27　　　a soul from the place where Judas is confined,[2]
the lowest, darkest, and most distant ring
　　　from the all-encircling heaven. I know this ground.
30　　　Fear not, I know the road we are following.
This powerfully reeking marsh runs all around
　　　the dolorous city, where we cannot go
33　　　without provoking wrath." I heard the sound
of further words, and yet I do not know
　　　what he said next, because my eyes were steered   *sensory overlay*
36　　　to the summit of the high tower, with its glow,
for on that spot had suddenly appeared
　　　three hellish Furies, who in shape and mien
39　　　resembled women, but they were blood-smeared
and girdled with hydras of the deepest green.
　　　They had horned vipers and small snakes for hair,
42　　　round their fierce temples. Handmaids of the queen
of eternal lamentation, all three were
　　　well known to him who turned and said to me:
45　　　"Behold the ferocious Erinyes up there.
That is Megaera on the left, and she
　　　is Alecto who is wailing on the right.
48　　　The one in the center is Tisiphone."[3]
They were clawing at their breasts with all their might,
　　　beating themselves and shrieking. I tried to hold
51　　　as close as I could to the poet in my fright.

1. In Book VI of Lucan's *Pharsalia*, Erichtho, a sorceress of Thessaly, reanimates a dead sol-
dier of Pompey's army at the behest of the general's son, Sextus, who wishes to learn in
advance the outcome of the campaign against Caesar (48 B.C.E.). There is no known
source for the incident that Virgil describes in lines 22–27, and it is generally assumed to
be of Dante's invention.
2. Judecca is the fourth and last region of the ninth and last circle of hell (see Canto XXXIV).
3. The Furies, also known as Erinyes or Eumenides, appear in many classical works, most
notably the *Oresteia* of Aeschylus, as avengers of crimes, especially those that violate the
bonds of kinship. They are presented as the gatekeepers of the city of Dis in Book VI of
the *Aeneid*.

"Now let Medusa[4] come! He'll be stone cold
    when she gets done!" they cried. "It was a poor
54   revenge we took when Theseus was so bold!"[5]
"Turn round and keep your eyes shut tight! Be sure
    that if the Gorgon shows herself to you
57   and you look at her, you will see the world no more!"
So my master cried, and with his own hands too
    he covered my eyes when he had turned me round,
60   as if not trusting what my hands could do.
O you who have intelligence that is sound,
    look through the veil of these strange lines and see
63   to where the hidden doctrine may be found.[6]
Now along the muddy waves there came to me
    a terrifying crash that made the shore
66   on either side start shaking violently,
like one of those wild winds born with a roar
    when two conflicting heats clash in the air,
69   that tears through forests sweeping all before,
smashing the branches, stripping the trees bare,
    driving on proudly in a cloud of dust,
72   scattering beasts and herdsmen everywhere.
My master said, removing the hands still pressed
    around my eyes: "Point the beam of your sight beyond,
75   where the fumes from this ancient scum are bitterest."
As frogs dart through the water to abscond
    from their enemy the serpent, till they lie
78   all huddled at the bottom of the pond,
so I saw many wasted souls slip by,
    more than a thousand, fleeing from one who strode
81   across the Styx with feet that were still dry.
He fanned his left hand often, to clear the load
    of fetid air with which the place was full.
84   This was the only weariness he showed.
I knew that he had come at heaven's will.
    I turned to my master then, who signified
87   that I should bow before him and keep still.
With high disdain, he opened the gate wide
    with a little wand he carried in his hand,
90   and there was no resistance from inside.
"Outcasts of heaven, miserable band,"

[handwritten in margin: "behold an angel"]

4. The Gorgons were three sisters, of whom the beautiful Medusa was the youngest. After her rape by Neptune (Ovid's *Metamorphoses,* Book IV), the goddess Minerva gave her serpents for hair, making her appearance so horrifying that all who saw her were turned to stone.

5. In the version followed by Dante, Theseus, king of Athens, entered the underworld to carry off Proserpine, wife of Hades, and was imprisoned there until Hercules rescued him.

6. Commentators are divided on the meaning of these lines, not only in their interpretations of "the hidden doctrine" but also on whether the "strange lines" are the ones preceding or following this address to the reader.

he called to those within from the terrible sill,
93   "why do you make so insolent a stand?
Why are you so recalcitrant toward the will
         that can never be balked, that has added to the weight
96   of your pain many times? Have you not had your fill?
What do you gain by butting against fate?
         The still-peeled throat and chin of your Cerberus
99   should tell you what those who try can anticipate."[7]
He turned away without a word to us.
         Seeming like one who was preoccupied
102   much more with other matters than he was
with our affairs, he crossed the filthy tide.
         Safe in the holy words and unafraid,
105   we approached the city and we went inside.
No one opposed the progress that we made.
         I was eager to observe the way things fare
108   behind such fortress walls, so my eyes strayed
in all directions once I entered there.
         There was an enormous plain, where I could see
111   great pain and savage torments everywhere.
Just as at Arles, where the Rhône flows sluggishly,
         as at Pola, with Quarnaro lying near
114   to hem Italy in and bathe her boundary,
where sepulchers make all the ground appear
         uneven, with some lower and some higher,[8]
117   so it was here, but so much harsher here.
Surrounded as they were by scattered fire,
         the tombs glowed with a heat much more intense
120   than any human purpose could require.
Their lids were raised, and from them came laments
         so wretched as to make me realize
123   these souls paid horribly for their offense.
"Master," I said, "who are these who agonize
         inside the arks, and in voices so abject
126   fill up the air with so many doleful sighs?"
And he: "The heresiarchs of every sect
         lie here with their followers. Every sepulcher
129   is packed more fully than you would suspect.
They are buried like with like. The temperature
         from tomb to tomb displays great variance."
132   He made a turn to the right, and soon we were
between the tortures and the battlements.

---

7. When Hercules came to hell to rescue Theseus (see note 5), he chained Cerberus and
dragged him on the ground.
8. These lines refer to ancient Roman cemeteries, with sarcophagi of varying heights, in
Provence and in Istria (Croatia).

Canto x

*The Epicureans in the Sepulchers; Farinata; Guelphs
and Ghibellines; Cavalcanti; Guido Cavalcanti is Evoked;
Knowledge of the Future and the Present by the Damned;
Frederick II*

My master walked a secret path that led
    between the great wall and the agonies
3   of the tortured souls. I followed him, and said:
"O highest virtue, revolving me as you please
    through all the unholy circles, satisfy
6   my wishes now and speak to me of these.
Is it possible to see the ones who lie
    in the sepulchers? The lids are raised, I see,
9   and nowhere is any watchman standing by."
"When they come from Jehoshaphat," he answered me,
    "with the bodies they left above at their demise,
12   the tombs will all be sealed eternally.[1]
Here in this section Epicurus lies,[2]
    surrounded by his followers, all those
15   who make the soul die when the body dies.
And therefore to the question that you pose
    you will soon have satisfaction, and have it too
18   to the other wish that you do not disclose."
And I: "I do not hide my heart from you,
    dear guide, except to speak in briefer space,
21   as you have inclined me previously to do."
"O living Tuscan, speaking with such grace
    and honesty as you go walking here
24   in the city of flame, will you please stop in this place?
You are a native son, as your speech makes clear,
    of that noble fatherland to which I have done
27   much damage, and perhaps was too severe."
This sound arising suddenly from one
    of the nearby arks so scared me that I drew
30   close to the side of my leader, whereupon
he said: "What are you doing? Turn round and view

---

1. According to Joel 3.2, Jehoshaphat, a valley between Jerusalem and the Mount of Olives, will be the site of the last judgment, when all will reclaim their bodies and return with them to heaven or hell.
2. The Greek philosopher Epicurus (342–270 B.C.E.) maintained that all events are subject to natural, not supernatural, explanation, and that the greatest good is pleasure (not sensuality, but freedom from pain and anxiety), which is achieved through virtue, temperance, and harmony of mind and body. His philosophy denied divine intervention and punishment and the immortality of the soul.

Farinata[3] who has risen now, upright.
33   From head to waist he stands in front of you."
His gaze and mine already were locked tight.
        He stood with chest thrown out and upturned head
36   as if hell itself were contemptible in his sight.
By my leader's bold and quick hands I was sped
        between the tombs toward him. "Now you must be
39   appropriate in your speech," my master said.
When I reached the foot of his tomb, he looked at me
        for just a moment, and then I heard him say,
42   as if disdainful, "Who were your family?"
And I, since I was eager to obey,
        held nothing back, but told him everything.
45   I saw his brows go up a little way,
then he said: "They were fierce foes, bedevilling
        my party, my house, and me. But on the attack
48   two separate times I sent them scattering."
"Though driven out, they managed to come back
        both times from where they were dispersed," I said,
51   "an art that those of your kind seem to lack."
Beside him rose another of the dead
        just then. This one was on his knees, I thought,
54   for all that he was showing was his head.
His eyes went all around, as if he sought
        someone else who might be there, but when he knew
57   that all his expectation was for naught,
he wept, and said: "If high genius lets you through
        to wander this prison where the light has died,
60   where is my son? and why is he not with you?"
"I have come not of myself. He who stands aside
        leads me through here to one that, it may be,
63   your Guido[4] had disdain for," I replied.

---

3. Manente degli Uberti, called Farinata, was born early in the thirteenth century, and in 1239 became leader of the Ghibellines, who expelled the Guelphs from Florence in 1248. The Guelphs returned three years later and in 1258 expelled the Ghibellines, who drove them out once again in 1260 at the bloody battle of Montaperti, near the river Arbia (see lines 85–86). After the battle, a council was held in Empoli, at which Farinata argued successfully against the intention of the Pisan Ghibellines to destroy Florence (see lines 91–93). Farinata died in 1264, the year before Dante's birth. In 1283, he and his wife, who had disbelieved in the resurrection of Christ, were posthumously branded heretics.
4. The shade to whom Dante is speaking is Cavalcante de' Cavalcanti (died c. 1280), a leader of the Guelphs. His son was the poet Guido Cavalcanti (whose works were translated by Dante Gabriel Rossetti and Ezra Pound). In La vita nuova, Dante had earlier described Guido as his "first friend." In an effort to heal political strife, Guido Cavalcanti was married to Farinata's daughter Beatrice. Farinata's later remarks (lines 100–105) explain why Cavalcante is unaware that his son Guido is alive in April 1300 (and that he will die in August of that year), while Farinata can apparently tell the future. Lines 61–63 are ambiguous, no doubt deliberately so. Even the syntax is not entirely clear, since the object of Guido's disdain can be either Virgil or, in the reading I have followed, the one to whom Virgil is conducting Dante—which can mean either Beatrice or God. The heretical views of the Cavalcanti family would seem to support the latter interpretation.

His words and the nature of his penalty
    had given his identity away
66   and allowed me to respond so thoroughly.
He suddenly stood up straight. "What's that you say?
    He 'had'? Is he no longer living then?
69   Are his eyes not struck by the sweet light of day?"
Noticing how I hesitated when
    he expected me to answer him, he dropped
72   down in his tomb and did not rise again.
That great soul at whose urging I had stopped,
    who had neither changed his look nor moved his head
75   nor turned to watch, once more picked up our cropped
discussion where it had been cut, and said:
    "An art they seem to lack? If that is the case,
78   I find it more tormenting than this bed.
But before the lady who reigns here has her face
    relit another fifty times, you will know
81   all about that art and just how much it weighs.[5]
And explain to me, so may you once more go
    to the sweet world, why your people's laws have spurned
84   my kind, and why you all despise us so."
"The carnage and the savagery that turned
    the Arbia's current crimson," I replied,
87   "are the reason for the prayers that we have learned
to pray in our temple." He shook his head and sighed:
    "I was not alone in that, and would not have thrown
90   in with the rest were it not justified.
But there was a time when with open face I alone
    dared defend Florence when the rest agreed
93   to raze the city down to the last stone."
"And now," I said, "so may peace find your seed,
    I beg you to resolve this knot for me
96   so that my understanding may be freed.
You seem to know of the things that are yet to be
    delivered by time, if what I hear is right,
99   but the present moment, that you cannot see."
He said: "We are like those with squinting sight.
    When things are far away, we see them clear.
102   The lord supreme still grants us that much light.
Our minds are dark when things are close, or here.
    As for the present, we know nothing but
105   what we are told about your human sphere.

5. "The lady who reigns here" is Hecate, or Proserpine, wife of Hades; she was commonly
identified with the moon. Fifty months or so after this prophecy, in the summer of 1304,
the Whites made their last, futile attempt to reenter Florence, after which Dante saw no
prospect of the end of his exile.

Now, therefore, you may comprehend just what
    our future holds. Our knowledge will go dead
108   that moment when the door of time is shut."[6]
It was compunction for my fault that led
    to my next words: "That other shade who fell,
111   tell him his son is still alive," I said.
"As for why I did not answer him, please tell
    of how my thought was wholly occupied
114   in that error you have clarified so well."
And now my master called me to his side,
    so to the shade I hastily appealed
117   to learn who were there with him, and he replied:
"More than a thousand in this part of the field,
    the second Frederick and the Cardinal . . . [7]
120   The names of all the rest I leave concealed."
And he hid himself. I turned toward the venerable
    poet my master, thinking anxiously
123   about those words that seemed to mean me ill.
We moved along, and then he said to me:
    "What has occurred to make you so unnerved?"
126   And I satisfied his curiosity.
"Let the words that were said against you be preserved
    in memory, but take heed," the sage commanded,
129   and then he raised his finger as he observed:
"When you stand in her sweet radiance whose splendid
    eyes can see all, then you will learn from her
132   the whole journey of your life till it is ended."
We turned to the left, from the walled perimeter
    to a central path on which we were to go
135   down into a valley. High up as we were,
we were sickened by the vile stench from below.

---

6. After the last judgment, time will no longer exist.
7. Ottaviano degli Ubaldini (d. 1273), who was suspected of unbelief and is reputed to have said, "If I have a soul, I have lost it a thousand times for the Ghibellines." His nephew Archbishop Ruggieri is among the most deeply damned (see Canto XXXIII and its first note). Frederick II (1194–1250), king of Sicily and Naples, Holy Roman Emperor, was known as *stupor mundi*, "the wonder of the world," for his political skills, his intellectual accomplishments and fostering of learning, and his open mind and humanistic spirit. Although himself a scourge of heretics, he was suspected of Epicureanism by the Guelphs; the latter part of his reign was marked by constant struggles with the papacy, and he was excommunicated.

Canto XI

Expositions of the Plan of Hell; Tripartite Division:
Incontinence (Outside of the City of Dis), Violence, and
Fraud in Lower Hell; Violence Is Punished in Three
Concentric Rings of the Seventh Circle; The Deceivers
Punished in Ten Concentric Ditches of the Eighth Circle;
Traitors in the Ninth Circle; Theory of Art as Work.

At the edge of a high bank formed by a ring
        of enormous broken rocks, we came to a halt
3   and looked down on a crueler gathering.
Choked by the overpowering assault
        of noxious stink that rose from the deep abyss,
6   we drew back to the lid of a large vault
on which I saw an inscription that said this:
        "Herein I hold Pope Anastasius, drawn
9   by Photinus from the path of righteousness."[1]
"We must tarry here before we can go on,"
        my master said, "till the sense has been resigned
12   to the foul breath, and the odor will seem gone."
"So the time will not be wasted, can we find
        some compensation?" I inquired of him,
15   and he replied: "That is what I have in mind."
So he thus began: "My son, inside the rim
        of the rocks, three smaller, narrowing circles lie,
18   like the ones through which we have already come.
All are filled up with damned spirits. So that I
        need only show them to you in due course,
21   I will tell you now how they are held and why.
The intent of every malice that heaven abhors
        is an injustice, and the result of it
24   is to do another harm, by fraud or force.
Because only human beings can commit
        a fraud, this is the sin God most resents.
27   These sinners endure more pain, in the lower pit.
The first circle holds the violent. Since violence
        may have three objects, the circle is split in three
30   and has one ring for each kind of offense.
To God or self or neighbor one may be

1. There is a possible confusion here between Pope Anastasius II (496–498) and the em-
peror Anastasius I (491–518). Photinus, a deacon of Thessalonica, is believed to have
persuaded the emperor to the heresy of Acacius, which denied the divinity of Christ. On
the other hand, Robert and Jean Hollander point out that Isidore of Seville, a possible
source for Dante's lines, says that Pope Anastasius was converted by Photinus, bishop of
Sirmium, to the Ebionite heresy, which claimed that Jesus was the purely human child of
Mary and Joseph (*Dante Alighieri: Inferno*, Doubleday, 2000).

violent, against his person or possession,
33   as I will now unfold it logically.
Wounding and death come of violent aggression
    on a neighbor's self. On his property one may bring
36   ruin, arson, or extortionate oppression.
You will see in separate groups in the first ring
    despoilers, plunderers, murderers, everyone
39   who used malicious force on man or thing.
To one's own person violence may be done,
    or to one's own goods. To the second ring are sent
42   all those who now must uselessly atone
for robbing themselves of the world, all those who went
    through their property with dice or dissipation,
45   all those who wept when they should have been content.
They are violent against God who feel negation
    and blasphemy at heart, who in bitterness
48   hate nature and the bounty of creation.
And thus the smallest ring with its impress
    seals Sodom and Cahors,[2] and those who say
51   evil of God within the heart's recess.
Fraud gnaws at every conscience, and a man may
    use fraud on one who trusts him or one who invests
54   no special confidence. In the latter way
he breaks the natural bond of love that exists
    among all humanity, and thus is sent
57   to the second circle, which contains the nests
of hypocrites, flatterers, thieves, those who were bent
    on sorcery, simoniacs and cheats,
60   swindlers and pimps and all such excrement.
But in the former way he violates
    not just this natural love, but what is worse,
63   a special bond and the trust that it creates.
Thus at the center of the universe
    is the seat of Dis, the smallest circle, where
66   all traitors are ravaged by the eternal curse."
"Master, your lucid words make me aware,"
    I said, "of how the abyss has been laid out
69   and the kinds of people that are kept down there.
But those in the thick marsh, those who are driven about
    by the wind, those in the rainfall and its mess,
72   and those who crash together and harshly shout,
why does the red-hot city not oppress
    those souls with pain, if they have earned God's hate?
75   If not, why are they set in such distress?"

---

2. A city in southern France that was notorious in the Middle Ages for usury. "Sodom": connotes sodomy.

"Why does your understanding deviate
    so far afield?" he said. "Has your mind been driven
78   by stray thoughts into some distracted state?
Do you forget the explanation given,
    in the pages of your *Ethics,*[3] of the three
81   dispositions that offend the will of heaven,
incontinence, malice, and mad bestiality?
    How it says there that incontinence will incur
84   less blame, offending God less grievously?
If you contemplate that saying and you stir
    your wits to recollect the souls you saw
87   punished above, just who and what they were,
you will see why justice has seen fit to draw
    a line between them and the evil souls below,
90   why they are less fiercely battered by God's law."
"O sun that clears the mists, your answers so
    content me that I am as gratified
93   to be perplexed by doubt as I am to know.
But please go back," I said, "to where you implied
    that one who practices usury offends
96   God's bounty. I would like that knot untied."
"Philosophy, to one who comprehends,
    makes clear," he said, "and not only in one part,
99   that the course of nature totally depends
upon divine intelligence and its art.
    If you read your *Physics*[4] carefully, then you
102   will find, not many pages from the start,
that art follows nature, as well as it can do,
    like a pupil with his master. It may be said
105   that your art is God's grandchild. It is by these two,
as you will recollect from having read
    the beginning of Genesis, that humans were
108   enjoined to make their way and earn their bread.[5]
By taking another road, the usurer
    puts his hope elsewhere, and in doing so
111   despises nature and her follower.
But now come follow me, for I wish to go.

---

3. Aristotle's *Nicomachean Ethics* is cited. For Aristotle, "bestiality," or brutishness, is a cat-
egory that transcends the normal range of human evil to encompass such things as can-
nibalism; since the *Inferno* groups violence and fraud under malice, there has been much
debate over what Dante intends by the term.
4. The reference is to the *Physics* of Aristotle, although this discussion of usury more likely
derives from the commentary of Aquinas on Aristotle's *Politics.*
5. See Genesis 3.19: "In the sweat of thy face shalt thou eat bread, till thou return unto the
ground."

The Wain has crossed over Caurus the north wind,
114   on the horizon the Fish begin to glow,
     and before us waits the cliff we must descend."[6]

Canto XII

*The Seventh Circle: The Violent; The Minotaur; The First Ring:
Violence against Others; The Centaurs; The River of Blood*

The place was of an alpine nature where   *rocky, treacherous*
     we were to go down, a place to be abhorred   *location (not*
     by every eye because of what was there.   *the fun Alps)*

3   As with the devastation that was poured
     on the bank of the Adige this side of Trent
     by a quake or by the land's being badly shored,[1]

6   where down the mountainside the turbulent
     rockslide has formed a pathway to allow
     the traveler to make a rough descent,

9   such was the slope that we had come to now.
     And stretched out near the shattered chasm's edge
     lay the thing that was conceived in the false cow,

12   the infamy of Crete.[2] Like one whose rage
     is tearing at his insides, he began
     to bite himself at the sight of us. My sage

15   called out to him: "Perhaps you think this man
     is the Duke of Athens, he who struck you dead   *Theseus*
     in the world above, coming after you again.

18   Beast, get away from here! He is not led
     by your sister's guidance,[3] but has come to see
     the punishments inflicted on your head."

21   And like a bull that suddenly breaks free
     when it takes its deathblow, and from side to side
     it leaps and wheels, careening crazily,

24   the Minotaur jumped up, and my wary guide
     called out to me: "Run for the opening there

---

6. The Wain is the Big Dipper, and the Fish are the constellation Pisces. It is now about four o'clock in the morning, and ten of the journey's twenty-four hours have elapsed.
1. The precipice of Slavini di Marco, south of Trent in northern Italy, was formed by a land-slide, c. 883, which diverted the Adige from its course.
2. Minos, king of Crete, failed to carry out the promised sacrifice of a bull to the sea god Poseidon, who afflicted Minos's wife, Pasiphaë, with an unnatural passion for a bull. She lured the bull by crouching inside a wooden cow covered with cowhide. From this union was born the Minotaur, which Minos kept imprisoned in an intricate labyrinth. It is usu-ally represented as having a bull's head and a human body.
3. Theseus, king of Athens, killed the Minotaur with the assistance of Ariadne, daughter of Minos and Pasiphaë, who provided him with a sword and a long thread by which to find his way back out of the labyrinth.

27   while his mad fury has him occupied!"
We picked our way down the scattered rockpile, where
     the stones beneath my feet were moved about
30   by the unaccustomed load I made them bear.
I was walking lost in thought, till he spoke out:
     "Are you thinking about this ruin, guarded by
33   that beastly wrath I just now put to rout?
You should be aware that the other time that I
     delved down into the deep hell's lowest ring,
36   this crag had not yet fallen from on high.
Not long before he came, by my reckoning,
     who carried off from Dis the great spoils of
39   the highest circle through his harrowing,
the deep and reeking pit so shook—above,
     below, on every side—that I began
42   to think the universe was moved by love,
by which, some say, the world has often been
     convulsed to chaos. These ancient rocks, both here
45   and elsewhere, all came crashing down just then.[4]
But look to the valley. All who interfere
     with others by violence, doing them injury,
48   are boiled in the river of blood that is coming near."
O senseless rage and blind cupidity,
     that in the short life stimulate us so
51   and in the eternal one drench us wretchedly!
I saw a broad ditch bending like a bow,
     just as my guide had said, with its wide embrace
54   surrounding the whole plain that lay below.
I saw a single file of centaurs race,[5]
     with arrows armed, between the ditch and hill,
57   as in the world they had galloped to the chase.
When they saw us coming down, they all stood still.
     Selecting arrows, three began to go
60   away from the others, approaching us, until
one called from afar. "You there! We want to know
     what punishment you are going to," he said.
63   "Tell us from there, or else I draw the bow."
My master answered: "We will reply instead
     to Chiron[6] beside you, when we come down there.
66   You have always harmed yourself with your hot head."
He nudged me. "That is Nessus, who died for the fair

4. In Matthew 27.50–53, the earth is convulsed by a mighty earthquake at the moment of Christ's death upon the cross.
5. The original centaurs, one hundred in number, were passionate and violent creatures, half man, half horse. They were born when Ixion, seeking to possess Hera, instead assaulted a cloud that Zeus had fashioned to resemble her, and the drops of his seed fell to the earth.
6. The son of Philyra and of Kronos, the sun god, who had turned himself into a horse to elude his wife's jealousy. Wise and just, Chiron was the tutor of Achilles, Jason, Asclepius, and others.

Deïanira, having managed first to stage
revenge for himself upon his very slayer.[7]
69
In the center, gazing at his chest, is sage
Chiron, who taught Achilles. The other one
72
is Pholus,[8] who was always full of rage.
They patrol the ditch in thousands, arrows drawn
to pierce any spirit who rises from the blood
75
higher than guilt allows." Then we moved on,
approaching where those nimble creatures stood.
Chiron took up an arrow, and with its notch
78
he brushed his beard aside until his broad
mouth was uncovered, and told the others: "Watch
the one who walks behind. Look, do you see it,
81
the way his feet are moving what they touch?   *feet!*
I have never seen that done by dead men's feet."
My good leader, who now stood before his breast,
84
that part of him where his two natures meet,
replied: "He is alive, as I'll attest.
Alone I must show him the dark vale, not for my
87
or his pleasure, but at necessity's behest.
One who was singing alleluia on high
came where I was, to give me this new command.
90
He is no thief, no cutpurse soul am I.
But by the power that through so wild a land
moves all my steps, I ask you now to spare
93
one who can guide us, a member of your band
to walk beside us and to show us where
the crossing is, and carry him astride,
96
for he is no spirit who can fly through air."   *he has a body*
Chiron told Nessus: "Go then, be their guide,"
as he turned on his right flank, "and if you see
99
another troop, then make them move aside."
With our trusty escort we walked the boundary
of the boiling crimson, where we heard the cries
102
of the boiled shades shrieking in their agony.
With some, the river rose above their eyes.
The great centaur said: "These gave themselves to fierce
105
plunder and carnage, living to tyrannize.
Here they lament their merciless careers.

7. Nessus, one of the sons of Ixion, carried Deïanira, wife of Hercules, across a stream. Attempting to rape her, he was shot by Hercules with a poisoned arrow. Dying, the centaur told her to keep some of his blood, which, he claimed, when smeared on a garment, would cause its wearer to love her. Hercules later fell in love with Iole, Deïanira gave him the garment, and its poison caused him such horrible suffering that he committed suicide (Ovid, *Metamorphoses,* Book IX).
8. Another of Ixion's sons, Pholus died accidentally when he dropped one of Hercules' poisoned arrows on his foot.

        Here is Alexander, cruel Dionysius too[9]
108   who gave Sicily so many painful years.
    This one upon whose head such black hair grew
        is Azzolino,[1] and that fairhaired one
111   is Opizzo d'Esti,[2] who—and this is true—
    was extinguished in the world by his stepson."
        I turned to the poet, who told me: "In this sphere
114   he leads, I follow. Thus let it be done."
    We approached a group whose heads and throats were clear
        of the stream. One spirit stood alone, away
117   from all of the other ones. As we drew near,
    the centaur stopped to point to him and say:
        "That one pierced through a heart, in God's own breast,
120   that drips blood above the Thames to this very day."[3]
    Then I saw some who stood up to the chest
        out of the current, and in this crowd I spied
123   many I recognized among the rest.
    Thus more and more I saw the bloody tide
        recede, till it cooked the feet alone, so low
126   that here we went across to the other side.
    "Just as you see the boiling river grow
        more and more shallow," the centaur said to me,
129   "here in this part of the plain, I would have you know
    that on the other side it constantly
        grows deeper till it completes its circle where
132   the tyrants are groaning in their misery.
    Heavenly justice stings Attila[4] there,
        who was a scourge upon the earth for years,
135   and Pyrrhus and Sextus.[5] And it stings that pair—
    the one from Corneto, and Pazzo—the two Riniers[6]

9. The likeliest identifications are Alexander of Macedonia, the Great (356–323 B.C.E.), and Dionysus the Elder, who ruled Syracuse from 405 to 367 B.C.E.
1. Ezzelino III da Romano (1194–1259), son-in-law of Frederick II, was a Ghibelline leader who committed atrocities, especially against the Paduans.
2. Obizzo II d'Este (1247–1293), lord of Ferrara and a Guelph, is believed to have been smothered by his son and successor, Azzo VIII. Various attempts have been made to explain "stepson": some see it as a hint at the infidelity of Obizzo's wife, others as a suggestion of the unnaturalness of his son's crime.
3. "That one" is Guy de Montfort (c. 1243–1298), of royal English blood. To avenge his father, Simon de Montfort, killed at the battle of Evesham in 1265 by the future Edward I, Guy stabbed Edward's cousin, Prince Henry of Cornwall, at mass in the church of San Silvestro in Viterbo in 1271. According to one source, Henry's heart was placed in a golden casket on a pillar at the end of London Bridge. It continues to drip because Henry's murder remains unavenged.
4. Attila (c. 406–453), king of the Huns c. 433–453, was known as the Scourge of God.
5. Both identifications are disputed, but Pyrrhus is probably the king of Epirus (318–272 B.C.E.) whose defeat of the Romans at Asculum in 279 was the original Pyrrhic victory, and Sextus is most likely Sextus Pompeius Magnus (d. 35 B.C.E.), younger son of Pompey the Great.
6. Rinier da Corneto and Rinier Pazzo were highway robbers of Dante's time, the former near Rome and the latter south of Florence.

who turned the public roads to fields of war,
138   for the bath unlocks and justice milks their tears."
Then he turned round and crossed the ford once more.

Canto XIII

*The Seventh Circle, Second Ring: The Violent against
Themselves; Wood of the Suicides; Pier delle Vigne; The Chase
of the Squanderers; The Anonymous Florentine*

Not yet had Nessus finished crossing there
     when we began to walk into a grim
3   forest without a pathway anywhere.
Not bright green leaves, but foliage dark and dim,
     not sturdy branches, but each a twisted bough,
6   not fruits, but poisoned thorns on every limb.
Not even the beasts that hate the lands men plow
     between Corneto and Cécina[1] can roam
9   through such rough, tangled brush as I saw now.
This wood is the foul, nesting Harpies' home,
     who drove the Trojans from the Strophades
12   with dread predictions of approaching doom.
With talons, broad wings, gross feathered paunches, these
     human-faced things sit uttering their lay   *human/bird*
15   of lamentation in the twisted trees.[2]
"Before going any further on the way,"
     said my good master, "I would have you know
18   you are in the second ring, where you will stay
till the horrid sand. Look closely as we go.
     Here are things that you would call impossible
21   if you had heard me tell you they were so."
I could hear wailing, deep and pitiful,
     but there was no one anywhere about,   *body-less*
24   and I grew so perplexed that I stood still.
I think that he was thinking that I thought
     that all those voices came from people who,
27   on seeing us approach, had quickly sought
to hide themselves. And so he said: "If you
     break off a little branch, you will soon see
30   that what you are thinking will be broken too."
Then I reached out, and from a great thorn tree

---

1. The reference is to the rough terrain of the Maremma in Tuscany, bounded on the north by
the river Cecina and on the south by the Marta, on which the town of Corneto is situated.
2. The Harpies, daughters of Thaumas and Electra, were usually represented as birds with
the faces of women and as defilers of food. In Book III of the *Aeneid*, they chase the Tro-
jans from the Strophades islands with prophecies of famine and starvation.

I tugged a branch until it snapped apart,
33   and the stem cried out: "Why are you tearing me?"
Where it was broken, I saw dark blood start.   *bodily*
        "Why are you mangling me?" it cried again.
36   "Have you no spirit of pity in your heart?
Now we are turned to stumps, but we were men
        when we were on the earth. Truly, your hand
39   should show more mercy, even if we had been
the souls of serpents." Just as a green brand
        will burn at one end, and the escaping air
42   will hiss as sap drips from the other end,
so from the stump words mixed with blood flowed where
        I had broken it. I dropped it suddenly,
45   and like someone terror-stricken I stood there.
"O wounded soul," my sage replied, "if he
        could have believed what previously he had met
48   only in the pages of my poetry,[3]
he would not have raised his hand to you, and yet
        the thing was so incredible that I came
51   to urge him on, which I myself regret.
So that he may make amends, let him know your name,
        that when, as he will be allowed to do,
54   he returns to earth, he may refresh your fame."
Said the stem: "Allured by such sweet words from you,
        I cannot stay silent. May it not displease
57   if I am enticed to speak a word or two.
I was the man who carried both the keys
        to Frederick's heart.[4] I turned them expertly,
60   locking, unlocking with such tender ease
that scarcely any shared his intimacy.
        True to the glorious office in my care,
63   I gave up sleep and my vitality.
That whore who never turns aside her stare,[5]
        keeping her sluttish eyes on Caesar's hall,
66   common vice and death of royal courts everywhere,
inflamed all minds against me, and they all,
        once so inflamed, then so inflamed Augustus
69   that my glad honors turned to mortal gall.
My mind, so filled with scorn and with disgust, was

3. In Book III of the *Aeneid*, Aeneas breaks the branch of a myrtle bush, and from it comes the
   voice of the murdered Polydorus, a son of King Priam, who is buried beneath the plant.
4. The speaker is Pier delle Vigne (c. 1190–1249), a trusted counselor and minister of Em-
   peror Frederick II. After a long and successful career, he was accused of treachery, blinded,
   and thrown into prison, where he committed suicide. His speech in this canto reflects the
   rhetorically ornate style both of his official documents, written in Latin, and of his vernacu-
   lar poetry.
5. The reference is to envy.

thinking through death to escape their scorn for me,
72   so myself to my just self did great injustice.
But I swear by the new and strange roots of this tree   *I swear by my new feet*
      that I never once betrayed my lord, who so
75   deserved all honor and all loyalty.
If it is true that one of you will go
      back to earth, restore my memory, which still
78   lies fallen from the force of envy's blow."
The poet paused for a little while, until
      he said: "Since he is silent, you should start
81   to use the time, and ask him what you will."
And I replied: "Now you must take my part
      and speak for me. I am unable to,
84   with so much pity tearing through my heart."
So he began: "That this man may freely do
      what you have begged, then satisfy his mind,
87   imprisoned spirit, if it pleases you
to tell us how the gnarled wood comes to bind
      the souls, and if you know whether one may be
90   set free again once it has been confined."
When he had done, the branch puffed mightily
      and then these words were fashioned from that breath: *how to speak*
93   "I will briefly answer what you ask of me.
When the ferocious soul is finished with
      the flesh from which it rooted itself out,
96   Minos sends it to the seventh hole in his wrath.
It falls into the forest, blown about
      where fortune flings it. After its descent
99   it roots at random. Like spelt it starts to sprout.
It grows to a sapling, then to a wild plant.
      The Harpies, feasting on its foliage then,
102   both give it pain and give the pain a vent.   *speak through open wounds*
We will come for our remains like other men,
      but not to wear them. It would not be fit
105   that what we steal from ourselves we have again.
We will drag our bodies here to this desolate
      forest, where they will hang forevermore,
108   each on the tree of the shade that murdered it."
We waited, thinking that he might say more,
      but then we were startled by a clamorous sound,
111   as when a hunter senses the wild boar
and the hounds hot on its heels as they all pound
      toward where he stands in wait, and hears the blare
114   of the beasts, and branches crashing all around.
And hard upon our left we saw a pair
      of scratched and naked figures running by
117   so fast they smashed the tangles everywhere.

"Come quickly, death, come quickly!" came the cry
    from the leader. Losing ground, the other one
120   called out: "Ah, Lano, your legs were not so spry
in the jousting at the Toppo!" Whereupon
    he knotted himself with a bush, as if to hide,
123   perhaps because his breath was nearly gone.[6]
A swarm of great black mastiffs in full stride
    filled up the wood behind them, like a pack
126   of starving swift greyhounds who have been untied.
They reached the bush and fell to the attack.
    They tore the one who crouched there limb from limb,
129   then seized the wretched pieces and ran back.
My escort took my hand, and I walked with him
    to stand before the torn bush where it bled,
132   weeping uselessly through every broken stem.
"O Jacopo de Sant'Andrea," it said,
    "you made me your screen, and what good did it do?
135   How am I to blame for the evil life you led?"
Then my master stood above it. "Who were you,"
    he asked, "who have words and blood now blowing out
138   through so many limbs that have been snapped in two?"
"O souls who arrived to see this shameful rout,"[7]
    it told us, "that has ripped the foliage from
141   my boughs, please bring the leaves that are strewn about
to the foot of this unhappy bush. My home
    was the city that chose the Baptist to replace
144   its ancient patron, who for all time to come
will therefore use his art to afflict our race.
    And if the Arno bridge did not still contain
147   some semblance of his visage at its base,
then those who made the city rise again
    out of the ashes left by Attila[8] when he
150   destroyed it would have done their work in vain.
I turned my house into my gallows tree."

6. Arcolano Maconi of Siena and Giacomo da Sant'Andrea of Padua were notorious spend-
thrifts and squanderers of their property. Maconi died in 1288 in a bloody encounter be-
tween the Sienese and the Aretines at the crossing of the Pieve del Toppo, reputedly
choosing to die in battle rather than to escape and live in poverty.

7. The speaker of lines 139–51 has not been positively identified. According to legend as re-
ported in the early commentaries, in pagan times the Florentines chose Mars, the god of
war, as their patron. When the city was converted to Christianity, Mars was replaced by
Saint John the Baptist, but the statue of Mars was preserved in a tower, in order to avoid
the god's displeasure. When Florence was destroyed by Attila in 450, the tower—and the
statue—fell into the Arno. When the city was rebuilt by Charlemagne early in the ninth
century, the statue was recovered and placed on a pillar by the river, where it remained
until it was swept away by a flood in 1333.

8. Florence was in fact besieged by Totila, king of the Ostrogoths, in 542, not by Attila nearly
a century earlier. There is no evidence that the city was destroyed by Totila—or by Attila
or by anyone else—and then rebuilt by Charlemagne.

Canto XIV

*The Seventh Circle, Third Ring: The Violent against God,
Nature, or Art; The Sandy Plain and the Rain of Fire;
Capaneus; The Rivers of Hell; The Old Man of Crete*

By the love of my native land I was bestirred
　　　to gather up the scattered leaves for him,
3　　whose voice had grown too feeble to be heard.
From there we moved on, coming to the rim
　　　that marks the second from the third ring, where
6　　the hand of justice is horrible and grim.
To explain these new things, I must now declare
　　　that we had come upon a plain which would
9　　permit no plant to root or flower there.
The plain is garlanded by the sad wood,
　　　just as the wood is girded by the band
12　　of the miserable ditch. We paused, and stood
at the very edge. I saw the ground was sand,
　　　arid and deep, and in its quality
15　　like that where Cato marched with his command.[1]
O vengeance of God almighty, they should be
　　　quaking in terror now who read of these
18　　horrors that were made manifest to me!
I saw naked souls bewailing their miseries,
　　　ranged in many herds, and every group seemed bound
21　　to suffer a separate set of penalties.
Some of them lay stretched out along the ground,
　　　some of them crouched and squatted, and others went
24　　unendingly meandering around.
Those who wandered were the largest complement.
　　　Fewer in number were the ones who lay
27　　on the ground, but they were loudest in lament.
Enormous flakes of fire made their way
　　　through the air, falling slowly over the whole expanse,
30　　like snow in the mountains on a windless day.
And just as Alexander[2] in the intense
　　　broiling heat of India saw fireballs fall
33　　to earth, intact, upon his regiments,

---

1. Cato the Younger (95–46 B.C.E.) led his army through the northern Sahara in Libya to es-
cape Caesar's forces after the defeat of Pompey. Dante adapts a reference from Lucan's
Pharsalia, in which Cato refuses to be carried, as was customary, and instead marches on
foot with his soldiers.
2. Dante here cites the *De meteoris* of Albertus Magnus (c. 1200–1280), who misrecalls an in-
cident in the (probably spurious) *Epistoli Alexandri,* in which Alexander the Great suppos-
edly describes to his tutor, Aristotle, how he had ordered his soldiers to trample the snow.

and had his men begin to trample all
     the soil around them, so as to contain
36   the flames while they were separate and small,
so I saw now with the everlasting rain.
     Just as flint will kindle tinder, it ignited
39   the sand and thus redoubled all the pain.
Here, there, the wretched hands danced an excited   *& forced*
     and constant dance as they brushed away the spate
42   of fiery flakes that endlessly alighted.
I said: "O master, you who eliminate
     all obstacles except that obstinate breed
45   of demons at the entrance to the gate,
who is that great one[3] who seems not to heed
     the flame, lying there with a scornful scowl instead,
48   who despite the rain remains an unripened seed?"
That very shade immediately said,
     knowing he was the one alluded to:
51   "What I was when I was alive, I still am, dead!
Though Jove wear out his smith, from whom he drew
     the sharpened bolt that on my final day
54   was hurled at me in rage and ran me through,
though he wear out one by one the whole array
     of dark Mongibello's[4] blacksmiths with the call
57   of 'Help me, good Vulcan, help me,' just the way
he did at the field of Phlegra,[5] and then with all
     his might fall down upon me, I guarantee
60   that his pleasure in his vengeance will be small."
And then my leader spoke more forcefully
     than I had ever heard him speak, and cried:
63   "Capaneus, your punishment's intensity
grows stronger with your unextinguished pride.
     No torment could be more appropriate
66   than your ravings, for the rage you have inside."
Then he turned to me, with his face less sternly set.
     "He was one of the seven kings, and with the rest
69   besieged Thebes. He held God—and seems to yet—

---

3. Capaneus was one of the seven against Thebes, as recounted in the *Thebaid*, an epic poem by Statius (Publius Papinius Statius, c. 40–96 C.E.). With the aid of an army and seven mighty champions, Polynices, son of Oedipus, besieged the city when his brother Eteocles refused to relinquish power to him as previously agreed. As he scaled the city wall, Capaneus defied Jove, who slew him with a thunderbolt.
4. Mongibello is Mount Etna in Sicily, where Vulcan had his forge.
5. At Phlegra, Jove defeated the giants who were storming Mount Olympus.

in high disdain, in low esteem at best.
　　　But his own rantings, as you heard me say,
72　　　are the fittest decorations for his breast.
　　Now follow me, and be careful not to stray
　　　to the burning sand, but let your feet be led
75　　　close to the forest the entire way."

[handwritten: Dante can be burned by the hell-sand]

　　We walked in silence till we reached the bed
　　　of a stream that spurted from the woods, whose look
78　　　makes me shudder even now, it was so red.
　　Down from the Bulicame[6] comes a brook
　　　that the sinful women share, just like the flow
81　　　of this rivulet that through the hot sands took
　　its steady course. Its bed was stone, and so
　　　were both its banks and both its margins too,
84　　　and I saw that this was the path we were to go.
　　"Of all the things that I have shown to you
　　　since we crossed the threshold of the wide gate where
87　　　no one is ever stopped from coming through,
　　not one among those marvels can compare
　　　to this stream that has the power to quench the fire
90　　　that comes raining down upon it through the air."
　　So my leader said, which led me to inquire
　　　if he would have the grace to furnish me
93　　　with the food for which he had furnished the desire.
　　"There is a land in the middle of the sea,
　　　a wasteland now, called Crete,"[7] my lord replied,
96　　　"under whose king the world lived virtuously.
　　It has a mountain, Ida, once supplied
　　　with plants and water bright beneath the sky,
99　　　deserted now like something cast aside.
　　There Rhea hid her son in days gone by,
　　　concealed in his safe cradle, and had each priest
102　　　make a loud clamor when the child would cry.[8]
　　In the mountain is a huge old man encased,
　　　who looks toward Rome as in a looking glass,
105　　　with his back to Damietta in the east.[9]

6. A hot spring, near Viterbo, where a spa developed. According to Boccaccio, a stream was
diverted from the spring to serve the needs of the many local prostitutes, who were not al-
lowed to use the public baths.
7. The Mediterranean island of Crete was once believed to be the center of the world. Ac-
cording to the *Aeneid,* it was the source of Trojan—and therefore of Roman—civilization.
Its king was Saturn (equivalent to the Greek Kronos).
8. Saturn devoured each of his children to prevent the fulfillment of the prophecy that he
would be overthrown by one of them. His wife, Rhea, hid their son Jupiter (or Jove) to
spare him this fate.
9. The statue is derived from the dream of Nebuchadnezzar (Daniel 2.31–35), but its place-
ment within Mount Ida is apparently Dante's invention. According to Charles S. Singleton,

His head is made of gold of the finest class,
    of purest silver are his arms and breast,
108   to where the legs fork he is solid brass.
From there he is choice iron, the very best,
    except for his right foot, which is baked clay.
111   On this, more than the other, his weight is pressed.
All the parts of him except the gold display
    great fissures. Constant tears seep from each crack
114   and cut through the floor of the cavern. Slipping away
to this valley as they drip from rock to rock,
    they form the Acheron, Styx, and Phlegethon.
117   Then they descend along this narrow track
till, where no more descending can be done,
    they form Cocytus.[1] I will not speak to you
120   of that pool, which your own eyes will look upon."
I asked him then: "And yet, if it is true
    that this stream starts up above, where the living are,
123   why does it only now come into view?"
"You know," he said, "that the place is circular,
    and going toward the bottom with your feet
126   turned always to the left, you have come far,
but the whole circle is not yet complete.
    So there needn't be such astonishment upon
129   your face at every new thing that we meet."
And I said: "Master, where are Phlegethon
    and Lethe? You have told me that one is fed
132   by this rain, and say nothing of the other one."
"All of your questions please me well," he said,
    "but you should find one solution in the roll
135   of the stream before you as it boils blood-red.
And you will see Lethe too, not in this hole
    but far from here, in the place where spirits go
138   to wash when penance has purged guilt from the soul.[2]
It is time for you to leave the wood, and so
    you must follow me closely through the fiery sand
141   on the margins, which do not burn, because the flow
quenches all the flames above it before they land."

---

the Egyptian city of Damietta may have been identified in the Middle Ages with Mem-
phis, the seat of the Pharaohs (*Dante Alighieri: The Divine Comedy. Inferno 2: Commen-
tary.* Princeton, 1970).
1. The frozen lake at the pit of hell (Cantos XXXIII–XXXIV).
2. In Latin poetry, Lethe is the river of forgetfulness, whose waters are drunk by souls about
    to be reincarnated. Dante places it at the summit of the Mount of Purgatory.

Canto XV

The Sodomites; Brunetto Latini; Other Clerks

Now the solid margin bears us as we go,
    and the vapor from the stream creates a shade
3   that keeps the flames from the banks and from the flow.
As Flemings from Wissant to Bruges, afraid
    of the rising tide as it rushes in headlong,
6   repel it with the bulwarks they have made,
and as the Paduans who live along
    the Brenta keep their towns and castles free
9   from the Carentana[1] thaw when the sun grows strong—
whoever the master builder here might be,
    he had made these walls, though not as high or wide,
12   with similar design and artistry.
We had moved so far along that, had I tried
    turning round and looking back where we had been,
15   I could not have seen the forest. Alongside
the embankment appeared a group of shades just then,
    and each one stared at us as they passed by
18   the way that men will stare at other men
at nightfall, with the new moon in the sky.
    Each knit his brows as an old tailor does
21   when he attempts to thread a needle's eye.
Looked over by the lot of them, I was
    recognized by one, who reached out suddenly
24   and grasped my hem and cried: "How marvelous!"
And I, when he held out his arm toward me,
    scanned his scorched visage and began to peer
27   at the baked features, till my memory
allowed their original image to come clear,
    and then I stretched my hand down toward his face
30   and answered: "Ser Brunetto,[2] are you here?"
"Let it not displease you if for a little space
    Brunetto Latini turns back with you, my son,"
33   he said, "and lets his band move on apace."
"With all my heart," I said, "let it be done,

---

1. Chiarentana is a mountainous region north of Padua. Wissant and Bruges are in Flanders. In both areas, dikes were constructed to prevent flooding.
2. Brunetto Latini (c. 1220–1294) was a notary (hence the title *ser*) and a prominent Guelph. He lived in France from 1260 to 1266, during a Ghibelline ascendancy, and was afterward active in public affairs in Florence. His principal volume was *Li Livres dou Tresor*, an encyclopedic work in French prose. His *Tesoretto* is a long allegorical and didactic poem in Italian, which influenced Dante in the writing of the *Comedy*. There is no other surviving or known source for the identification of Brunetto as a homosexual.

or I will sit with you, if you desire,
    if it pleases him with whom I journey on."
36
"My son, if one stops for a second, the laws require
    that he lie for a hundred years on the burning plain,
39   forbidden to brush away the falling fire.
I will follow at your hem, and then regain
    my company where they wander in their woe,
42   loudly bewailing their eternal pain."
I did not dare to leave the path and go
    to his level, but like one in reverence
45   I walked beside him with my head bowed low.
And he began: "What destiny or chance
    brings you down here before your dying day,
48   and who points out the road by which you advance?"
I said: "In the pleasant life I lost my way
    before the fullness of my age had come.
51   It was in a valley that I went astray.
Yesterday morning I was fleeing from
    that place when I turned back, and he came to me.
54   And now along this path he leads me home."
"Follow your star and you will certainly
    come to a glorious harbor, if it is true
57   that in the sweet life I had power to see,"
he said, "and seeing heaven so kind to you,
    if I had not died so soon, I surely would
60   have sustained you in the work you seek to do.
But that people of malice and ingratitude
    who came down from Fiesole so long ago,
63   though the mountain and the rock still rule their blood,
will despise you for your good work—rightly so,
    for it is not fit that the sweet fig should abide
66   and bear its fruit where bitter sorb trees grow.
A race of envy, avarice, and pride,
    they are blind, as the world has said since olden days.
69   Of their customs let yourself be purified.
The honors fortune holds for you will raise
    a hunger in both factions for your doom,
72   but the grass grows far from where the goat will graze.
Let the wild beasts from Fiesole consume
    themselves for fodder, and let them not molest
75   that plant—if any bit of it still bloom
in their manure—that preserves the best,
    the sacred seed of the Romans who chose to stay
78   when the city was turned into corruption's nest."[3]

3. As did Farinata in Canto X, Brunetto prophesies Dante's exile from Florence. These lines
   draw upon the legend, retold by Brunetto in his *Tresor,* that Florence was founded by the

"If I could have the things for which I pray,"
  I said to him, "then you would not yet be
81   banished from our humanity this way.
Forever fixed in poignant memory
  is the kind, paternal, loving face I knew
84   when in the world above you instructed me
from time to time in what a man must do
  to become eternal. I must proclaim with pride,
87   for as long as I still live, my debt to you.
I will write what you have told of my fortune's tide
  with another text, which a lady[4] will understand
90   and make clear to me, if I ever reach her side.
But know this much: as long as I can stand
  upright, with conscience clear, I will undergo
93   unafraid whatever Fortune may have planned.
This prophecy is not new to me, and so
  let Fortune turn her wheel as she sees fit
96   and let the peasant likewise turn his hoe."
At these last words my master turned a bit
  round to his right and looked at me and said:
99   "He listens well who makes a note of it."
I did not give an answer, but instead
  asked Ser Brunetto who were the most renowned
102   and the highest born in that circle of the dead.
"It is good to learn of some who share this ground,"
  he said, "but the rest require reticence,
105   for the time for so much talk cannot be found.
In short, they all were men of great eminence,
  all of them clerics and men of letters who
108   were one and all befouled by the same offense.
Here Priscian[5] moves amid the wretched crew,
  with Francesco d'Accorso[6] also among the reviled,
111   and had you a taste for mange, you might see too
the one whom the servant of servants had exiled
  from the Arno to the Bacchiglione, where
114   he left the distended nerves he had defiled.[7]

Romans after the siege of nearby Fiesole, where Catiline had fled after the failure of his
conspiracy (63 B.C.E.), and that the Fiesolans, including Catiline's followers, intermin-
gled with the Roman settlers.
4. Beatrice; "another text": the prophecy of Farinata.
5. A celebrated Latin grammarian of the early sixth century. The little that survives con-
cerning him says nothing about homosexuality.
6. Francesco d'Accorso (1225–1293) was born in Bologna, where he became—as his father
had been in Florence—a lawyer and a professor of civil law. In 1273, he went to England
at the invitation of Edward I, and was for a time a lecturer at Oxford.
7. Andrea de' Mozzi was bishop of Florence from 1287 to 1295, when he was transferred to
Vicenza on the Bacchiglione because of his scandalous ways. He died in February 1296.
Since the pope who transferred him was Boniface VIII, the traditional description of the
pontiff as "the servant of servants" has a satirical application here.

There is more that I could say, but I do not dare
    speak or stay with you longer, for I see
117   a new smoke rising from the sand out there.
People are coming with whom I must not be.
    But let my *Treasure*, where I still live on—
120   I ask no more—live in your memory."   *specific rememb rance*
Then he doubled back, like one of those who run
    for the green cloth at Verona, and as my eyes
123   followed him, he seemed not to be the one
who loses, but the one who wins the prize.[8]

Canto XVI

The Boundary of the Seventh Circle; Three Florentines; The Mighty Precipices; The Pilgrim's Girdle; Geryon Appears

In that place to which we had already come,
    the water falling into the next ring
3   resounded like a beehive's steady hum,
when all at once three shades came hurrying
    across the sand as they broke free from the rest
6   of a band beneath the rain's tormenting sting.
All three cried out with one voice as they pressed
    toward where we were: "Stop, you who seem to be
9   from our wicked land, by the way that you are dressed."
Alas, what old and fresh wounds I could see
    burned in their members, etched into their skin.
12   Remembering it now still saddens me.
My teacher attended to their cries, and then
    turned to me, saying: "Here courtesy is due.
15   You must wait, and be respectful to these men.
Were it not for all the flames that fly here through
    the nature of this place, then I would feel
18   this haste suits them much less than it suits you."
They resumed their old refrain as we turned heel
    to wait for them. They reached us, and at once
21   all three combined themselves into a wheel.
As oiled and naked wrestling champions
    circle warily, seeking grip and vantage place
24   before the thrusting and the blows commence,
so each one fixed his eyes upon my face,
    and his head and feet as he was turning there
27   went in opposite directions with each pace.

8. The race in question, in which the runners competed naked, was established in 1207 and held on the first Sunday in Lent.

One said: "If our charred faces, singed of hair,
    and the misery of this barren sand compel
30   contempt for us and for our every prayer,
then let our fame prevail on you to tell
    who you are, who walk with living feet that show
33   such confidence upon the floor of hell.
This one whose steps I trample must now go
    naked and peeled, but in the days that were
36   he was of higher station than you know.
The good Gualdrada[1] was his grandmother.
    He was Guido Guerra.[2] His good works combined
39   the deeds of a counselor and those of a warrior.
The other one, who treads the sand behind,
    is Tegghiaio Aldobrandi.[3] Wise words from him
42   the world above would have done well to mind.
And I, who am set upon the cross with them,
    was Iacopo Rusticucci.[4] The savagery
45   of my wife did much to bring me where I am."
Could I have braved the flames without injury,
    I would have flung myself down from the wall,
48   and I think my guide would not have hindered me,
but since I would have burnt and baked, the pall
    of fear held back my good will from achieving
51   its greedy impulse to embrace them all.
Then I began: "It was not contempt, but grieving
    for your eternal misery that lay—
54   so heavily it will be a long time leaving—
upon my heart when I heard my master say
    respectful words that conveyed the eminence
57   of the men that we saw hurrying our way.
I am from your land. With what fond sentiments
    I have always loved to hear and to retell
60   your honored names and high accomplishments.
I will leave the gall, to go where sweet fruits dwell,
    as my honest leader promised me, although
63   I must first go down to the very core of hell."

1. The daughter of Bellincione Berti, and when young supposedly impressed Emperor Otto IV with her beauty, intelligence, and modesty. Unfortunately for legend, she was married in 1180, twenty years before Otto became emperor and nearly thirty before he visited Florence.
2. A Guelph leader (1220–1272) on the field of battle. He advised the Florentine Guelphs against the planned Sienese campaign of 1260; his counsel was disregarded, with disastrous results.
3. Another leader of the Florentine Guelphs, who also counseled against the Sienese expedition.
4. Jacopo Rusticucci was apparently a middle-class merchant, and thus the social inferior of his two companions. According to early commentators, his wife was so shrewish that he sent her back to her family.

"So may your body for a long time go
    still guided by your soul," that one replied,
66   "so may your fame even afterward still glow,
tell us if valor and courtesy abide
    in our city as they did in olden days,
69   or if such customs have been cast aside.
Guiglielmo Borsiere,[5] walking in these ways
    of pain as a newcomer to our band,
72   has told us things that fill us with malaise."
"New people and sudden wealth have brought your land
    so much excess and so much vanity,
75   O Florence, the time of weeping is at hand,"
I cried with my face uplifted. And all three
    took this to be my answer, and began
78   exchanging looks that men wear when they see
the truth. They said: "If at other times you can
    speak with so little cost and with such flair
81   to satisfy others, you are a happy man.
And if you escape these dark lands to go where
    you may gaze upon the lovely stars again,
84   when you take pleasure in saying 'I was there,'
be sure to speak of us to living men."
    And then they broke their circle, whereupon
87   they fled on legs that seemed like wings. *Amen*
could not be said by the time that they were gone
    from sight, so quickly did they disappear.
90   My master thought it best that we move on.
I followed, and in a short time we could hear
    the sound of water falling with such force
93   that, if we spoke, not one word would be clear.
As that river (the Acquacheta at its source,
    but at Forlì it leaves that name behind)
96   which is the very first to take its course
from Monte Viso eastward and to wind
    down the Apennines' left slope to its low bed,
99   at floodtide when the waters are combined
above San Benedetto dell'Arpe[6] is sped
    so mightily that it makes one cataract where
102   there might otherwise be a thousand rills instead,
here too there was such a roaring in the air
    of dark water dropping steeply that the din
105   would have hurt our ears if we had lingered there.
Wrapped around me was a cord which I had been

---

5. Little is known of Guiglielmo Borsiere, whose surname suggests "pursemaker." He is the
   protagonist of one of the tales in Boccaccio's *Decameron*.
6. A monastery near the source of the Montone, a river northeast of Florence that runs to
   the Adriatic.

      hoping to make good use of previously,
108   to catch the leopard with the painted skin.
   My leader ordered me to work it free.
         I passed the cord from my hand into his
111   wound in a coil, and taking it from me
   he flung it well beyond the precipice
         when he had turned a little to his right,
114   and down it fell into the deep abyss.
   "This strange signal that he follows with his sight,"
         I told myself, "now in response to it
117   surely some strange new thing will come to light."
   How careful men should be with those whose wit
         can see not only what we say and do
120   but has the power to pluck the intimate
   thoughts from our heads! He said: "The thing that you
         are dreaming in your mind, the thing that I
123   am looking for, will soon come into view."
   When the truth he wants to tell has the face of a lie,
         a man should be silent. Though he does no wrong,
126   some shame will still attach to him thereby.
   But, reader, here I cannot hold my tongue.
         By the notes of this very comedy, I swear—
129   so may the favor that it finds be long—
   that even those of stoutest heart would stare
         in amazement at the sight that greeted me,
132   floating up through the dark and heavy air
   the way that one who has worked the anchor free
         from a rock or another obstacle will go
135   back to the surface, rising through the sea
   with arms stretched high and feet drawn in below.

Canto XVII

*Geryon as Image of Fraud; The Usurers; Virgil and
Dante Descend on Geryon's Back*

   "Behold the beast with the pointed tail,[1] who can pass
         over mountains, who breaks walls and weaponry,
3   who makes the world a festering morass!"

---

1. The monster is identified as Geryon at line 97 of the canto. In classical mythology, he was
the treacherous three-headed or three-bodied king of an island in the far western stream
Oceanus and the possessor of a fabled herd of cattle. He was killed by Hercules as part of
his tenth labor, that of the oxen of the sun. He is mentioned in the *Aeneid* and in Ovid's
Heroides. Dante's depiction of him draws upon his tripartite nature, but incorporates de-
tails from the plague of locusts in Revelations and from the manticore as described in
Pliny's *Historia naturalis* and in the *Tresor* of Brunetto Latini.

These were the words my master said to me
  while beckoning him to the cliff's edge, near the place
6 where the marble pathway ended suddenly.
Fraud's filthy image came to us apace,
  beaching head and torso at my master's sign
9 but leaving his tail to dangle into space.
His face was the face of a just man, so benign
  was the outward aspect that it chose to wear,
12 but beneath it his long trunk was serpentine.
To the armpits his two paws were thick with hair.
  His breast and back and both sides were arrayed
15 with painted knots and ringlets everywhere.
Never was cloth that Turks or Tartars made
  so colorful in design and background, nor
18 did Arachne ever weave such rich brocade.[2]
The way a boat will lie along the shore
  half in the water and half upon the ground,
21 the way the beaver settles in for its war
in the swilling Germans' land, was the way I found
  that worst of all beasts perched upon the ring
24 of rocky ledge by which the sand is bound.
The entire length of his tail was quivering
  in the emptiness and lifting its forked end,
27 which had its point armed like a scorpion's sting.
"And now," my leader told me, "we must bend
  our way a bit so that it will bring us where
30 that beast is lying." We started to descend
on the right side of the marble path, taking care
  to walk ten steps out on the cliff and be
33 clear of the burning sand and the fiery air.
When we had reached the creature, I could see
  that some people sat on the sand near the abyss
36 a short way off, and my master said to me:
"To take the whole experience of this
  circle away with you, you ought to go
39 and learn from them what their situation is.
Speak to them briefly, and while you are doing so,
  I will see if I can persuade this one to stretch
42 his mighty shoulders and carry us below."
So I walked on by myself along the ledge
  of the seventh circle and approached that band
45 of wretched people sitting near the edge.

---

2. Arachne challenged the goddess Athena (Minerva to the Romans) to a weaving competition. Arachne's tapestry depicted the amours of the gods. Angered by its subject, unable to find any flaw in its craftsmanship, Minerva destroyed the design of Arachne, who hanged herself. The goddess, however, saved her and changed her into a spider. Ovid tells the story in Book VI of the *Metamorphoses*.

Their pain was bursting through their eyes. One hand
　　　or another would fly now here, now there, to stay
48　　　　the falling fire or the scorching sand,
in the same way that a dog on a summer day,
　　　with its paws in motion now, and now its snout,
51　　　　tries to drive the horseflies, fleas, or flies away.
There were none among those people sitting out
　　　under the flames that I could recognize,
54　　　　but each of them had a great purse hung about
his neck, and each of them seemed to feast his eyes
　　　upon the moneybag that he was wearing.
57　　　　Each one had its own color and device.
The first I saw as I moved among them, staring,
　　　was a yellow purse with an azure form that would
60　　　　have been a lion by its shape and bearing.[3]
Whiter than butter was the goose that stood
　　　on a sack a little further off, displayed
63　　　　against a background that was red as blood.[4]
And one who wore a white purse, which portrayed
　　　a gross blue sow,[5] saw me there and raised a cry:
66　　　　"Get out of here, whoever you are who've strayed
to this ditch! And know, since you have yet to die,
　　　that my townsman Vitaliano[6] will appear
69　　　　and will sit here at my left side by and by.
I am Paduan, and all these others here
　　　are Florentines who keep shouting, the whole crew,
72　　　　'Let him come down, the sovereign cavalier[7]
who will bring the purse with the three goats!'" Then he drew
　　　his mouth in a grimace and thrust out his tongue
75　　　　the way an ox that licks its nose will do.
I turned, and spent no further time among
　　　those weary souls, lest I provoke my guide,
78　　　　who had cautioned me that I should not be long.
I found that he already was astride
　　　the savage creature's rump. He said to me:
81　　　　"Be bold, and let your soul be fortified.

3. The azure lion on a yellow background was the heraldic device of the Gianfigliazzi family
of Florence, prominent Black Guelphs and accused usurers.
4. The white goose on the blood-red field denotes the Ubriachi family, Ghibelline bankers
and moneychangers.
5. The white purse with the blue sow signifies the Scrovegni family of Padua. The speaker is
usually identified as Reginaldo degli Scrovegni, who became very wealthy through the
practice of usury and died around 1290.
6. This line is customarily understood to refer to Vitaliano del Dente, who was appointed
mayor of Padua in 1307, and was described as a moneylender.
7. Assumed to be Giovanni Buiamonte, of the Becchi family of Florence, a moneylender who
was made a knight sometime before 1298.

From this point on, our going down will be
　　　on such stairs. Mount in front, here I will sit
84　　　to keep his tail from doing you injury."
As one with quartan draws so near his fit
　　　that his nails grow pale and shade can make him start
87　　　to tremble at the very sight of it,
such terror did those words of his impart.
　　　But shame, which gives a servant courage when
90　　　he stands before a good lord, reproved my heart.
I scaled the hideous shoulders and I began
　　　to try to say (though my voice did not accord
93　　　with my intent): "Be sure you hold me then."
But he, who had at other times restored
　　　my heart through other dangers, gripped me tight
96　　　and steadied me once I had climbed aboard.
He said: "Now, Geryon, carry us from this height.
　　　And, remembering the new burden that you bear,
99　　　make great wide circles and a long, slow flight."
As bit by bit a boat backs out from where
　　　it is moored, just so did Geryon begin
102　　　to move, and when he sensed he was in the air
he turned his tail round where his breast had been
　　　and stretched it out, and it wriggled like an eel,
105　　　and with his paws he gathered the air in.
Such fear, I think, did no one ever feel,
　　　not Phaëton when he dropped the reins that day
108　　　and burned the sky with a scar still visible,[8]
nor wretched Icarus when he went astray
　　　and the wax began to melt and his father cried:
111　　　"You are going wrong!" and his feathers fell away.[9]
Not even they could have been as terrified
　　　as I with nothing but the beast in view
114　　　and nothing but thin air on every side.
The wind upon my face and the wind that blew
　　　from beneath were the only ways I had to know
117　　　that, wheeling, dropping, Geryon slowly flew.
And now I heard a horrid roaring grow
　　　from the whirlpool underneath us, on our right,
120　　　so I stretched out my neck to look below.

8. Phaëton persuaded his father, the sun god Helios, to let him drive the chariot of the
　　sun. He was unable to control the horses, and Zeus slew him with a thunderbolt to keep
　　the earth from catching fire. The scar on the sky is the Milky Way. The story is related in
　　Book II of the *Metamorphoses*.
9. On a second flight, Icarus ignored the warnings of his father, Daedalus, and flew too near
　　the sun, which melted the wax that held the feathers of his wings, and he fell into the sea
　　and drowned (*Metamorphoses*, Book VIII).

Then I was filled with even greater fright,
 seeing fires and hearing cries of misery,
123 and, trembling in every part, I held on tight.
Now for the first time I could really see
 the turn and descent. On every side my eyes
126 took in onrushing scenes of agony.
As when a falcon for a long time flies
 without catching sight of any bird or lure
129 ("You're already coming down?" the master cries)
and, after a hundred weary circles where
 it had taken off so swiftly, comes back down,
132 sullen and angry, far from the falconer,
so, when we were discharged by Geryon
 at the very base of the jagged cliff, far below
135 where we began, he turned and he was gone,
vanishing like an arrow from the bow.

Canto XVIII

The Eighth Circle: The Fraudulent; Malebolge; The First
Ditch: Panderers and Seducers; Caccianemico; The Second
Ditch: The Flatterers

In hell there is a region that is known
 as Malebolge.[1] Like the cliff by which it's sealed,
3 it is all made of iron-colored stone.
In the very center of this evil field
 is a deep, wide pit, and in the proper place
6 its structure and its use will be revealed.
The belt descending from the high cliff's base
 to the pit is circular. Ten valleys lie
9 near the bottom, just above that gaping space.
As the walls of a castle are protected by
 concentric rings of moats, just such a row
12 of patterned circles now impressed my eye
as I gazed upon the scene that stretched below,
 and as lines of little bridges will project
15 from the walls to the outer bank, here long crags go
through the ditches and embankments to connect
 the cliff to the lip of the pit, which gathers them
18 and cuts them off before they intersect.

---

1. A word ("Evilditches") coined by Dante, combining the terms for "evil" (*male*) and "ditch" or "pouch" (*bolgia*).

This is where we were when we were shaken from
    Geryon's back. Now the poet began to stride
21   off to the left, and I walked after him.
I saw new miseries now on the right side,
    new tortures, new tormentors with long whips,
24   with which the ditch was abundantly supplied.
The sinners were naked, moving through the depths.
    The nearer file faced us, while the others went
27   the same way we did, but with longer steps,
just as the Romans, for the management
    of the huge crowds in the Year of Jubilee,
30   have a plan by which the opposing rows are sent
across the bridge, with one line constantly
    facing the mount, while their opposite numbers wind
33   in the direction of Saint Peter's as they see
the castle before them.[2] Here the dark rock was lined
    at stages by horned demons who drove the herd
36   of sinners along by lashing them from behind.
With the first crack of the whip each one was spurred
    to pick his heels up! No one seemed to care
39   to linger for the second or the third.
As I walked, one met my eyes with a moment's stare,
    and I said at once when I saw him: "I have not
42   always been starved of the sight of that man there."
My gentle leader stopped with me on that spot
    and let me go back a bit, with steps that led
45   to the one whose face I was trying to make out.
The scourged soul sought to hide, with lowered head,
    but it was all in vain for him to try.
48   "You there with your eyes upon the ground," I said,
"I know you, for unless your features lie,
    Venedico Caccianemico[3] is your name.
51   You are cooked in spicy sauces now, but why?"
He said: "I can hear the world from which I came
    in your plain speech, and though I would keep still,
54   I feel compelled to answer all the same.
I was the one—however they may tell

2. In February 1300, Pope Boniface VIII proclaimed that year to be one of Jubilee (the first
such in the Church's history), during which indulgences would be granted to those who
visited the basilicas of Saints Peter and Paul. The heavy traffic on the Ponte Angelo over
the Tiber (it is estimated that as many as 200,000 people visited Rome that year) was con-
trolled in the manner described here: one file of pilgrims crossing the bridge with the
Castel Sant'Angelo directly in view, on their way to Saint Peter's, and the other file cross-
ing toward Monte Giordano and Saint Paul's.
3. Venedico Caccianemico (born c. 1228) was for many years a leader of the Bolognese
Guelphs. Although Dante apparently believes that he was dead by 1300, documents indi-
cate that he survived until 1302 or early 1303.

the vile tale—who brought Ghisolabella to
57   the marchese, so that she might do his will.[4]
I am far from the only Bolognese who
    laments here. There are more of us than they breed
60   to say *sipa* from the Sàvena clear through
to the Reno.[5] If it's assurance that you need,
    some token or testimony, just keep clear
63   in your mind that we are famous for our greed."
And as he spoke, a demon standing near
    lashed him and cried: "Keep moving, panderer!
66   There are no women for the coining here!"
I soon rejoined my escort, and we were,
    in a few steps, at a place where from the ledge
69   a reef was jutting outward like a spur.
With easy steps we climbed onto that bridge.
    We left the eternal circlings, and we made
72   a turn to the right across the jagged ridge.
The ditch was wide to make room for all the flayed.
    My leader said, as we watched them from on high:
75   "Stop here and let this opposite parade
of misbegotten wretches strike your eye.
    Their faces will be new to you, for they
78   were going the same way as you and I."
From the old bridge we could see the whole array
    as they came toward us, and like the opposing row
81   these spirits were being flogged along their way.
Before I had even asked what I wished to know,
    my guide said: "See that great one there, and see
84   how he seems to shed no tear for all his woe.
His face still wears an air of majesty.
    That is Jason, who purloined the Colchian
87   ram through his cunning and his bravery.
On his way, he sailed to the isle of Lemnos, when
    the bold and merciless women of that place
90   had all laid murderous hands upon their men.
There, with love tokens and with words of grace
    he deceived Hypsipyle, the maiden who
93   had deceived the other women of her race.
He left her pregnant and bereft. Here you
    may see the punishments such vices cause,
96   and here Medea has her vengeance too.[6]

4. Venedico was rumored to have procured his sister, "the lovely" Ghisola, for Obizzo II, the marchese d'Este (see note 2 to Canto XII, p. 46), either for a bribe or in order to win favor.
5. The Sàvena and Reno rivers mark the western and eastern boundaries of the city. *Sipa*: old Bolognese dialect for "yes."
6. Jason, leader of the Argonauts, was promised the throne of Iolcus if he could return with the golden fleece belonging to King Aeëtes of Colchis. On the way, he stopped at the island

All such deceivers move here without pause.
    That is all you need to know of this first ditch
99   and of all the souls that are gripped within its jaws."
And while he spoke, we came to the point at which
    our narrow path reached the next embankment, where
102   it arched once more to form another bridge,
over the next pouch. We heard people there
    hitting themselves and uttering loud cries
105   and snuffling with their muzzles at the air.
From down inside this ditch rank vapors rise
    that cling to the rockface, causing mold to grow,
108   and that wage a constant war with nose and eyes.
Here the bottom is so deep that we had to go
    up to the bridge's highest point, between
111   the embankments, so that we could see below.
From that great height we stared down at the scene
    of a swarm of people plunged into a mess
114   that looked as if it came from a latrine.
My eyes, as they went picking through that press,
    saw one whose head was so besmeared with shit,
117   whether he was priest or layman, who could guess?[7]
He called to me: "Your greedy eyeballs sit
    on me more than the other pigs here. Why?"
120   And I: "Because, if I remember it
rightly, I saw you when your hair was dry,
    and you are Alessio Interminei[8]
123   from Lucca. That is why you caught my eye."
Then he began to smack his gourd and say:
    "How have I sunk to this disgusting place
126   through the flatteries my ready tongue would spray!"
And my leader said: "Now let your vision trace
    a path a little way ahead, then drop
129   your eyes till they can clearly see the face
of that vile disheveled slut who cannot stop
    scratching herself with her shitty nails as she
132   stands up now, and now squats down in the slop.
That is Thaïs, the whore. 'Are you greatly pleased with me?'[9]

---

of Lemnos, where the women had massacred all the men. Hypsipyle, the daughter of King Thoas, had deceived the other women by hiding her father and pretending to have killed him. Jason won the fleece with the aid of Aeëtes's daughter Medea, whom he brought back with him and married. He later deserted her for Glauce, daughter of King Creon of Corinth. On their wedding day, Medea killed the bride and her own two children by Jason.

7. Under ordinary circumstances, a priest's tonsure would distinguish him from a layman.

8. The Interminei (or Interminelli) family were prominent members of the White party in Lucca. Little is known of Alessio.

9. A flattering courtesan in *Eunuchus*, a comedy by Terence (Publius Terentius Afer, c. 195–159 B.C.E.).

her paramour once asked her, and she stated:
135 'Just "greatly"? Why, you please me marvelously!'
With that sight, we will let our eyes be sated."

[handwritten: sin of prostitution lies in its fake flattery]

Canto XIX

[handwritten: buying & selling of ecclesiastical privileges]

The Third Ditch: The Sin of Simony; Pope Nicholas III;
Reference to Pope Boniface VIII; Invective against Acts of
Simony and against the Donation of Constantine

[handwritten: e.g. verkoop van ambten]

O Simon Magus![1] and many more besides,
  his wretched followers, who have whored and sold
3   the things of God, which ought to be the brides
of righteousness, for silver and for gold,
  now must the trumpet sound for you, I say,
6   because the third pouch has you in its hold.
We had climbed the reef and reached the part that lay
  directly above the middle of the ditch
9   containing the next tomb along the way.
O highest wisdom, how great your art, with which
  the heavens, the earth, and the evil world resound,
12   and how justly does your power deal with each!
Along the bottom and the sides I found
  in the livid stone a multiplicity
15   of identical holes that were all completely round.
By their dimensions they reminded me
  of my San Giovanni. They all were the same size
18   as the fonts in that beautiful baptistery,
one of which I had to break once, otherwise
  someone would have drowned inside it—and here let
21   this be the seal to open all men's eyes.[2]
Protruding from each hole there was a set
  of feet, with legs up to the calves in view.
24   All the rest was in the hole, pressed into it.
The soles of their feet were burning, and their legs flew
  so hard in convulsive thrashings that their throes
27   could have broken withes or even ropes in two.

---

1. In Acts 8.9–24, Simon the magician was converted to Christianity by the preaching of Philip. When he saw Peter and John summon the Holy Spirit, he offered them money to acquire this power for himself, and was sternly rebuked. From his name comes the word "simony," which signifies a trafficking in holy things, especially the buying and selling of ecclesiastical offices.
2. There is no documentation of the incident that Dante describes here. Some have argued the unlikelihood of his gratuitously interpolating a self-defense against a charge of sacrilege, and have instead suggested that the last clause has larger thematic and theological implications. For one such interpretation, see Mark Musa, *Dante Alighieri's Divine Comedy. Inferno: Commentary* (Indiana, 1996), pp. 257–59.

On any oily substance fire flows
    along the surface, and here it was the same
30   as the flames licked at their feet from heels to toes.
"Master," I said, "I would like to know his name
    who is twitching more than any other one
33   and whose feet are leeched by a much redder flame."
And he: "If you wish, I will carry you down upon
    that sloping bank so you can hear him tell
36   who he is and of the evil he has done."
And I: "Your pleasure pleases me as well.
    You are my lord, you know that I embrace
39   your will, and you know every syllable
of what is unsaid." So we approached the place
    where the fourth bank is, moving leftward as we went
42   toward the ditch's narrow, perforated base.
He held me to his hip in our descent,
    and soon we were standing right before that man
45   whose legs were flailing in a fierce lament.
"Whoever you are, sad spirit," I began,
    "stuck in like a pole, with the upper part interred
48   where the lower end should go, speak if you can."
I stood there like a friar who has heard
    the confession of a killer who, placed inside,[3]
51   calls him back so his death may be a bit deferred.
"Are you standing up there, Boniface," he cried,
    "are you standing there already? What was stated
54   was wrong by several years, and the writ has lied.
Have all of your spoils left you so quickly sated?
    When you coveted them, you dared use guile to win
57   the lovely lady that you lacerated."[4]
I stood like those who think they may have been
    made fools of, not understanding the response
60   they have heard, not knowing how they should begin
to answer. Virgil said: "You must say at once:
    'I am not who you think I am, I am not he,'"
63   and I responded with obedience.
At that the spirit's feet thrashed furiously,
    and then he sighed, and in a tearful tone
66   he said: "What is it that you want from me?

---

3. In the Middle Ages, an assassin would be executed by being placed upside down in a ditch
   and buried alive.
4. Pope Boniface VIII (Benedetto Caetani, 1235–1303) is the subject of numerous gibes in
   the course of the poem. The speaker mistakes Dante for Boniface, who is not due to ar-
   rive for another three and a half years. The lovely lady that he tore to pieces by his corrupt
   practices is, of course, the Church; "guile" alludes to the common belief that Boniface
   had persuaded his predecessor, Celestine V (see note 3 to Canto III), to resign, and then
   won the support of King Charles II of Naples in his effort to become pope himself.

If it means so much to you that for this alone
>   you have come down here, to hear what I have to tell,
69   then know that the great mantle was my own.[5]
But I was a son of the she-bear, and strove so well
>   to advance the cubs that on earth I pocketed
72   my spoils, and now I pocket myself in hell.
My predecessors are pressed below my head,
>   simoniacs all, and all of them flattened through
75   the fissures hollowed in the rock's deep bed.
When my turn comes I will be flattened too,
>   pressed down when he arrives, that other soul
78   that I took you for when I started to question you.

simoniacs are buried by other simoniacs

I have spent more time already in this hole
>   with cooked feet, upside down, than he will pass
81   stuck here with *his* feet glowing like lumps of coal.
A lawless shepherd, his crimes more odious,
>   will come from the west, and he will prove indeed
84   a proper cover for the two of us,
a new Jason, like the one of whom we read
>   in Maccabees, whose king showed him deference,
87   as to this one France's ruler will pay heed."[6]
I do not know whether in my vehemence
>   I grew too bold in the thoughts that I expressed
90   in this measure: "Tell me, on what recompense,
on how much treasure did our Lord insist
>   before he placed the keys in Peter's hand?

Dante scolds a sinner again

93   'Follow me,' I'm certain, was his sole request.
Nor did Peter or the other ones demand
>   gold or silver from Matthias[7] when it befell
96   that he took the bad soul's place in their holy band.
So stay here in your fitting spot in hell.
>   As for those ill-gotten gains that made you bold
99   toward Charles, be certain that you guard them well.[8]

---

5. The speaker is Giovanni Gaetano degli Orsini (whose surname means "little bears"), Pope Nicholas III (1277–1280).
6. Nicholas has been dead for nearly twenty years, and must wait another three for his replacement, Boniface, whose own feet will be exposed and aflame for only eleven years until he is pushed along by the arrival of the even more corrupt Clement V in 1314. Clement, born Bertrand de Got in Gascony, intrigued with King Philip IV of France to win the papacy, offering him a share of the Church's revenues. Upon his accession, Clement moved the papal see to Avignon (where it remained until 1377) and created nine new French cardinals. In 2 Maccabees 4–5, Jason becomes high priest of the Jews by bribing King Antiochus of Syria and proceeds to introduce corrupt practices. He is soon displaced, however, by Menelaus, who offers the king an even greater bribe.
7. In Acts 1.13–26, Matthias is selected by lot to take Judas's place among the Apostles.
8. This is probably a reference to the now discredited assumption that Nicholas III was bribed to support Giovanni da Procida, a force behind the bloody uprising known as the Sicilian Vespers (1282), which liberated Sicily from the rule of Charles I of Anjou.

And if this intensity were not controlled
    by my deep reverence for the sacred keys
102   that in the happy life you used to hold,
I would speak in even stronger words than these,
    for your greed, grinding down the good, giving glory to
105   the wicked, afflicts the world with its disease.
And when the Evangelist had that beast in view
    who sits on the waters whoring wantonly
108   with kings, he was thinking of shepherds just like you.
She had seven heads when she was born, and she
111   drew her strength from the ten horns, but it was gone
    when her spouse lost his delight in purity.[9]
With your gold and silver god, what you have done
114   differs from the idolators in this alone:
    you worship a hundred, they worship only one.
Ah, Constantine, how much evil seed was sown,
117   not with your conversion, but your dowry, which
    the first rich father had from you as his own."[1]
Perhaps it was his rage that made him twitch
120   or his conscience, but his two feet kicked like mad
    as I sang these notes to him with a rising pitch.
I am sure this pleased my guide, because he had
123   a look of satisfaction on his face
    as he listened to the truthful words I said.
Thereupon he swept me up in his embrace
126   and held me to his breast, and once again
    walked the incline that had brought us to that place.
Nor did he tire of holding me. Only when
129   we stood upon the arch that spanned the fosse
    between the fourth and fifth walls, only then
did he gently put me down. He was gentle because
132   the reef was steep and rugged, so much so
    that goats would find it difficult to cross.
And I saw another valley stretched below.

[handwritten margin note: Virgil approves of Dante's scold]

9. In Revelations 17, John gives his vision of pagan Rome, which Dante applies to the corrupt papacy. The seven heads are here understood to be the sacraments, and the ten horns are the commandments, whose power waned when the Church's husband, the pope, turned away from virtue.

1. Constantine I (c. 274–337), known as the Great, was Roman emperor from 306 to 337. Dante alludes to the Donation of Constantine, a document forged in the papal curia and believed genuine for seven hundred years until its fraudulence was demonstrated in the fifteenth century. It claims that, in return for Constantine's being cured of leprosy by Pope Sylvester I (see note 3 to Canto XXVII, p. 103), this "first rich father" and all succeeding popes were granted temporal sovereignty over the western part of the empire, including Italy.

Canto xx

The Fourth Ditch: Diviners; Digression on Manto and Mantua

In this, the twentieth canto of the first
    canzone, describing souls submerged by sin,
3   the new punishment I saw must now be versed.
I was leaning forward, ready to look within
    the depth of the ditch that lay visible to me,
6   whose floor was awash with anguished tears, wherein
I saw a line of spirits silently
    weeping as they approached us, keeping the slow
9   pace of the living praying a litany.
And as my line of vision dropped below
    their heads, I saw they were horribly distorted
12   between the chin and where the chest should go.
Each head was turned to the rear, and thus contorted
    they all were walking backward, bit by bit,
15   for their power to look before them had been thwarted.
Such distortion may have happened in a fit
    of palsy sometime, but never to my eye,
18   and I put no faith in the likelihood of it.
So may God bestow the fruits of your reading, try
    to imagine yourself, reader, in my state,
21   and ask how I could keep my own cheeks dry
when confronted close at hand with such a fate,
    our form so twisted that their tears rolled down
24   to the cleft where the two buttocks separate.
I leaned my face upon the projecting stone
    and let my tears flow down, till my guide said:
27   "I see the fools still claim you for their own!
Here piety lives when pity is truly dead.
    What is more wicked than spurning God's command
30   to heed the promptings of one's heart instead?
Look up and see the one for whom the land
    opened up when all the Thebans raised the call:
33   'Amphiaraus,[1] where are you running? Stand
and fight the battle with us!' But his fall
    continued till he landed among the shades
36   at the feet of Minos, who seizes one and all.
He who wished to see too far forward now parades

---

1. The seer Amphiaraus was one of the seven against Thebes (see note 3 to Canto XIV). As he had foreseen, he died in battle during the siege, when the earth opened to swallow him as he was retreating.

backward and looks behind him in damnation,
39   making a new chest of his shoulder blades.
      See Tiresias,[2] who made an alteration
         of his looks from masculine to feminine,
42   and whose members made a similar transformation.
   When he came upon the coupling snakes, he then
      had to strike them with his staff anew, to obtain
45   the plumage of his manhood once again.
   Backed up to that one's belly in the chain
      is Aruns.[3] Up in the Luni hills worked by
48   the peasants who dwell upon Carrara's plain,
   he lived in a cave in the marble cliffs, his eye
      delighted by the unobstructed view
51   of the sea below and the stars up in the sky.
   And she whose breasts are turned away from you
      and covered by the long tresses that she wore,
54   with all of her hairy parts on that side too,
   was Manto,[4] who searched through many lands before
      she came to my birthplace. And I wish to say
57   some words on this subject for a moment more.
   After her father the prophet passed away
      and the city of Bacchus fell into slavery,
60   she roamed the earth's domains for many a day.
   Below Tiralli, in lovely Italy
      lies a lake known as Benaco, at the base
63   of the Alps that form the border of Germany.
   The water of a thousand springs that race
      through Val Camonica and Pennino flows
66   to Garda, and it gathers in that place.
   An island sits in the middle. Three bishops, those
      of Brescia, Trent, and Verona, would have the right
69   to give the blessing there if they so chose.
   The low point of the lakeshore is the site
      of striking, strong Peschiera, built to restrain
72   the spread of Bergamese and Brescian might.

---

2. The Theban Tiresias was turned into a woman when he struck a pair of copulating snakes. After seven years, he struck them again and was returned to his male form. When summoned to settle a dispute between Zeus and Hera over whether males or females enjoyed lovemaking more, he agreed with Zeus, stating that women experienced ten times as much sexual pleasure. For this, Hera struck him blind, and Zeus compensated him with the gift of prophecy. His story is told in Book III of Ovid's *Metamorphoses*. He appears most famously in Sophocles' *Oedipus the King* and T. S. Eliot's *The Waste Land*, as well as in the *Odyssey* (as a shade) and several plays by Euripides.
3. An Etruscan soothsayer who, in Lucan's *Pharsalia*, foresaw but did not fully communicate the consequences of the war between Caesar and Pompey. According to Lucan, he lived in the ruins of Luni and divined by, among other things, examining entrails. It is Dante who situates him in a nearby cave and makes him, by implication, an astrologer.
4. The daughter of Tiresias. In Book X of the *Aeneid*, Manto is described as coming to Italy after her father's death and the fall of Thebes, and giving birth to Ocnus after mating with the river god Tiber.

The water Benaco's bosom cannot contain
  is collected at that point and begins to flow
75   in a river running down through the green plain.
 No longer Benaco now, but Mincio
  once the current starts to run, it travels then
78   to Govèrnolo,[5] where it drops into the Po,
 and soon it spreads into a marsh, and when
  the summer's heat afflicts that level ground
81   it is turned into a miserable fen.
 In passing there, the untamed virgin found
  a stretch of dry land in the marshes where
84   no one had farmed and no one was around.
 She settled with her servants in that bare
  forbidding spot, shunned people while she plied
87   her arts, then left her empty body there.
 The people of those parts, when she had died,
  came together on that ground secure from foes,
90   defended by the marsh on every side.
 There, over those dead bones, the city rose.
  For her who came there first, with no divination
93   Mantua was the name the people chose.[6]
 At one time it had a larger population,
  till idiot Casalodi fell victim to
96   the cunning Pinamonte's calculation.[7]
 Therefore, should another story come to you
  concerning my city and its establishment,
99   do not let lies devalue what is true."[8]
 "Master," I said, "I feel so confident
  in the sureness of your account that, should they try,
102   their words would be like coals that have been spent.

5. The town of Governolo is some twelve miles from Mantua. Benaco was the Latin name for Lake Garda, at the foot of the Tyrolean Alps. The city of Garda is on its eastern shore. Valcamonica is a valley west of the lake. The term "Pennino" alludes to the Alpine range (although precisely which part of it is alluded to is a matter of some dispute). The boundaries of the dioceses of Brescia, Trent, and Verona meet at a point in the middle of Lake Garda, at the southern end of which stand the fortress and town of Peschiera.
6. By some accounts, it was customary in the ancient world to determine the names of cities through the casting of lots.
7. Alberto da Casalodi, a Guelph count from Brescia, was ruler of Mantua in 1272 and much resented by the native population. The Ghibelline Pinamonte Bonacolsi duped him into thinking that he could hold on to power only by exiling the city's noble families, which he did to such an extent that he deprived himself of his own supporters. Pinamonte led a revolt that resulted in the exile of Casalodi and the murders of the remaining nobles.
8. This statement of Virgil's has occasioned much comment, especially since his account here contradicts the one in the *Aeneid* (see note 4 above). The matter is further complicated by the mention of "the daughter of Tiresias" as one of the souls in Limbo (*Purgatorio*, Canto XXII), in contrast to Virgil's identification of her here among the soothsayers.

But speak to me about those who are passing by,
    if any have stories worthy to be heard,
105   for my mind goes back to them." And his reply:
"Then look upon that one there, with the spreading beard
    from his cheeks to his brown shoulders, for he was
108   augur when all the Greek males disappeared,
leaving even the cradles empty in the cause.
    He decided with Calchas when the time should be
111   to cut the first cable at Aulis. Eurypylus
was his name, and in my lofty tragedy
    I sing of him, as you are well aware,
114   who know the whole of it so thoroughly.[9]
This other one, with thighs so thin and spare,
    was Michael Scot.[1] In the tricks of magic fraud
117   he was a practitioner beyond compare.
See Guido Bonatti. Asdente,[2] who if he could
    would stick to his last and practice his devotions,
120   but repentance comes too late to do him good.
See the sad hags who left their threads and notions
    for the false divining of the divine will,
123   who cast their spells with poppets and with potions.
But let us move along. While we stand still,
    Cain, carrying his thornbush,[3] casts his light
126   where hemispheres meet, on the wave below Seville.
The moon was already round and full last night,
    as you must recall, for you came to no harm then
129   in the deepest wood, when she was shining bright."
So he spoke to me, and we walked on again.

9. This passage presents additional difficulties. Eurypylus is indeed mentioned in the *Aeneid* (Book II), but the details there are very different from what Dante has Virgil claim. Calchas was the augur when the Greek fleet set sail from Aulis to lay siege to Troy. In the *Aeneid*, Eurypylus is a soldier sent to consult the oracle of Apollo to determine the most propitious time for the Greeks to sail home from Troy. (In fairness to Dante, it should be pointed out that Calchas does figure briefly in this incident also.)

1. Michael Scot (c. 1175–c. 1235), so called because of his national origin, was a philosopher and astrologer at the court of Frederick II (see note 7 to Canto X) at Palermo. He wrote a number of works dealing with the occult sciences and translated Arabic versions of Aristotle into Latin.

2. Benvenuto, called Asdente ("toothless"), was a shoemaker from Parma who was said to possess magical powers. The astrologer and soothsayer Guido Bonatti was a rooftiler from Forlì; he is believed to have been in the service of Guido da Montefeltro (see note 2 to Canto XXVII, p. 101).

3. Equivalent to the man in the moon, Cain with his thornbush is above the point of demarcation between the northern hemisphere (land) and the southern (water). It is now about six in the morning.

Canto XXI

The Fifth Ditch; Grafters; Malacoda; The Devil's Wiles

We went from bridge to bridge, exchanging talk
    of which my comedy does not wish to sing,
3   and at the highest point we stopped our walk
to see the Malebolge's next opening
    and hear the vain cries of the miserable.
6   An eerie darkness covered everything.
Just as when, flanked by boiling cauldrons full
    of sticky pitch, the worn-out vessels wait
9   to be worked on at the Venice Arsenal,
since winter means they cannot navigate:
    some make their ships new, some recaulk the bow
12   or the ribs of one that has carried many a freight,
some hammer at the stern or at the prow,
    and some carve oars, or twist lines, or repair
15   the jibs and mainsails—so it was just now,
but for the fact there was no fire there.
    Through heavenly art the pitch boiled endlessly
18   and spread its gluey coating everywhere.
I could see the pitch, but all that was clear to me
    inside it were the bubbles on its tide
21   as it rose and fell in one great heaving sea.
"Look out, look out!" my leader quickly cried
    and suddenly reached out and pulled me near
24   from where I was standing to peer down inside.
I turned like one who wants to have a clear
    look at the thing he has been warned to shun,
27   who is taken by an overwhelming fear
and flees, but looks while he keeps moving on,
    and then I saw a great black demon race
30   up the crag behind us, coming at a run.
How savage were his bearing and his face!
    With wings spread, what ferocity he showed
33   with every step, keeping up his rapid pace,
moving lightly on his feet! He bore the load,
    on his high, sharp shoulder, of a sinner's thighs,
36   and he gripped the ankle tendons as he strode.
He called from our bridge: "Hey, Evilclaws, here's a prize,
    one of Saint Zita's Elders![1] Dunk him under,
39   while I go back there for some fresh supplies.

1. Zita (d. 1270s) was a servant woman of Lucca, to whom miracles were attributed; she was
known as Saint Zita, although she was not canonized until 1690. The Elders were the city's
magistrates, ten in number, chosen for two-month terms. The dead soul (identified by an
early commentator as Martino Bottaio, a Luccan politician who died the day on which this
canto is set) is, like the others here, guilty of barratry, the buying and selling of public offices.

That town is ripe for plucking, and no wonder.
       Except for our friend Bonturo,[2] everyone
42   is a grafter, changing *no* to *yes* for plunder."
He tossed the soul down, turned, and then was gone.
       Never did any hound that has been untied
45   move faster after a burglar on the run.
The soul resurfaced, showing his backside,
       and the devils beneath the bridge began to crow.
48   "This is no place for the Holy Face!"[3] they cried.
"The swimming that you did in the Serchio[4]
       is not the fashion here. If you don't care
51   to be stuck with grappling hooks, then stay below."
With a hundred prongs they bit him everywhere.
       "Undercover dancing's what our minions do,"
54   they said, "so, if you're able, graft down there."
And they did what cooks will set their scullions to
       when with forks they plunge the meat down in the pot
57   to keep it under so it will cook through.
My master said: "It is better that you not
       be seen just now. Screen yourself behind a near
60   outcrop of rock and crouch down on the spot.
I know the way they do things. Never fear,
       no matter how outrageous their offense,
63   for once before I tangled with them here."
He crossed the bridgehead and he passed at once
       to the sixth embankment, needing now to be
66   steady in manner and in countenance.
With all the clamor and the savagery
       of mastiffs rushing a poor mendicant
69   who freezes and starts begging instantly,
from beneath the little bridge, all at a sprint
       and pointing their hooks at him, came the whole crew,
72   but he called out: "There's no need to be violent!
Before you grapple me, let one of you
       come forth and hear me out, and then you may
75   decide if you still wish to run me through."
"Send Wickedtail!" I heard the demons say.
       Then one stepped forward, saying: "I wonder what
78   he expects to gain by carrying on this way."
"Do you think that you would see me in this spot,"

---

2. This line is highly ironic, since Bonturo Dati, who died in 1325, was reputed to be the most corrupt official in Lucca.
3. An ancient crucifix in Lucca, carved from dark wood.
4. A river that flows near Lucca. According to the early commentaries, it was a popular site for swimming in summer.

           my master told the one called Wickedtail,
81   "secure so far against each plan and plot,
     without God's will and a fate that cannot fail?
              So let us pass, for it is heaven's command
84   that I lead another on this savage trail."
       The fiend was so crestfallen that his hand
              let go his grappling hook. "Now let him be,
87   let no one strike at him," he told his band.
       My leader called: "O you who fearfully
              crouch on the bridge, it is safe now to appear
90   from the cover of your crag and come to me."
       I rushed to him, and I began to fear
              whether the fiends would keep the pact they'd made,
93   from the way they all pressed round and crowded near.
       Once I had seen a line of troops parade
              out of Caprona[5] amid their enemies.
96   Despite the pledge of truce, they looked afraid.
       I stood beside my leader and tried to squeeze
              against him, keeping the fiends under close watch,
99   for their looks were far from putting me at ease.
       They aimed their hooks, and one said: "Should I scratch
              his butt for him?" and another one replied:
102   "Sure, why not stick it to him in the notch?"
       But the demon speaking with my leader cried
              aloud as he turned around to face them: "No!
105   At ease there, Tangletop, put your hook aside."
       Then he said to us: "It's impossible to go
              along this crag, for the sixth arch is long gone.
108   It's lying in pieces in the pit below.
       But if it is still your pleasure to go on,
              I know another way that you can take.
111   Nearby is a spur that you can cross upon.
       About five hours from now, it's going to make
              twelve hundred and sixty-six years and one day
114   since the road was broken by a mighty quake.[6]
       I was about to send a squad that way
              to see if anyone's drying out in the air.
117   You'll be safe with them." And then he turned to say:
       "Step forward, Tramplefrost, and Droopwing there.
              And Baddog, I want you to join the hunt.
120   Let Spikebeard lead the ten. And let that pair

---

5. A castle about five miles from the city of Pisa, Caprona was surrendered to Tuscan
   Guelph forces (Florentines and Lucchese) in August 1289. Dante was a member of the
   invading army.
6. See note 4 to Canto XII, p. 44. It is now about seven o'clock on Saturday morning.

Lusthoney and Dragonsnout step to the front,
    and Pigface with the tusks, and Scratchbitch too,
123   and Littlehoof and crazy Rubicant.
Search round the edges of the boiling glue,
    get these two safely to the next precipice
126   that bridges all the ditches and runs clear through."
"Master," I said, "surely something is amiss.
    Let us go on, just the two of us alone,
129   if you know the way. I don't like the looks of this.
Where is the caution that you've always shown?
    Do you not see their threatening brows and hear
132   their grinding teeth, that may grind me to the bone?"
"I would not have you suffer needless fear,"
    he told me. "Let their teeth grind. That is what
135   they do to scare the wretches stewing here."
They all turned round to face left on the spot,
    first pressing their tongues between their teeth en masse
138   to signal their leader, who sounded the charge, but not
as you'd think—he made a trumpet of his ass.

Canto XXII

Games of the Devils; Ciampolo's Autobiography; His Escape; Virgil and Dante Escape

I have seen cavalry break camp and ride out,
    or make assaults or muster on command,
3   or retreat to save themselves when put to rout,
I have seen coursers dash across your land,
    O Aretines, seen raiding parties there,[1]
6   watched tournaments and jousting near at hand,
signaled by ringing bells or trumpets' blare
    or drumbeats, castle signals near and far,
9   our own and foreign, sound and sign and flare,
but never to a bagpipe so bizarre
    have I seen horsemen move, or infantry,
12   or a ship set forth by landmark or by star.
We walked with the ten fiends. Savage company,
    but in the church with saints, as people say,
15   in the tavern with the drunkards on a spree.

---

1. According to a letter that has not survived, Dante was a cavalryman at the battle of Campaldino on June 11, 1289, in which the Aretine Ghibellines were defeated by the Florentine Guelphs.

The sea of pitch was where my attention lay,
    to learn what the pit was like and to take note
18   of the souls inside it as it boiled away.
Like dolphins swimming near a ship or boat
    whose arching backs make sailors realize
21   that they have to act to keep their craft afloat,[2]
from the pitch a sinner's back would sometimes rise
    to ease the pain, then plunge down into it
24   faster than lightning streaks across the skies.
As frogs with only their muzzles showing sit
    at the water's edge inside a ditch and hide
27   their feet and all their bulk, so in the pit
I could see surfaced heads on every side,
    but when the souls saw Spikebeard come their way
30   they plummeted below the boiling tide.
I saw—and my heart still shudders to this day—
    one head still up, as sometimes when you look
33   one frog will dive and another one will stay.
And Scratchbitch, who was closest to him, took
    the soul by his pitch-soaked hair and hauled him high.
36   To me he seemed like an otter on the hook.
I was familiar with their names, for I
    had watched them when they were chosen for this run
39   and listened to what they called each other by.
The godforsaken gang cried out as one:
    "Hey, Rubicant, get out your claws and play,
42   and flay his carcass till the skin is gone!"
"Master," I said, "I wonder if I may
    learn who he is, this luckless miscreant
45   hanging helpless before his enemies this way.
Please speak to him." And so my leader went
    to the soul and asked about his origins.
48   "I was born in the kingdom of Navarre,[3] and sent
by my mother to serve a lord," he answered, "since
    she had had me by a wastrel, one who threw
51   his property and his body to the winds.
Then I joined the good King Thibaut's retinue,[4]
    where I became so skilled a barrator
54   that in this heat I'm paying back what's due."

---

2. It was believed that the surfacing of dolphins near a vessel signified an approaching storm.
3. Once an independent kingdom, Navarre is now divided between northern Spain and southwestern France. The speaker was named in early commentaries as one Ciampolo, but nothing is known of him.
4. Thibaut II, king of Navarre from 1253 to 1270, was highly regarded for his justice and generosity.

Then Pigface, who had tusks just like a boar
    that protruded from his snout on either side,
57   let him feel the way that one of them ripped and tore.
Cruel cats had trapped the mouse. Now Spikebeard cried
    as he ringed his arms around the soul: "Look smart!
60   Stand back while I enfork him!" Then to my guide
he turned and said: "I think you'd better start
    asking now if there's anything else you want to know,
63   before the others tear him all apart."
So my leader said: "Among the souls below,
    under the pitch, are there any Italians here?"
66   And the soul replied: "Just a little while ago
I was with someone from there, or very near.
    I wish I were still hidden where he is,
69   then there'd be no hooks or claws for me to fear."
Lusthoney yelled: "We've had enough of this!"
    And then he raked the sinner's arm and took
72   a sinew out with that vicious hook of his.
Now Dragonsnout was gesturing with his hook
    at the sinner's legs, but turning toward his crew
75   their captain faced them down with an evil look.
As they grew still, my leader turned back to
    the soul, who was staring at his mangled limb,
78   and started in to question him anew:
"Who was it that you parted from to swim
    to so miserable an outcome on the banks?"
81   "Fra Gomita of Gallura.[5] I was with him,"
said the soul, "a receptacle of fraud who ranks
    at the head of the list, a first-class barrator.
84   From his master's foes he garnered praise and thanks.
As he has said, he took their money for
    a smooth release when he had them in his hand.
87   A silky trick, and he had a hundred more.
And there's one from Logodoro who's his friend,
    Don Michel Zanche.[6] Once they start to jaw
90   about Sardinia, there isn't any end.
How that demon grinds his teeth! They're like a saw!
    I want to go on, but I can't say a word,
93   I'm afraid he'll scrub my mange and rub me raw!"
Littlehoof's eyes were rolling as he was spurred
    by a zeal to strike, but his provost suddenly

5. Around 1294, Fra Gomita was appointed chancellor by Nino Visconti (see note 1 to Canto XXXIII), a Pisan who was the judge of Gallura, one of the four judicial districts of Sardinia. Visconti ignored all complaints against Gomita until he discovered that the friar had helped prisoners to escape, whereupon he had him hanged.
6. Governor of Logudoro, another of the four judicial districts of Sardinia. He was murdered by his son-in-law, Branca d'Oria (see note 1 to Canto XXXIII, p. 128).

96   wheeled round and barked: "Get back, you noxious bird!"
    "If it's Lombards that you'd like to hear or see,
            or Tuscans," the frightened soul began to say,
99   "then let me call for them, and here they'll be.
    Let the Evilclaws drop back a little way,
            so the souls won't fear the things that they might do.
102   Just one of me sitting here—and here I'll stay—
    will make sure that seven souls come out for you
            when I whistle. That's the way we do it when
105   any one of us gets free from the hot glue."
    And Baddog lifted up his muzzle then,
            shook his head, and said: "Don't fall into the snare!
108   It's a trick so he can jump back in again."
    The spirit, who had trickery to spare,
            said: "I must be really tricky then, if I
111   am procuring some new pains for my friends down there."

solidarity amongst souls?

    Droopwing, against the others, stood idly by
            no longer, but told the soul: "If you make a break,
114   I won't come running after you, I'll fly,
    beating my wings above the boiling lake.
            We'll go hide behind the bank. In any event,
117   we'll see how much of a match for us you make."
    Here, reader, is new sport. The whole complement
            looked off to the ridge, and the first to turn was he
120   who had raised his voice the loudest in dissent.
    The Navarrese had it measured perfectly.
            He planted his feet and broke from the embrace
123   of the leader in one leap, and he was free.
    They all were mortified at their disgrace,
            and most of all the one who had caused the error.
126   "You're caught!" he called as he started to give chase,
    but his flapping wings could not outdistance terror.
            The one dove in and the other had to go
129   looping swiftly upward as the pitch came nearer,
    like the angry falcon left with nothing to show
            for his efforts when the wild duck he pursues
132   eludes him with a rapid plunge below.
    Tramplefrost, who was seething at the ruse,
            took wing, but hoped his quarry would abscond
135   and provide him with a pretext he could use
    to pick a fight. With the barrator beyond
            their reach, he turned and dug his claws into
138   his fellow demon right above the pond.
    But the other was a full-fledged hawk who knew
            how to give it back to him, and as they fought
141   they dropped right down into the boiling glue.

There the heat shocked them apart, but when they sought
    to fly away, their wings were so besmeared,
144   as if with lime, that they were truly caught.
Lamenting with his fellow fiends, Spikebeard
    sent four of them flying toward the other shore.
147   Two landed on each side and quickly steered
their hooks above the lake to grapple for
    their limed companions, who'd already been
150   baked in their crusts and cooked through to the core.
We left them to the mess they were stewing in.

Canto XXIII

The Sixth Ditch: The Hypocrites; Two Evil Friars; Catalano; Caiaphas

We walked with no companions and no sounds,
    with one before and one behind, the way
3   that Friars Minor[1] do upon their rounds.
I was reminded by the demons' fray
    of Aesop's fables, the one in which we see
6   the story of the frog and mouse.[2] I say
that *now* is no closer to *immediately*
    than these two cases, if we scrutinize
9   beginnings and conclusions carefully.
Out of one thought another one will rise,
    and that one bred another one that was
12   making my fear grow twice its former size.
I thought: They have been tricked because of us,
    so hurt and humiliated that I swear
15   by now they must be truly furious,
and if their spite is blended with a share
    of anger, they will follow where we've led
18   more fiercely than a dog destroys a hare.
My scalp already tingled with cold dread
    and my senses fastened on what might appear
21   behind us at any moment. "Master," I said,
"unless you conceal us now, I greatly fear

1. The Franciscans. Following the example of their founder, St. Francis of Assisi, they culti-
vated poverty and humility. They made their begging rounds in pairs, the younger friar
walking behind the elder.
2. In most versions of this fable, a mouse asks a frog to carry him across a stream; before do-
ing so, the frog ties the mouse to his leg, and during the crossing he tries to drown the
mouse by submerging; the ensuing commotion attracts a hawk, who carries them off, eat-
ing the frog and freeing the mouse.

the Evilclaws. I know they are in our wake.
24   I fear them so, it sounds as if they're here."
He said: "Were I leaded glass, I could not take
    your outer form more quickly than I do
27   the image that your inward motions make.
A moment ago, I felt these thoughts from you
    mingle with mine, the same movement and same face,
30   so that I have drawn one counsel from the two.
If we follow the right slope down to its base
    we will reach the next ditch, in my expectation,
33   and so escape from this imagined chase."
He had not finished with his explanation
    when I saw the demons with their wings outspread
36   behind us, bent on our annihilation.
My leader drew me to him, and he sped
    like a mother wakened by the noise and seeing
39   the rising flames as they crackle by her bed
and then picking up her child and quickly fleeing
    without stopping even to put on a shift,
42   more concerned for his than for her own well-being.

maternal Virgil

Supine, he gave himself up to a swift
    slide on the hard ridge that slopes down below
45   to form the outer wall of the next cleft.
Never did water make such a rapid flow
    to the bottom of the sluice where it ends its run
48   by hitting the paddles to make the millwheel go
as my master sledded down the rock upon
    his back, and all the while he clasped me tight,
51   not just as a companion, but as a son.

architecture

As we reached the base, I looked back to the height
    and saw the entire troop of fiends appear,
54   but now there was no cause for further fright,
for that high providence that placed them here
    to rule the fifth ditch makes them powerless
57   ever to pass beyond their proper sphere.
Below there were painted people in distress,
    weeping, and trudging slowly, with an air
60   of great oppression and great weariness.

bureaucracy of Hell, even amongst monsters

Large cloaks were worn by all the sinners there,
    with cowls that hid their eyes, and cut like those
63   that are fashioned for the Cluny monks[3] to wear.
Though the eye was dazzled by these gilded clothes,
    they were lead inside, and sat so heavily
66   they made the ones that Frederick would impose

3. The abbey of Cluny in Burgundy was founded by the Benedictines in 910.

seem straw.[4] A weary cape for eternity!
    Turning left once more, we walked with that parade
69   and listened to their moans of misery.
The leaden capes with which they were arrayed
    so weighed them down and made their steps so slow,
72   we saw new faces with each stride we made.
I told my guide: "Please look round as we go,
    to see if there are people anywhere
75   of whom, by name or deed, I ought to know."
And hearing my Tuscan speech, one trudging there
    cried after us: "Don't go at such great speed,
78   you who are hurtling through the dusky air!
Perhaps I can provide you what you need."
    My leader said: "Till he overtakes you, stay,
81   then match your pace to his, and so proceed."
I stopped. There were two whose faces showed that they
    had minds that raced to join me, but they were balked
84   by their burden and by the narrowness of the way.
They looked at me askance when they had walked
    to where I was, and silently took note.
87   Then they turned to one another, and they talked:
"He seems alive, from the workings of his throat.
    And if they are dead, by what authority
90   are they exempted from the heavy coat?"
Then to me: "O Tuscan, who have come to see
    the college of sad hypocrites, we implore
93   that you not disdain to tell us who you might be."
And I: "The great city on fair Arno's shore
    is where I was born and where my youth was spent,
96   and I wear the body that I always wore.
But who are you, whose misery has sent
    its distillations down along your cheek,
99   and why do you wear this glittering punishment?"
Then one of the two souls began to speak:
    "The orange cape's thick lead weighs down our frame,
102   which is its balance scale, and makes it creak.
We were Jolly Friars, and Bolognese. My name
    is Catalano and his is Loderingo.
105   Chosen jointly by your city, we became
maintainers of the peace, a post for a single
    appointee in most times. How well we tried

---

4. According to his enemies (although there is no confirmation), Emperor Frederick II pun-
ished treason by having the offender be boiled in a cauldron while wearing a lead cape;
the cape, when it melted, peeled away the traitor's skin.

108　　　can still be seen in the region of the Gardingo."[5]
　　"O friars, your wicked—" I started. The rest died
　　　　in my throat as my eye was caught by someone nailed
111　　　right into the ground with three stakes, crucified.
　　He began to writhe when he saw me, and exhaled
　　　　great sighs in his beard. Catalano, carefully
114　　　observing, said: "The one who is impaled
　　advised the Pharisees that it would be
　　　　expedient that one man be made to die
117　　　in order that the people might go free.
　　And just as you see before you, he must lie
　　　　naked and stretched in the middle of the road
120　　　under the weight of each one who passes by.
　　Transfixed with spikes and racked in the same mode,
　　　　his father-in-law lies elsewhere in this fosse,
123　　　and the others of that council, those who sowed
　　so much evil for the Jews."[6] Seeming at a loss,
　　　　Virgil was staring at the one who lay
126　　　in such vile eternal exile, as on a cross.
　　Then he turned and spoke to the friar: "I hope it may
　　　　not displease you, if the laws down here permit,
129　　　to let us know if there is any way
　　on the right by which we two can leave this pit
　　　　without our having to depend upon
132　　　the black angels to deliver us from it."
　　"Much closer than you hope, making its run
　　　　from the massive outer wall, there is a ridge
135　　　linking all the savage valleys—except this one,
　　where it is broken and there is no bridge,"
　　　　the friar replied, "but you may climb instead
138　　　on the pile of the ruin up to the next ledge."
　　My leader stood for a moment with bowed head,
　　　　then said: "The one who hooks sinners up on that rise

directions out of this circle

---

5. The Knights of the Blessed Virgin Mary were a religious order whose charge was to rec-
oncile factions and disputes and to protect the weak. They were known sarcastically as
the Jolly Friars because of the laxity of their rules and their reputation for corruption.
Among the founders of the order were Catalano di Guido di Ostia (c. 1210–1285), a
Guelph, and Loderingo degli Andalò (c. 1210–1293), a Ghibelline, who served jointly as
maintainers of public order in Bologna in 1265. Having arranged a truce between warring
factions, they were appointed in 1266 to a similar function in Florence at the behest of
Pope Clement IV, whose secret intent was to establish the Guelph party at the expense of
the Ghibellines. In 1267, the Ghibellines were driven out of Florence, their property con-
fiscated, and the houses of some of the more prominent familes destroyed, including
those of the Uberti family in the Gardingo section of the city.
6. Caiaphas, the high priest of the Jews, urged that Jesus be turned over to the Romans, os-
tensibly for the public good but secretly because Jesus' teachings posed a threat to the
established leadership. In this he was abetted by his father-in-law, Annas, and other mem-
bers of the Sanhedrin, the supreme council. From this betrayal, as Dante sees it, followed
the destruction of Jerusalem and the diaspora.

141   gave a bad account of this." And the friar said:
"In Bologna once, I heard men philosophize
    on the devil's vices, and someone put the case
144   that he is a liar, and even the father of lies."
A spot of anger darkened my guide's face
    as he strode away, and I no longer stayed
147   among those weighted souls, but left that place
to follow in the steps his dear feet made.

Canto XXIV

The Seventh Ditch: The Thieves; The Metamorphosis; Vanni Fucci; Prophecy of Florentine Civil Strife

In that part of the young year when the sun's rays
    are tempered beneath Aquarius, and when
3   the nights grow shorter, equaling the days,[1]
and when her white sister's image once again
    appears upon the ground as copied by
6   the hoarfrost with her quickly dulling pen,
the peasant, with the loss of his supply
    of fodder, goes outside in anxiety
9   to see the whitened fields, and smites his thigh
and mutters and starts to pace distractedly
    like a wretch whose mind can find no resting place,
12   then grows hopeful, going out again, to see
how rapidly the world has changed its face,
    and taking staff in hand walks forth once more
15   to lead his sheep to graze. Such was my case,
because the troubled look my master wore
    distressed me deeply, but he soothed my pain
18   when he quickly put the plaster to the sore.
At the ruined bridge I saw his face regain,
    when he turned to me, the sweet look I first knew
21   at the base of the mountain on the desert plain.
He looked carefully at the ruin, then he drew
    into himself in silent contemplation,
24   and then took hold of me. Like someone who
while working keeps a constant calculation
    and thus is able to anticipate,
27   he would look ahead and make an estimation
as he lifted me from rock to rock, and state:
    "Take hold of this one, but be sure to test

1. The sun is in Aquarius between January 21 and February 21.

30   beforehand whether it will bear your weight."
That was no road for anybody dressed
        in a lead cloak. Rock by rock we had to grope,
33   he weightless and I half-carried, toward the crest.
And happily upon that side the slope
        was shorter than on the other, or else I—
36   I cannot speak for him—would have had no hope.
All of the rungs of the Malebolge lie
        on an incline toward the deep well's mouth, and so
39   one wall is always low and one is high
in each of the ten troughs along the row.
        But in the end we made our way to where
42   the last rock had broken free and dropped below.
My aching lungs had been so milked of air,
        when I finally reached the top, that I had to sit,
45   feeling unable to go on from there.
"Now you must rouse yourself, for never yet
        has anyone come to fame," my master cried,
48   "sitting on cushions or under a coverlet.
He who consumes his life, when he has died
        without fame, leaves the world with the impress
51   of smoke in the air or foam upon the tide.
Rise. Let your soul overcome your breathlessness,
        for, unless the heavy body lets it fail,
54   the soul will always prove victorious.
There is still a longer ladder we must scale.
        It is not enough to have left the rest, and so
57   act for your good, if you know what these words entail."
Then I stood up and said, with a greater show
        of breath than what I really felt within:
60   "I am strong and I am ready. Let us go."
So we took up our journey once again.
        The ridge was narrow, difficult, and rough,
63   much steeper than the previous one had been.
I was talking as I walked, to keep up the bluff
        of vigor, when a voice with little skill
66   in forming words came from the nearby trough.
Although I had reached the high point of the hill
        made by the arch, I could not tell what was said
69   and I sensed the speaker was not standing still.
Because of the darkness, even my riveted
        eyes could not see to the bottom of the ring,
72   so I said: "Master, let us walk ahead
and descend the wall, for I am listening
        without understanding what I hear, and
75   I am looking without seeing anything."
He said: "A right request should be followed by

male-bolge from above (architecture)

the deed itself without words' embellishment,
78   and so the doing is my sole reply." *he is kind of a pretenti*
At the end of the bridge, we two made our descent *prick, isn't h*
to the eighth embankment, and from where we stood
81   what was down there in the ditch was evident.

Hell
make up

In it I saw a horrible multitude
of serpents, of such weird variety
84   that thinking about them now still chills my blood.
Let Libya boast no more of phareae
and jaculi and chelydri in her sands,
87   and cenchres with amphisbaena, because she,
with all Ethiopia or the Red Sea's lands,[2]
has never bred a pestilence of such scope
90   or such malignancy. Here naked bands
of terrified souls were running, with no hope,
amid this savage swarm, that they would find
93   a crevice where they could hide, or a heliotrope.
With serpents each one's hands were bound behind,
and the ends poked through his loins and gathered tight
96   in a knot at front, with head and tail entwined.
Not far from where we stood, I beheld the sight
of a serpent darting at a sinner's nape,
99   transfixing him where shoulders and neck unite.
Never did pen so quickly make the shape
of an *o* or *i* as he flared and burned before
102   he turned to ash and fell into a heap.
And when he lay destroyed on the ditch's floor,
the loose dust gathered by itself and then
105   quickly assumed its former shape once more.
In such fashion, as affirmed by learned men,
when its five hundred years are near complete
108   the phoenix dies and then is born again.
Tears of balsam and of incense are its meat,
not grass or grain, and when it comes to die
111   spikenard and myrrh are its final winding-sheet.
Just as when someone falls without knowing why,
seized by a devil hidden from his eyes
114   or a blockage that a man may be stricken by,
and looks around him as he starts to rise,
stunned by the anguish that he undergoes,
117   and in his great bewilderment he sighs,

2. Libya (the ancient term for northern Africa, exclusive of Egypt), Ethiopia (from Egypt
south to Zanzibar), and Arabia ("the Red Sea's lands") were considered to be largely un-
inhabitable and filled with exotic creatures. All the species of serpents mentioned here
are taken from Book IX of Lucan's *Pharsalia*.

such was the soul before us as he rose.
    O power of God, so rigorously applied,
120   that in its vengeance showers down such blows!
My leader asked who he was, and he replied:
    "Not long ago I was rained from Tuscany
123   down to this savage gullet. I enjoyed
a beast's, not a man's life, mule that I used to be.
    I am Vanni Fucci,[3] beast. Pistoia was
126   a proper den for an animal like me."
I said to my guide: "Tell him not to slip from us,
    and ask what sin has thrown him down here, since
129   I knew him to be bloody and furious."
The soul had heard me, and with no pretense
    fastened on me with his face and with his mind,
132   and said, as sad shame colored his countenance:
"It pains me more to be caught by you in the bind
    of this misery than it did a short while ago
135   to be snatched away from the life I left behind.
I cannot deny the thing you wish to know.
    I am this far down because I was the one
138   who stole the sacristy's ornaments, although
others were wrongly blamed for what I'd done.[4]
    But lest this sight please you, if you ever do
141   escape this land that never sees the sun,
open your ears and hear what I'm telling you.
    Pistoia puts out its Blacks, then Florence makes
144   its population and its ways anew.
Mars goes to Val di Magra, where he takes
    a vapor wrapped in dense clouds, and the might
147   of a violent and a bitter tempest breaks
on Campo Piceno, where there is a fight
    till the vapor rends the mist above the plain
150   all of a sudden, striking every White.
And I have told you this to give you pain."[5]

3. The illegitimate son ("mule") of Fuccio dei Lazzari and an extreme partisan of the Blacks in Pistoia. He was notorious for his rage and was known to have committed at least one murder (thus Dante's surprise, in lines 128–29, at finding him here and not among the violent).
4. The theft of sacred objects from the sacristy of the chapel of San Jacopo caused a sensation in Pistoia in 1293. Fucci revealed his involvement in this crime in order to save the life of one Rampino di Francesco Foresi, who was about to be hanged for it.
5. Fucci's prophecy alludes to the following events: In May 1301, the Pistoian Whites, with the aid of their Florentine counterparts, expelled the Blacks from their city. In November of that year, the Blacks began an uprising in Florence that led to their recapture of the city the following year and the banishment of the Whites, which would result in Dante's permanent

Canto XXV

The Seventh Ditch, continued; Cacus;
Infernal Metamorphosis; Puccio Sciancato

When he had finished speaking, the thief threw
    his arms up, making figs with both his hands,
3   and shouted: "Take these, God, they're aimed at you!"
From that moment on, the serpents were my friends,
    for one approached his neck and circled it,
6   as if to tell him "Now your talking ends,"
and another retied him with so tight a fit,
    knotting itself in front, that he could not free
9   his arms to even wriggle them a bit.
Pistoia, Pistoia, why do you not decree
    the flames of your own destruction and downfall,
12   since you surpass your seed in villainy?[1]
I saw no soul so proud toward God through all
    the murky rings of hell, not even the one
15   who assaulted Thebes and fell from the high wall.[2]
He fled without a word, and on the run
    came a raging centaur who was calling out:
18   "Where is he, where's the unripe spirit gone?"
I believe not even Maremma[3] has such a rout
    of snakes as I saw upon him, from the rear
21   to the part where our human shape begins to sprout.
A dragon with its wings stretched out was here
    across his shoulders, crouched behind his head,
24   spitting fire and burning anyone who was near.
"That centaur there is Cacus,"[4] my master said.

---

exile from Florence (see note 3 to Canto VI). The vapor—or hot wind, which clashes with the cold, moist clouds to produce the storm—is generally understood to be Moroello Malaspina, from the region of Val di Magra, a highly effective military leader of the Blacks. Campo Piceno refers to a field near Pistoia, believed to be the site of Catiline's defeat in 63 B.C.E., and also the location of a raid by Malaspina against the Whites.

1. The "seed" of Pistoia was presumed to be the remains of the defeated army of Catiline; see note 3 to Canto XV, for similar presumptions regarding the origins of Florence.
2. The reference is to Capaneus (see Canto XIV, lines 43–72).
3. The Maremma (see note 1 to Canto XIII) was, in addition to its other harsh features, swampy and snake-infested.
4. Son of Vulcan and Medusa, a fire-breathing monster who lived in a cave beneath Mount Avetine and preyed upon travelers. In Book VIII of the *Aeneid*, Virgil describes him as "half-human"; Dante has adapted these details to make him a centaur with a fire-breathing dragon on his back. Cacus stole some of the cattle that Hercules had taken from Geryon (see note 1 to Canto XVII), for which he was slain by Hercules—strangled, according to Virgil; clubbed, according to Ovid. Other centaurs guard the violent who are punished in the river of blood (Canto XII), but Cacus, even though he has something of a guard's function here, is punished with the thieves.

"Below the rock of Mount Avetine, blood flowed
27   because of him into frequent lakes of red.
And owing to the craftiness he showed
         when he stole the great herd grazing near his den,
30   he and his brothers are not on the same road.   *explanation*
That brought the end of his crooked dealings when   *for his*
         Hercules clubbed him down, although he may,   *lower*
33   of a hundred blows, have felt not even ten."   *place in*
While he said these words, the centaur ran away   *Hell*
         and three souls came to stand below us two,
36   although neither my guide nor I perceived that they
were there until they called out: "Who are you?"
         We stopped what we were saying, and we were
39   attentive to them. I couldn't make out who
these three might be, but as it will occur
         by chance sometimes, at that moment it occurred
42   that one of them had occasion to refer
to someone else—"Where's Cianfa?"[5]—at which I stirred,
         and I placed a finger on my lips to show
45   my leader we should watch without a word.
Reader, it is no wonder if you are slow
         to credit what comes next, for I was there
48   and I hardly can believe that it was so.
As I fixed upon those three with a steady stare,
         all at once I saw a six-legged serpent race
51   up to one and fasten on him everywhere.
Its front feet moved to pin his arms in place,
         its middle feet gripped his belly like a vise
54   while it sank its fangs in both sides of his face,
and between his legs its tail began to rise
         and it curved up to secure him from behind
57   after its rear feet spread apart his thighs.
Never did any strand of ivy bind
         its clinging roots more closely to a tree
60   than the limbs of that disgusting beast entwined
round the soul's. The two seemed like hot wax to me
         as their colors mingled and they were stuck tight,
63   and neither kept its own identity.
In the same way, when a paper is alight,
         ahead of the flame a dark hue starts to spread
66   that is not yet black but already no longer white.
The other two were watching, and they said:

---

5. Cianfa (died c. 1289) appears to have been a member of the Donati family of Florence.
   He is the serpent who comes running up at line 50.

"Alas, Agnello,[6] how fast you are defaced,
69   neither two nor one, but something else instead."
Where there had been two heads, they were replaced
     by a single one, and in the face it wore
72   all the details of their own two were erased.
Now two arms sprouted where there had been four,
     and thighs, legs, chests, and bellies mixed and grew
75   into members that were never seen before.
All of their features had disappeared into
     a perverse thing that was both and neither one,
78   that with slow steps went trudging out of view.
As across the lane you may see a lizard run
     like a lightning flash as it darts from hedge to hedge
81   when the dog days scourge the earth with a burning sun,
so I saw a little serpent in a rage,
     as fiery and as black as pepper, bound
84   toward the bellies of the two beneath our ledge.
Lunging, it bit one where that part is found
     through which we all take in our earliest food,
87   and then fell back, stretched out upon the ground.
The one it had bitten made no sound. He stood
     gazing and yawning, as if he had been hit
90   with a sleepy or a feverish lassitude.
The serpent looked at him and he looked at it.
     Thick smoke poured from its mouth, and met and mixed
93   with smoke from his belly, where the reptile bit.
Let Lucan be still, who tells us in his text
     of poor Sabellus and Nasidius,
96   and let him wait to hear what is sent forth next.[7]
Let Ovid be still. If he tells how Cadmus was
     made a snake, how Arethusa came to be
99   a fountain,[8] I do not envy him, because
in all his transmutations we never see
     two different natures facing one another
102   whose forms exchange their substance instantly.
The two responded readily to each other,
     so that the serpent split its tail in two
105   and the wounded spirit drew his feet together.

6. A member of the Brunelleschi family, Ghibellines of Florence. There is little historically reliable information about him.
7. In Book IX of *Pharsalia*, Lucan tells of Sabellus, a soldier in Cato's army who was bitten by a snake in the Libyan desert and became a festering mass, and of Nasidius, another of Cato's soldiers, also bitten by a serpent, whose body became so swollen that it burst.
8. Cadmus, son of King Agenor of Phoenicia, and his wife, Harmonia, were turned into serpents for killing a dragon sacred to Mars (*Metamorphoses*, Book IV), and the nymph Arethusa was transformed to a fountain to escape the river god Alpheus, who nonetheless mingled his waters with hers (Book V).

Then his legs, from thigh to ankle, also drew
    together, and they were joined so seamlessly
108   that soon the juncture disappeared from view.
The cloven tail took on the anatomy
    the other abandoned, and the serpent's hide
111   grew soft as the other's skin grew leathery.
I saw the spirit's arms drawn up inside
    at the armpits, while the serpent's short feet surged
114   and correspondingly grew long and wide.
While its hind feet, which had twisted and converged,
    became the member man hides, from within
117   the wretch's member two small feet emerged.
As the smoke began to envelop each one in
    a different color and to generate
120   on the one the hair it stripped from the other's skin,
the one fell down and the other stood up straight.
    Neither turned his pitiless lamps aside, and so
123   each watched the other's features modulate
to his own. The standing one made its muzzle go
    in toward its temples and made its cheeks express
126   ears from the shifted matter's overflow.
With what it still retained of that excess,
    in the middle of its face a man's nose grew
129   and its lips plumped to a human fleshiness.
Meanwhile, the one who had fallen started to
    push out a snout and pull his ears inside,
132   as a snail when it retracts its horns will do.
His tongue, which had been fit for speech and wide,
    now forked. The other's tongue, which had been split,
135   became one. And I saw the smoke subside.
The new-formed beast went scampering through the pit,
    emitting hissing noises as it fled.
138   The other one was spitting after it.
He turned his new shoulders toward the third and said:
    "Now I'll let Buoso[9] have the degradation
141   of running on six legs the way I did."
Thus the mutation and the transmutation
    in the seventh dump. Put it down to my surprise
144   at the strangeness, if I err in my narration.
My mind had been bewildered and my eyes
    had been confused, but no matter how furtively
147   they fled away, I could clearly recognize

9. Variously identified, Buoso is believed to have been Buoso di Forese Donati (died c. 1285; not the Buoso Donati mentioned in Canto XXX, line 43).

Puccio Sciancato.[1] Of the original three
    he was the only one to undergo
150   no transformation. The other one was he
on whose account, Gaville,[2] your tears still flow.

Canto XXVI

The Eighth Ditch, continued: Evil Counselors;
Ulysses' Last Journey

Florence, rejoice at how great you have grown,
    beating your wings over land and sea, with fame
3   that has spread through hell! I found five of your own
among the thieves,[1] and such to inflict a shame
    that is clinging to me still, and I say to you
6   that the fact adds no great honor to your name.
But if the things we dream toward dawn are true,[2]
    then you will feel, in a time that is soon to come,
9   what Prato[3] craves for you, as others do.
It were not too soon had it already come.
    I could wish it had, since it must surely be,
12   and will grieve me more the older I become.
We left that place, going up where previously
    we had descended on the crags we found.
15   My leader mounted first, then lifted me.
We made our solitary way around
    the rocks and the projections as we went.
18   Without the hand, the foot could gain no ground.
I lamented then, and once more I lament
    over what I saw, and here I have denied
21   my genius its full freedom, to prevent
its wandering where virtue does not guide.
    If my good star or an even higher grace
24   has given this gift, it should not be misapplied.[4]
In the season when the light-giver turns his face

---

1. Puccio Galigai, called Sciancato ("lame"), was a member of a Ghibelline family and appears to have had the reputation of a gentleman thief.
2. Francesco de' Cavalcanti, called Guercio ("squinting" or "cross-eyed"), was murdered by people from Gaville, a town near Florence. The Cavalcanti avenged his death by killing many of Gaville's inhabitants. There is no solid evidence that he was a thief.
1. The five thieves were all members of upper-class families.
2. There was a common belief that morning dreams are prophetic in nature.
3. The reference may be either to Cardinal Niccolò da Prato, who excommunicated the city's inhabitants in 1304 after failing to reconcile its rival factions, or to the town of Prato, eleven miles northwest of the city, which expelled its Black Guelphs in 1309.
4. See note 6 to Canto IV, p. 16.

the least from us, at the hour when flies yield
27   to mosquitoes that have come to take their place,
as many as are the fireflies revealed
    to the peasant as he rests upon the height,
30   looking down where he harvests grapes and tills the field,
with so many flames the eighth pouch was alight,
    as I could see upon arriving where
33   the bottom of the ditch came into sight.
As the one who was avenged by bears was there
    to see the chariot of Elijah rise
36   when the horses strode right up into the air,
but found he could not follow it with his eyes,
    seeing nothing but the fire in its glide
39   toward heaven like a cloudlet through the skies,[5]
so it was here, where all the fires hide
    their theft, as through the gullet of the ditch
42   each steals away with a sinner hidden inside.
In my zeal to see, I had risen up on the bridge,
    and had I not grasped a rock, I have no doubt
45   that without a push I'd have fallen from the ledge.
My leader said, when he saw me leaning out:
    "Inside the fire the spirits are confined.
48   With a burning sheet each wraps himself about."
"Master, your words confirm what I was inclined
    to assume was so already," I replied,
51   "and already I had this question in my mind:
Who is in that flame whose top parts so divide
    that it seems to surge up from the funeral pyre
54   where Eteocles was laid at his brother's side?"[6]
He answered: "Joined in torment in that fire
    Ulysses and Diomed endure the force
57   of vengeance, as they once were joined in ire.
There they bemoan the ambush of the horse
    which made the gate that the noble seed of Rome
60   passed through as it set forth upon its course,
and lament the deceit that took Achilles from
    Deidamía, who mourns him still, though dead.
63   And there they pay for the Palladium."[7]

---

5. When the prophet Elisha cursed forty-two young boys who had mocked his baldness, two bears came from the forest and tore them to pieces (2 Kings 2.23–24). Elisha also beheld the prophet Elijah borne to heaven in a whirlwind by fiery horses and a fiery chariot (2 Kings 2.7–14).

6. In the siege of Thebes (see note 3 to Canto XIV), the warring sons of Oedipus, Eteocles and Polynices, killed one another. The dividing of the flame of their mutual pyre communicated their undying hatred.

7. The condemnation of the Greek heroes Ulysses (Odysseus) and Diomedes among the fraudulent is based on three incidents, the first and third of which are drawn from Book II of the *Aeneid*, the second from the unfinished *Achilleid* of Statius: (1) They devised the

"If they can speak within those sparks," I said,
    "Master, I pray you fervently, and I pray
66   that you hear a thousand prayers in this one's stead,
that you not deny me my desire to stay
    till that two-pronged flame approaches. You can see
69   how eagerly I am leaning out that way."
"Your prayer deserves much praise," he said to me,
    "and I accede to it. But you should restrain
72   your tongue just now and listen quietly.
Leave speech to me. There is no need to explain
    what you wish to know. But since those two were Greek,
75   any words from you might be greeted with disdain."
The fire came nearer, leaving him to seek
    the appropriate place and moment to pursue
78   his purpose. Then I heard my leader speak:
"O you who are in one flame and yet are two,
    if I earned merit with you while I drew breath,
81   if I earned merit great or small with you
when I wrote my lofty verses, then herewith
    remain, and let the one of you tell where
84   he went, when he was lost, to find his death."
Humming, the greater of the horns that share
    that ancient fire fluttered like a flame
87   struggling against a current in the air,
and its tip began to wriggle with the same
    undulations as a tongue engaged in speech,
90   and a voice was flung from it, and these words came:[8]
"When I was freed at last from Circe's reach,
    who had detained me for a year or more
93   near Gaeta, as Aeneas would name that beach,[9]
neither reverence for an aged father, nor
    a son's sweetness, nor the love I should profess
96   to Penelope, which she would be happy for,

[handwritten margin note: Also Dante doesn't speak Greek]

Trojan horse, whose role in the fall of Troy made it the portal through which the surviving
Trojans passed to become the founders of Rome. (2) They went to Scyros to lure the
beardless Achilles out of hiding among the women—where his mother, the goddess
Thetis, had placed him—because he would be needed for success against the Trojans; the
news of his death in Troy would cause Deidamia, the mother of his son, to die of grief. (3)
They sneaked into Troy by night to steal the statue of Pallas Athena, upon which the city's
safety was believed to depend.

8. Ulysses' speech was the primary inspiration for Tennyson's great monologue "Ulysses." It
is fascinating to observe how the same material is made to yield opposite conclusions:
where Dante in lines 91–142 presents Ulysses' final journey as a failure of familial re-
sponsibilities and a hubristic flouting of divinely imposed limitations, Tennyson cele-
brates the spirit of quest and daring without which there would be no human progress.

9. Gaeta, a town on the southeastern coast of Italy, was named by Aeneas for his nurse, Cai-
eta, who died there (*Aeneid*, Book VII). Dante would have known the story of Ulysses'
entanglement with the enchantress Circe from Ovid's *Metamorphoses*, Book XIV.

could overcome my ardor to possess
    experience of the world and humanity
99   in all its worth and all its wickedness.
But I set forth upon the open sea
    with just one vessel from my fleet's remains
102   and those few men who had not deserted me.
We sailed both shores, Morocco's coast and Spain's.
    As far as to Sardinia did we go,
105   and the other islands which that sea contains.
My mariners and I were old and slow
    when at last we reached that narrow channel lined
108   by Hercules with his marks so men would know
that they must not go beyond the bounds assigned.
    On the starboard side Seville now disappeared,
111   on the other Ceuta already lay behind.[1]
'Through a hundred thousand dangers we have steered,
    my brothers,' I said, 'to reach these western gates.
114   Now has the brief vigil of our senses neared
its close, so let us not forswear our fates
    but embrace experience, tracing the sun's route
117   to the uninhabited region that awaits.
Consider your origins. Living like a brute
    is not the destiny of men like you,
120   but knowledge and virtue ever our pursuit.'
With these few words of mine, my shipmates grew
    so eager to go on that even I
123   could not have stopped them had I wanted to.
Setting our stern against the morning sky,
    we turned our oars to wings in our mad flight,
126   gaining always on the left as days flew by.[2]
The other pole and all its stars showed night
    their faces now, and so near was our own
129   to the ocean's floor that it barely was in sight.[3]
Five times already had the light that shone
    below the moon been lit and then quenched once more
132   since we had sailed into the vast unknown,
when in the distance on the course we bore
    a huge dark mountain loomed, that seemed to be
135   taller than any I had seen before.

[handwritten margin note: several months]

1. The narrow channel is the Strait of Gibraltar. The Pillars of Hercules are Calpe in Spain and Abyla on the African promontory. In legend, they were originally one mountain, which was torn apart by Hercules, marking the point beyond which no one may sail and survive. Seville here connotes southern Spain, near Gibraltar. Ceuta is on the north coast of Morocco opposite Gibraltar.
2. They are sailing southwest, toward the point on the globe that is exactly opposite Jerusalem, where Dante locates Mount Purgatory (line 134).
3. The ship has now crossed the equator into the Southern Hemisphere.

Our joy was quickly turned to misery
        as a whirlwind rose from the land where we were bound
138   and rammed the prow of our vessel violently.
With the churning sea it spun the ship around
        three times, and on the fourth time the stern rose,
141   as it pleased another, and the prow was downed,
and over us we saw the waters close."

Canto XXVII

*The Eighth Ditch, continued: Guido de Montefeltro;
Guido's Evil Advice to Pope Boniface VIII;
Disputation between Saint Francis and the Devil*

Its speaking done, the flame stood straight and still,
        and then it went away when allowed to take
3   its leave of us through the gentle poet's will.
Another one came following in its wake.
        We looked to its tip because of the sputtering
6   and garbled noises that we heard it make.
And as the Sicilian bull[1] (whose bellowing
        began with the cries—and this was justified—
9   of the artisan whose file had shaped the thing),
although it was fashioned out of brass, still cried
        as if transfixed with pain, with a voice that came
12   from the victim who was sealed in its inside,
with these miserable words it was much the same.
        When at first they found no path or outlet, they
15   were translated to the language of the flame.
But when at last the sounds had pushed their way
        to the tip of the fire and then forced it through
18   the movements the tongue had made, we heard it say:
"O you at whom I aim my voice, and who
        just now spoke Lombard, for I could discern
21   the words 'Now go, I ask no more of you,'
perhaps I have come late, but before you turn
        may it not displease you to converse with me.
24   It does not displease me, even though I burn!
If you have just now left sweet Italy,
        out of which I bring my guilt, and are dropped below
27   to this blind world, tell me what there is to see

---

1. Several classical sources tell of Phalaris, tyrant of Agrigentum in the sixth century B.C.E.,
who had the Athenian Perillus fashion a bronze bull in which victims would be roasted
alive, with their muffled cries passing through pipes that made them sound like the bel-
lowing of a bull. Phalaris tested the device with Perillus himself as subject.

in Romagna: peace or war? I wish to know
    for I come from the mountains between Urbino and
30   the chain in which the Tiber starts its flow."[2]
And then my leader, when he saw me stand
    intently forward, touched me on the side
33   and said: "You speak to him. He is of your land."
I did not delay, but readily replied
    with an answer there was no need to prepare.
36   "O spirit down below whom the fires hide,
today in your Romagna war is where
    it has always been, in her tyrants' hearts," I said,
39   "but when I left, there was no fighting there.
Polenta's eagle sits brooding overhead
    at Ravenna, where things are still as they have been,
42   and as far as Cervia his wings are spread.[3]
The city that piled up Frenchmen's corpses when
    it resisted the long siege it suffered through
45   finds itself beneath the green paws once again.[4]
The mastiffs of Verrucchio, old and new,
    who sank their teeth into Montagna's throat,
48   still ply those fangs as they are wont to do.[5]
The white-laired lionet has the towns on both
    the Lamone and the Santerno beneath his sway.
51   As summer turns to winter, he turns his coat.[6]
And the city on the Savio lies today
    between tyranny and freedom, as it lies
54   between the plain and mountain.[7] Now I pray

2. Romagna is a district in northeastern Italy stretching from the Po south to the eastern Apennines, the range that includes Mount Coronaro, where the Tiber originates. The speaker, who is never identified by name, is Guido da Montefeltro (c. 1220–1298), perhaps the greatest of the Ghibelline commanders, who kept Romagna under Ghibelline rule when most of Italy, including the papacy, was Guelph-dominated. The bane of several popes, he was excommunicated in 1289, but was later reconciled to the Church and joined the Franciscan order (the "corded friars" of lines 67–68) in 1296.
3. Guido da Polenta, whose coat of arms displayed an eagle, had ruled Ravenna since 1275. Cervia is a town on the Adriatic, southeast of Ravenna. Guido was the father of Francesca da Rimini (see note 8 to Canto V) and the grandfather of Guido Novello, who was Dante's host in Ravenna in 1321.
4. Forlì, the central city of Romagna, held off a yearlong siege by a Guelph army, of French and Italian troops, sent by Pope Martin IV. The successful defense of the city was directed by Guido da Montefeltro, whom Dante is addressing. "Green paws" alludes to the escutcheon of the Ordelaffi family, who despotically ruled Forlì at the end of the thirteenth century.
5. In 1295, when the Ghibellines of Rimini were defeated by Malatesta da Verrucchio, the Ghibelline leader, Montagna de' Parcitati, was captured and then killed by Malatesta's son Malatestino. Malatesta ruled until his death in 1312, at the age of 100, when he was succeeded by Malatestino, who was succeeded in 1317 by his brother Pandolfo. Malatesta's other sons were Gianciotto, the husband of Francesca da Rimini, and Paolo, her lover.
6. Faenza is on the Lamone River, Imola on the Santerno. In 1300, they were under the control of Maghinardo de' Pagani da Susinana, here called the lionet because of his coat of arms. He was known for his political inconsistency.
7. Cesena was ruled by the relatively benign Galasso da Montefeltro, Guido's cousin.

to know who you are. Be as free in your replies
    as another has been with you, so may your name
57   remain forever vivid in men's eyes."
After the fire had bellowed in the same
    way as before, its pointed tip went through
60   its movements once again, and these words came:
"If I thought my answer were to someone who
    might see the world again, then there would be
63   no more stirrings of this flame. Since it is true
that no one leaves these depths of misery
    alive, from all that I have heard reported,
66   I answer you without fear of infamy.[8]
I was a man of arms, and then a corded
    friar, to make amends, and all seemed well
69   and would have been, but that my hopes were thwarted
by the high priest—may his spirit rot in hell—[9]
    who pulled me back to those first sins I had known,
72   the how and the *why* of which I wish to tell.
While I still had the form of flesh and bone
    that my mother gave to me, it was the style
75   of the fox, not the lion, that I made my own.
All covert ways and every kind of wile
    I mastered, and did such fine things in that art
78   that reports went round the earth of my great guile.
When I saw myself arriving at that part
    of the life of every man when it is best
81   to strike the sails and coil the ropes, my heart
was pained by what had pleased it. I confessed,
    repented, and turned friar, and all of these,
84   alas, would have secured my interest.
Ah, but the prince of the new Pharisees
    was waging war hard by the Lateran.
87   Neither Jews nor Saracens were his enemies.
His foes were Christians, every single one,
    and none had gone to conquer Acre or
90   been a merchant where the sultan's will is done.[1]

---

8. Lines 61–66, untranslated and unidentified, were used by T. S. Eliot as the epigraph to
"The Love Song of J. Alfred Prufrock."
9. The corrupt pope alluded to here is Boniface VIII.
1. There was endless strife, erupting into armed conflict in 1297, between Boniface and the
powerful Colonna family, whose residences were not far from his own, the Lateran
Palace. The Colonna refused to accept the abdication of Celestine V (see note 3 to Canto
III) and thus denied the legitimacy of Boniface's papacy. Here Boniface is attacked for
launching a crusade against his fellow Christians, while doing nothing to oppose the
Saracens who had in 1291 conquered Acre, the last Christian stronghold in the Holy
Land, or to punish those who defied the order, imposed by Pope Nicholas IV after the fall
of Acre, forbidding all commerce with Muslim lands.

He heeded neither the great keys that he bore
    nor his holy orders, nor my friar's cord,
93   which had made its wearers thin in times before.[2]
As Constantine sent to Soracte and implored
    Sylvester to cure his leprosy,[3] so I
96   had been sent for to be doctor to this lord,
for the fever of his pride was burning high.
    He solicited advice from his physician,
99   but his words seemed drunken, so I did not reply.
Then he said: 'Your heart need harbor no suspicion.
    I absolve you on the spot, so you must state
102   how I may cause Penestrino's demolition.[4]
For I can lock and unlock heaven's gate,
    as you know, with these two keys that I display,
105   which my predecessor failed to venerate.'
These weighty reasons convinced me that to stay
    silent would be the worst response of all,
108   so I said: 'Father, since you wash away
the sin in which I am about to fall,
    you will hold your throne in triumph if you provide
111   long promise, but make the keeping short and small.'[5]
Saint Francis came to get me when I died,[6]
    but one of the black cherubim came along,
114   saying: 'Leave him! He's mine! Justice will be denied
if he does not join my miserable throng
    because of the fraudulent counsel he presented.
117   I've been at his hair since the instant of that wrong,
for no one can be absolved who has not repented,
    and repent what he still wills, no one can do.
120   The inherent contradiction must prevent it.'
O wretched me! how I shivered when he threw
    his hands upon me, saying: 'Did you fail
123   to realize that I know logic too?'

---

2. The cord worn by the Franciscan friars made its wearers thin through their adherence to the vows of poverty and abstinence; "in times before" is an attack on the corruption of the contemporary Church.
3. It was widely believed during the Middle Ages that Constantine, afflicted with leprosy for his persecution of Christians, sent for Pope Sylvester I, who was hiding in a cave on Mount Soracte; Constantine was cured instantly upon being baptized by Sylvester and, according to the fraudulent Donation of Constantine, gave the Church temporal power in the western part of the empire (see note 1 to Canto XIX, p. 72).
4. Palestrina (Praeneste in ancient times) is a city some twenty miles east of Rome, where the Colonna resisted Boniface's siege until September 1298, when they surrendered under promise of amnesty. Supposedly, although their lives were spared, the Colonna were ruined and the city was destroyed.
5. It is not clear whether Guido actually gave Boniface such advice, since later chroniclers may have had Dante as their only source for the story.
6. According to Singleton, "The transition is the more effective for being so abrupt. Guido in fact did die in September 1298, the month in which Boniface tricked the Colonna."

calculation of punish-ment

He dragged me down to Minos, who wrapped his tail
    eight times round his hard back, and in an excess
126   of rage he bit it and began to rail:
'This sinner goes to the thieving flames!' And thus
    have I come to perdition, robed in the array
129   you see before you, going in bitterness."
When he had finished what he had to say,
    with its pointed tip still twisting to and fro
132   the grieving fire slowly went away.
My guide and I walked on from there, to go
    as far as the bridge the next pouch stretches under.
135   The souls sent here to pay the debt they owe
take their burden on by putting things asunder.

Canto XXVIII

The Ninth Ditch: The Schismatics; Mohammed; Fra Dolcino; Curio; Bertran de Born; The Law of contrapasso

Even in words not bounded by rhyme's law,
    through many repetitions of the tale,
3   how could the blood and wounds that I now saw
be fully told? Every tongue would surely fail,
    because our powers of speech and memory
6   are not meant to comprehend on such a scale.
If all of Apulia's battle dead[1] could be
    assembled, those of that battered country who
9   bewailed blood spilled by Trojan infantry,
and those in the long war who fell victim to
    the immense spoils of the rings (so does Livy say
12   in his history, where what he tells is true),[2]
and those who felt the heavy blows when they
    resisted Robert Guiscard's[3] steady press,
15   and those whose bones are still piled up today

---

1. Puglia is the southeastern corner of Italy, the heel of the boot. Dante uses the term, as was common in his time, to denote the entire southern portion of the peninsula. He alludes to several battles, ancient and modern, that were fought there, beginning with the invasion by Aeneas and his forces.
2. According to Livy (Titus Livius, 59 B.C.E.–17 C.E.) in his monumental history of Rome, *Ab urbe condita*, Hannibal had his soldiers remove the rings of Roman officers they had killed at the battle of Cannae (216 B.C.E.), an Apulian village, and sent them to the Carthaginian senate to demonstrate the magnitude of his victory. The "long war" was the second Punic War (218–201 B.C.E.).
3. Robert Guiscard (1015–1085), brother of the duke of Normandy, was made ruler of Apulia and Calabria by Pope Nicholas II. He spent twenty years battling the Greeks and Saracens in southern Italy, and is cited in Canto XVIII of the *Paradiso* among warriors for the faith.

at Ceprano, failed by Apulian faithlessness,[4]
  and there near Tagliacozzo where the old
18   Alardo won the victory weaponless,[5]
and one showed his pierced limb and one made bold
  to display his stumps, it all would not begin
21   to approach the loathsomeness of the ninth hold.
A cask, when its midboard or its cant has been
  removed, is not so open as one I saw
24   whose body was split apart right from the chin
to the farthole. Down between his legs his raw
  entrails spilled out, with his vitals visible
27   and the sorry sack where what goes through the maw
is turned to shit. I was looking at him, full
  of awe and wonder, when he saw me stare
30   and spread his breast open, saying: "Watch me pull,
see mangled Mohammed tear himself![6] And there
  walking before me and weeping is Alì,[7]
33   with his face split from his chin right to his hair.
And since all of these other sinners that you see
  sowed scandal and schism in their lives, now they
36   are ripped apart in reciprocity.
Back there a devil waits to hack and flay
  each one of us with the sharp edge of his blade,
39   cleaving anew, each time we pass his way,
every member of this miserable parade,
  for by the time we have circled the whole pit
42   we are healed of the cuts he has already made.
But who are you? Are you putting off for a bit,

---

4. The forces of King Manfred of Sicily met the invading army of Charles of Anjou near
Benevento (not Ceprano) on February 26, 1266. When his Apulian allies fled the field,
Manfred chose to die in battle rather than flee. Because he had been excommunicated,
he was buried in unconsecrated ground and subsequently disinterred (according to some,
on the orders of Pope Clement IV). In Canto III of the *Purgatorio*, Manfred is the first
penitent soul Dante encounters as he begins his ascent of the mountain.
5. In 1268, Charles of Anjou fought Conradin, nephew of Manfred and grandson of Freder-
ick II, near Tagliacozzo. Charles was advised by the chevalier Érard de Valéry (c. 1200–c.
1277) to hold back his reserves as long as possible, which strategy turned the tide of bat-
tle in his favor.
6. Ronald L. Martinez and Robert M. Durling state: "In the Christian polemics that were
Dante's sources of information, Mohammed was said to have been a Nestorian Christian
(the Nestorians denied that Christ's divine and human natures were united) before found-
ing Islam; thus he was thought both a heretic and a schismatic, having drawn one third of the
world's believers away from the true faith" (*The Divine Comedy of Dante Alighieri. Volume I:
Inferno*, Oxford, 1996). According to Mark Musa, Dante's treatment of Mohammed "reflects
the medieval belief that Mohammed was responsible not only for a schism but the invasion
of Palestine and the dismantling of Christian power and influence in the Middle East. Opin-
ion in Dante's day ignored the fact that Mohammed was a monotheist in a pagan culture and
that his split from Christianity followed the development of its trinitarian dogma."
7. Ali (c. 592–661) was Mohammed's cousin and son-in-law. Controversy over his assump-
tion of the caliphate in 656 led to the splitting of Islam into the Sunni and Shiite sects.

by musing upon the bridge, the punishments
45 pronounced on you for the sins you must admit?"
"Death has not found him," my guide said. "No offense
brings him here for torment, but in order to
48 provide him with a full experience,
it is fitting that I, who am dead, conduct him through
ring after ring of hell, and every word
51 is as true as that I am speaking them to you."
More than a hundred in the ditch were stirred
to gape at me, forgetting their agony
54 as they stood amazed at what they had just heard.
"Tell Fra Dolcino, since you may shortly see
the sun again, that if he still wants to live
57 before joining me, he should fill his armory
with provisions, lest the grip of snow should give
to the Novarese a victory that they
60 might otherwise find difficult to achieve."[8]
Before Mohammed had turned to me to say
these words, he had raised his foot into the air,
63 and now he put it down and went away.
A soul with his throat pierced through was standing there.
His nose had been cut off to the brows, his head
66 had only one ear left. He had stopped to stare,
amazed with the rest at what my guide had said.
Before the others, he stuck his fingers in
69 and pulled apart his throat, which was all red,
and spoke: "O you who are not condemned by sin,
and whom I sometimes saw in Italy
72 unless there is someone who could be your twin,
you know the sweet plain sloping tenderly
from Vercelli to Marcabò. If you see it again,
75 keep Pier da Medicina[9] in memory.
Tell Guido and Angiolello, Fano's best men,
that if our foresight here is in accord
78 with what will be, the time is coming when
they'll be bound with weights and then thrown overboard
near La Cattolica, sunk without a trace
81 through the machinations of an evil lord.

8. Dolcino Tornielli of Novara was known as Fra Dolcino because of his association with the Apostolic Brethren, who sought to bring the Church back to the simplicity of its earliest times, the days of the Apostles. After the death of the group's founder, Gherardo Segarelli, Dolcino took command of the Brethren. He was accused of holding heretical views, and in 1305 Pope Clement V preached against the sect. Dolcino and a large group of his followers, including his companion and presumed mistress, Margaret of Trent, held out for some time in the hills between Novara and Vercelli, but were driven out by hunger and repeated attacks. Dolcino and Margaret were captured in June 1307 and burned at the stake.
9. Medicina is a town between Bologna and Imola. Pier has not been positively identified. The "sweet plain" is the entire Po valley.

Neptune has never seen a crime so base
    from Cyprus to the isles that lie near Spain,
84   neither by pirates nor the Argive race.
That one-eyed traitor, who holds as his domain
    the city from whose sight one at my side
87   could wish he had been able to abstain,
will call them there to parley, but provide
    such treatment that they will need no vow or prayer
90   that Focara's perilous wind be pacified."[1]
I said: "Tell me who he is, and show me where,
    who found the city bitter to his eye,
93   if you wish me to carry news of you up there."
Then he grabbed the jaw of one who stood nearby
    and pulled it so the mouth came open, stating:
96   "Here he is, and he doesn't talk. He was forced to fly
from Rome, and when he saw Caesar hesitating,
    he extinguished Caesar's doubts. 'A man prepared,'
99   he said, 'can only hurt himself by waiting.'"
I was shocked to see him looking lost and scared,
    his tongue hacked out right down to his throat's base,
102   this Curio whose speech had always dared.[2]
And one with both hands lopped began to raise
    his stumps in the dusky air imploringly
105   so that they spattered blood upon his face.
He cried: "And Mosca too! Remember me
    who said 'What's done is finished,' the seed that had
108   such ill effects for all of Tuscany—"
"—and that killed off your whole line,"[3] I was quick to add,
    at which, piling pain on pain, he turned to go
111   like a man that misery has driven mad.

1. The incident in question, for which there is no definite, historical authority, is believed to have occured around 1312. Guido del Cassero and Angiolello di Carignano were leaders of opposing political parties in Fano. La Cattolica is midway between Fano and Rimini on the Adriatic coast. The references to Cyprus and Majorca signify the entire extent of the Mediterranean; the Argives are the people of Argos—broadly speaking, the Greeks. The "one-eyed traitor" is Malatestino, ruler of Rimini (see note 5 to Canto XXVII, p. 101).
2. Gaius Scribonius Curio the Younger was a follower of Pompey, then went over to Julius Caesar, and in the ensuing civil war led the campaign that drove Cato's army out of Sicily. Dante follows Lucan in claiming that it was on the advice of Curio that Caesar decided to cross the Rubicon at Rimini, which action marked the beginning of the civil war.
3. In 1215, Buondelmonte de' Buondelmonti, a Florentine noble, broke his engagement to a daughter of the Amidei for what he considered a better offer. When allies of the Amidei discussed how best to avenge the shame, Mosca dei Lamberti spoke the words signifying that the matter should be resolved with finality, by the death of Buondelmonte, and himself took part in the murder. Although there had previously been tension between the Guelphs and Ghibellines, this killing crystallized the hostility that was to plague the city thereafter. Dante's taunt in line 109 refers to the expulsion of the Lamberti from Florence in 1258, after which they no longer figured in the affairs of the city. In Canto VI, line 80, Dante had asked Ciacco about Mosca's posthumous whereabouts.

I stayed to watch the multitude below
> and saw a sight that I would not have revealed
114   without more proof that it was really so,
but, knowing that I saw it, I am steeled
> by conscience, a just man's support and stay
117   whose sense of right protects him like a shield.
Truly I saw, as I can see today,
> a headless body with the others there,
120   trudging like them along the dismal way.
It held its severed head up by the hair,
> swinging it like a lantern in the night
123   as it cried "Oh me!" and caught us with its stare.
Out of itself it had made for itself a light.
> They were two in one and one in two. How this
126   could be is known to him who in his might
ordains it. When he stood right under us,
> beneath the bridge, he held his arm up straight
129   to bring us closer so we would not miss
these words: "Behold my miserable fate.
> Live man among the dead, in your journeying
132   try to find another punishment so great.
Know I am Bertran de Born, so you may bring
> news of me back with you. I am the one
135   who counseled wickedness to the young king.
Because of me, the father fought the son.[4]
> Ahithophel did no worse when he instigated
138   wickedly with King David and Absalon.[5]
Two who were one, by me were separated.
> I carry my brain separated from its source
141   inside this trunk. In me is demonstrated
how the law of retribution takes its course."[6]

---

4. Bertran de Born (c. 1140–c. 1215) was one of the greatest of the Provençal troubadors. Ezra Pound adapted or loosely translated several of his poems, including the "Planh for the Young English King," Bertran's elegy for Prince Henry (1155–1183), second and oldest surviving son of King Henry II and called "the young king" because he was twice crowned during his father's lifetime. Encouraged by his mother, Eleanor of Aquitaine, and King Louis VII of France, Prince Henry rebelled against his father, demanding that he be given a substantial portion of his patrimony. The ensuing conflict lasted until "the young king" died of a fever; unlike his younger brothers, Richard and John, he never attained the throne.

5. In 2 Samuel 15–17, Ahithophel counseled Absalom to rebel against his father, King David, a course of action that led to Absalom's death and Ahithophel's suicide.

6. This line is the poem's only direct mention of the *contrapasso*, the principle of fitting the punishment to the nature of the offense.

Canto XXIX

The Ninth Ditch, continued; Geri del Bello;
The Tenth Ditch: Falsifiers; Alchemists;
Griffolino; Capocchio

So many souls with wounds so red and raw
    made my besotted eyes desire to stay
3   and weep for the mutilation that they saw.
"What are you staring at?" I heard Virgil say.
    "Why do you keep your sight so riveted
6   on those maimed and miserable shades this way?
You have not done that with all the other dead.
    This ring is twenty-two miles around, and so
9   keep that in mind if you mean to count each head.
The moon is beneath our feet, and we must go.
    Our allotted time grows short, and you will find
12   there is more to see than what you see below."
"If you had realized why I was so inclined
    to stand and look down there," I told him then,
15   "perhaps you would have agreed to stay behind."
He had taken up the journey once again,
    and I followed in his footsteps while I made
18   my answer, adding: "There, where I have been
staring so hard, I believe I saw the shade
    of one of my kinsmen in the crowd that cry
21   the guilt for which they have so dearly paid."
My master said: "Your attention should not lie
    in that direction. Let him stay there, and switch
24   your thoughts to other things as we pass by.
He was pointing at you as he stood beneath the bridge,
    thrusting his finger threateningly, the one
27   called Geri del Bello[1] by others in the ditch.
At that moment you were all intent upon
    the soul that once held Hautefort.[2] When you came
30   to look where he'd been standing, he was gone."
"My leader," I said, "his violent death, whose claim
    for vengeance is not yet satisfied by those
33   who have been implicated in the shame,
made him indignant: I think that is why he chose
    to go away without any word to me,
36   and that is why my pity for him grows."

1. Geri del Bello degli Alighieri was a first cousin of Dante's father. According to Dante's son Pietro, he was murdered by Brodaio dei Sacchetti, a murder that was not avenged until many years later, in 1310. Peace between the feuding families was not arranged until 1342. Vengeance for the murders of one's kinsmen was sanctioned by both law and custom.
2. The castle of Bertran de Born.

We spoke these words as we moved gradually
    to the crag overlooking where the next valley lies,
39   right to the bottom, were there light to see.
And now, from where we stood upon the rise,
    Malebolge's final cloister was unveiled,
42   with its lay brothers visible to our eyes.
Weird lamentations, barbed with pity, assailed
    my ears so horribly that my hands flew
45   to cover them against the souls that wailed.
Such pain as there would be all summer through
    if the sick from Maremma's hospitals, as well
48   as those from Sardinia's and Valdichiana's too,[3]
were piled into a single ditch to dwell,
    such pain was here, and all the air was rank
51   with putrefaction's flesh-decaying smell.
Still turning left, we moved along the flank.
    I saw the depths more clearly as we wound
54   our way down to the long reef's final bank.
Infallible Justice, God's minister, is found
    meting punishment to the falsifiers there
57   whose sins she has recorded above ground.
I do not believe that it was worse to bear
    the sight of Aegina when all its people fell
60   victim to such contagion in the air
that along with every other animal
    even the worm succumbed (but the ancient men,
63   as the poets who believe the story tell,
from the seed of ants sprang into life again)[4]
    than to see these spirits heaped in disarray
66   like sheaves as they languished there in that dark den.
One lay on another's belly, and one lay
    across another's shoulders, and one went
69   crawling on all fours down the dismal way.
With slow steps, without speaking, all intent,
    we watched and heard the sick, who could not put
72   themselves upright. Two who were sitting leant
against each other, looking, as I thought,
    like two pots set to keep warm side by side,
75   and both were marked with scabs from head to foot.

---

3. Like the island of Sardinia, the Tuscan areas of the Maremma (see note 1 to Canto XIII, and note 3 to Canto XXV) and the Valdichiana are swampy, and in medieval times all were breeding grounds for malaria in the summer.
4. As the story is told in Book VII of the *Metamorphoses*, Aeacus was the son of Jupiter (Zeus) and the nymph Aegina, and ruler of the island that bore his mother's name. After Juno (Hera) devastated the island with a plague, Zeus repopulated it by turning its ants into men (hence the name Myrmidons for the inhabitants, from the Greek for "ant"). Aeacus was the father of Peleus and the grandfather of Achilles.

I have never seen a currycomb being plied
  by a groom who against his will is still awake
78 or a stableboy whose master waits to ride
so fiercely as I saw these sinners rake
  their own flesh, because nothing else avails
81 against the burning itch. The scabs would flake
when they were dragged by the sinners' fingernails,
  the way a knife will scrape a carp or do
84 the same to a fish with even larger scales.
My leader spoke to one of them: "O you
  whose fingers undo your chain mail bit by bit
87 and now and then turn into pincers too,
tell us if any Italian sinners sit
  among you, so may your nails be vigorous
90 and for the work at hand prove ever fit."
"We that you see disfigured, both of us
  are Italian," said the soul, who now began
93 to weep. "And you, who are so curious?"
Said my leader: "I conduct this living man
  ever deeper through the regions of the dead.
96 To show him all hell's levels is my plan."
They broke their shared support and each turned his head,
  trembling, to look at me. Among the rest
99 who had heard the echo of what Virgil said,
many did likewise. My good master pressed
  close to me, saying: "Say what you would say,"
102 and I began, in accord with his request:
"So may the thought of you not fade away,
  up in the first world, from man's memory
105 but live instead for many and many a day,
tell me who you are and of what ancestry.
  Do not let your hideous penalty and its shame
108 keep you from speaking." And one said to me:
"Born in Arezzo, I was put to the flame
  at Albero of Siena's will,[5] although
111 why I died is not the reason why I came
to this. I told him: 'I can fly, you know,'
  thinking to have myself a bit of fun,
114 and he, who was eager but whose wits were slow,
demanded that I show him how it was done.
  Because I could not make him Dedalus,
117 he had me burned by one who called him son.

---

5. Early commentators identify the Aretine as one Griffolino, who was burned at the stake
 for heresy around 1272. The credulous Albero was the protégé and perhaps the actual son
 of the bishop of Siena.

What brought me to this tenth and last pit was
    alchemy. Minos damned me to this place,
120   whose judgment cannot be erroneous."
To the poet I said: "Has there ever been a race
    so empty-headed as the Sienese?
123   They're far worse than the French, in any case."
The other leper, listening to these
    remarks of mine, responded: "Even so,
126   you must make an exception for Stricca, if you please,
that moderate spender, and for Niccolò,
    who showed how clove and costliness could sit
129   together in the garden where such seeds grow,
and that club where Caccia d'Asciano once saw fit
    to squander his vineyard and his woodland too
132   and Meo the pixilated showed his wit.[6]
But let your eye grow sharp to show you who
    seconds you on Sienese stupidity,
135   so that my face may also answer you.
I am Capocchio's shade.[7] Through alchemy
    I gave the metals a deceptive shape.
138   And you, if I have eyed you properly,
will recall how skilled I was as nature's ape."

Canto XXX

The Tenth Ditch, continued: Impersonators; Gianni Schicchi;
Myrrha; Counterfeiters: Master Adam;
False Witnesses: Sinon; Potiphar's Wife

In days when Juno burned with indignation
    at the Theban blood because of Semelè,
3   showing her wrath on more than one occasion,
Athamas suffered such insanity
    that when he saw his wife, who was holding one
6   of their sons in each arm, he cried violently:
"See the lioness and her cubs! Before they run

6. Stricca (line 126), about whom nothing is known for certain, has been tentatively identi-
fied with Stricca di Giovanni de' Salimbeni, whose brother Niccolò was a member of the
brigata spendereccia ("spendthrifts' club"), a group of young Sienese nobles who dedi-
cated themselves to squandering their wealth as lavishly as possible, and were believed to
have run through their entire fortunes in less than two years. Some claim that Niccolò in-
troduced cloves, then extremely expensive, to the "garden" of Siena. Other spendthrifts in
good standing were Caccia d'Asciano and Bartolommeo dei Folcacchieri, called Ab-
bagliato, or "bedazzled." Meo was fined in 1278 for drinking in a tavern.
7. Capocchio was burned alive at Siena in 1293. Some early commentators claim that he
and Dante knew one another as students.

to the pass, spread out the nets along the ground!"
9   And then with ruthless claws he seized his son
    Learchus and began to whirl him round
          and smashed him on a rock. She, horrified,
12   leaped in the sea with her other charge and drowned.[1]
    When Fortune leveled the all-daring pride
          of the Trojans by inflicting the long war
15   in which the king and all his kingdom died,
    Hecuba, lost, enslaved, her heart made sore
          to see Polyxena dead and then to find
18   her Polydorus stretched upon the shore,
    was driven to such madness that she declined
          to howling and barking like a dog because
21   the weight of the great grief had so wrenched her mind.[2]
    But frenzy never showed so furious
          a face in Thebes or Troy, inciting men
24   or beasts with such ferocity as was
    shown by two souls that came running up just then,
          naked and pale, biting everything around
27   like pigs that have been turned out of the pen.
    Sinking its tusks into his nape, one downed
          Capocchio and dragged him on ahead
30   so that his belly scraped the solid ground.
    "That lunatic is Gianni Schicchi,"[3] said
          the Aretine, who was shivering with fear.
33   "Like a rabid dog he rips the other dead."
    "So may its fangs not find you, please make clear,"
          I said to him, "who the other one may be
36   before it turns and runs away from here."
    "That is the ancient shade," he answered me,
          "of wicked Myrrha, who came to love her father
39   beyond the bounds of all propriety.[4]

---

1. Semele was the daughter of Cadmus, founder of Thebes, and one of the many loves of
   Zeus. After Semele was accidentally killed by lightning when Zeus manifested himself to
   her in his godly form, their unborn child was saved, placed in Zeus's thigh and ultimately
   born there, and then given to Semele's sister, Ino. Her wrath unabated, Hera maddened
   Athamas, Ino's husband, making him kill their son Learchus; Ino then leaped into the sea
   with their other son, Melicertes (*Metamorphoses*, Book IV).
2. Hecuba, widow of King Priam of Troy, and her daughter Polyxena were enslaved by the
   conquering Greeks. Hecuba was driven mad by the sacrifice of Polyxena on the tomb of
   Achilles and her discovery of the body of her murdered son Polydorus, which had washed
   up on the shore.
3. According to early commentators, after Buoso Donati died intestate, his nephew Simone
   enlisted Gianni Schicchi (died c. 1280), of the Cavalcanti family, to impersonate the
   dead man and dictate a will in Simone's favor. During the impersonation, Schicchi pro-
   ceeded to make lavish bequests to himself of Donati's property. The story is the basis of
   Giacomo Puccini's one-act opera, one of the components of his *Trittico*.
4. For her refusal to honor the goddess Aphrodite, Myrrha was afflicted with an incestuous
   passion for her father, King Cinyras of Cyprus. After she seduced him by impersonating

She counterfeited the image of another
    so she might dare to lie with him in sin,
42   much like the demon running off, that other
who counterfeited Buoso Donati to win
    the lady of the herd, and even made
45   a will with the proper language all put in."
When those rabid two on whom my eyes had stayed
    were gone at last, I turned round to survey
48   the ranks of many a misbegotten shade.
There was one shaped like a lute, so I would say,
    if the part below the groin where man is split,
51   forking in two, had here been cut away.
Because of the dropsy, in which the humors sit
    so ill-mixed that the members are badly blended,
54   with face and belly disproportionate,
his lips spread like a hectic's when distended
    by racking thirst, with both of them thrusting out,
57   one curling up while the other one descended.
"O you who are here in this horrid world without
    any punishment," he said, "though I cannot see
60   just why that is, behold me and take note
of Master Adam[5] in his misery.
    Alive I had everything I wished, and here
63   one drop of water would be all to me.
The streams of Casentino, cool and clear,
    flowing softly from the green hills as they race
66   down to the Arno, constantly appear
before me, and not vainly, in this place.
    The image of them parches me much more
69   than this disease that wastes away my face.
The rigid justice prodding at my core
    uses the place where I misused my wit
72   and makes my sighs fly faster than before.
Romena is there, where I learned to counterfeit
    the coins stamped with the Baptist, and was thrown
75   on the flames and burnt alive because of it.
I would rather see one of those brothers moan—
    Alessandro, Guido, the other one—at my side
78   than have the Fonte Branda for my own.

---

her mother, he threatened to kill her. She fled, and was turned into a myrtle (or myrrh) tree, from whose trunk Adonis was born (*Metamorphoses*, Book X).

5. A Master Adam, an Englishman, was identified in a 1277 document as a member of the household of the Conti Guidi of Romena, a village in the region of the Casentino, east of Florence. In 1281, someone in their employ was burned alive for coining florins with twenty-one carats of gold instead of twenty-four; the first gold florin had been coined in 1252, and soon became the standard gold coin throughout Europe. The Guidi were four brothers in all; the two not named in line 77 were Aghinolfo and Ildebrandino. The reference in line 80 must be to Guido, who also died in 1281; the other three were still alive in 1300. There is a Fonte Branda in Romena and a more famous one in Siena; it is not clear which one is meant.

If the rabid souls who run around have not lied,
    one of the three is already here below.
81   What good is that to me, whose limbs are tied?
Were I still light enough that I could go,
    every hundred years, one inch along the ground,
84   I would have set out already, even though
this circle is eleven miles around
    and half a mile across, to find that man
87   down here where the disfigured ones abound.
Because of them I am numbered in this clan.
    The striking of the florins with the three
90   carats of alloy—it was all their plan."
I said: "And who might these two wretches be,
    steaming like wet hands in the winter chill,
93   lying close by your western boundary?"
And he: "I found them there, completely still,
    when I was first rained down into this trench.
96   They have never moved, and I think they never will.
Joseph's accuser is that lying wench,[6]
    and this is Sinon, Troy's false Greek.[7] The drought
99   of fever makes them give off such a stench."
And perhaps annoyed at being talked about
    with such dark insinuation, one of them
102   punched him right where his solid paunch puffed out.
It sounded like the beating of a drum.
    Then Master Adam smacked him in the face
105   with an arm that was just as hard, and said to him:
"My limbs may keep me fastened to this place
    because they are so heavy, but at my side
108   I have a free arm fit for such a case."
"When you were burned," the other one replied,
    "there wasn't very much that arm could do,
111   but it worked just fine for the coins you falsified."
And the dropsical: "What you're saying now is true,
    but you didn't give such truthful testimony
114   the day the Trojan leaders questioned you."
"My words were false. You falsified the money,"
    said Sinon. "One sin brought me here. Yours were
117   a multitude. What demon did so many?"

6. The wife of Potiphar, an officer of Pharaoh, made repeated attempts to seduce Joseph, who was her husband's overseer. Spurned by him, she made the false accusation that he had tried to assault her sexually, and he was imprisoned (Genesis 39.6–20).
7. Sinon allowed himself to be captured by the Trojans, claiming falsely that he had escaped his fate as an intended sacrifice by the Greeks and that the Trojan horse was meant as an atonement to Athena for the theft of the Palladium (see note 7 to Canto XXVI). On the basis of his lies, the Trojans took the horse into the city.

And the paunch: "Recall the horse, you perjurer.
  May it stretch you on the rack to realize
120   the whole world knows you for a lying cur."
"May you be racked by the thirst that cracks and dries
  your tongue," the Greek said, "and the rancid fen
123   that makes your gut a hedge before your eyes."
"Your sickness spreads your big mouth, which has been
  your bane before," said the coiner. "I am sick
126   with thirst, and humors make me swell, but then
your head aches and your limbs burn. You'd be quick
  to give, without much need for an invitation,
129   the mirror of Narcissus a good lick."8
I was following this with all my concentration
  when my master told me: "Watch some more, I say,
132   and then you will answer to my indignation."
And when I heard him speak to me that way
  in anger, I turned to face him hurriedly
135   with a shame that shakes me to this very day.
As one who dreams he is in jeopardy
  and, dreaming, wishes it were a dream, and thus
138   wants what is real as if it were fantasy,
so I became, all speechless there, because
  I wanted to seek pardon, and I did
141   seek pardon without knowing that I was.
"Less shame would wash away," my master said,
  "a greater fault than yours, so do not fear,
144   and let your sadness dissipate. Instead,
remember that I always will be near
  if it ever should befall that fortune brings
147   such arguments as this one to your ear,
for it is low to want to hear such things."

Canto XXXI

The Giants (Nimrod, Ephialtes, Briareus, and Antaeus);
Descent to Cocytus

I had been pricked by one and the same tongue,
  making my two cheeks tingle and turn red,
3   which then supplied the balm where it had stung.

---

8. The reference is to a surface of water, like that of the fountain in which the beautiful youth Narcissus became enamored of his own image, ultimately dying of despair over his inability to possess it.

In much the same way, I have heard it said,
      where the spear of Achilles and his father hit
6   came a sad gift, then a good one in its stead.[1]
We turned our backs upon the dreadful pit
      and then without a word we climbed the height
9   of the embankment that surrounded it.
Here it was less than day and less than night.
      I could hardly see ahead as we went on,
12   but then I heard a horn blast with such might
that thunder is quiet in comparison.
      My eyes were drawn to one spot as I traced
15   the sound right back to where it had begun.
Not even Roland blew so fiercely,[2] faced
      with the dolorous rout of Charlemagne's brigade
18   when the ranks of the holy guardsmen were laid waste.
And shortly after I had turned my head
      to look that way, I saw what seemed to be
21   a host of enormous towers, so I said:
"Master, what is that city there?" And he:
      "You pierce the darkness from too far, and stray
24   in your imaginings of what you see.
When you are near, your vision will display
      how distance makes the sense misunderstand,
27   so spur your footsteps on along the way."
Then, as he took me lovingly by the hand:
      "Lest the strangeness overwhelm you, you should know
30   before we cross the intervening land
that those are giants, not towers, where we must go,
      and from the waist down they are standing where
33   the bank surrounds them, in the pit below."
As when a mist whose vapor packs the air
      begins to dissipate, and bit by bit
36   the eye makes out more clearly what is there,
as I came nearer and nearer to the pit,
      cutting the dark and thick air with my sight,
39   my error fled and fear succeeded it.
For just as Montereggione[3] crowns the height
      of its long round wall with towers in the sky,

---

1. The spear of Achilles had the power to heal the wounds that it inflicted. Homer asserts that the spear had previously belonged to Achilles' father, Peleus. But Dante, who did not know Greek, seems, like other medieval poets, to have made this association through a misreading of Ovid, mistaking a reference to Mount Pelion for an allusion to Peleus.
2. As recounted in the *Chanson de Roland*, Ganelon, the stepfather of Roland, betrayed the rear guard of Charlemagne's army to the Saracens at Roncesvalles in 778. Roland blew his horn to summon the main force to their rescue, but Ganelon dissuaded Charlemagne from responding, and Roland and all his companions were killed.
3. A heavily fortified castle outside Siena. Fourteen towers, each over sixty feet tall, were added to its walls after the battle of Montaperti (see note 3 to Canto X).

42   so here the horrible giants, whom Jove's might
     still threatens when he thunders from on high,[4]
          betowered with half themselves the bank that drew
45   a circle round the pit. Already I
     saw the face of one of them come into view,
          his dangling arms, his shoulders and his chest,
48   and the upper portion of his belly too.
     Nature, when she decided to desist
          from making them, and took such instruments
51   away from Mars, was acting for the best.
     Although she does not repent of elephants
          and whales, those who consider it will find
54   that she demonstrates more justice and good sense,
     for if she added faculty of mind
          to power and malevolence, our race
57   would be helpless against creatures of such kind.
     His face was as big as the pinecone Rome displays
          before Saint Peter's on the holy ground,[5]
60   and his bones were in proportion to his face.
     The bank, which was an apron all around
          his lower parts, revealed his upper shape
63   and length, so that three Frieslanders[6] would sound
     an empty boast if they thought to reach his nape,
          for I noted thirty spans[7] of him, or more,
66   downward from where a man will tie his cape.
     "Raphèl maì amècche zabì almi!" tore[8]
          from his raw throat, and that fierce cry seemed to be
69   the sweetest psalm his mouth was fitted for.
     And then my leader: "Mass of stupidity,
          keep to your horn for venting your frustration
72   when these rages come upon you suddenly!
     Tower of confusion, make an examination
          of your own neck till you find the strap you wear
75   that holds it on your huge chest like a decoration."
     Then he said to me: "That self-accuser there

---

4. Jove still thunders because of the giants' assault on Mount Olympus (see Canto XIV, lines 52–60, and note 5).
5. The bronze pinecone, now located in the Belvedere Gardens of the papal palace, is about thirteen feet high.
6. Frieslanders, or Frisians, inhabitants of the Frisian Islands in the North Sea, were known for their great height.
7. A span is the width of an outstretched hand, roughly nine inches.
8. A number of attempts have been made to decipher Nimrod's words, despite the clear indication in lines 80–81 that they are unintelligible.

is Nimrod. Through his evil thought alone
78   there is not one common language everywhere.[9]
Let us not waste breath, but leave him on his own.
          All languages will sound to him as will
81   his tongue to us, which is totally unknown."
Then, turning to the left, we walked until
          we had gone as far as a crossbow shot and found
84   the next one, far more fierce and huger still.
Just who the master was who had him bound
          I cannot say, but he was shackled tight
87   by a chain that ringed his neck and wrapped around
to pin his left arm before him and his right
          behind his back, then coiled five times before
90   it wound below his waist and out of sight.
"This proud one tried his strength by making war
          upon almighty Jove," said my leader then,
93   "and here you see the fruit his efforts bore.
He, Ephialtes, struck the great blows[1] when
          giants made gods afraid. Then they swung free,
96   those arms of his, but they did not move again."
And then I said to him: "If it could be,
          these eyes of mine would wish to gaze upon
99   Briareus in his immensity."[2]
"You will see Antaeus[3] not much further on,
          who can speak and who is also unrestrained.
102   He will set us down where the guiltiest have gone.
The one you want is far off," he explained.
          "Though his face is more ferocious, his limbs take
105   the shape of this one's, and he too is chained."
Never did nature cause the earth to quake
          and make a tower tremble with such might
108   as when Ephialtes now began to shake.
Now more than ever, death filled me with fright,
          and the fear alone would have furnished the event
111   had I not seen the chains that held him tight.

---

9. Nimrod, king of Babylon, is described in Genesis 10.9 as "a mighty hunter before the Lord," which may account for his horn. According to tradition, it was he who built the tower of Babel.
1. In an attempt to scale the heavens during the assault on the gods, Ephialtes and his brother Otus tried to pile Ossa on Olympus and Pelion on Ossa, but were killed by Zeus.
2. Briareus is another of the giants who made war on Olympus. In the *Aeneid*, he is described as fifty-headed and hundred-handed. By deflecting Dante from viewing him and by characterizing him as normally shaped, Virgil seems to implicitly acknowledge the absurdity of that depiction.
3. The son of Neptune and Gaea (Earth), who retained his great strength by maintaining contact with his mother. He wrestled Hercules (lines 131–32), who lifted him off the ground and crushed him to death. His unfettered state may be a result of his not participating in the assault on Olympus, which took place before he was born.

Then we came upon Antaeus as we went.
    He rose a full five ells above the ground,
114   with his head not counted in the measurement.
"O you who, in the fateful vale that crowned
    Scipio heir of glory on the day
117   when Hannibal and his army turned around,[4]
once took a thousand lions as your prey,
    through whom, had you joined your brothers in the field
120   in their high war, there are many who still say
that the sons of earth would have forced the gods to yield,
    now lower us, not disdaining to do so,
123   to the cold in which Cocytus[5] has been sealed.
Do not curl your lip, but bend. Do not make us go
    to Tityus or Typhon.[6] Be assured
126   this man can give what is longed for here below.
Through him your earthly fame may be restored,
    for he lives, and expects a long life, unless graced
129   by an early summons to his last reward."
So spoke my master. The other one in haste
    held out the huge hands in whose vigorous
132   clutches had Hercules once been embraced.
When Virgil felt their grip, he called me thus:
    "Come here to me, so I may gather you,"
135   and made one bundle of the two of us.
As the Garisenda[7] seems to someone who
    stands under it when a cloud comes overhead
138   athwart the way the tower leans, so too
Antaeus seemed as he stooped with his hands spread
    to pick me up. Just then I wished we were
141   descending by another road instead.
Where the bottom swallows Judas and Lucifer
    he set us down, and waited not at all,
144   but as soon as we were clear began to stir
and like a ship's mast rose up straight and tall.

4. Scipio defeated Hannibal at Zama in North Africa in 202 B.C.E., resolving the second Punic War in favor of Rome.
5. The frozen lake of the ninth circle of hell; in Cocytus are embedded the worst of all sinners.
6. Typhon, who had a hundred fire-breathing serpent heads, was killed by the thunderbolts of Zeus. Tityus was a giant killed by Apollo and Artemis when he attempted to rape their mother, Leto.
7. Built c. 1110, the Garisenda, is the smaller of two leaning towers in Bologna.

Canto XXXII

The Ninth and Last Circle: The Treacherous Freezing
in Cocytus; The First Ring of the Traitors: Caïna
(Traitors to Kindred); The Second Ring: Antenora
(Traitors to Country or Faction)

With harsh and clacking rhymes that could convey
    the nature of that hole of misery
3   on which all other rocks converge and weigh,
I would press out the juice more thoroughly
    from my conception. Lacking them, I fall
6   to the work at hand with some anxiety.
To try to describe the very floor of all
    the universe is nothing to attract
9   an idle mind, no task for tongues that call
to mama and papa. May my attempts be backed
    by those ladies that inspired Amphion[1] when
12   he walled Thebes, that my words may hold the fact.
O most misbegotten rabble in that den
    so hard to speak of, better far had you
15   been born as sheep or goats instead of men!
Down in the dark pit we'd been carried to,
    far beneath the giant's feet, I was standing where
18   I had the enormous wall still fixed in view
when I heard a voice that said to me: "Take care
    not to step upon the poor heads, as you pass,
21   of the weary brothers who are lying there."
Then I saw around me, under me, a mass
    of solid water, a lake so frozen over
24   that it looked much less like water than like glass.
Never in Austria did the Danube river
    or the distant Don, where winter is most bleak,
27   provide their currents with so thick a cover
as there was here, and if the entire peak
    of Tambernic or Pietrapana[2] were
30   to fall on it, not even the edge would creak.
As when the croaking frogs will barely stir,
    with mouths out of water, while the peasant will
33   dream of the gleaning that means so much to her,

---

1. The Muses helped Amphion wall Thebes by inspiring him to play so beautifully upon the lyre that the stones came down from Mount Cithaeron to form the walls themselves.
2. Mount Pietrapana is in the Apuan Alps; Tambernic is most likely Mount Tambura, in the same range.

so the dolorous souls in the ice were livid till
    their heads emerged with faces shame had dyed.
36   Their teeth were clicking like the stork's long bill.
Each face looked down. Their mouths all testified
    to the bitter cold, and all their eyes were signed
39   with the depths of misery that gnawed inside.
I looked about, and then glanced down to find
    two who were pressed together so intimately
42   that the hair upon their heads was intertwined.
"Tell me," I said to them, "who you may be,
    frozen chest to chest." They craned their necks, and when
45   they turned their faces up to look at me,
their eyes, which had been only moist within,
    now overflowed. Tears trickled down and froze,
48   and locked them even tighter than they'd been.
Two boards were never clamped as close as those
    two souls. Like goats they butted head to head
51   because such anger held them in its throes.
Face down nearby was another of the dead,
    whose ears had broken off in the bitter air.
54   "Why reflect yourself in us so long?" he said.
"If you really want to know about that pair,
    the valley of the Bisenzio was their father's,[3]
57   who was called Alberto. Then it was theirs to share.
They came from the same womb, and there are no others—
    search all Caïna and you'll see it's true—
60   more fit to set in aspic than those brothers.
Not him whose breast and shadow were run through
    by Arthur, not Focaccia[4] certainly,
63   and not this one whose head blocks off my view,
who was Sassol Mascheroni[5]—which should be,
    if Tuscany is the land from which you came,
66   all you have to hear to know his history.
So that I need speak no more, know that my name
    was Camiscion de' Pazzi.[6] I'm waiting till
69   Carlino comes to mitigate my blame."

---

3. Alessandro and Napoleone were the sons of Count Alberto of Mangona. According to the early commentators, they fought over their inheritance and wound up killing one another sometime in the 1280s.

4. The nickname of Vanni de' Cancellieri, who murdered his cousin Detto di Sinibaldo Cancellieri in 1293. "Arthur": King Arthur was killed by Mordred, his treacherous nephew (or son). In their mutually fatal encounter, Arthur pierced him through with his lance, inflicting so gaping a wound that a ray of light passed through Mordred's body.

5. He murdered one of his relatives over an inheritance. In punishment for the crime, he was rolled through the streets of Florence in a nail-filled cask and then beheaded.

6. Of Alberto Camicione de' Pazzi of Val d'Arno, all that is known for certain is that he murdered a relative named Ubertino. In 1302, Carlino de' Pazzi, another kinsman of his, would accept a bribe to betray the castle of Piantravigne to the Black Guelphs. Camicione's guilt

Then I saw a thousand faces that the chill
    had purpled, and I shudder to this day
72   when I cross a frozen stream, and I always will.
And I was shivering as we made our way
    through the endless cold to find that central place
75   where all gravity collects. I cannot say
whether will or fate or pure chance was the case,
    but, passing among the heads, my foot swung out
78   and kicked one hard, directly in the face.
He wailed at me and then began to shout:
    "What is this? If you're not here to heap on
81   revenge for Montaperti,[7] why knock me about?"
"Master," I said, "let me linger with this one
    so that I may satisfy a mental craving.
84   I will walk as fast as need be when I'm done."
Then I turned back to the soul, who was still raving,
    while my leader stopped. "Just who are you," I said,
87   "to criticize how others are behaving?"
"Stomping through Antenora to kick the head
    of anyone that you please, just who are you?"
90   he asked. "It would be too much, if you weren't dead."
"I'm not dead," I replied, "and if it's true
    that you crave fame, it's worth your while to know
93   that among the others I will name you too."
He said: "I crave the opposite. Now go,
    get out of here, and leave me to my share,
96   since you don't know how to flatter souls this low."
I answered, as I seized him by the hair
    upon his nape: "Now tell me what you're called,
99   or else you won't have a tuft left anywhere."
And he replied: "Go ahead and strip me bald!
    I won't tell, or show my face, not if you land
102   on my head a thousand times and leave it mauled."
I took his hair and wrapped it round my hand
    as he barked and looked straight down to hide his brow,
105   and I'd already pulled more than one strand
when another shouted: "Bocca, what ails you now?
    Your flapping jaws are hard enough to endure.
108   Now barking? What devil's got you anyhow?"
"I don't want to hear another word from your
    damned traitor's mouth! To your lasting shame," I cried,

---

will be mitigated because his cousin's treachery will be of a more serious kind than his
own and qualify him for the next zone, Antenora (named for Antenor, who in Dante's time
was believed to have betrayed Troy to the Greeks).
7. At the battle of Montaperti in 1260 (see note 3 to Canto X), Bocca degli Abati, a Ghi-
   bellino infiltrator, cut off the hand of the Guelph standard-bearer, creating a panic that
   led to a crushing defeat for the Guelphs.

111   "I will spread the news of you, you can be sure!"
          "Tell what you want. Just go away," he replied.
              "But if you escape this place, take my advice
114   and speak of him who just stretched his mouth so wide.
          He took French silver. Now he pays the price.
              'I saw the one from Duera,'[8] you can tell it,
117   'in the bowl where they keep the sinners packed in ice.'
          And if they ask what others help to fill it,
              right by your side's a Beccheria,[9] the one
120   the Florentines paid back with a slit gullet.
          Gianni de' Soldanieri and Ganelon[1]
              are further along. Tebaldello[2] is another.
123   He opened up Faenza before the dawn."
          After we left him, I saw two together
              frozen so close in one hole that the head
126   of the one was like a hood upon the other.
          I stood and watched the higher one imbed
              his teeth in the other's nape and brain, and eat
129   the way a starving man devours bread.
          Not even Tydeus[3] in his savage heat
              gnawed Menalippus's head more passionately
132   than this one did to the skull and the soft meat.
          "O you who show such wild hostility,
              attacking him with bestial violence,
135   tell me why," I said, "and if it seems to me
          that you are justified by his offense
              to take such vengeance, then before I die
138   in the world above you shall have recompense,
          unless my tongue should wither and turn dry."

---

8. Buoso da Duera of Cremona, a Ghibelline leader, was allegedly bribed by the French in
   1265 to allow the forces of Charles of Anjou to pass unresisted through Lombardy on
   their way to Naples to attack Manfred (see note 4 to Canto XXVIII, p. 105).
9. Tesauro de' Beccheria was abbot of Vallombrosa and papal legate of Alexander IV. After
   the Ghibellines were expelled from Florence in 1258, he was accused of conspiring with
   them, and was subsequently tortured and beheaded.
1. See note 2 to Canto XXXI, p. 117. When the Florentines rebelled against their Ghibelline
   rulers in 1266, Gianni de' Soldanieri deserted his party and joined the Guelphs in an un-
   successful attempt to advance himself politically.
2. Tebaldello belonged to the Zambrasi, a Ghibelline family of Faenza. Because of personal
   hostility to members of the Lambertazzi, Ghibelline exiles from Bologna who had taken
   refuge in Faenza, he opened the gates of the city to their Guelph enemies in the predawn
   hours of November 13, 1280.
3. Tydeus, one of the seven kings besieging Thebes (see note 3 to Canto XIV), exchanged fa-
   tal blows with the Theban Menalippus. According to Statius, the dying Tydeus called for
   the head of Menalippus and proceeded to gnaw it in his rage.

Canto XXXIII

Ugolino; Archbishop Ruggieri; Fra Alberigo;
The Third Ring: Ptolomea (Traitors to Guests)

He paused in his savage meal and raised his head
   from the one he was destroying in his fit,
3   and wiped his mouth upon its hair, and said:
"What you ask revives a grief so desperate
   that its recollection tears my heart, even though
6   I have yet to tell one single word of it.
But if my words are a seed from which will grow
   the fruit of this vile traitor's evil fame,
9   then I shall speak, and weep while doing so.
I do not know who you are, or how you came
   among us, but from your speech you seem to be
12   a Florentine. I should tell you that my name
was Count Ugolino,[1] and this one next to me
   is Archbishop Ruggieri. Now I shall explain
15   why I am such a neighbor as you see.
How I was seized, and executed then,
   having trusted him while he betrayed and lied—
18   there is no need to tell that tale again.
But of what you cannot know—the way I died,
   the cruelty of it—hear what I have to say.
21   Whether he wronged me, you may then decide.
A narrow opening in the Mew that they
   call Hunger now in memory of my plight,[2]
24   where prisoners are still to be shut away,
had shown me more than once the new moon's light
   when the bad dream came to me that tore in two
27   the veil that hides the future from our sight.
This man was there, as the lord and master who
   pursued the wolf and his young cubs as they sped
30   on the mountain that blocks Lucca from the view[3]

1. Ugolino della Gherardesca, Conte di Donoratico (c. 1220–1289) belonged to a noble Ghibelline family of Pisa. He was banished after the failure of his intrigue with the Guelph leader Giovanni Visconti in 1275, but returned to Pisa the following year and quickly reassumed a position of power. He conspired with the archbishop, Ruggieri degli Ubaldini, also a Ghibelline, to rid the city of Nino Visconti, who was a judge, a Guelph, Ugolino's grandson, and a friend of Dante's. After they had driven Visconti out of Pisa in 1288, Ruggieri turned on Ugolino, accusing him of betraying the city because he had, in 1285, ceded castles to Florence and to Lucca. Whether Ugolino's action was intended to betray Pisa or to preserve it by conciliating its powerful foes is open to question. In any event, he was imprisoned in the summer of 1288 with two sons and two grandsons, the youngest of whom was fifteen (not the four young sons that Dante gives him). All five were starved to death early in 1289.
2. The Torre della Fame, or "Tower of Hunger," was used as a prison until 1318.
3. Monte San Giuliano stands between Pisa and Lucca.

of the Pisans. Trained hounds, lean and eager, led
    while Gualandi, Sismondi, and that other one,
33   Lanfranchi,[4] had been set to run on ahead.
The wolves were weary after a short run,
    and then I saw the dogs as their sharp fangs ripped
36   into the flesh of the father and every son.
It was not yet dawn, but I no longer slept.
    My sons were there with me. Though still asleep,
39   they called to me to give them bread, and wept.
You are cruel indeed if you can know the deep
    dread that I felt, and not yet shed a tear.
42   If not this, what could ever make you weep?
The time of our morning meal was drawing near.
    My children were awake. Their dreams had stirred
45   in each of them uneasiness and fear.
From the base of the horrible tower I now heard
    the door being nailed shut, and I looked into
48   the faces of my sons, without a word.
I did not weep. I was turned to stone all through.
    They wept. And Anselmuccio spoke up when
51   he saw my face, saying: 'Father, what's troubling you?'
I shed no tears and I gave no answer then,
    and all that day and night I sat like stone,
54   until the sun lit up the world again.
As soon as a small ray of sunlight shone
    in the miserable prison, and I could see
57   from their four faces the aspect of my own,
I bit my hands in grief and agony.
    And they, assuming that I acted thus
60   for hunger, quickly rose and said to me:
'Eat of us, Father. It will hurt us less.
    From you we have this wretched flesh we wear.
63   Now it is yours to take away from us.'
I calmed myself, to stay them from despair.
    Alas, hard earth, you should have opened wide!
66   Two more days passed while we sat silent there.
And when it was the fourth day, Gaddo cried:
    'Father, why don't you help me!' I watched him fall
69   outstretched before my feet. And there he died.
Just as you see me now, I saw them all,
    between the fifth and sixth days, one by one,
72   drop down and die. Now blindness cast its pall,

---

4. Gualandi, Sismondi, and Lanfranchi were prominent Ghibelline families of Pisa who
supported Ruggieri in his actions against Ugolino.

and for two more days I crawled from son to son,
  calling to them, who were already dead.
75   Then fasting did what misery had not done."
With eyes asquint, having finished what he'd said,
  as a dog attacks a bone he turned back to
78   his gnawing of the other's wretched head.
Pisa, disgrace of all the peoples who
  fill the fair land where *sì* is heard, who show
81   no readiness to rise and punish you,
let Capraia and Gorgona[5] shift, and go
  to dam the Arno's mouth so that it may
84   drown all your citizens with its overflow!
Even if Count Ugolino did betray
  your castles as was reputed, you did wrong
87   to put his sons upon the cross that way.
New Thebes,[6] there is no guilt in those so young
  as Uguiccione or Brigata or
90   the two already mentioned in my song.
We came to another place, where we found more
  who were covered with coarse frost in the bitter chill,
93   but these faced up, unlike the ones before.
Here tears themselves make tears impossible.
  The grief is blocked, turning inward when it tries
96   to express itself, making pain more painful still,
for knots are formed by the first tears each soul cries,
  resembling a crystal visor as they spread
99   to fill the hollows that surround the eyes.
Although, as with a callus that is dead
  to all sensation, the cold was so severe
102   that all the feeling in my face had fled,
I thought I felt a wind come blowing clear.
  "Master," I turned to ask, "what forces drive
105   this current? Aren't all vapors dead down here?"
He answered: "Very soon you will arrive
  where your own eyes will give you your reply,
108   with what rains down to keep this breath alive."
One wretch inside the cold crust gave a cry:
  "O you two souls, so cruel that you have been
111   assigned to go where the very basest lie,
pry the hard veils from my face, so that I can
  vent my heart-soaking pain for a bit before
114   my tears begin to turn to ice again."

5. Capraia and Gorgona are Mediterranean islands then belonging to Pisa.
6. Thebes had a reputation as the worst city of the ancient world for violence and bloodshed.

"Tell me who you are," I answered, "who implore.
　　If I fail to help you then, may I be made
117　　to go to the bottom of the icy floor."
"I am Fra Alberigo,[7] and I displayed
　　the fruits of the evil orchard," he replied.
120　　"Now, for my figs, with dates I am repaid."
And I to him: "Oh, you've already died?"
　　"I have no information here," he said,
123　　"how my body fares up there, on the other side.
It often happens that a soul is sped—
　　such is Ptolomea's[8] privilege—to this place
126　　while Atropos has yet to cut its thread.[9]
So that you may scrape the glazed tears from my face
　　more readily, let me also say to you
129　　that as soon as the soul betrays, as in my case,
its body is taken by a devil who
　　will be master over it in everything
132　　until its allotted time on earth is through.
To this cistern then the soul comes plummeting.
　　Still walking the earth, perhaps, is the body of
135　　this one who is here behind me wintering,
as you must know if you just came from above.
　　He is ser Branca d'Oria,[1] and I'll attest
138　　that he has been here many years." "Enough,"
I said to him, "I believe you are in jest.
　　I know that Branca d'Oria is not dead.
141　　He eats and drinks, he sleeps, and he gets dressed."
"Above, in the ditch of the Evilclaws," he said,
　　"where the sea of sticky pitch is boiling hot,
144　　Michel Zanche was not yet deposited
when this one, dropping down here like a shot,
　　left a devil to fill his body in his place,
147　　as did his kinsman who was in the plot.

7. A member of the Manfredi family of Faenza and of the Jolly Friars (see note 5 to Canto
XXIII). A close relative of his named Manfred struck him in the course of an argument
over the lordship of Faenza. Alberigo pretended to forgive the insult. In 1285, he invited
Manfred and one of his sons to dinner. His calling to his servants to bring in the fruit was
a signal for assassins to rush into the room and kill Manfred and his son. The comment
made by Alberigo (who was still alive in 1300) at line 120 turns on the fact that dates
were more expensive than figs.
8. The third of the four zones of Cocytus, named either for Ptolemy XII, king of Egypt, who
allowed his guest, Pompey, to be murdered, or for the Ptolemy who killed Simon the Mac-
cabee and two of his sons at a banquet (1 Maccabees 16.11–16).
9. The Fates, described by Hesiod as daughters of the night, are represented as spinning
women: Clotho winds the yarn on the distaff of Lachesis, and Atropos cuts the thread of
life.
1. A member of a Ghibelline family of Genoa who murdered his father-in-law, Don Michel
Zanche (see note 6 to Canto XXII) at a banquet to which he had invited him. Branca (who
lived until at least 1325) was assisted in the murder by one of his relatives, either a cousin
or a nephew.

So, now reach out your arm and clear my face
    of the ice around my eyes." But I refused.
150   Betrayal was true courtesy in this case.
Genoans, strangers to the customs used
    by all good men, and filled with every vice,
153   how are you still here on the earth you have abused?
For, with Romagna's worst, there in the ice
    was one of you, who for his crimes was hurled
156   to Cocytus, where even now he pays the price
while his body goes on walking in the world.

Canto XXXIV

The Fourth Ring: Judecca (Traitors to Lords and Benefactors);
Satan; Brutus, Cassius, and Judas; Climb from the Bottom
of Hell, Past the Earth's Center, to the Southern Hemisphere

"*Vexilia regis prodeunt inferni*[1]
    toward where we are," I heard my master say.
3   "Look forward now and see if you discern him."
When our hemisphere grows dark at close of day
    or when a thick fog breathes, there still may be
6   a turning windmill seen from far away.
Just such a structure I now seemed to see.
    Then I walked behind my leader. The wind was raw
9   and there was nothing else to shelter me.
I tremble to make verse of what I saw.
    The souls were covered over in this place
12   in ice like glass-embedded bits of straw.
Some are lying flat, some standing in their space,
    some with heads and some with soles in the ascent,
15   one like a bow with feet bent toward his face.
We continued moving forward. On we went
    till we reached a place at which it pleased my guide
18   to show me the creature once so radiant.
He moved from before me, bade me stop, and cried:
    "Behold Dis! Here behold the place where you
21   must summon courage and be fortified."
I cannot, reader—do not ask me to—
    describe the way I felt, for I know that I
24   lack words to tell how cold and weak I grew.

---

1. "Vexilia regis prodeunt" ("The banners of the King advance") is the first line of a hymn
   written in 569 by Venantius Fortunatus, bishop of Poitiers.

I did not live and yet I did not die,
    deprived of both states. You may realize
27   what I then became, if you have the wit to try.
From midbreast he stood out above the ice,
    the emperor of that realm of misery.
30   And I compare more favorably in size
with the giants than would any giant be,
    compared with just his arm. With such a limb,
33   how monstrous must be his entirety.
If he was fair as he is foul and grim,
    and dared defy his maker, it is well said
36   that all suffering and sorrow flow from him.
I stared to see three faces on his head,
    one of the greatest wonders I had seen yet.
39   The middle one faced forward and was red.
The other two were joined to it and set
    above each shoulder's midpoint, and they went
42   up to his crown, where all three faces met.
The right one had a whitish yellow tint.
    The left one had the appearance of the race
45   that comes from where the Nile starts its descent.
Two enormous wings spread out below each face,[2]
    well scaled to such a bird. Never did I see
48   such sails on any ship in any place.
His wings were featherless and leathery
    just like the long wings of a bat, and since
51   he flapped the six of them incessantly,
all Cocytus was congealed by three cold winds.
    Tears from his six eyes, mixing with a flow
54   of bloody slobber, dripped down his three chins.
Just as a hackle mangles flax, a row
    of teeth in each mouth gripped a soul. He made
57   three spirits suffer unremitting woe.
The one in the front mouth was far less afraid
    of his biting than the raking of his nails.
60   At times the spirit's back was wholly flayed.
My master said: "That one whose fate entails
    the greatest pain is Judas Iscariot.
63   His head is in the mouth, while his body flails.
Of the other two, whose heads are hanging out,
    that is Brutus in the black face, whose control
66   keeps his tongue silent as he writhes about,

---

2. Satan, or Lucifer, had belonged to the angelic order of the Seraphim: "In the year that King Uzziah died I saw also the Lord sitting upon a throne, high and lifted up, and his train filled the temple. Above it stood the seraphims: each one had six wings; with twain he covered his face, and with twain he covered his feet, and with twain he did fly" (Isaiah 6.1–2).

and Cassius is that other, sinewy soul.
    Now the night is rising once again, and we
69   must take our leave, for we have seen the whole."
I clasped his neck, as he commanded me.
    Then he, when the monstrous wings were opened wide,
72   making use of place and time efficiently,
took hold of the shaggy fur on the devil's side
    and climbed down clump by clump, conveying us
75   between the frozen crust and the matted hide.
The moment we came to where the thigh joint was,
    the point at which the haunches spread, was when
78   my leader with movements pained and strenuous
brought his head round to Satan's shanks and then,
    just like a climber, grappled on the hair.
81   I thought we had turned back toward hell again.
He spoke like a weary man who gasps for air:
    "Hold tight. We need such stairs to leave this place
84   where there is so much evil everywhere."
And after that, he came out through the space
    in a rock, upon whose edge he seated me.
87   Then he moved toward me with a cautious pace.
I raised my eyes, expecting I would see
    Lucifer just as he had last appeared,
90   but his legs were tapering upward endlessly.
How perplexed I was by this I will let the herd
    of dullards judge for themselves, who do not know
93   what point I'd passed and what had just occurred.
"The sun returns now to mid-tierce,[3] and so
    you must now stand up again," my master said.
96   "The road is hard and we have far to go."
It was no palace hall that lay ahead,
    but a natural cellar with a rugged floor
99   and little light to show us where it led.
"Master," I said when I arose, "before
    I uproot myself from the abyss, I pray
102   that you help me understand a little more.
Where is the ice? And why is he set this way,
    turned upside down? And how did the sun spin
105   so short a transit from the night to day?"
And he: "You think we are still where we have been,
    on the other side, where I took hold of the hair
108   of the evil worm who gnaws the world from within.

---

3. Tierce is the first of four three-hour periods of the day (6:00 to 9:00 A.M.). Virgil had said
in line 68 that the moon was rising, but it is now about 7:30 A.M., since he and Dante
have crossed the earth's midpoint and are now in the Southern Hemisphere, where it is
day when it is night on the other, inhabited side of the world.

As long as I climbed down, you were still there.
     When I turned myself, you were where the halves divide,
111   at the center that draws all weights from everywhere.
You are under the hemisphere on the opposite side
     from the one that canopies the vast dry land,
114   beneath whose zenith he was crucified
who was born and lived his life without the brand
     or taint of sinfulness. This little sphere
117   is Judecca's other face, where your feet now stand.
It is evening there when it is morning here,
     and he whose hair we made a ladder of
120   is still secured where you saw him appear.
He fell upon this side from the heavens above,
     and the land, in terror as he plummeted,
123   used the ocean for a cover as it strove
toward our hemisphere. And what was here may have fled,
     rushing upward[4] as he hurtled through the sky
126   and leaving this great cavern in its stead."
As far from Beelzebub[5] as it could lie
     within his tomb is a space that no one knows
129   by sight, whose presence is detected by
the sound of a trickling rivulet that flows
     through a hollow in the rock that it has lined,
132   gently wandering and sloping as it goes.
We entered on that hidden road to find
     our way once more into the world of light.
135   My leader walked ahead and I behind,
without a pause to rest, till we were in sight
     of a hole that showed some few particulars
138   of those heavenly things that beautify the night.
From there we came outside and saw the stars.[6]

4. The earth's interior, which rushed upward to avoid the fall of Satan, then formed the Mount of Purgatory. These lines thus create a transition to the *Purgatorio*.
5. Although others see them as separate devils, Dante uses the name Beelzebub here to refer to Satan.
6. The journey to the surface, encapsulated in the previous two tercets, has taken nearly twenty-four hours. In this concluding line, Virgil and Dante emerge to see the dawn sky. "Stars" (*stelle*) will also be the last word of each of the other two parts of the *Comedy*.

BACKGROUNDS
AND CONTEXTS

Dante in His Own Voice

DANTE ALIGHIERI

[Love and the gracious heart]†

Love and the gracious heart are a single thing,
    as Guinizelli tells us in his poem:
    one can no more be without the other
    than can the reasoning mind without its reason.
5   Nature, when in a loving mood, creates them:
    Love to be king, the heart to be his home,
    a place for Love to rest while he is sleeping,
    perhaps for just a while, or for much longer.

And then the beauty of a virtuous lady
10   appears, to please the eyes, and in the heart
    desire for the pleasing thing is born;
    and this desire may linger in the heart
    until Love's spirit is aroused from sleep.
    A man of worth has the same effect on ladies.

---

† From *Dante's Vita Nuova*, trans. Mark Musa. Copyright © 1973 by Indiana University Press. Reprinted by permission of Indiana University Press. The *Vita nova (New Life)* was written in Italian between 1292–1300. Also a work of prosimetrum, a series of poems accompanied by prose commentaries, it recounts Dante's earthly encounters with Beatrice, all the while demonstrating how romantic love is the first step toward divine love.

DANTE ALIGHIERI

[The Tower of Babel]†

❊   ❊   ❊

I. VII

O how shameful it is to repeat the ignominy of the human race![1] Yet since I cannot proceed without passing through it, I shall hurry through despite the reddening of my face and the recoil of my soul.

O human nature ever prone to sin, wicked from time immemorial and forever![2] Was it not sufficient punishment for your first transgression to be deprived of light and exiled from your homeland? Was it not sufficient that because of the lasciviousness and violence of all your kind except for one family, all that was yours perished in the Flood, and that animals of the sky and earth atoned for the sins committed by you? Indeed this should have been enough. But as the proverb says, "You won't ride till the third attempt," and you wretches preferred to mount a wretched horse again and again.[3] Behold now, reader, how mankind, forgetting or overlooking previous lessons and turning its eyes from the scars remaining, rose up for the third time to get its beating, in presumption and vain stupidity.

Thus incorrigible man presumed in his heart, persuaded by the giant Nimrod,[4] to surpass by his skill not only Nature but even Nature's creator, who is God, and began to build a tower on Sennaar,[5]

---

† From De Vulgari Eloquentia, Dante's Book of Exile, trans. Marianne Shapiro. Copyright © 1990 by the University of Nebraska Press. De vulgari eloquentia (Of the Vernacular Language), an unfinished work composed in Latin between 1303–05, describes and lauds the usage of the vernacular.

1. Virgil, Aeneid 2.3: "Infandum, regina, iubes renovare dolorem." Cf. Inferno 5.121–23; 33.4–5.
2. Geoffrey of Vinsauf advocates the topic of Adam, Eve, and the exile from Paradise as a standard rhetorical exercise of rhetorical colors (Edmund Faral, Les arts poétiques du xiie et du xiiie siècles: Recherches et documents sur la technique littéraire du moyen âge [Paris: 1923], 212–13).
3. Marigo, 40 n.10, believes the "horse" to have been a standard mode of punishment for recalcitrant schoolboys: one straddles another, who holds him in place while he is beaten by the master (Aristide Marigo, ed., De vulgari eloquentia [Florence: Le Monnier, 1968]).
4. For Nimrod as the instigator of the Tower, De civitate Dei 16.14, also Tresor 1.24: "Et sachies ke au tens Phalech, ki fu de la lignie Sem, cil Nembrot edefia la tor Babel en Babilone, ou avint la diversités des parleures et de la confusion des langues" (St. Augustine, The City of God, trans. Marcus Dods [New York: Modern Library, 1950]; Brunetto Satini, Li livres dou Tresor, ed. F. J. Carmody [Berkeley: University of California Press, 1948]).
5. Genesis 11.2, 4, 9; De civitate Dei 16.4. Inferno 5.54 links the sin of lust with Babel in the person of Semiramis, the Babylonian empress "of many languages" (di molte favelle), under the rubric of Confusion; see Marianne Shapiro, "Semiramis in Inferno 5," Romance Notes 16 (1974), 455–56.

which was later called Babel, or "Confusion." By this tower he hoped to ascend to Heaven with the mad purpose not only to equal but to surpass his own Maker. O infinite clemency of the heavenly Power! What father would have borne such insults from a son? Yet he rose up with his scourge, one already used to dealing blows, and like a father, not an enemy, punished his rebellious son compassionately but memorably.

Virtually all of the human race had united in this iniquitous enterprise. Some gave orders; some did the planning; some raised the walls; some straightened them with rule and line; some smoothed mortar with trowels, some concentrated on cutting stone and others on transporting it by land and by sea.[6] Thus diverse groups applied themselves in various ways, when they were struck by Heaven with so great a confusion that though all had been using the same language in their work, they abandoned their work, made strangers to one another by the diversity of tongues, and never again succeeded in working together. Only each group that had been working on one particular task kept one and the same language: for example, one for all the architects, one for all the stone-movers; for all the stone-cutters, and so on with every trade. And now as many languages separated the human race as there were different kinds of work; and the more excellent the type of work, the more crudely and barbarically did they speak now.[7]

But those to whom the sacred language remained had not been present nor did they condone the work, but profoundly condemning it, derided the stupidity of the builders. Yet as I conjecture, this minority was of the seed of Sem, the third son of Noah;[8] and from it arose the people of Israel, who continued to use the most ancient language until their dispersion.

6. The description of the construction of Babel is influenced by *Aeneid* 1.423–40, the building of Carthage. Genesis 11.8 states that "God divided" the builders throughout the world.
7. The form of retribution Dante accords to the tower-builders resembles certain punishments in *Inferno* which more closely approximate the *contrappasso*: for example, that of Bertran de Born and the other schismatics in *Inferno* 28, which directly metaphorizes their sin.
8. Genesis 10.21, for Sem, Noah's third son; 22.28 for "Israel" as the name given to Jacob, which passed to the Hebrew people.

DANTE ALIGHIERI

[On knowledge; literature; government]†

Book One

CHAPTER I

As the Philosopher says at the beginning of the *First Philosophy*, all men by nature desire to know.[1] The reason for this can be and is that each thing, impelled by a force provided by its own nature, inclines towards its own perfection. Since knowledge is the ultimate perfection of our soul, in which resides our ultimate happiness, we are all therefore by nature subject to a desire for it. Many are, however, deprived of this most noble perfection by various causes within and outside of man which remove him from the habit of knowledge. Within man there exist two kinds of defects which impede him, one pertaining to the body, the other to the soul. That pertaining to the body occurs when its parts are not properly disposed, so that it can receive nothing, as is the case with the deaf, the dumb, and the like. That pertaining to the soul occurs when malice overcomes it, so that it becomes the follower of vicious pleasures, by which it is so deceived that because of them it degrades the worth of all things. Likewise outside of man two causes may be discerned, one of which subjects him to necessity, the other to indolence. The first consists of family and civic responsibilities, which properly engage the greater number of men, so that they are permitted no time for contemplation. The other is the handicap that derives from the place where a person is born and bred, which at times will not only lack a university but be far removed from the company of educated persons.

Two of these causes, namely the first from within and the first from outside, are not to be blamed but excused and are deserving of pardon; the other two, although one more than the other, deserve our censure and scorn. Anyone therefore can plainly see upon careful reflection that there remain few who are capable of achieving the habit of knowledge desired by all, and that the handicapped who live forever starved of this food are almost too numerous to count. Blessed are the few who sit at the table where the bread of the an-

---

† From Dante's *Il Convivio* (*The Banquet*), trans. Richard H. Lansing. Copyright © 1990 by Richard H. Lansing. The *Convivio*, or *Banquet*, was written in Italian between the years 1304–1308. It is an unfinished, prosemetric work that deals with ethics and the question of authority.

1. Aristotle, whom Dante refers to by antonomasia throughout, following the traditional practice of his age. The *First Philosophy* is his *Metaphysics*, and the citation is to the opening line of Book I, Ch. 1.

gels is eaten, and most unfortunate those who share the food of sheep![2]

But since man is by nature a friend of all men, and every friend is grieved by defects found in the one he loves, they who are fed at so lofty a table are not without compassion toward those whom they see grazing about on grass and acorns in animal pastures. And since compassion is the mother of generosity, they who possess knowledge always give liberally of their great riches to the truly poor and are like a living fountain by whose waters the natural thirst referred to above is quenched.[3] Therefore I (who do not sit at the blessed table, but, having fled the pasture of the common herd, gather up a part of what falls to the feet of those who do sit there, and who know the unfortunate life of those I have left behind, for the sweetness that I taste in what I gather up piece by piece, and moved by compassion, though not forgetting myself) have set aside for those who are unfortunate something that I placed before their eyes some time ago, by which I have increased their desire.[4]

Wishing now to set their table, I intend to present to all men a banquet of what I have shown them and of the bread which must necessarily accompany such meat, without which it could not be consumed by them. This banquet, being worthy of such bread, offers meat which I intend should not be served in vain. Therefore I would not have anyone be seated there whose organs are ill-disposed because he lacks teeth, tongue, or palate, nor anyone addicted to vice, for his stomach is so full of poisonous and contrary humors that it would not be able to retain my meat. But let come here all those whose human hunger derives from domestic or civic responsibilities, and let them sit at the same table with others likewise handicapped; and at their feet let all those place themselves who do not merit a higher seat because of their indolence; and let each group partake of my meat with bread, for I will have them both taste of it and digest it. The meat of this banquet will be prepared in fourteen ways: that is, in fourteen canzoni, whose subject is both love as well as virtue. By lacking the present bread they possessed some degree of obscurity, so that to many their beauty was more pleasing than their goodness. But this bread (that is, the present explanation) will be the light that renders visible every shade of their meaning.

If in the present work, which is called *The Banquet*, as I wish it to

2. A metaphor signifying wisdom.
3. The thirst for knowledge of truth. The same metaphor reappears in *Purg.* XXI, 1 ("La sete natural").
4. Dante had written the three canzoni, placed at the beginning of the second, third, and fourth books, some ten years earlier, and now seeks to make their meaning more accessible by extended commentaries, which comprise the prose portion of these books (or treatises). The "meat" is the poetry, the "bread" the commentary.

be, the subject is treated more maturely than in *The New Life*, I do not intend by this in any way to disparage that book but rather more greatly to support it with this one, seeing that it understandably suits that one to be fervid and passionate, and this one tempered and mature.[5] For it is proper to speak and act differently at different ages, because certain manners are fitting and praiseworthy at one age which at another are unbecoming and blameworthy, as will be shown below with appropriate reasoning in the fourth book. I wrote the former work at the threshold of my youth, and this one after I had already passed through it. Since my true meaning was other than what the previously mentioned canzoni outwardly reveal, I intend to explain these canzoni by means of an allegorical exposition, after having discussed the literal account, so that both arguments will be savored by those who have been invited to this supper. And if the banquet does not fulfill their expectations, I ask them to attribute every shortcoming not to my will but to my capability; for here it is my desire to be a disciple of complete and loving generosity.

Book Two

CHAPTER I

Now that by way of a preface my bread has been sufficiently prepared in the preceding book through my own assistance, time calls and requires my ship to leave port; thus, having set the sail of my reason to the breeze of my desire, I enter upon the open sea with the hope of a smooth voyage and a safe and praiseworthy port at the end of my feast. But so that this food of mine may be more profitable, I wish to show, before it appears, how the first course must be eaten.

As I stated in the first chapter, this exposition must be both literal and allegorical. To convey what this means, it is necessary to know that writings can be understood and ought to be expounded principally in four senses. The first is called the literal, and this is the sense that does not go beyond the surface of the letter, as in the fables of the poets. The next is called the allegorical, and this is the one that is hidden beneath the cloak of these fables, and is a truth hidden beneath a beautiful fiction. Thus Ovid says that with his lyre Orpheus tamed wild beasts and made trees and rocks move toward him, which is to say that the wise man with the instrument of his voice makes cruel hearts grow tender and humble and moves to his will those who do not devote their lives to knowledge and art; and those who have no rational life whatsoever are almost like stones.

---

5. Dante's first literary work (c. 1295), the *Vita Nuova*, which celebrates his youthful and passionate love for Beatrice. Like the *Convivio*, it collects a number of poems written at an earlier time and supplies a commentary on their meaning.

Why this kind of concealment was devised by the wise will be shown in the penultimate book. Indeed the theologians take this sense otherwise than do the poets; but since it is my intention here to follow the method of the poets, I shall take the allegorical sense according to the usage of the poets.[1]

The third sense is called moral, and this is the sense that teachers should intently seek to discover throughout the scriptures, for their own profit and that of their pupils; as, for example, in the Gospel we may discover that when Christ ascended the mountain to be transfigured, of the twelve Apostles he took with him but three, the moral meaning of which is that in matters of great secrecy we should have few companions.[2]

The fourth sense is called anagogical, that is to say, beyond the senses; and this occurs when a scripture is expounded in a spiritual sense which, although it is true also in the literal sense, signifies by means of the things signified a part of the supernal things of eternal glory, as may be seen in the song of the Prophet which says that when the people of Israel went out of Egypt, Judea was made whole and free.[3] For although it is manifestly true according to the letter, that which is spiritually intended is no less true, namely, that when the soul departs from sin it is made whole and free in its power. In this kind of explication, the literal should always come first, as being the sense in whose meaning the others are enclosed, and without which it would be impossible and illogical to attend to the other senses, and especially the allegorical. It would be impossible because in everything that has an inside and an outside it is impossible to arrive at the inside without first arriving at the outside; consequently, since in what is written down the literal meaning is always the outside, it is impossible to arrive at the other senses, especially the allegorical, without first arriving at the literal.

Moreover, it would be impossible because in every natural or artificial thing it is impossible to proceed to the form unless the subject on which the form must be imposed is prepared first—just as it is impossible for a piece of jewelry to acquire its form if the material

---

1. What Dante means by distinguishing between the allegory of the poets and the allegory of the theologians is not entirely clear and has given rise to endless speculation. The theologians insist on the veracity of all four levels of meaning and conceived of the allegorical levels (the typological, tropological, and anagogical) to depend on a literal level which was historically true. In the allegory of the poets, as exemplified by the allusion to the myth of Orpheus, the literal level is a "bella menzogna," a beautiful fiction having no basis in historical reality. In the allegory of the theologians, moreover, the second level always refers to some aspect of Christ's historical being, of which he is the ideal type, which is not the case with the poets. The third and fourth levels are shared in common by both modes of allegory.
2. The apostles Peter, James, and John (see Matthew 17:1–8, Mark 9:1–7, Luke 9:28–36).
3. The reference is to Psalm 113, *In exitu Israel de Egypto*. Dante employs this same psalm in his *Letter to Cangrande* to illustrate the various levels of allegory, and the souls of the saved sing this psalm upon entering Purgatory.

(that is, its subject) is not first arranged and prepared, or a chest to
acquire its form if the material (that is, the wood) is not first
arranged and prepared. Consequently, since the literal meaning is
always the subject and material of the other senses, especially of the
allegorical, it is impossible to come to an understanding of them be-
fore coming to an understanding of it. Moreover, it would be impos-
sible because in every natural or artificial thing it is impossible to
proceed unless the foundation is laid first, as in a house or in study-
ing; consequently, since explication is the building up of knowledge,
and the explication of the literal sense is the foundation of the oth-
ers, especially of the allegorical, it is impossible to arrive at the other
senses without first arriving at it.

Moreover, even supposing it were possible, it would be illogical,
that is to say out of order, and would therefore be carried out with
great labor and much confusion. Consequently as the Philosopher[4]
says in the first book of the *Physics*, nature wills that we proceed in
due order in our learning, that is, by proceeding from that which we
know better to that which we know not so well; I say that nature
wills it since this way of learning is by nature innate in us. Therefore
if the senses other than the literal are less understood (which they
are, as is quite apparent), it would be illogical to proceed to explain
them if the literal had not been explicated first. For these reasons,
therefore, I shall on each occasion discuss first the literal meaning
concerning each canzone, and afterwards I shall discuss its allegory
(that is, the hidden truth), at times touching on the other senses,
when opportune, as time and place deem proper.

Book Four

CHAPTER 4

The root foundation underlying the Imperial Majesty is, in truth,
man's need for human society, which is established for a single end:
namely, a life of happiness, which no one is able to attain by himself
without the aid of someone else, since one has need of many things
which no single individual is able to provide. Therefore the Philoso-
pher says that man is by nature a social animal.[1] And just as for his
well-being an individual requires the domestic companionship pro-
vided by family, so for its well-being a household requires a commu-
nity, for otherwise it would suffer many defects that would hinder
happiness. And since a community could not provide for its own
well-being completely by itself, it is necessary for this well-being
that there be a city.

4. See St. Thomas's commentary to *Phys.* I, lect. 1.
1. Aristotle, *Politics* I, 2.

Moreover, a city requires for the sake of its culture and its defense mutual relations and brotherhood with the surrounding cities, and for this reason kingdoms were created. Since the human mind does not rest content with limited possession of land but always seeks to achieve glory through further conquest, as we see from experience, discord and war must spring up between one kingdom and another. Such things are the tribulations of cities, of the surrounding cities, of the communities, and of the households of individuals; and so happiness is hindered. Consequently, in order to do away with these wars and their causes, it is necessary that the whole earth, and all that is given to the human race to possess, should be a Monarchy[2]— that is, a single principality, having one prince who, possessing all things and being unable to desire anything else, would keep the kings content within the boundaries of their kingdoms and preserve among them the peace in which the cities might rest. Through this peace the communities would come to love one another, and by this love all households would provide for their needs, which when provided would bring man happiness, for this is the end for which he is born.

In regard to this argument we may refer to the words of the Philosopher when he says in the *Politics* that when many are directed to a single end, one of them should be a governor or a ruler, and all the rest should be ruled or governed. This is what we observe on a ship, where the different offices and objectives are directed to a single end: namely, that of reaching the desired port by a safe route. Just as each officer directs his own activity to its own end, so there is one individual who takes account of all these ends and directs them to their final end: and this is the captain, whose commands all must obey. We see this in religious orders, in armies, and in all things, as has been said, which are directed to an end. Consequently it is evident that, in order to bring to perfection the universal social order of the human species, it is necessary to have a single individual who, like a captain, upon considering the different conditions in the world, should have, in order to direct the different and necessary offices, the universal and indisputable office of complete command. This pre-eminent office is called the Empire, without qualification, because it is the command of all other commands. And thus he who is placed in this office is called the Emperor, since he is the commander of all other commands; what he says is law for all and ought to be obeyed by all, and every other command gains strength and

---

2. The concept of monarchy as the ideal form of government will be more fully developed in the Latin treatise *Monarchia* (1312), where Dante will reiterate the notion that the monarchy, being exempt from greed by virtue of its possessing universal jurisdiction on earth, is founded on absolute justice.

authority from his. And so it is clear that the imperial majesty and authority are the highest in the fellowship of mankind.

Nevertheless someone might quibble by arguing that although the world requires an imperial office, there is no sound reason why the authority of a Roman prince should be supreme—which is the point we seek to prove—because the power of Rome was acquired neither by reason nor by decree of universal consensus, but by force, which appears to be the opposite of reason. To this we may easily reply that the election of this supreme officer must in the first place derive from that wisdom which provides for all men, namely God; for otherwise the election would not have been made on behalf of everyone, since prior to the officer named above there was no one who attended to the general good. And because no nature ever was or will be more tempered in the exercise of rule, stronger in its preservation, and more clever in acquiring it than that of the Latin race (as can be seen from experience), that sacred people in whom was mingled the lofty blood of the Trojans, namely Rome, God chose this people for that office. Therefore since this office could not be attained without the greatest virtue, and since its exercise required the greatest and most humane kindness, this was the people best disposed to receive it. Consequently the Roman people secured it originally not by force but by divine providence, which transcends all reason.

Vergil concurs in this in the first book of the *Aeneid* when, speaking in the person of God, he says: "To these (namely the Romans) I set no bounds, either in space or time; to these I have given empire without end."[3] Force was therefore not the moving cause, as our quibbler supposed, but rather the instrumental cause, as the blows of a hammer are the cause of a knife, while the mind of the smith is the efficient and moving cause; and thus not force but reason, and moreover divine reason, must have been the origin of the Roman Empire. Two very distinct reasons may be adduced to prove that this city is imperial and had an origin and progress that were especially arranged by God. But since this subject could not be treated in this chapter without undue length, and long chapters are the foe of memory, I will extend my digression to another chapter to set forth the reasons indicated above, not without profit and much delight.

---

3. *Aeneid* I, 278.

DANTE ALIGHIERI

[On nobility and government]†

* * *

II. III

On this question I therefore affirm that it was by right, and not by usurping, that the Roman people took on the office of the monarch (which is called 'empire') over all men. This can be proved firstly as follows: it is appropriate that the noblest race should rule over all the others; the Roman people was the noblest; therefore it was appropriate that they should rule over all the others. The major premiss is proved by an argument from reason: for since "honour is the reward for virtue"[1] and every position of authority is an honour, every position of authority is the reward of virtue. But we know that men become noble through virtue,[2] either their own virtue or that of their forebears. For "nobility is virtue and ancient wealth", as Aristotle says in the *Politics*;[3] and according to Juvenal:

> nobility of mind is the sole and only virtue.[4]

These two sayings refer to two kinds of nobility, i.e. a man's own nobility and that of his ancestors. Therefore the reward of a position of authority is appropriate to the noble by reason of the cause of their nobility.[5] And since rewards should be commensurate with deserts, as we read in the words of the Gospel: "With the same measure you have applied to others you will be measured",[6] it is appropriate that the most noble should have the highest position of authority over

---

† From *Dante, Monarchia*, trans. and ed. Prue Shaw. Copyright © 1995 by Cambridge University Press. *On World-Government* (*De monarchia*), written in Latin between 1310–1313, expresses Dante's belief in the necessity of a single ruling power separate from the Church.
1. Aristotle, *Ethics* 4, 3 1123b 35.
2. Dante analysed the relationship between nobility and virtue in his poem *Le dolci rime d'amor* [sweet love poetry] on which Book IV of the *Convivio* provides his own extended commentary. A brilliant and exhaustive analysis of the poem and the concepts it deals with is provided in K. Foster and P. Boyde, *Dante's Lyric Poetry, Volume II, Commentary*, Oxford, 1967, pp. 210–28.
3. *Politics* 4, 8 1294a 21–2; this definition is discussed in *Conv.* IV, iii, 6f., where it is attributed to the Emperor Frederick II.
4. *Satires* 8, 20. The line is slightly different in modern critical editions of the text, see Nardi's commentary *ad loc*. Dante may be quoting from memory, as he seems to do elsewhere, see n. 9.
5. The cause of nobility is virtue, therefore if *prelatio* [preference] is due to virtue it will be due to the noble.
6. Matthew 7, 2; Luke 6, 38.

others. The minor premiss[7] is supported by the testimony of the an-
cients; for our divine poet Virgil bears witness throughout the whole
of the *Aeneid*, to his everlasting memory, that the father of the Ro-
man people was that most glorious king Aeneas; and Titus Livy, the
illustrious chronicler of Roman deeds, confirms this in the first part
of his book,[8] which takes as its starting-point the capture of Troy. It
would be beyond me to give a full account of just how noble this
supremely victorious and supremely dutiful father was, taking into
account not only his own virtue but that of his forebears and his
wives, whose nobility flowed into him by hereditary right: "but I
shall trace the main outlines of the facts".[9]

Now as far as his own nobility is concerned, we must listen to our
poet when in the first book he introduces Ileoneus as he petitions in
this manner:

> Aeneas was our king; no man more just
> In piety, nor greater in war and arms.[1]

Let us listen to him too in the sixth book, when he speaks of the dead
Misenus, who had served Hector in battle and who after Hector's
death had entered the service of Aeneas; he says that Misenus "fol-
lowed no less a hero",[2] comparing Aeneas with Hector, whom Homer
glorifies above all others, as Aristotle relates in that book of the
Ethics which deals with behaviour to be avoided.[3] As far as hereditary
nobility is concerned, we find that each of the three regions into
which the world is divided[4] made him noble, both through his ances-
tors and through his wives. For Asia did so through his more immedi-

---

7. *Subassumptam*: the minor premiss, i.e. 'the Roman people were the noblest'. This is cer-
   tainly the correct reading, *pace* Nardi (see his translation and commentary): the argu-
   ment developed in this chapter is absolutely clear, and consists of proving that the
   content of the syllogism enunciated in par. 2 is true. The major premiss is proved in pars.
   3–5; the minor premiss occupies the remainder of the chapter: pars. 6–16 establish the
   nobility of Aeneas and hence of the Romans, using the key testimony of Virgil, the princi-
   pal witness to Rome's greatness, corroborated by others; par. 17 recapitulates, and re-
   minds us, in case we have lost the thread during this extended review of the evidence,
   that it bears on the proof of the minor premiss (*ad evidentiam subassumpte*).
8. *Ab urbe condita* I, 1, 11. It is uncertain whether Dante had a firsthand knowledge of Livy.
   The evidence is exhaustively reviewed by A. Martina in *Livio, ED* III, pp. 673–7.
9. *Aeneid* I, 342. Again Dante is either quoting from memory, or from a text with the variant
   reading *vestigia* instead of *fastigia*.
1. *ibid.* I, 544–5.
2. *ibid.* VI, 170.
3. *Ethics* 7, I 1145a 20–3. In Book 7 Aristotle expounds the three-fold division of sinful be-
   haviour which provides the conceptual framework for the *Inferno* and which Virgil will
   echo when he explains the structure of Hell to Dante-character in *Inf.* XI, 79–83: Non ti
   rimembra di quelle parole / con le quai la tua *Etica* pertratta / le tre disposizion che 'l ciel
   non vuole, / incontinenza, malizia e la matta/ bestialitade? ("Do you forget the explanation
   given, / in the pages of your *Ethics* of the three / dispositions that offend the will of
   heaven, / incontinence, malice, and mad bestiality?")
4. This tripartite division of the world derives from Orosius, *Hist.* I, 1; cf. also Alberti Magni *De
   natura loci*, Tract. 3 Cap. 5: De distinctione trium partium orbis: Asiae, Europae et Africae.

ate forebears, such as Assaracus and the others who ruled over Phrygia, a region of Asia; hence our poet says in the third book:

> After the Gods saw fit to overthrow
> The might of Asia and Priam's guiltless race.[5]

Europe did so with his most ancient male forebear, i.e. Dardanus; Africa did so too with his most ancient female forebear Electra, daughter of King Atlas of great renown; our poet bears witness concerning both of them in his eighth book, where Aeneas speaks in these words to Evander:

> Dardanus,
> First father and founder of the city of Troy,
> Born of Electra, as the Greeks maintain,
> Comes to the Teucrians; mighty Atlas begat her,
> Who bears the spheres of heaven on his shoulders.[6]

That Dardanus was of European birth our bard[7] proclaims in the third book:

> There is a land the Greeks call Hesperia,
> Ancient, mighty in arms and fertile soil.
> Oenotrians lived there; a later generation
> Has called the nation Italy after their leader:
> This is our homeland; Dardanus was born here.[8]

That Atlas came from Africa is confirmed by the mountain there which bears his name. Orosius in his description of the world tells us it is in Africa in these words: "Its furthest boundary is Mount Atlas and the islands they call Fortunate" ('its' meaning 'Africa's', because he is talking about Africa).[9]

In similar fashion I find that he was also made noble by marriage. For his first wife, Creusa, the daughter of king Priam, was from Asia, as may be gathered from what was said earlier. And that she was his wife our poet bears witness in his third book, where Andromache questions Aeneas as a father about his son Ascanius in this way:

> What of your boy Ascanius,
> Whom Creusa bore when Troy was smouldering?
> Is he alive and does he breathe earth's air?[1]

---

5. *Aeneid* III, 1–2.
6. *ibid.* VIII, 134–7.
7. The word *vates* underlines Virgil's prophetic function, reiterated in the verb *vaticinatur* in par. 15.
8. *Aeneid* III, 163–7.
9. *Hist.* I, 2. Mount Atlas is on the NW coast of Africa; the Fortunate Isles are Madeira and the Canaries.
1. *Aeneid* III, 339–40. Line 340 (quem tibi iam Troia . . . ?) is the only incomplete line in the *Aeneid* where the sense is incomplete (Servius *ad Aen.* III, 340 draws attention to the incomplete sense). In medieval manuscripts the lacuna is occasionally filled as Dante fills

His second wife was Dido, queen and mother of the Carthaginians in Africa; and that she was his wife our bard proclaims in the fourth book, for he says there of Dido:

> Dido no longer thinks of a secret love:
> She calls it marriage; this name conceals her sin.[2]

The third was Lavinia, mother of the Albans and the Romans, the daughter of King Latinus and his heir as well, if our poet is to be believed in his last book, where he introduces the defeated Turnus making supplication to Aeneas in these words:

> You have won; the Ausonians have seen
> The vanquished man stretch forth his upturned hands:
> Lavinia is your wife.[3]

This last wife was from Italy, the most noble region of Europe. When these facts in support of the minor premiss are borne in mind, who is not satisfied that the father of the Roman people, and as a consequence that people itself, was the noblest in the world? Or who will fail to recognize divine predestination in that double[4] confluence of blood from every part of the world into a single man?

* * *

---

it here (inappropriately, as Ascanius was born long before the destruction of Troy). Andromache's question to Aeneas about his son is famously echoed in the *Comedy* in Cavalcante's anguished questioning about the fate of his son Guido: non viv'elli ancora? / non fiere li occhi suoi il dolce lome? ("Is he no longer living then? / Are his eyes not struck by the sweet light of day?"), *Inf.* X, 68–9.

2. *Aeneid* IV, 171–2.
3. *ibid.* XII, 936–7.
4. *duplici* (not *triplici* as in Rostagno's conjectural emendation, which has no manuscript support). Dante is making a genealogical not a geographical point, positing a 'double confluence' from ancestors and wives, not a 'three-fold conflux' from the three parts of the world, as Ricci (following Vianello and Toynbee) demonstrated, *EN*, p. 181.

Sources and Influences

VIRGIL

From the Aeneid†

Book I

I sing of warfare and a man at war.
From the sea-coast of Troy in early days
He came to Italy by destiny,
To our Lavinian western shore,
5 A fugitive, this captain, buffeted
Cruelly on land as on the sea
By blows from powers of the air—behind them
Baleful Juno in her sleepless rage.
And cruel losses were his lot in war,
10 Till he could found a city and bring home
His gods to Latium, land of the Latin race,
The Alban lords, and the high walls of Rome.
Tell me the causes now, O Muse, how galled
In her divine pride, and how sore at heart
15 From her old wound, the queen of gods compelled him—
A man apart, devoted to his mission—
To undergo so many perilous days
And enter on so many trials. Can anger
Black as this prey on the minds of heaven?
20 Tyrian settlers in that ancient time
Held Carthage, on the far shore of the sea,
Set against Italy and Tiber's mouth,
A rich new town, warlike and trained for war.
And Juno, we are told, cared more for Carthage
25 Than for any walled city of the earth,

---

† From *The Aeneid*, trans. Robert Fitzgerald. Copyright © 1981, 1982, 1983 by Robert Fitzgerald. Virgil wrote the epic Latin poem the *Aeneid* between c. 29 B.C.E.–19 B.C.E. Excerpts included here are the opening verse and introduction to Aeneas, Juno's Carthage, and the destiny of the founding of Rome (1.1–49); the shipwreck and Aeneas's encouraging speech to his men (1.270–304); Dido and her desire for Aeneas (4.1–120).

More than for Samos, even. There her armor
And chariot were kept, and, fate permitting,
Carthage would be the ruler of the world.
So she intended, and so nursed that power.
30   But she had heard long since
That generations born of Trojan blood
Would one day overthrow her Tyrian walls,
And from that blood a race would come in time
With ample kingdoms, arrogant in war,
35   For Libya's ruin: so the Parcae spun.
In fear of this, and holding in memory
The old war she had carried on at Troy
For Argos' sake (the origins of that anger,
That suffering, still rankled: deep within her,
40   Hidden away, the judgment Paris gave,
Snubbing her loveliness; the race she hated;
The honors given ravished Ganymede),
Saturnian Juno, burning for it all,
Buffeted on the waste of sea those Trojans
45   Left by the Greeks and pitiless Achilles,
Keeping them far from Latium. For years
They wandered as their destiny drove them on
From one sea to the next: so hard and huge
A task it was to found the Roman people.

                             *   *   *

270   "Friends and companions,
Have we not known hard hours before this?[1]
My men, who have endured still greater dangers,
God will grant us an end to these as well.
You sailed by Scylla's rage, her booming crags,
275   You saw the Cyclops' boulders. Now call back
Your courage, and have done with fear and sorrow.
Some day, perhaps, remembering even this
Will be a pleasure. Through diversities
Of luck, and through so many challenges,
280   We hold our course for Latium, where the Fates
Hold out a settlement and rest for us.
Troy's kingdom there shall rise again. Be patient:
Save yourselves for more auspicious days."

So ran the speech. Burdened and sick at heart,
285   He feigned hope in his look, and inwardly
Contained his anguish. Now the Trojan crews

---

1. Aeneas speaks to his fellow Trojans, who have been shipwrecked.

Made ready for their windfall and their feast.
They skinned the deer, bared ribs and viscera,
Then one lot sliced the flesh and skewered it
290   On spits, all quivering, while others filled
Bronze cooking pots and tended the beach fires.
All got their strength back from the meal, reclining
On the wild grass, gorging on venison
And mellowed wine. When hunger had been banished,
295   And tables put away, they talked at length
In hope and fear about their missing friends:
Could one believe they might be still alive,
Or had they suffered their last hour,
Never again to hear a voice that called them?
300   Aeneas, more than any, secretly
Mourned for them all—for that fierce man, Orontës,
Then for Amycus, then for the bitter fate
Of Lycus, for brave Gyas, brave Cloanthus.

                *   *   *

Book IV

The queen, for her part, all that evening ached
With longing that her heart's blood fed, a wound
Or inward fire eating her away.
The manhood of the man, his pride of birth,
5   Came home to her time and again; his looks,
His words remained with her to haunt her mind,
And desire for him gave her no rest.
                        When Dawn
Swept earth with Phoebus' torch and burned away
Night-gloom and damp, this queen, far gone and ill,
10   Confided to the sister of her heart:
"My sister Anna, quandaries and dreams
Have come to frighten me—such dreams!
                        Think what a stranger
Yesterday found lodging in our house:
How princely, how courageous, what a soldier.
15   I can believe him in the line of gods,
And this is no delusion. Tell-tale fear
Betrays inferior souls. What scenes of war
Fought to the bitter end he pictured for us!
What buffetings awaited him at sea!
20   Had I not set my face against remarriage
After my first love died and failed me, left me
Barren and bereaved—and sick to death
I could perhaps give way in this one case

To frailty. I shall say it: since that time
25 Sychaeus, my poor husband, met his fate,
And blood my brother shed stained our hearth gods,
This man alone has wrought upon me so
And moved my soul to yield. I recognize
The signs of the old flame, of old desire.
30 But O chaste life, before I break your laws,
I pray that Earth may open, gape for me
Down to its depth, or the omnipotent
With one stroke blast me to the shades, pale shades
Of Erebus and the deep world of night!
35 That man who took me to himself in youth
Has taken all my love; may that man keep it,
Hold it forever with him in the tomb."

At this she wept and wet her breast with tears.
But Anna answered:
                              "Dearer to your sister
40 Than daylight is, will you wear out your life,
Young as you are, in solitary mourning,
Never to know sweet children, or the crown
Of joy that Venus brings? Do you believe
This matters to the dust, to ghosts in tombs?
45 Granted no suitors up to now have moved you,
Neither in Libya nor before, in Tyre—
Iarbas you rejected, and the others,
Chieftains bred by the land of Africa
Their triumphs have enriched—will you contend
50 Even against a welcome love? Have you
Considered in whose lands you settled here?
On one frontier the Gaetulans, their cities,
People invincible in war—with wild
Numidian horsemen, and the offshore banks,
55 The Syrtës; on the other, desert sands,
Bone-dry, where fierce Barcaean nomads range.
Or need I speak of future wars brought on
From Tyre, and the menace of your brother?
Surely by dispensation of the gods
60 And backed by Juno's will, the ships from Ilium
Held their course this way on the wind.
                                        Sister,
What a great city you'll see rising here,
And what a kingdom, from this royal match!
With Trojan soldiers as companions in arms
65 By what exploits will Punic glory grow!
Only ask the indulgence of the gods,
Win them with offerings, give your guests ease,

And contrive reasons for delay, while winter
Gales rage, drenched Orion storms at sea,
70 And their ships, damaged still, face iron skies."

This counsel fanned the flame, already kindled,
Giving her hesitant sister hope, and set her
Free of scruple. Visiting the shrines
They begged for grace at every altar first,
75 Then put choice rams and ewes to ritual death
For Ceres Giver of Laws, Father Lyaeus,
Phoebus, and for Juno most of all
Who has the bonds of marriage in her keeping.
Dido herself, splendidly beautiful,
80 Holding a shallow cup, tips out the wine
On a white shining heifer, between the horns,
Or gravely in the shadow of the gods
Approaches opulent altars. Through the day
She brings new gifts, and when the breasts are opened
85 Pores over organs, living still, for signs.
Alas, what darkened minds have soothsayers!
What good are shrines and vows to maddened lovers?
The inward fire eats the soft marrow away,
And the internal would bleeds on in silence.

90 Unlucky Dido, burning, in her madness
Hit by an arrow shot from far away
By a shepherd hunting in the Cretan woods—
Hit by surprise, nor could the hunter see
His flying steel had fixed itself in her;
95 But though she runs for life through copse and glade
The fatal shaft clings to her side.
                                    Now Dido
Took Aeneas with her among her buildings,
Showed her Sidonian wealth, her walls prepared,
And tried to speak, but in mid-speech grew still.
100 When the day waned she wanted to repeat
The banquet as before, to hear once more
In her wild need the throes of Ilium,
And once more hung on the narrator's words.
Afterward, when all the guests were gone,
105 And the dim moon in turn had quenched her light,
And setting stars weighed weariness to sleep,
Alone she mourned in the great empty hall
And pressed her body on the couch he left:
She heard him still, though absent—heard and saw him.
110 Or she would hold Ascanius in her lap,
Enthralled by him, the image of his father,

As though by this ruse to appease a love
Beyond all telling.

*   *   *

AUGUSTINE

From The Confessions[†]

13

But I still cannot quite understand why I hated the Greek which I had to study as a boy. For I was very fond of Latin, not the elementary grammar but the literature. As to the rudiments—reading, writing, and arithmetic—I found these just as boring and troublesome as all my Greek studies. And how can this be explained except from the sin and vanity of life, because I *was flesh, and a breath that passeth away and cometh not again?* For by means of these rudiments I acquired and still retain the power to read what I find written and to write what I want to write myself; they are therefore undoubtedly better, because more reliable, than those other studies in which I was forced to learn all about the wanderings of a man called Aeneas, while quite oblivious of my own wanderings, and to weep for the death of Dido, because she killed herself for love, while all the time I could bear with dry eyes, O God my life, the fact that I myself, poor wretch, was, among these things, dying far away from you.

What indeed can be more pitiful than a wretch with no pity for himself, weeping at the death of Dido, which was caused by love for Aeneas, and not weeping at his own death, caused by lack of love for you, God, light of my heart, bread of the inner mouth of my soul, strength of my mind, and quickness of my thoughts? You I did not love. Against you I committed fornication, and in my fornication I heard all around me the words: "Well done! Well done!" *For the love of this world is fornication against Thee* and when one hears these words: "Well done! Well done!" they have the effect of making one ashamed not to be that sort of person. But this was not what I wept for; I wept for dead Dido "who by the sword pursued a way extreme," meanwhile myself following a more extreme way, that of the most extremely low of your creatures, having forsaken you, and being

† From *The Confessions of Saint Augustine*, trans. Rex Warner. New York: Copyright © 1963 by Rex Warner. The *Confessions* (c. 400) is the autobiographical Latin work of Augustine of Hippo. The selection here from Book 1, chapters 13–14, describes his study of Greek and Latin literature.

earth going back to earth. And if I were forbidden to read these things, I would be sad at not being allowed to read what would make me sad. And this sort of madness is considered a superior and richer form of learning than learning how to read and write!

But now let my God cry out in my soul; let your truth speak to me and say: "Not so, not so at all. Those first studies were very much better." For obviously I would rather forget about the wanderings of Aeneas and everything of that sort than how to read and write. True enough that curtains are hung at the doors of Schools of Literature. Why? Rather as a covering for error than as a mark of the distinction of some special knowledge. These professors of literature, of whom I am no longer afraid, need not cry out against me as I confess to you, my God, what my soul wishes to confess and as I find rest in the condemnation of my evil ways in order that I may love those good ways of yours. There is no need for either the buyers or sellers of literary knowledge to cry out against me. For suppose I were to ask them: "Is it really true that, as the poet says, Aeneas came at some time to Carthage?" the more ignorant ones will reply: "We don't know," and the more learned: "No, it is not true." But if I ask: "What is the correct spelling of the name 'Aeneas,'" all who have learned it will give me the correct answer, an answer in accordance with the general agreement which men have made among themselves for the use of these signs. And again if I were to ask: "Which would have the worse effect on man's life; to forget how to read and write, or to forget all these imaginary stories of the poets?" is it not obvious what everyone not quite out of his mind would reply? I sinned, therefore, in my boyhood when I showed greater affection for these empty studies than for the others that were more useful; or, it would be truer to say, I loved the former and I hated the latter. At that time "One and one make two; two and two make four" was a horrible kind of singsong to me. What really delighted me were spectacles of vanity—the Wooden Horse full of armed men, the Burning of Troy, and "there the very shade of dead Creüsa."

14

But why, then, did I hate Greek literature, which is full of such things? For Homer too is full skillful at putting together this sort of story and there is great sweetness in his vanity; yet when I was a boy he was not to my taste. I think that Greek children must feel just the same about Vergil, when they are forced to study him as I was forced to study Homer. No doubt it was a question of difficulty; and this difficulty of mastering a foreign language was like bitter gall sprinkled over all the sweetness of Greek stories and fables. For I simply did not know the words, and strict measures were taken, punishments and cruel threats, to make me learn them. There had been a time too, of course, in my infancy, when I did not know any Latin words either; yet simply by paying attention I learned Latin without any fears or torments; I learned it in the caressing language of my nurses and in the laughter and play and kindness of those about me. In this learning I was under no pressure of punishment, and people did not have to urge me on; my own heart urged me on to give birth to the thoughts which it had conceived, and I could not do this unless I learned some words; these I learned not from instructors but from people who talked to me and in whose hearing I too was able to give birth to what I was feeling. It it clear enough from this that free curiosity is a more powerful aid to the learning of languages than a forced discipline. Yet this discipline restrains the dissipation of that freedom: and this, God, is through your laws, your laws which, from the master's cane to the martyr's trials, have the power to make a blend of healthful bitterness, calling us back to you from these deadly pleasures in the enjoyment of which we become separated from you.

BERTRAN DE BORN

I take great pleasure in the joyous season of spring[†]

   I.   I take great pleasure in the joyous season of spring
        which makes leaves and flowers burst forth,
        and I am pleased when I listen to the gaiety
        of the birds, which make their song
5   resound through the woodlands;
        and I am pleased when I see across the meadows
        tents and pavilions pitched;
        and I feel great joy
        when I see lined up through the fields
10   armed knights and horses.

  II.   And I am pleased when the scouts
        put people to flight with their riches;
        and I am pleased when I see, following them,
        large crowds of armed men come together;

† From *Troubador Lyrics: A Bilingual Anthology*, ed. and trans. Frede Jensen. Copyright © 1998 by Peter Lang Publishing Inc., New York. Reprinted by permission of Peter Lang Publishing. This political sirventes "Be'm platz lo gais temps de pascor" ("I take great pleasure in the joyous season of spring") from the troubadour Bertran de Born (c. 1140–c. 1214) glorifies war, and illustrates Dante's conception of him as a "sower of discord" (*Inferno* XXVIII).

15   and it pleases me in my heart
when I see strong castles besieged
and the ramparts broken and fallen down,
and I see the host at the river's edge
surrounded on all sides by moats
20   protected by palisades of strong stakes.

III.   And I am also pleased with the lord
when he opens the battle
on horseback, armed, without fear,
for thus he makes his men take heart
25   from his own bravery.
And when the battle is under way,
each man must be ready
to follow him willingly,
for no man is worth anything
30   until he has taken and dealt many blows.

IV.   Maces and swords, colored helmets,
shields being broken and shattered,
we shall see at the beginning of the battle,
and many vassals clashing together,
35   and thus horses of the dead and wounded
shall roam aimlessly.
And when each man of noble lineage
has entered into battle,
let him think of nothing but breaking heads and arms,
40   for it is better to be dead than alive and defeated.

V.   And I tell you that I do not find such pleasure
in eating or drinking or sleeping
as I do when I hear people shout: "At them!"
from both sides, and I hear riderless horses
45   neighing in the shade,
and I hear people cry out: "Help! Help!",
and I see falling alongside the moats
the low and the mighty in the grass,
and I see the dead who, through their ribs,
50   have stumps of lances with silk pennons.

VI.   Barons, pawn your
castles, towns and cities
before you cease to make war on one another.

VII.   Papiol, go with good will and quickly
55   to Lord Yes-and-No
and tell him that he has been too long at peace.

GUIDO GUINIZELLI

Love returns always to a noble heart†

1. Love returns always to a noble heart
    Like a bird to the green in the forest.
    Nature did not make love before the noble heart,
    Nor the noble heart before love.
5   As soon as the sun appeared,
    Brightness shone forth,
    But it did not exist before the sun.
    And love takes its place in true nobility
    As rightly
10 As heat in the brightness of fire.

2. Love's fire catches in the noble heart,
    Like the power of a precious stone
    Whose potency does not descend from the star
    Until the sun makes it a noble object:
15 After the sun has drawn out
    Everything base with its own force,
    The star confers power on it.
    In such a way, a lady,
    Like the star, transforms the heart
20 Chosen by Nature and made pure and noble.

3. Love remains in the noble heart for the same reason
    That fire shines on the tip of a candle
    Clear and refined in its own delight.
    Nor could it be any other way—it is so proud.
25 Thus a baser nature
    Opposes love, just as water quenches
    Burning fire with its coldness.
    Love takes its place in the noble heart
    As its rightful dwelling
30 Like a diamond in a vein of ore.

4. Sun strikes the mud all day long;
    It remains base, nor does the sun lose heat.
    A proud man says, "I am made noble by birth."
    I liken him to the mud and noble worth to the sun.

† From *The Poetry of Guido Guinizelli*, ed. and trans. Robert Edwards. Copyright © 1987 by Robert Edwards. In this canzone "Al cor gentil rempaira sempre amore" ("Love returns always to a noble heart"), Guido Guinizelli (ca. 1230–1276) likens the lady to an angel and equates love as belonging only to the noble heart: two essential themes lent to the Dolce stil novo (the *Sweet New Style*).

35   No man should believe
      That nobility exists outside the heart
      By right of lineage,
      Unless he has a noble heart disposed to virtue,
      Just as water carries the sunray
40   And the sky holds the stars and their brightness.

5.   God the Creator shines in the Intelligence
      Of the heavens, more than even the sun in our eyes.
      It understands its maker beyond the sky
      And, turning the sky, prepares to obey Him;
45   And much as the blessed realization
      Of the just God follows instantly,
      So truly should the beautiful lady,
      When she shines in the eyes of her noble lover,
      Inspire a wish that he will never
50   Cease in his obedience to her.

6.   Lady, God will say to me when my soul
      Stands before Him, "How could you presume?
      You went past heaven, coming finally to me,
      And tried to compare Me to a vain love.
55   All praises are due to me alone
      And to the Queen of this noble realm
      Through whom all evil ends."
      But I shall say to Him, "She had the likeness
      Of an angel from your kingdom.
60   It's not my fault if I fell in love with her."

GUIDO CAVALCANTI

A lady bids me[†]

A lady bids me, and so I would speak
Of an accident that is often unruly
And so haughty that it is called love:
   Would that he who denies that were able to feel its truth!
   And for the present purpose I want someone nobly
5   knowledgeable,

[†] From *The Poetry of Guido Cavalcanti*, ed. and trans. Lowry Nelson, Jr. Copyright ©
1986 by Garland Publishing, Inc. "Donna me prega" ("A lady bids me") are the first
words from the ornate Italian canzone written by Dante's older contemporary and
"primo de li miei amici" (*Vita nuova* III), Guido Cavalcanti (ca. 1259–1300). In the poem
he describes love's workings.

As I do not expect that anyone base-hearted
   Could bring knowledge to such an argument:
For without philosophical demonstration
I have no intention of wishing to establish
10 Where it resides and who makes it exist,
   And what its virtue and potency may be,
Its essence next and each of its stirrings,
And the pleasurableness that makes it called love,
And whether one can show it to be visible.

15   In that part where memory resides,
[Love] takes its place—given its form, just as
Transparency is by light, by a darkness
   That comes from Mars—and makes its abode;
It is created and has a sensate name,
20 Is a habit of the soul and an intention of the heart.
   [Love] derives from a seen form that becomes intelligible,
That takes up place and dwelling
In the possible intellect as in a substance.
In that part [love] never has any power.
25   Since [the possible intellect] does not derive from quality,
It shines in itself as perpetual effect;
It does not have pleasure but rather contemplation;
And thus it cannot create an image.

   [Love] is not a faculty, but comes from that [faculty]
30 Which is a perfection (for so it is posited),
Not the rational do I mean, but the sensory;
   [Love] keeps its judgment independent of well-being,
Since intention is operative in place of reason:
It discriminates poorly for one to whom vice is a friend.
35   Death often follows on [love's] potency
If ever the [rational] power should be obstructed
That furthers the contrary course:
It is not because [love] is against nature
   But so far as by chance one is diverted from the perfect good,
40 One cannot say that one is alive,
For one has not established self-mastery.
A like result can obtain when one forgets [love].
   [Love's] mode of being is when desire is so strong
That it goes beyond nature's measure,
45 In that it never takes refreshment in rest.
   It goes about making the color change, turning
      laughter into tears,
And through fear it puts the image to flight;
It stays a brief while; moreover, you will see
   That it is to be found mostly in people of worth.

50 The extraordinary quality [of love] provokes sighs
And it desires that one gaze upon an unformed object,
Arousing one's anger that gives off fire
    (Who has not felt it cannot imagine it),
And that one not move at all when one is attracted,
55 And that one not turn elsewhere for enjoyment:
Of course one's mind has neither much nor little learning.

From a like temperament [love] draws a glance
That makes pleasure seem certain:
It cannot stay hidden once it is thus conjoined.
60 Beauties, but not uncouth ones, are an arrow,
For such longing is dispelled by fearing:
The spirit that is pierced gets its reward.
And [love] cannot be known by sight:
Perception of white is no help in perceiving such an object;
65 And (O he who listens well) form cannot be seen:
Even less, therefore, [love] that proceeds from [form].
Lacking in color, separate from being,
Set in dark surroundings, [love] eliminates light.
Without any deception, I say, as one worthy of trust,
70 That only from [such love] is favor born.

You, song, can safely go
Where you like, for I have so embellished you
That your argument will be greatly praised
By those persons who have understanding:
75 You have no desire to be with the others.

BONIFACE VIII

The One Holy, i.e., Church[†]

Boniface, Bishop, Servant of the servants of God. For perpetual remembrance:—

Urged on by our faith, we are obliged to believe and hold that there is one holy, catholic, and apostolic Church. And we firmly believe and profess that outside of her there is no salvation nor remission of sins, as the bridegroom declares in the Canticles, "My dove, my undefiled, is but one; she is the only one of her mother; she is

[†] From *History of the Christian Church* by Philip Schaff (vol. VI). Copyright © 1910 by Charles Scribner's Sons. *Unam sanctam*, (The One Holy, i.e. Church) a controversial papal bull decreed in 1302 by Pope Boniface VIII (1294–1303), postulates the supreme earthly and spiritual authority of the pope.

the choice one of her that bare her." And this represents the one
mystical body of Christ, and of this body Christ is the head, and
God is the head of Christ. In it there is one Lord, one faith, one bap-
tism. For in the time of the Flood there was the single ark of Noah,
which prefigures the one Church, and it was finished according to
the measure of one cubit and had one Noah for pilot and captain,
and outside of it every living creature on the earth, as we read, was
destroyed. And this Church we revere as the only one, even as the
Lord saith by the prophet, "Deliver my soul from the sword, my dar-
ling from the power of the dog." He prayed for his soul, that is, for
himself, head and body. And this body he called one body, that is,
the Church, because of the single bridegroom, the unity of the faith,
the sacraments, and the love of the Church. She is that seamless
shirt of the Lord which was not rent but was allotted by the casting
of lots. Therefore, this one and single Church has one head and not
two heads,—for had she two heads, she would be a monster,—that
is, Christ and Christ's vicar, Peter and Peter's successor. For the
Lord said unto Peter, "Feed my sheep." "My," he said, speaking gen-
erally and not particularly, "these and those," by which it is to be un-
derstood that all the sheep are committed unto him. So, when the
Greeks or others say that they were not committed to the care of Pe-
ter and his successors, they must confess that they are not of
Christ's sheep, even as the Lord says in John, "There is one fold and
one shepherd."

That in her and within her power are two swords, we are taught in
the Gospels, namely, the spiritual sword and the temporal sword.
For when the Apostles said, "Lo, here,"—that is, in the Church,—
are two swords, the Lord did not reply to the Apostles "it is too
much," but "it is enough." It is certain that whoever denies that the
temporal sword is in the power of Peter, hearkens ill to the words of
the Lord which he spake, "Put up thy sword into its sheath." There-
fore, both are in the power of the Church, namely, the spiritual
sword and the temporal sword; the latter is to be used for the
Church, the former by the Church; the former by the hand of the
priest, the latter by the hand of princes and kings, but at the nod
and sufferance of the priest. The one sword must of necessity be
subject to the other, and the temporal authority to the spiritual. For
the Apostle said, "There is no power but of God, and the powers that
be are ordained of God"; and they would not have been ordained un-
less one sword had been made subject to the other, and even as the
lower is subjected by the other for higher things. For, according to
Dionysius, it is a divine law that the lowest things are made by
mediocre things to attain to the highest. For it is not according to
the law of the universe that all things in an equal way and immedi-
ately should reach their end, but the lowest through the mediocre

and the lower through the higher. But that the spiritual power excels the earthly power in dignity and worth, we will the more clearly acknowledge just in proportion as the spiritual is higher than the temporal. And this we perceive quite distinctly from the donation of the tithe and functions of benediction and sanctification, from the mode in which the power was received, and the government of the subjected realms. For truth being the witness, the spiritual power has the functions of establishing the temporal power and sitting in judgment on it if it should prove to be not good.[1] And to the Church and the Church's power the prophecy of Jeremiah attests: "See, I have set thee this day over the nations and the kingdoms to pluck up and to break down and to destroy and to overthrow, to build and to plant."

And if the earthly power deviate from the right path, it is judged by the spiritual power; but if a minor spiritual power deviate from the right path, the lower in rank is judged by its superior; but if the supreme power [the papacy] deviate, it can be judged not by man but by God alone. And so the Apostle testifies, "He which is spiritual judges all things, but he himself is judged by no man." But this authority, although it be given to a man, and though it be exercised by a man, is not a human but a divine power given by divine word of mouth to Peter and confirmed to Peter and to his successors by Christ himself, whom Peter confessed, even him whom Christ called the Rock. For the Lord said to Peter himself, "Whatsoever thou shalt bind on earth," etc. Whoever, therefore, resists this power so ordained by God, resists the ordinance of God, unless perchance he imagine two principles to exist, as did Manichæus, which we pronounce false and heretical. For Moses testified that God created heaven and earth not in the beginnings but "in the beginning."

Furthermore, that every human creature is subject to the Roman pontiff,—this we declare, say, define, and pronounce to be altogether necessary to salvation.

* * *

1. This passage is based almost word for word upon Hugo de St. Victor, *De Sacramentis*, II. 2, 4.

CRITICISM

JOHN FRECCERO

Dante's Prologue Scene[†]

In the shadowy world of the prologue scene, things both are and are
not what they seem. For all its familiarity, the scenery seems to have
no real poetic existence independent of the allegorical statement it
was meant to convey. Moreover, the statement itself, judging from
the vast bibliography dedicated to it, is by no means obvious to the
contemporary reader. The ambiguous nature of the moral landscape
lends itself too readily to arbitrary allegorization, but scarcely to for-
mal analysis. In this respect, the prologue is radically unlike any
other part of the *Commedia* and matches the abortive journey of the
pilgrim with an apparent failure that is the poet's own.

The Region of Unlikeness

Any fresh interpretation of the prologue, if it is to contribute meas-
urably to our understanding, must not only attempt an exploration
of this well-travelled critical terrain, but also account for the pres-
ence, in this most substantial of poetic visions, of a region whose
outlines are decidedly blurred. It is such an accounting that I hope
to offer. My thesis is that the landscape in which the pilgrim finds
himself bears a striking, indeed at times a textual, resemblance to
the "region of unlikeness" in which the young Augustine finds him-
self in the seventh book of the *Confessions*. Moreover, the resem-
blance is not simply an isolated fact of purely historical interest but
is also of some significance for an interpretation of the poem. If the
point of departure, as well as the goal, of Dante's spiritual itinerary
deliberately recalls the experience of Augustine in the *Confessions*,
then it may be that we are to regard Dante's entire spiritual autobi-
ography as essentially Augustinian in structure.

There is good evidence, apart from the prologue scene, for consid-
ering Dante's poem as a spiritual testament in the manner of Augus-
tine. Toward the end of the *Purgatorio,* at a moment that is of great
dramatic importance, Beatrice calls to the pilgrim by name:

> in su la sponda del carro sinistra,
>   quando mi volsi al suon del nome mio,
>   che di necessità qui si registra,
> vidi la donna . . . (XXX, 61–64)

† From *Dante Studies* 84 (1966): 1–25. Copyright © 1966. Reprinted by permission of the
author.

Thus, in defiance of medieval convention, the author identifies him-
self with his protagonist, insisting that he does so "di necessità." The
apology is so pointed and the word "necessità" so strong that the
passage seems to call for some interpretation. It happens that in the
Convivio Dante had discussed the circumstances under which it
might be considered necessary to speak of oneself. One of his exam-
ples, precisely the *Confessions,* is described in terms that seem al-
most to herald Dante's own "testament":

> Per necessarie cagioni lo parlare di sè è conceduto: e intra l'al-
> tre necessarie cagioni due sono più manifeste. L'Una è
> quando sanza ragionare di sè grande infamia o pericolo non si
> può cessare . . . L' Altra è quando, per ragionare di sè, gran-
> dissima utilitade ne segue altrui per via di dottrina; e questra
> ragione mosse Agostino ne le sue confessioni a parlare di sè,
> *chè per lo processo de la sua vita, lo quale fu di [non] buono in*
> *buono, e di buono in migliore, e di migliore in ottimo, ne diede*
> *essemplo e dottrina, la quale per sì vero testimonio ricevere non*
> *si potea.*[1]

Critics have usually been content with rather generic explanations
for Dante's mention of his own name in the *Purgatorio,* none of
which seem as relevant as does this passage in the *Convivio.*[2] It is
clear from the beginning of the poem that Dante, like Augustine, in-
tends his work to have exemplary force for "*nostra* vita." Elsewhere
Dante makes this explicit, when he says that he writes "in pro del
mondo che mal vive" (*Purg.* XXXII, 103). By naming himself at the
moment of his confession, however, he gives to the abstract *exem-
plum* the full weight of *vero testimonio,* exactly as had St. Augustine
before him. Furthermore, the three stages of Augustine's progress
are described in the *Convivio* in terms that are partially echoed in
the *Paradiso:*

> È Bëatrice quella che sì scorge
>   *di bene in meglio,* sì subitamente
>   che l'atto suo per tempo non si sporge. (X, 37–39)

The phrase "di bene in meglio," for all of its apparent banality, has
technical force,[3] describing the second stage of the pilgrim's progress.

---

1. *Convivio* I, ii, 12.
2. See, for example, Natalino Sapegno. After quoting some early commentators, he con-
   cludes: "Qui insomma il nome esplicitamente pronunciato del protagonista non è segno
   di vanità, ma serve ad accrescer vergogna" [Here, in brief, the protagonist's name, explic-
   itly mentioned, is not a sign of vanity: it works as a way of increasing his shame]. *La Div.
   Com.* a cura di N.S. (Milano-Napoli: Ricciardi, 1957), *ad. loc.*
3. Richard of St. Victor uses an analogous phrase in a context where "transitus" means "con-
   version": "Qui transit de malo ad bonum, bene quidem transit; et qui transit de bono ad
   optimum, bonum et ipse transitum facit." *De exterminatione mali* I (*Patrologia Latina*
   196, 1074).

Beatrice is virtually defined here as the guide for the second stage of spiritual progress[4] in terms that the *Convivio* had used for the second stage of Augustine's conversion from sinner to saint: "di buono in migliore." It seems likely that in the *Convivio* Dante perceived in Augustine's life the same pattern of conversion that he was later to read retrospectively in his own experience.

Dante speaks of Augustine's life as giving an "essemplo," implying the transformation of personal experience into intelligible, perhaps even symbolic, form. We may observe in passing that it is the exemplary quality of the *Confessions* that distinguishes it from its modern descendants. Augustine's purpose is not to establish his own uniqueness (nor, therefore, innocence, in terms of the standards by which ordinary men are judged), but rather to demonstrate how the apparently unique experience was, from the perspective of eternity, a manifestation of Providence's design for all men. The scholarly debates about the historicity of Augustine's conversion scene, where a real garden in Milan seems to enclose the fig tree of Nathanael (John 1:48),[5] are paralleled by the scholarly debates about Beatrice who, on one hand, was a woman of flesh and blood and yet, on the other hand, seems to be surrounded at Dante's confession scene with unmistakably Christological language and mystery. The point is that in the "then" of experience, grace came in intensely personal form, whereas in the "now" of witness, the particular event is read retrospectively as a repetition in one's own history of the entire history of the Redemption. For both Dante and Augustine the exegetical language seems to structure experience, identifying it as part of the redemptive process, while the irreducibly personal elements lend to the *exemplum* the force of personal witness. Together, *exemplum* and experience, allegory and biography, form a confession of faith for other men.

Conversion, a death and resurrection of the self, is the experience that marks the difference between such confessions and facile counterfeits. In the poem, the difference between the attempt to scale the mountain, the journey that fails, and the successful journey that it prefigures is a descent in humility, a death of the self represented by the journey through hell. Augustine alludes briefly to a similar *askesis* in order to describe his suffering during his stay in Rome:

4. For Beatrice as guide for the second stage of Dante's spiritual progress, see C. S. Singleton, *Dante Studies 2: Journey to Beatrice* (Cambridge: Harvard University Press, 1958).
5. For the arguments against the *literal* historicity of the scene, see Pierre Courcelle, *Recherches sur les "Confessions" de Saint Augustin* (Paris: E. de Boccard, 1950), esp. pp. 188 ff. Courcelle answers some of his critics in *Les "Confessions" de Saint Augustin dans la tradition littéraire: Antécédents et postérité* (Paris: Etudes Augustiniennes, 1963), 191 ff. Both works were essential in the preparation of this study. Indeed, the present article might be considered simply an application of Courcelle's conclusions to the *Divine Comedy*.

And lo, there was I received by the scourge of bodily sickness, and I was going down to Hell, carrying all the sins which I had committed, both against Thee, and myself, and others, many and grievous, over and above that bond of original sin, whereby we all die in Adam. . . . So true, then, was the death of my soul, as that of His flesh seemed to me false; and how true the death of His body, so false was the life of my soul.[6]

The descent into hell, whether metaphorical as in the *Confessions,* or dramatically real as in Dante's poem, is the first step on the journey to the truth. It has the effect of shattering the inverted values of this life (which is death, according to Christian rhetoric) and transforming death into authentic life. The inversion of values is represented in Dante's poem by the curious prefiguration in the first canto of the ascent of the mountain of purgatory: the light at the summit, the mountain itself, the attempted climb. Although the landscape is analogous to the scenery that comes into sharper focus in the second *cantica,* all directions are reversed. What seems up is in fact down; what seems transcendence is in fact descent. Just as the reversed world of Plato's myth in the *Statesman* represented a world of negative values, so the reversed directions of the prologue stand for spiritual distortion. Augustine alludes in the seventh book to Plato's myth when he describes his spiritual world before his conversion as a "regio dissimilitudinis."[7] Although Dante nowhere uses the phrase, he borrowed several of Augustine's topographical details to describe his own spiritual condition.

Augustine's journey to God, like Dante's, is immediately preceded by a journey that fails, an attempt at philosophical transcendence in the seventh book of the *Confessions* that amounts to a conversion *manquée.* Lost in what he refers to as a "region of unlikeness," Augustine turns to the light of Platonic vision, only to discover that he is too weak to endure it. He is beaten back by the light and falls, weeping, to the things of this world. At that point in the narrative, the author asks himself why God should have given him certain books of neoplatonic philosophy to read before leading him to Scripture. He answers: "[So that] I might know the difference between presumption and confession; between those who saw where they were to go, yet saw not the way, and the way itself, that led not to behold only, but to

---

6. *Confessions* V, chap. 20. The translation is by E. B. Pusey (New York: Collier Books, 1961), p. 72.
7. For the "region of unlikeness" from Plato (*Statesman* 272e ff.) to Gide, see Courcelle's "répertoire" in *Les "Confessions"* . . . Appendice V, pp. 623–640. For relevant bibliography, see, by the same author, "Tradition néo-platonicienne et traditions chrétiennes de la 'région de dissemblance,'" in *Archives d'histoire doctrinale et littéraire du Moyen Age* XXXII–1957 (1958), 5–33.

dwell in the beatific country."[8] The answer applies exactly to the dramatic purpose of Dante's prologue scene.

There are some excellent reasons for believing Dante meant that first ascent to be read as a purely *intellectual* attempt at conversion, where the mind sees its objective but is unable to reach it. After the pilgrim's fear is somewhat quieted, the poet uses a famous simile:

> E come quei che con lena affannata,
> uscito fuor del pelago a la riva,
> si volge a l'acqua perigliosa e guata,
> così *l'animo mio, ch'ancor fuggiva,*
> si volse a retro a rimirar lo passo
> che non lasciò già mai persona viva.
> Poi ch'èi posato un poco *il corpo lasso,*
> ripresi via per la piaggia diserta,
> sì che 'l piè fermo sempre era
> 'l più basso. (I, 22–30)

Charles Singleton has called our attention to the shift, in these lines, from the flight of an *animo,* the mind of the pilgrim, to the lagging of a *corpo lasso,* a tired body.[9] He was primarily concerned with the radical shift in poetic tone, the beginning of what he referred to as Dante's vision "made flesh." It should be observed that such a shift, besides being a radical poetical departure, has a precise conceptual significance in this context. The whole reason for the failure of all such journeys of the mind resides precisely in that laggard body. The *animo* is perfectly willing, but it is joined to flesh that is bound to fail.

The phrase "l'animo mio ch'ancor fuggiva" has an unmistakable philosophical ring. For one thing, the word *animo* is decidedly intellectual, rather than theological in meaning, quite distinct from the more common *anima.* For another, the phrase recalls, or at least would have recalled to the Church fathers, the flight of the soul from the terrestrial to the spiritual realm according to the Platonists and especially to Plotinus. In the *Enneads,* the latter urges such a flight: "Let us therefore flee to our dear homeland . . . But what manner of flight is this? . . . it is not with our feet that it can be accomplished, for our feet, no matter where they take us, take us only from one land to another; nor must we prepare for ourselves a team of horses or a ship . . . it is rather necessary to change our sight and look with the inner eye."[1]

---

8. *Conf.* VII, 20. Pusey, p. 112.
9. *Dante Studies 1: Commedia: Elements of Structure* (Cambridge, Mass.: Harvard University Press, 1954), pp. 11–12.
1. *Enneads* I, 8. Courcelle's chap. III, "La découverte du néo-platonisme chrétien" in his *Recherches* is dedicated to Ambrose's borrowing from Plotinus and its influence on Augustine. Section 2 (pp. 106 ff) in particular is devoted to the influence of this chapter from the *Enneads* on Ambrose and Augustine. The text we quote is cited by Courcelle, p. 111.

This flight of the soul by means of the "interior eye" was destined to have an interesting history. It is perhaps the ancestor of Dante's abortive journey. The point of it is that the Plotinian sage can safely ignore his body in his attempts at ecstasy. By chance this passage was well known in the Middle Ages, having been paraphrased, indeed almost translated, as Pierre Courcelle has shown, by St. Ambrose. In one of his sermons, he adds an interesting detail to Plotinus' exhortation: "Let us therefore flee to our true homeland . . . But what manner of flight is this? It is not with our bodily feet that it is accomplished, for our steps, no matter where they run, take us only from one land to another. Nor let us flee in ships, in chariots, or with horses that stumble and fall, but let us flee with our minds (*fugiamus animo*), with our eyes or with our interior feet."[2] It is not essential, for my purposes, to suggest that Dante knew this passage, although there is no reason why he could not have. The phrase *fugiamus animo* is not so bizarre that its resemblance to Dante's phrase could establish it as the poet's source. But even if Dante did not know it, the point can still be made that since Ambrose's phrase was meant to sound Platonic, it is likely that the similar phrase, "l'animo mio ch'ancor fuggiva," especially in a context of failure, was likewise meant by Dante to have philosophical rather than theological force.

The division between body and soul was of course a commonplace in ancient "flights" of the soul. For Christians, however, it was not the body *per se* that constituted the impediment, but rather the fallen flesh. It is not physical reality that the soul must flee, but sin itself. Before looking at Augustine's view of the dichotomy, it might be well to show how a less original thinker saw the effect of the division of body and soul in the psychology of conversion. Gregory the Great provides us with the kind of theological context in which I believe we are to read the "animo" and "corpo" of Dante's verses. His remarks are suggestive, too, for a reading of the impediments that beset the pilgrim:

> Indeed, one suffers initially after conversion, considering one's past sins, wishing to break immediately the bonds of secular concerns, to walk in tranquillity the ways of the Lord, to throw off the heavy burden of earthly desires and in free servitude to put on the light yoke of God. Yet while one thinks of these things, there arises a familiar delight in the flesh which quickly takes root. The longer it holds on, the tighter it becomes, the later does one manage to leave it behind. What suffering in such a situation, what anxiety of the heart! *When the spirit calls and the flesh calls us back.* On one hand the intimacy of a

---

2. *Liber de Isaac et anima* VIII, 79 (*PL* 14, 559), Courcelle, *Recherches*, p. 111.

new love invites us, on the other the old habits of vice hold us back.[3]

This is the "flesh" that was ignored by Plotinus in his rather optimistic invitation to the soul to fly to the Truth.

To return to Ambrose's influential statement for a moment, we notice that he added the detail of the "interior feet" to Plotinus' remarks. No reader of Dante's first canto can fail to remember that after resting his tired body, the pilgrim sets off to his objective "sì che 'l piè fermo sempre era 'l più basso." In another essay, * * * I attempt to explain the meaning of that verse in terms of the allegory of the "interior feet" of the soul.[4] The "piè fermo" signifies the pilgrim's will, unable to respond to the promptings of the reason because of the Pauline malady, characteristic of fallen man whose mind far outstrips the ability of a wounded will to attain the truth. The fallen will limps in its efforts to reach God. Augustine, who uses the theme in a submerged way, was himself very probably Dante's direct source for the image of an *homo claudus,* unable to advance to the summit. In a passage from the *Confessions* paraphrasing precisely the Plotinian, then Ambrosian passage, Augustine insists upon the inability of a crippled will to complete the journey. He does so with an extended comparison of the movement of the limbs with the movement of the will:

> I was troubled in spirit, most vehemently indignant that I entered not into Thy Will and Covenant, O my God, which all my bones cried out unto me to enter, and praised it to the skies. And therein we enter not by ships, or chariots, or feet, nor move not so far as I had come from the house to that place where we were sitting. For, not to go only, but to go *in* thither was nothing else but to will to go, but to will resolutely and thoroughly; not to turn and toss, this way and that, *a maimed and half-divided will, struggling, with one part sinking as another rose.*[5]

In this magnificent passage, Augustine uses Platonic words and turns them against the Platonists. The goal is not some world of Ideas, but the covenant of Jehovah. Moreover, the problem is not of

3. *Moralia* XXIV, cap. XI [*Rec.* VII], PL 76, 300. It is clear from the context that Gregory is talking about the first stage of conversion, presumably before the reception of sanctifying grace. In the figure of Exodus which he subsequently applies to his analysis (col. 301), this stage corresponds to the crossing of the desert, between the crossing of the Red Sea and the crossing of the Jordan. This is precisely the stage at which the pilgrim finds himself here. See Singleton, "In Exitu Israel de Aegypto," 78*th Annual Report of the Dante Society* (1960), reprinted in *Dante: A Collection of Critical Essays,* ed. J. Freccero (Englewood Cliffs, New Jersey: Prentice-Hall, 1965), p. 105, where Singleton quotes a passage further on in this chapter of the *Moralia.*
4. Freccero, "Dante's Firm Foot . . ." *Harvard Theological Review,* LII, 3 (October, 1959), 246–281.
5. *Conf.* VIII, 8; Pusey, p. 126.

the body as a purely physical impediment, but rather of the fallen and crippled will, shortcomings the Platonists had not considered. As Augustine was unable to achieve the ecstasy of the Platonists, so Dante's pilgrim is unable to reach the truth of the mind with a will that "sempre era 'l più basso." The parallel is close enough to suggest on Dante's part a conscious evocation.

Apart from the parallels between Dante's journey and Augustine's with respect both to the need for the journey and to the fatal flaws in the wayfarers, there are also parallels to be drawn with regard to the objective. The light of God, even as perceived with the neoplatonic eyes of the soul, proves too much for Augustine in the seventh book of his *Confessions:* "And Thou didst beat back the weakness of my sight, streaming forth Thy beams of light upon me most strongly, and I trembled with love and awe: and I perceived myself to be far off from Thee, in the region of unlikeness, as if I heard this Thy voice from on high: 'I am the food of grown men, grow, and thou shalt feed upon Me.'"[6] In spite of his repeated attempts to reach the light, the weight of "fleshly habit" causes him to fall back, "sinking with sorrow into these inferior things—*ruebam in ista cum gemitu.*"[7] Dante might well have been remembering that phrase when he described himself as beaten back by the wolf: "i' rovinava in basso loco." Augustine seems to hear the voice of God in the light that he sees. The synaesthetic effect is rhetorically appropriate in this interior journey, for all of the senses here stand for movements of the mind, moved by a single God in all of His various manifestations. It may not be purely coincidental that Dante also insists on a mystical synaesthesia in his experience. After he is beaten back to the dark wood, he describes it as the place "dove 'l sol tace." The implication is that the light which he saw before spoke to him with a voice that was divine.

Pierre Courcelle has traced Augustine's "vain attempts at Plotinian ecstasy" back to their neoplatonic sources.[8] What emerges clearly from his study is that the ancients saw no need for a guide on such a journey. Plotinus explicitly says that one requires self-confidence to reach the goal, rather than a guide.[9] This self-confidence was precisely what Augustine interpreted as philosophical pride, the element that in his view vitiated all such attempts. His own interior journey begins with an insistence upon his need for help: "And being thence admonished to return to myself, I entered even into my inward self, *Thou being my Guide:* and able I was, for *Thou wert become my Helper.* And I entered and beheld with the eye of my soul (such as it

6. *Ibid.* VII, 10; Pusey, p. 107.
7. *Ibid.* 17; p. 109–110.
8. *Recherches,* pp. 157–167: "Les vaines tentatives d'extases plotiniennes."
9. *Enneads* I, 6; Courcelle, *Les "Confessions,"* p. 49.

was), above the same eye of my soul, above my mind, the Light Un-
changeable."[1] Christian virtue, unlike Socratic virtue, is more than
knowledge and vice is more than ignorance. The Platonic conver-
sion toward the light is doomed to failure because it neglects to take
account of man's fallen condition. To put the matter in Platonic
terms, the pilgrim must struggle even to reach the cave from which
Plato assumed the journey began. That struggle, the descent in hu-
mility, helps remove the barrier that philosophy leaves intact. God's
guidance, represented dramatically in the poem by the pilgrim's
three guides, transforms philosophical presumption into Christian
confession. St. Bernard, an outspoken critic of philosophical pre-
sumption, speaks of the opposition between humility and pride in
the itinerary to God. His remarks serve as an excellent illustration of
how familiar Augustine's struggle was in the Middle Ages and of how
readily the struggle lent itself to dramatization in terms that are
strikingly like Dante's:

> "Who dares climb the mountain of the Lord or who will stand
> in His holy place?" . . . Only the humble man can safely climb
> the mountain, because only the humble man has nothing to
> trip him up. The proud man may climb it indeed, yet he cannot
> stand for long . . . The proud man has only one foot to stand
> on: love of his own excellence . . . Therefore to stand firmly, we
> must stand humbly. So that our feet may never stumble we
> must stand, not on the single foot of pride, but on the two feet
> of humility.[2]

There can be scarcely any doubt that Dante's pilgrim climbs the
mountain in the same tradition.

The final passage from Augustine's seventh book provides a series
of images which offer the closest analogue to the landscape with
which Dante begins his poem. The theme is humility, which pro-
vides a transition to the eighth book, from attempts at Plotinian ec-
stasy to the conversion under the fig tree. Speaking of Christ against
the philosophers he says:

> They disdain to learn of Him, because He is gentle and humble
> of heart; for these things hast Thou hid from the wise and pru-
> dent, and hast revealed them unto babes. For it is one thing,
> from a wooded mountain-top (*de silvestre cacumine*) to see the

---

1. *Conf.* VII, 10; p. 107. Courcelle (*Les "Confessions,"* p. 51) shows that in his insistence on
the need for a guide, Augustine is much closer to Philo than to Plotinus. In the *De migra-
tione Abraham,* Philo states that it is precisely because they were not presumptuous but
were guided by God that Moses and Abraham were able to see the light (*De migr. Abr.* VII,
ed. Cadiou, *Sources chrétiennes* XLVII [Paris, 1957], p. 70).
2. St. Bernard, Letter to William, Patriarch of Jerusalem, No. 217 in his *Letters,* trans. B. S.
James (London: Burns, Oates, 1953), p. 296. I am indebted to Professor Morton Bloom-
field of Harvard for having first drawn my attention to this passage.

land of peace and to find no way thither; and in vain to essay
through ways unpassable, opposed and beset by fugitives and
deserters, under their captain the lion and the dragon: and an-
other to keep on the way that leads thither, guarded by the host
of the heavenly General (*cura caelestis imperatoris*); where they
spoil not who have deserted the heavenly army (*qui caelestem
militiam deseruerunt*)[3]

The Augustinian phrase, "de silvestre cacumine," may at first seem a
trifle remote as an analogue for the "selva oscura," but if we read on
in the *Confessions* we find that Augustine elaborates on the descrip-
tion of his former life with an alternate image: "In this so vast
wilderness [*immensa silva*], full of snares and dangers, behold many
of them I have cut off and thrust out of my heart."[4] Of greater sig-
nificance is the fact that elements of the former passage echo not
only in the first canto of the *Inferno,* but perhaps also in the eighth
canto of the *Purgatorio.* In other words, there seem to exist between
the two authors not only analogies of detail but also of structure, for
in these few lines Augustine distinguishes between success and fail-
ure in the journey to God by a series of oppositions that match the
opposition between the journey of the prologue and the successful
journey that it foreshadows. One need only paraphrase Augustine
in Dantesque terms in order to make this apparent: it is one thing
to be beset by wild beasts and quite another to be guarded by the
"essercito gentile" (*Purg.* VIII, 22) of the "imperador che là sù
regna" (*Inf.* I, 124), safe from the chief deserter, " 'l nostro avver-
saro" (*Purg.* VIII, 95).

A further word must be said here about the most famous image of
the prologue scene, that of the "selva oscura." If we are in fact deal-
ing in the prologue with an attempt at transcendence that is neopla-
tonic in origin, then the temptation is strong to identify Dante's
"selva" with the prime matter of Plato's *Timaeus,* the traditional en-
emy of philosophical flights of the soul. The Greek word for matter,
hylē, was rendered into Latin as "silva" by Chalcidius and the phrase
"silva Platonis" became proverbial in the Middle Ages. Bernardus
Silvestris uses the word with a force that sometimes suggests a to-
tally unchristian equation of matter with evil: *silva rigens, praepon-
derante malitia, silvestris malignitas.*[5] Some critics recently have
attempted to associate Dante's "selva" with the Platonic "silva,"
thereby reviving a gloss that goes back to the Renaissance commen-

3. VII, 21; Pusey, pp. 113–114. (I have corrected Pusey's rendering of the phrase "de sil-
vestre cacumine.")
4. X, 35; Pusey, p. 181.
5. On Bernardus and the question of his dualism, as well as relevant bibliography, see E.
Garin, *Studi sul platonismo medievale* (Florence: Le Monnier, 1958) pp. 54 ff.: "Le 'cos-
mogonie' di Chartres."

tary of Cristoforo Landino.[6] The gloss runs the risk, however, of leading to a serious misunderstanding. In the dark wood, we are not dealing with man's hylomorphic composition, but rather with *sin*. Landino's facile equation, "corpo, cioè vizio" will not do for the "selva," for it obscures the fundamental point of Christianity's quarrel with metaphysical dualism. Ultimately, to obscure the difference between "corpo" and "vizio" is to forget the doctrine of the Incarnation and this Dante was no more likely to forget than was Augustine, who spent much of his life refuting the Manicheans.

Nevertheless, it is possible to show that Dante used the opposition "selva–luce" in exactly the same way that he used the opposition "corpo–animo"; that is, as a Platonic commonplace used to signify a struggle of which the Platonists were unaware. The distinctive characteristic of the dark wood in Dante's poem is not that it is a *selva*, but rather that it is *oscura*, as the following textual parallel reveals:

Già m'avean transportato
    i lenti *passi*
dentro a *la selva antica*
    tanto, ch'io
	Nel mezzo del *cammin*
	    di nostra vita
	mi ritrovai per *una*
	    selva oscura

	. . . . .

non potea rivedere *ond'*
    io mi 'ntrassi;
	Io non so ben ridir com'
	    i' v'intrai

	. . . . .

ed ecco più andar mi tolse
    un rio
    (*Purg.* XXVIII, 22–25)
	Ed ecco, quasi al cominciar
	    de l'erta
	    (*Inf.* I, 1–2, 10, 31)

The resemblance can hardly be fortuitous. Dante's descent into hell and his ascent of the mountain of purgatory bring him to a point from which he can begin his climb to the light, his entrance into sanctifying grace, without fear of the impediments that blocked his way before. That new point of departure, the garden of Eden, was the home of man before the fall. Through Adam's transgression, the prelapsarian state of man was transformed into the state of sin. In poetic terms, Adam transformed the *selva antica* into a *selva oscura*. Although the "rio" forever separates the pilgrim from original justice and Matelda, he can, with the help of Beatrice, go far beyond:

> "Qui sarai tu poco tempo *silvano;*
>   e sarai meco sanza fine cive
> di quella Roma onde Cristo è romano.
>   (*Purg.* XXXII, 100–102)

6. For a most recent view, as well as bibliography, see the forthcoming article by F. X. Newman, "St. Augustine's Three Visions and the Structure of the *Commedia*," in *Modern Language Notes*, LXXXII, No. 1 (Jan. 1967).

To say that the pilgrim is a *silvano* is to say that he still inhabits the *selva* of human existence; only in the *selva* darkened by sin, what Dante called "la selva erronea di questa vita,"[7] does it become impossible to follow the path to the heavenly city.

Augustine chose to describe the impediments on his journey to the mountain top in terms of the wild beasts of the Psalms, the lion and the dragon. Dante, on the other hand, described them in terms of the three beasts of Jeremiah 5:6. I take these to be the basic wounds to the rational, irascible, and concupiscent appetites suffered by all men as a result of the fall. * * * [8] What is of particular poetic interest here is that in the text of Jeremiah, those three beasts are said to be enemies of all the sinners of Jerusalem. The question is, why should the three beasts associated with Jerusalem, the promised land, be the obstacles to the pilgrim in his climb?

The answer, I believe, resides in the fact that the pilgrim's goal is in a sense Jerusalem, or at least the heavenly Jerusalem, although he cannot know that until he reaches it, which is to say, until he assumes the perspective of the poet. Earlier I suggested that both Augustine and Dante used scriptural exegesis in order to structure their experience, superimposing (or discovering, they would insist) a biblical pattern of meaning upon their own history. Thus far I have tried to compare the shadowy world of the pilgrim with Augustine's region of unlikeness. There is nothing shadowy abut the interpretative view of the poet, however, for, as Charles Singleton has shown, part of the poet's strategy is to introduce into both the prologue and the *Purgatorio,* superimposed upon the narrative, the *figura* which was considered to be the pattern of conversion.[9] We have already cited the verses that relate the emergence from the dark wood to the crossing of a "passo" through the open sea. Again, as the pilgrim struggles up the slope of the mountain, the poet refers to him as being in a "gran diserto," as far from woods or water as can be imagined. Finally, when the wolf blocks the pilgrim's passage, Lucy, looking down from heaven, sees him as though he were standing before a flooded river of death, weeping and unable to cross.[1] In the sea, desert, and river, any medieval exegete would discern the three stages of the exodus of the Jews, en route from Egypt to Jerusalem, the promised land.

In this respect too, Dante probably owed much to the Augustinian tradition. For the representation of his attempts at purely intellectual conversion, Augustine drew upon the traditional neoplatonic

---

7. *Convivio* IV, xxiv, 12.
8. Freccero, "Dante's Firm Foot," p. 274 ff.
9. "In Exitu," p. 105.
1. J. Freccero, "The River of Death: *Inf.* II, 108," in *The World of Dante,* ed. Chandler and Molinaro (Toronto: Toronto University Press, 1966), pp. 25–42.

motifs of the conversion to the light. At the same time, he reinter-
preted those motifs in the light of Revelation. On at least one occa-
sion, the death of Monica, his allusion to the figure of exodus is
explicit: "May they [God's servants] with devout affection remember
my parents in this transitory light, my brethren under Thee our Fa-
ther in our Catholic Mother, and my fellow-citizens in that eternal
Jerusalem which Thy pilgrim people sigheth after from their Exo-
dus, even unto their return thither."[2] There may be as well an allu-
sion to the exodus in the passage in the seventh book, which seems
so important for Dante's representation: "For it is one thing, from
the wooded mountain top to see the land of peace and to find no
way thither." In the sixteenth century, the passage was annotated
with a reference to Deut. 32:48–52, where Moses is permitted by
God to see the land of Canaan from the mountain, but not to reach
it: "Yet thou shalt see the land before thee; but thou shalt not go
thither unto the land which I give the children of Israel."[3]

These references are admittedly too few to enable us to demon-
strate that the presence of the figure of exodus is of importance in
Augustine's narrative, but if Augustine was merely allusive with re-
spect to the figure, commentators on his work throughout the Mid-
dle Ages were explicit. Courcelle's repertory of commentaries on the
"region of unlikeness" provides many citations that are suggestive for
the interpretation of Dante's prologue scene. Among them are sev-
eral which specifically relate Augustine's conversion to the tradi-
tional biblical figure of conversion. Richard of St. Victor will serve
as an example:

> The first miracle was accomplished in the exodus of Israel from
> Egypt (*In exitu Israel de Aegypto*), the second was in the exodus
> of Israel from the desert. Who will give me the power to leave
> behind the region of unlikeness? Who will enable me to enter
> the promised land, so that I may see both the flight of the sea
> and the turning back of the Jordan.[4]

Richard makes clear, first of all, that Egypt is a state of mind, and,
secondly, that even after leaving it, the soul must traverse a desert
region which is precisely like the "gran diserto" in which the pilgrim
is blocked: "Coming forth from the darkness of Egypt, from worldly
error to the more secret places of the heart, you discover nothing
else but a place of terror and vast solitude. This is that desert land,
arid and unpassable . . . filled with all terrible things."[5] In this desert

2. *Conf*. IX, 13; Pusey, pp. 151–152.
3. The annotation is contained in the translation of William Watts (1631), reprinted in the
Loeb Library edition of the *Confessions* (Cambridge, 1951) I, 399.
4. *Op. cit*. (a propos of Psalm 113), col. 1073, cited in part by Courcelle, *Les "Confessions,"*
p. 635.
5. *Ibid*., col. 1076.

place, where "all is confused, all is disturbed; where nothing is in its proper place, nothing proceeds in proper order,"[6] the impediments one encounters are the vices and passions (usually three-fold, according to Augustine's commentators)[7] to which man is subject, since "vulnerati sumus ingredientes mundum"[8] (we are already wounded when we enter the world).

RENATO POGGIOLI

Tragedy or Romance? A Reading of the Paolo and Francesca Episode in Dante's *Inferno*†

I

As every schoolboy knows, Dante classified the sins punished in the *Inferno* in descending order, going from transgressions caused by the abuse of our normal instincts down to the graver violations involving perfidy and malice, which both deface the nobility of the human soul and sever us from our fellow men. So, even before crossing the passage from the first to the second circle, we know that there we shall find damned souls worthy still of tears of pity. The damned of the second circle, carnal sinners, are men and women who have subjected their nobler impulses to the animal urges of the flesh. Foremost in the ranks of these stand Paolo and Francesca, and their story is in a certain sense the first truly infernal episode.

The scene is one of tender pity, but not of forgiveness or indulgence. Dante does not absolve those whom God has condemned for eternity. Here Dante the protagonist of his own poem is just beginning his "pilgrim's progress." Only gradually will he learn and accept the stern lesson of the wages of sin. Dante the author and narrator of his own metaphysical experience sees already with perfect fullness the absolute harmony between God's justice and God's will. Thus what to the heart of Dante the pilgrim may still appear as the "tragedy" of human life, for the mind of Dante the poet has become but a minor interlude in the sublime "comedy" of the divine order.

6. William of St. Thierry, *De nat. et dign. amoris* XI, 34 (*PL* 184, 401); Courcelle, *Ibid.*, p. 625.
7. Usually, *voluptas, concupiscentia, inanis gloria*, or *concupiscentia carnis, concupiscentia oculorum, superbia vitae*, following Augustine in Book X. See the texts of Courcelle, *Ibid.*, pp. 632–633.
8. St. Bernard, *De diversis sermo* XLII, 2 (*PL* 183, 661); Courcelle, *Ibid.*, p. 627.
† From *PMLA* 72 (1957): 313–58. Copyright © 1957 by MLA. Reprinted by permission of the Modern Language Association of America.

The author is morally detached, but artistically involved, and produces therefore one of the most moving episodes in the poem. One could say that the entire Paolo and Francesca story is based on a continuous tension between the ethos of contemplation and the pathos of experience. The artistic achievement lies in the fact that the poem reconciles within itself Dante the witness of the wretched misery of man, and Dante the beholder of the awful majesty of God.

II

The very opening of the episode rings with a sharply pathetic accent:

> Ora incomincian le dolenti note
> a farmisi sentire; or son venuto
> là dove molto pianto mi percote.[1]

The verb by which Dante suggests the impression made on him by the vocal grief of the sinners ("smites me," *mi percote*) is the same by which he will later describe the torments inflicted on the damned by the storm preying on them: and this parallelism indicates that pity itself acts on man as a kind of blow.

After this prelude, the poet represents in stark outlines the place which in the meantime he has finally reached:

> Io venni in luogo d'ogni luce muto,
> che mugghia come fa mar per tempesta,
> se da contrari venti è combattuto.

The place is devoid of light, but full of the sound and fury of a formidable hurricane. The expression *d'ogni luce muto*, "mute of all light," combining, as it does, optical and acoustic impressions, is powerfully suggestive, since the absolute absence of light, its "silence," as the poet says, parallels and balances the deafening roar of the elements. That hurricane, after all, is not a normal or natural one: and Dante tries to approximate its supernatural power by comparing it to a sea storm, battled by opposing blasts and streams. The similitude is quite proper since the ravaging force of the convulsed air mass carries along on the crest of its invisible waves the floating souls of the damned, tossing them around like the victims of a shipwreck:

> La bufera infernal, che mai non resta,
> mena li spirti con la sua rapina:
> voltando e percotendo li molesta.

---

1. All quotations from the episode (*Inferno* v.25–142) follow the text of the Società Dantesca Italiana as published in *Le opere di Dante* (Florence, 1921).

Unlike the tempests raging over our earth, the infernal hurricane knows neither interruption nor end: so that the sinners can expect neither that their ordeal will cease, nor that the implacable wind whirling and smiting them will grant respite:

> Quando giungon davanti alla ruina,
> quivi le strida, il compianto, il lamento:
> bestemmian quivi la virtù divina.

The suffering of the damned is made worse by the awareness that any time the rotating hurricane rejoins a given point within the walls of the second circle, their torture will rise again to a pitch of intolerable acuteness. This happens when the surge of the storm breaks against what Dante calls *la ruina* or "the landslide": perhaps a breach in the rocky side of the infernal abyss, which suddenly changes the gale into an aerial maelstrom. It is here that the shrieks of the sinners, up to now hardly audible over the noise of the blast, resound even higher than the crash of the storm. Dante evokes this shouting and crying with a threefold series of words, forming, by a varied gradation of intensity and meaning, a kind of musical diminuendo. The first to wound our ears are the *strida,* or loud cries, of the sinners; then the *compianto,* or their choral plaint; finally, the *lamento,* or faint groan. The line built around these three words ends by giving, paradoxically, also a crescendo effect: its slow rhythm, prolonged in a waning and softening trail of sounds, conveys powerfully the sinners' total powerlessness and exhaustion, and the merciless cruelty of the wind. Yet any further insistence on the plight of the damned would provoke a sense of insufferable anguish: so, to avoid a new excess of pathos, the poet hastens to remind us that that shouting and crying is also a "gnashing of teeth," something lower and viler than an articulate expression of human grief. Those souls are not guileless martyrs, but victims of their own guilt: and they show their everlasting wickedness by still rebelling in thoughts and words against the "divine virtue," by cursing the hand that chastizes them for their sins. Dante acknowledges all this, and recognizes them for what they are:

> Intesi ch' a cosí fatto tormento
> enno dannati i peccator carnali,
> che la ragion sommettono al talento.

Without explanation from Vergil, Dante has immediately guessed they are men and women who submitted the high claims of human reason to the yearnings of the brute. This recognition is based on the law of *contrapasso,* or "retribution," wherein the punishment fits the crime, by a parallel or contrasting analogy with the very nature of the sin. Since the tempestuous violence of their lust led them astray, they are punished by being dragged by a wind which, unlike the storms of our flesh and blood, will never pause or rest. The infernal hurricane is thus to be understood as a reality both physical and metaphysical, operating on the literal as well as on the figurative plane. The immediacy of Dante's realization is meaningful also in another subtler and more private sense. It may suggest a discreet autobiographical hint, and act as an implied confession that the poet as a man knew all too well the temptations of concupiscence and all too often yielded to them. Such are the manifold allusions contained in the simple opening verb, in the little word *intesi*: "I understood."

III

Up to now Dante has devoted his almost undivided attention to the massive, anonymous, elemental violence of the storm, as shown by the frequence of such words as *tempesta*, "gale"; *bufera*, "hurricane"; *rapina*, "rapine"; and *ruina*, "landslide." Now he is looking instead at the human prey of that violence: and he describes the crowd of the sinners as if they were a flock of birds, flying along with the wind. The main part of the canto's imagery will be based on a recurring bird motif, developed in three successive, and almost contiguous, similitudes, each one of which compares the sinners with a different species of birds. Since the souls hover forever in the air, so the birds are always described in a similar state of suspension: not as they appear when at rest, or when they stay on the ground. In this first simile the spirits are likened to a flock of starlings; and in order to make the likeness even more striking, the poet emphasizes the size of the flock, thus anticipating further statements as to the swarming multitude of the souls:

> E come li stornei ne portan l'ali
> nel freddo tempo a schiera larga e piena,
> cosí quel fiato li spiriti mali.[2]

One of the new things we learn from the image is that Dante and Vergil, who in the meanwhile must have come to a standstill, are now staring at the sinners from a particular point of view. The epithets by which Dante gives the first visual impression of the "troop" are "large and full" (*schiera larga e piena*). They indicate that the

---

2. This is the only point where I fail to follow the text of the Dantesca. Instead of closing the verse just quoted with a period, as I have done on the authority of other editors, the Dantesca joins the final sentence with the opening line of the following verse, in this way:

> E come li stornei ne portan l' ali
> nel freddo tempo a schiera larga e piena,
> cosí quel fiato li spiriti mali
> di qua, di là, di giú, di su li mena . . .

crowd of the damned is now facing the travelers in a sort of front formation, unfolding itself in the dimension of breadth, so that the eyes of the two pilgrims are now perceiving only the wide and thick first line of the troop, while they may only glimpse or guess the rows or files arrayed behind it. But the simile also contains references to things we already know. So the allusion to the bleakness of the season, to the *freddo tempo* or "cold weather" in which the flight of the starlings is taking place, suggests a similarity between that climatic condition and the darkness of the air of the second circle, a detail to which Dante attracts the reader's attention in several passages of the canto. The poet completes this series of correspondences between the scene and the image by developing the most important of all their common traits; and he does so by describing the motion of the birds in terms identical with the motion of the shades, or as a passive rather than as an active process. Since the sinners do not move on their own power, but are pushed and pulled by the wind, so likewise the movement of the starlings is seen as caused not by their will, but by the automatic action of their wings, which are treated as organs different from and independent of the birds themselves. Yet this willful and arbitrary equivalence is deliberately misleading, since it distracts our attention from the devastating power of the hurricane, thus attenuating the impression of its irresistible force. This new, implicit diminuendo is made evident by the use of the term *fiato*, "breath," to indicate, by way of understatement, the action of the wind.[3]

Such a softening of the elemental brutality of the punishing and torturing storm betrays a new undercurrent of pathos in the poet's mood: but Dante reverses that trend immediately by breaking the equivalence between the vision and its metaphorical vehicle, and by recalling to himself and his readers that those men and women are "evil spirits" (*spiriti mali*), not innocent birds. So, quite naturally, the opening line of the following stanza, with its merciless beat, evokes again the inexorability of the hurricane, hurling the souls in all directions, as if they were senseless things, while the remainder of the terzina conveys again the hopelessness of damnation, the absolute despair of a condition which admits neither end nor relief:

> Di qua, di là, di giú, di su li mena;
> nulla speranza li conforta mai,
> non che di posa, ma di minor pena.

After having restrained the string of pathos, Dante slightly relaxes it again. As we have already noticed, the mainstream of this canto

---

3. *Fiato* means in Italian also "wind," but hardly "blast," as Norton renders it in his *Translation* (Boston, 1891–93).

waves and shifts between the opposite poles of the stern acceptance of the designs of God's justice, and a feeling of compassion for the objects of God's wrath. The spectacle of the sinners' fate brings in, in the usual alternation, another wave of pity, and along with it a new comparison with another troop of birds. This time the damned are likened to a flight of cranes:

> E come i gru van cantando lor lai,
> faccendo in aere di sé lunga riga,
> cosí vidi venir, traendo guai,
>
> ombre portate dalla detta briga . . .

Since Dante's sensitive attention is now attuned to the lamenting voices of the tormented, the detail standing out from this second simile concerns the singing of those birds, and the sadness of their song. Such is the suggestion contained in the word *lai*, "lays," which Dante uses both in its general sense of complaint, and in a more special and technical meaning, designating a particular kind of medieval poetry, which in Provençal verse takes the form of the lyrical and melancholic re-evocation of an adventure of love. This all too significant allusion is but the first among the frequent literary references of the canto: and like almost all of them it reiterates the underlying pathos of the story. So the poet checks again the natural tendency of both the simile and the literary reference to idealize the situation: and achieves such a controlling effect by introducing a qualifying parallel between the singing of the cranes and the lamenting of the sinners, by degrading the "lays" of the former to the level of the latter's *guai* or "wails." Despite this shift to a lower key, even in this case the comparison obtains an absolute equivalence between the referential tenor and the emblematic vehicle. Such a harmony between trope and object is made even more evident by the metrical symmetry of the first and third lines, the one evoking the singing of the birds, and the other suggesting, as a confused and trailing echo, the less musical, and yet equally rhythmical, human plaint. Like the preceding bird simile, also, the crane image has a dynamic function besides the metaphorical one: it helps us to visualize the positions successively taken by the crowd of sinners, and to localize them in space and time. From the comparison with the starlings we learned that at the moment the shades were moving toward Dante and Vergil in frontal formation: from the new comparison we learn that after a long wide turn the wind is now driving them in such a way that the two travelers, still standing motionless, see the troop through a longitudinal perspective, rather than a transverse one. Now the army of the spirits is deployed in the sense of length, as we realize from the phrase "making in air a long line of themselves"

(*faccendo in aere di sé lunga riga*): and the extension of the forma-
tion, as well as the duration of the passage, are suggested by the lin-
gering effect of the rhythm, by the dragging quality of the sounds,
and, even more, by the overflow of the metrical and syntactical
phrase beyond the stanzaic structure, while normally each terzina is
divided from the next by a long and clear-cut strophic caesura.

IV

At this point the two pilgrims are able to see clearly enough at least
some of the individual shades. The descriptive phase of the canto
thereupon comes to an abrupt end. And now Dante the character, a
man curious like ourselves, asks of his master the very question we
would ask:

> per ch' i' dissi: 'Maestro, che son quelle
> genti che l'aura nera si castiga?'

Dante now wants personal identifications, not abstract examples
of the divine vengeance, and betrays his desire in an indirect manner:
in his question to Vergil he avoids calling those men and women sin-
ners or shades, and uses instead the simple and human term *quelle
genti*, "those people."

Vergil understands the questioner's intent, and answers straight-
forwardly by singling out among the sinners those whose memory is
still alive and who will serve the edifying purpose of teaching an ex-
emplary moral lesson to all of us, both high and low. He successively
identifies, almost in chronological order, a few outstanding figures,
giving us a typical medieval catalogue of famous persons, which, al-
though of no great interest in itself, performs an important function
in the economy of the canto, and acts as a kind of break in its narra-
tive structure. As a matter of fact, the catalogue is meaningful also in
the context of the Paolo and Francesca episode, and a re-examination
of the former will at the proper time throw a significant light on the
latter.

The first among the catalogue's figures, as they are listed by Vergil,
is Semiramis, who is dealt with at greater length than any other char-
acter, and whose name, to create an effect of suspense, or to offer
the learned reader the opportunity of recognizing the Queen of As-
syria by himself, appears only in the opening line of the last of the
three terzinas devoted to her. Vergil notes at the beginning and at
the end of his treatment of that figure that she ruled an empire of
many nations and tongues, and that she reigned not only over Baby-
lon, but also over Egypt, which is now one of the Sultan's domains.
The widow of King Ninus, she succeeded him on his throne; and
she was so dissolute (in the poet's drastic words, *sí rotta a vizio di*

lussuria, "so broken to the vice of lust,") as to marry her son. Thus Vergil accuses her of changing *libito* into *licito,* of making "the lustful lawful," or of legalizing incest:

> 'La prima di color di cui novelle
> tu vuo' saper,' mi disse quelli allotta,
> 'fu imperadrice di molte favelle.
>
> A vizio di lussuria fu sí rotta
> che libito fé licito in sua legge
> per tòrre il biasmo in cui era condotta.
>
> Ell'è Semiramís, di cui si legge
> che succedette a Nino e fu sua sposa;
> tenne la terra che 'l Soldan corregge.'

The second figure is Dido, whom Dante's master had sung yet fails to mention, perhaps out of a sense of modesty. Yet she is easily identifiable through the brief periphrasis alluding to the passion that led her to suicide, after having led her to betray the promise made on the grave of her husband Sichaeus: and such a violation of the vows of widowhood is conveyed by the same verb, *rompere,* "to break," by which Dante had already referred to the dissoluteness of Semiramis. After having so devoted two thirds of the terzina to his own heroine, Vergil uses the last line to evoke Cleopatra, fully portrayed by the single and final epithet, meaning "lascivious," and stretched to the abnormal length of five syllables by an emphatic dieresis (*lussuri-o-sa*):

> 'L'altra è colei che s' ancise amorosa
> e ruppe fede al cener di Sicheo;
> poi è Cleopatràs lussuriosa.'

The closing lines of the catalogue open with the last woman on the list, Homer's Helen, briefly described as the cause of much grief and ill, and immediately followed by the first masculine character, Achilles. Achilles appears here because Dante follows not the Homeric tradition, but a later legend, according to which the hero of the *Iliad* ended his life while pursuing a love affair instead of fighting enemy hosts.[4] The catalogue terminates with the figures of Paris and Tristan, or rather with their mere names, the echo of which seems to linger for a while beyond the caesura of the line, where Vergil's speech, as directly reported, unexpectedly breaks in the middle, far before its end:

---

4. Norton refers to this legend in the following way: "According to the post-Homeric account of the death of Achilles, which was current in the Middle Ages, he was slain by Paris in the Temple of Apollo in Troy, 'whither he had been lured by the promise of a meeting with Polyxena, the daughter of Priam, with whom he was enamoured'."

> 'Elena vedi, per cui tanto reo
> tempo si volse, e vedi il grande Achille
> che con amore al fine combattèo.
>
> Vedi París, Tristano' . . .

The poet, with a perfect sense of both timing and balance, soon stops his review of the procession, shortly after it started. This does not mean that the procession ends at this point, but merely that Dante chooses to reproduce only part of Vergil's speech. With great artistic economy he cuts that speech short, simply informing the reader that his guide went on showing to him one by one many and many other shades who, like Dido and Achilles, as well as Paolo and Francesca, died of love and by love:

> e piú di mille
> ombre mostrommi, e nominommi, a dito
> ch' amor di nostra vita dipartile.

Dante's statement that his guide identified for him "more than a thousand" (*piú di mille*) souls is but a verbal exaggeration or poetic licence, through which he conveys a sense of the immensity of their numbers, considering that most of them must have remained unrecognized and nameless. The vastness of the figure stated by Dante, as well as the unknown total quantity it implies, will also suggest the unusual amount of time spent by the pilgrim in getting acquainted with the souls of the second circle, thus betraying the peculiar intensity of his interest. It is in this manner that the poet starts unveiling his own personal and psychological curiosity in matters of love, to be later more clearly and fully manifested by the question he dares to ask of Francesca, while revealing at the same time the deep admiration he feels for the passionate heroes and the pathetic heroes he now beholds. When at the beginning of his list, Vergil had referred to Dante's desire "to have knowledge" *saper novelle*, of those spirits, he had shown his awareness that the information sought by his disciple was also purely factual, or historical, in character. In this sense, the catalogue is a tribute paid to the greatness and grandeur of a past forever gone. Such an intent is clearly intimated in the phrase by which Dante will define all the famous persons he has just seen: *le donne antiche e' cavalieri*, "the knights and the ladies of old." The suggestion of the splendor and glamor which those figures still radiate among men makes even more poignant the spectacle of their plight, and the realization that their misery will never end. The contrasting impact of these opposite feelings provokes in the poet a new and stronger wave of pity, that bewilders and almost overwhelms him:

Poscia ch' io ebbi il mio dottore udito
nomar le donne antiche e' cavalieri,
pietà mi giunse e fui quasi smarrito.

This sudden spell of pity is so intense that Dante seems about to swoon: and the present bewilderment prepares us for the fainting fit of the pilgrim at the close of the episode, when he is unable to resist the surge of compassion stirred in his soul by Francesca's words. The parallelism between these two moments of emotional weakness is striking, because in this case also the poet abandons himself to the violence of his feelings only after having listened up to the end to what is being said to him. The heart has its reasons, and reason may well be unaware of them: but Dante acknowledges his heart's claims only when his mind has first asserted its demands. Now that his yearning for knowledge has been satisfied, he can give free rein to his emotional needs; now only may pathos prevail again.

I have already stated that this procession of souls acts as a kind of break in the course of Dante's narrative. Later we must return to it, to see *its function within the entire episode*. Strictly speaking, the episode of Paolo and Francesca begins just after Vergil has ended his list, and as Dante recovers from its painful impact. Now *in medias res*, the main section of the canto is fittingly opened by the poet's desire to speak to two shades. At this stage, Dante gives no hint whether he knows those two spirits. Further in the canto, he calls the woman by name, but only after she has told enough of her story to be easily identified by anyone. Yet internal and external evidence strongly indicates that the pilgrim recognizes them at first sight. The external evidence is historical: we know for instance that Paolo Malatesta spent some time in Florence as *Capitano del Popolo;* and it is almost certain that Dante, who was then very young, saw or met Paolo on that occasion. This took place in 1282 or 1283; shortly after, probably in 1285, he must have heard that Paolo and Francesca had been killed by Gianciotto Malatesta, the Lord of Rimini, his brother and her husband: and this bloody event undoubtedly left a lasting impression on Dante's mind. A long time after completing the composition of the *Inferno*, when he was already working on the *Paradiso*, the poet settled in Ravenna. His generous and honored host was Guido Novello da Polenta, but it seems that Dante had been in friendly contact with that family for a long time; and through such a contact he may have learned very early the full story of Francesca, still alive in the memory of her family, and of all her father's descendants. As a matter of fact, his kind treatment of Francesca in this canto of the *Inferno*, the only part of the *Commedia* then already published, may have endeared him even more to her relatives. At any rate, it is on a more convincing kind of evidence, internal and poetic in character, that I base my assurance that Dante recognizes at first sight not only Paolo, but also Francesca: and that he immediately identifies in the two shades those whom only at the beginning of the following canto he will call "the two in-laws," (*i due cognati*).[5] Although decisive, the proof I have in mind is negative in character: Vergil, who has mentioned and described to his companion "more than a thousand" among the souls of the second circle, significantly neglects to give "a local habitation and a name" solely to Paolo and Francesca. This clearly means that any identification or explanation was in this case totally unnecessary, at least for his own disciple. At a later stage, any identification or explanation would be almost equally superfluous for the reader, especially of Dante's time. Even before reaching the point when in his question to Francesca Dante utters her name (and her name alone), the medieval reader would have already silently uttered more than once the same name. Dante presupposes so widespread a knowledge of the story's background as to feel free to paint it in bold strokes rather than in minute details. Yet it remains equally true that anyone reading the canto for the first time is able to recognize Paolo and Francesca only at second sight; and this adds an element of curiosity and suspense to the narrative:

> I' cominciai: 'Poeta, volontieri
> parlerei a quei due che 'nsieme vanno
> e paion síal vento esser leggeri.'

With a powerful artistic synthesis Dante describes his sudden vision of Paolo and Francesca only through the words by which he will later convey to his master his desire to speak to those two he has just perceived and recognized. When he does so, he singles them out on the strength of two distinctive traits: first, that, unlike their fellow sinners, they go together; second, that they seem to yield to the violence of the wind more gracefully and willingly than the others. Since the poet adds no details, the reader at this stage has no ground to surmise that one of them is a man, and the other a woman— although he will spontaneously guess that such is the case. In his words to Vergil, with tactful modesty Dante understates the intensity of his desire to talk with the two shades, and avoids referring to either their story or their names. Yet whether or not Vergil identified them by name is irrelevant. Of the two poets only one was a poet of love. Vergil, the heroic poet, sang *arma virumque*, and only in passing of the passion of Dido; but Dante, at least in his youth, had been a *fedele d'amore*, and a practitioner of the *dolce stil nuovo*. So it will be only fitting for Dante to address the two lovers: and Vergil grants

5. See *Inferno*, vi.1–2:

> Al tornar della mente, che si chiuse
> dinanzi alla pietà de' due cognati . . .

him willingly this privilege. He merely advises him to wait until the wind brings the two spirits a little nearer; and then to turn to them with his request:

> Ed elli a me: 'Vedrai quando saranno
> piú presso a noi: e tu allor li prega
> per quello amor che i mena, ed ei verranno.'

Vergil suggests that the request be made in the name of that love which still seems to lead the two shades, and foresees that they will come in response to such a request. Vergil's words, although addressed to Dante, are already words of entreaty and endearment, even of flattery; since love may be the power that still binds the two souls together, but it is the vengeance of God that spurs them in their ordeal. The first force operates in accordance, and the second in contrast, with their will. Vergil here seems to allude again to the impression they give of assisting, rather than resisting, the rush of the wind: yet he reveals that the impression is only illusory by using for the operation of love the same verb and the same form (*mena*, from *menare*, "to lead,") by which Dante had already indicated the action of the storm. Dante tacitly acknowledges the wisdom of his teacher's counsel, and follows his advice at least in part, imitating Vergil's delicacy in thoughts as well as in words. I say in part, because he fails to refer to love as Vergil had suggested to him. So as soon as the wind turns the spirits toward them, the pilgrim sends the two lovers a moved and moving call:

> Sí tosto come il vento a noi li piega,
> mossi la voce: 'O anime affannate,
> venite a noi parlar s' altri nol niega!'

Strangely enough, in his appeal the poet addresses the two in such a way as not to distinguish them from the other sinners. The apostrophe: "O wearied souls . . . !" (*O anime affannate* . . . !), could apply to all the spirits in the flying crowd: so that we may easily imagine that it was accompanied by an unmistakable, beckoning gesture. Or perhaps the plural was enough, because Paolo and Francesca are the only spirits of the second circle who are not exclusively absorbed in their individual plight, who suffer as two souls in one. To make his request even more respectful and courteous, Dante, who in his previous words to Vergil has stated his wish in terms of *his* speaking to them, now that he addresses the two spirits, restates that wish in terms of *their* speaking to his companion and himself. Finally, in the conditional sentence by which the poet avows fear that his request may not be agreeable to God, he expresses that thought in such a way as least to offend them. Even here the poet follows his steadfast rule according to which the name of God is never uttered in Hell, but chooses to replace that name by the vaguest possible term. Instead of saying "unless God forbids," he merely says: "if another deny it not" (s'altri nol niega). Clearly discretion cannot go farther than this.

The souls immediately heed Dante's appeal, exactly because they immediately feel, more in its tone than in its words, the loving charity of that sudden call. So they leave the swarm of sinners—which Dante describes here with words to be understood not as a qualifying statement, but rather as a compliment to Vergil, as la schiera ov'è Dido, "the troop where Dido is"—so the two spirits move easily and slowly toward the two pilgrims, who are waiting for them on the same spot, to remain there up to the end of their talk. To suggest the action and movement of Paolo and Francesca, Dante introduces here the third and last bird simile of the canto, and compares them to a pair of doves who suddenly abandon the large flock of their kind to rejoin their little ones, and to return to their nest:

> Quali colombe dal disio chiamate,
> con l'ali alzate e ferme al dolce nido
> vegnon per l'aere dal voler portate;
>
> cotali uscir della schiera ov' è Dido,
> a noi venendo per l'aere maligno,
> sí forte fu l'affettuoso grido.

The doves are carried through the air not so much by the force of their wings, or even of the wind, but by the power of their volere, which means "wish," rather than "will." Thus, in harmony with the previous similitudes of the same kind, which had represented the birds in a state of passive motion, this one too describes the flight of the doves in terms of what the French call vol plané. Like Paolo and Francesca, descending toward Vergil and Dante through the wicked air of Hell, so the doves do not fly, but rather glide, toward their nest: and that gliding is clearly suggested by the beautiful detail of their "steady" and "raised" wings.[6] The pertinence of the metaphor becomes even more striking if we consider that doves are traditionally held as the most tenderly loving, and the most tenderly lovely, of all birds. The spontaneous ease of the image must not lead us to forget that what is happening in the meanwhile is nothing less than a miracle, even if Dante prefers to understate, even to ignore, the strangeness of the event. It is clear that God has granted Dante's wish, that he has allowed the two sinners to heed his friendly and

---

6. The textual tradition has preserved another variant, according to which the wings of the doves are not "raised," alzate, but "open," aperte. The change does not affect the visual content of the image, nor does it detract in any way from its power or fitness. The metaphor itself is consciously patterned after a famous simile in the Aeneid (v.213–217).

tender call. For this very reason the action of Paolo and Francesca is described as the almost unconscious effect of a sympathetic and reciprocal attraction, as the operation of an "elective affinity," rather than as the unilateral decision of their will, which is no longer free. All this seems to be suggested by the repetition of the verb *venire*, which in Italian has often a strong affective undertone, meaning not merely "to come" or "to go," but to go where one's heart is.

The psychological and spiritual force of the poet's "passionate call" (or "cry," as the Italian *grido* also means), coincides with the longing of the two spirits without conflicting with God's will: thus it operates its wonder, and joins together the two visitors and the two souls. Dante neglects to say who is speaking, and to whom: yet the reader understands that the speaker is a woman, and that it is to Dante that she turns. Her language is not only feminine, but ladylike, revealing delicacy of feeling, as well as refined tact. She behaves as a well-born gentlewoman even in Hell; nay, as a princess, or at least as someone accustomed to command. Notwithstanding her tenderness and benevolence, despite the fact that her misery and her love place her on a level with Dante, she still stands on ceremony; her courtesy remains courtly, and she impresses the poet and the reader with the consciousness of her exalted station, of the privileged position she once held among men. She treats Dante as an equal, even better, as a friend: yet her familiarity is never informal, and her attitude seems to be inspired by the graciousness and generosity of a great lady condescending to honor someone of a lower status or lineage than herself. All her acts, gestures, and words, even when they are most captivating, betray a controlled pride, a sense of feudal dignity. This may lead us to think that she acts in this way in order to play the role expected from a woman of her status and breeding in a society which was educated in the cult of the "eternal feminine," and which raised all noblewomen (especially if married, as was the case in Provençal culture)[7] on a kind of pedestal. There may be something in this: but perhaps it is simply because she recognizes at first sight that Dante is not her equal that she does not ask him who he is and where he comes from, and that she greets him with the acknowledgment, not of the nobility of his blood, but merely of the nobility of his soul. Such is the meaning of the apostrophe by which she designates Dante as a living creature full of benevolence and good will:

> 'O animal grazioso e benigno,
> che visitando vai per l'aere perso
> noi che tignemmo il mondo di sanguigno . . .'

7. A main difference between the Troubadours and the poets of "the sweet new style" is that the former celebrate the bride, and the latter, the maiden. The Italians, moreover, unlike the Provençals, do not prize nobility per se.

Francesca's native pride manifests itself in the long relative clause
following the apostrophe, with its implication that the pilgrim's
journey through Hell was meant as a visit not to the sinners of all
circles, but only to Paolo and herself, whom she defines extrava-
gantly, in terms of their own tragic end, as those "who painted the
world blood-red." The line reveals Francesca's total absorption in the
event that dominated her life and brought her to her death. After all,
not Paolo and Francesca alone, but all the shades of this circle saw
their worldly existence cut short by jealousy, hatred, passion, or lust:
while all the circles of Hell (without mentioning the abodes of pur-
gation and bliss), are full of numberless spirits who suffered a vio-
lent death. Yet it seems to Francesca that the whole earth is still
stained by the blood which once flowed in Paolo's veins, and in hers.
The disproportion between the import of the event and the measure
by which she estimates its effects is so great as to escape nobody's
attention, excepting her own. The modern reader may assess that
disproportion by employing a concept which T. S. Eliot introduced
for the first time in modern criticism, and may conclude that there
is no "objective correlative"[8] between Francesca's emotions and the
remote experience which forever stirs those emotions in her memory
and soul. Yet in this case psychological imbalance is easily corrected
by artistic equilibrium: we must not forget that the metaphorical ex-
aggeration of Francesca's words is a characterizing device, through
which the poet projects the passion of his heroine rather than feel-
ings of his own. Yet the moving emphasis of Francesca's words
brings along a new flow of pathos, which for a while threatens to be-
come a flood. An emotional outburst of that kind, which would look
unseemly and improper if it were part of the poet's statement, be-
comes acceptable and forgivable as the effusive expression of the
grief filling Francesca's heart. The powerful impact of the heroine's
allusion to the manner of her death is not only due to its rhetorical
emphasis, but also to what the very image tacitly implies or sug-
gests. The metaphor of the world painted red by human blood ap-
pears also in Shakespeare's *Macbeth*. There the image always fulfills
a tragic function, since it recurs in the protagonist's mind as the
most obsessive detail of the murder he once committed, which he
continuously rehearses in his memory, and relives in his remorse.
But in Dante the same image produces a pathetic effect: the blood
of which Francesca says that it stained, not only the sea, but the
whole world, was shed by no others than Paolo and herself. The
blood reappearing in the nightmares of Macbeth is the blood of his
victims; the blood still haunting the memory of Paolo and Francesca

8. In the essay "Hamlet and His Problems" (1919), reprinted in *Selected Essays* (New York,
1932), pp. 121–126.

is but their own. In Aristotelian terms, one could say that in the Shakespearean version of the same trope terror overwhelms pity, while in Dante's variant the self-pity of the heroine and the poet's compassion triumph over terror itself.

Contrasting as it does with Francesca's previous reference to the *aere perso*, to the "black air" of Hell, that blood image strikes us with a lasting impression of vividness, as a bright spot, or a gush of color, suddenly lighting up the dark background of a landscape painted at dusk. Still both the metaphor and the line carrying it are but an incidental sentence and nothing more. Francesca does not insist on it, since she wishes to return to the task at hand, which is to thank Dante for his affectionate interest, for the pity he feels toward what she ambiguously calls *il nostro mal perverso*, a phrase which may equally mean "our wicked evil" or "our wretched ill." Yet Francesca cannot express her gratitude except in words, since her damnation denies her the highest human right, which is to pray God for the eternal peace of both the living and the dead:

> 'se fosse amico il re dell'universo,
> noi pregheremmo lui della tua pace,
> poi ch' hai pietà del nostro mal perverso.'

As the words quoted show, Francesca does not say merely "we would pray God for you if we could." Like Dante, she dares not utter the name of God, which would always be uttered in vain in Hell. But unlike Dante, who had previously alluded to God by the vague and anonymous pronoun, *altri*, "another," she refers to Him in very concrete, although indirect terms. So, quite simply and naturally, she introduces the noble periphrasis defining God as "the king of the universe." By describing God as the supreme sovereign she reveals again her aristocratic bent, her feudal frame of mind. By the very clause *se fosse amico*, "if only He were our friend," Francesca indicates that she conceives of God's blessing or God's curse in terms of courtly grace or disgrace, as honors or privileges which a crowned head may bestow on his subjects, or withdraw from them. In the same way, she seems to consider Paolo and herself as if they were two vassals who, having lost their king's personal favor, have also lost the right to intercede with him in behalf of others. Thus, by two brief conditional sentences, she succeeds in projecting the hierarchical idea of the feudal order into God's universe. All this is stated, or rather suggested, in thoughts and words both spontaneous and restrained, regretful and respectful at the same time. But if Francesca has lost her standing with God, she has not lost, even in Hell, her standing with her fellow men; so, with perfect composure, with the self-mastery of an accomplished lady, she gracefully grants the two pilgrims licence to converse with Paolo and with her:

'Di quel che udire e che parlar vi piace,
noi udiremo e parleremo a vui
mentre che 'l vento, come fa, ci tace.'

Francesca continues to speak in the first person plural, while
shifting from the second singular to the second plural in her form
of address. Thus she uses the pronouns "we" and "you": yet the
first sounds rather like a *pluralis majestatis*, and the second means
more Dante than Vergil. And to respect good manners, she pre-
tends to leave to the visitors the choice of the subject to be dis-
cussed: she seems to hold them on a footing of absolute equality.
Although declaring willingness to listen as well as talk, she will be
in reality, at least for some time, the only speaker: so, without wait-
ing for a word or even a nod, she speaks out on the only topic
which interests her. There is no time to lose: the wind has just qui-
eted, but the storm may rage again at any moment. With an elo-
quent understatement, hardly more than an expressive gesture,
she acknowledges the minor miracle now taking place for their
benefit. Let us talk, she says, "as long as the wind, as it does, will
keep silent for us" (*mentre che'l vento, come fa, ci tace*).[9] This dis-
creet reference to the truce suddenly granted by the storm adds a
charming aspect to the scene: the personification of the wind
seems to intrude for a while from one of the corners of the picture,
playing the role of a willing and helpful partner, hushing his voice
and bending his ear, so as not to disturb an elegant conversation in
which he has no right to take part.

v

Now Francesca introduces herself in a manner which again shows
the pride she feels in her ancestry. Posterity knows her as Francesca
da Rimini, from the abode of her husband and lover, from the city
where she died as well as sinned; but she still thinks of herself as
Francesca da Ravenna, from the city where she was born an off-
spring of renowned lineage. This is the aristocratic, feudal, royal
way of naming oneself: the great historical or legendary figures in
Shakespeare's plays are called by their princedoms, dukedoms, king-
doms, or realms. Thus, although extended for three lines, Francesca's
statement amounts to: "I am Ravenna." As she avoids uttering her
name, so she avoids mentioning directly her native city, but refers to
it through a long periphrasis, placing her "town" (such is the mean-
ing of the Old Italian *terra*) on the map:

---

9. Such is the interpretation I have chosen to give to *ci tace*: although most of the commen-
tators prefer to interpret the particle in its adverbial and locative sense, as meaning
"here," "on this spot," rather than in the pronominal one, as meaning "to us," "for us."

'Siede la terra dove nata fui
su la marina dove 'l Po discende
per aver pace co 'seguaci sui.'

What Francesca has just told is merely that her birthplace lies on the Adriatic coast, not far from the Po's mouth. Yet the connotations of this merely geographical reference are far richer and more complex than its denotative content. First of all, Ravenna does not "lie" on the seashore, but "sits" (*siede*) on it, and a lofty throne image seems to be implied in the choice of such a verb. Then, the purely physical phenomenon of the overflowing of the river into the wide expanse of the sea is evoked in terms of the "pathetic fallacy": Francesca humanizes and spiritualizes that blind natural force by comparing its consummation to the wish fulfillment of our soul, longing for an eternal peace denied to the damned, which Francesca would beseech for Dante, if she could pray God. Finally, the river marching to its own serene death, within a body of water far greater than itself, is seen as going to its peaceful end not alone but accompanied by its tributaries and affluents, thus likened to a retinue of loyal vassals following their lord to his destination.

After employing a full terzina to reveal her identity, Francesca now devotes almost three terzinas to tell what happened to her companion and herself. She re-evokes the most important event in their lives with a threefold statement, in terms of what love did first to each one, and later, to both of them. Each one of the three parts of her statement occupies a terzina, or part of it. The final part, as a matter of fact, is made of two parallel sentences, taking only two lines, as symmetrically related to each other as the preceding terzinas are. In the first of these Francesca describes how Paolo fell in love with her; and in the second, how she fell in love with him. In the two concluding lines, which act as the closing crescendo of her statement, she first simply asserts that their love led them to a joint death; and then she states the revengeful assurance that their killer, who is still alive, will be damned like them: that he will suffer eternally in Caina, that section of the ninth circle where those whose murderous hand broke the sacred ties of blood are punished. At this point Francesca has no more to tell, and Dante rounds off the last of the three terzinas by saying that the words he has just reported were uttered by the two shades to Vergil and himself:

'Amor, ch' al cor gentil ratto s' apprende,
prese costui della bella persona
che mi fu tolta; e' l modo ancor m'offende.

Amor, ch' a nullo amato amar perdona,
mi prese del costui piacer sí forte,
che, come vedi, ancor non m' abbandona.

> Amor condusse noi ad una morte:
> Caina attende chi a vita ci spense.'
> Queste parole da lor ci fu porte.

The opening line of each one of the first two stanzas begins with
the word "Love," which we must always envision as being capital-
ized, and which is immediately followed, in the rest of the line, by a
brief general definition of its modes of operation. The second line
describes how passion suddenly mastered one or the other of the
two lovers, while the third indicates, from Francesca's viewpoint, the
present or lasting effects of their love. Each one of the two terzinas
rises toward its climax in the middle, but at the end its tension re-
laxes somewhat. The action of love, as well as the consequences of
that action, are always suggested by such violent verbs as "to catch,"
"to seize," and the like. The first stanza is dominated by Francesca's
feeling of grief for the cruel and degrading way the feminine and
youthful loveliness of her "handsome body" (*bella persona*) was de-
faced by the vengeful hand of her outraged husband and lay disfig-
ured in death. The second is dominated instead by a feeling of
possessive pride at the thought that her love survived life itself: that
even Hell has been unable to destroy it, and to separate her lover
from her. In each stanza she refers to him by the pronoun *costui*,
"that one," which in Italian, when used in direct speech, indicates
someone who is more obviously visible to the listener than to the
speaker; and by the mere use of such a pronoun the poet helps us to
visualize the scene. Thus our imagination realizes that while speak-
ing, Francesca looks steadily at Dante, without ever turning her gaze
toward her companion, as if she could not even doubt that he is still
at her side. Francesca's speech seems to increase gradually in emo-
tional pitch, as may be easily shown by comparing the alternate lines
alluding to Love. In the first, Love is described as a natural attrac-
tion for every "noble" and sensitive heart,[1] in the second, as a fatal
necessity forcing its object to return the passion it has stirred in an-
other soul; in the third, as a tragic consummation, which in their
case brought both of them to a single death. After this nothing fur-
ther could be said, except, since we are in the all too human world of
Hell, words of hatred and revenge against the man who, by giving
them no time to repent, was also the unconscious instrument of
their damnation, of their "second death." Yet those words of hatred
and revenge sound so unexpected and sudden that many inter-
preters attribute them to Paolo, rather than to Francesca. They ar-

---

1. It is perhaps unnecessary to remark that in Dante's language, or, more generally, in Old
Italian, *gentile* means almost without exception "noble," "well born," "of high birth," and
the like.

gue that the reference to Caina is more proper in the mouth of him who was the brother of the man whom he wronged, and who wronged him in his turn; and find support for their claim in the plural forms which Dante uses at the end of this passage: "such words were brought to us from them" (*queste parole da lor ci fu porte*), and at the beginning of the following one: "When I heard those injured souls" (*quand' io intesi quell' anime offense*). But the great majority of the critics maintain, I believe rightly, that Dante merely means that Francesca and Paolo are two souls in one: and that the woman, even when she speaks in the first person singular, speaks always for both of them.

VI

The passage following acts as an interlude between the two speeches of Francesca, serving to calm the heroine's rekindled emotions, as well as the reader's excited imagination. This braking pause, sounding like the andante of a concerto, gives the poet the opportunity to describe the effect which Francesca's talk has produced on him. While listening to her words Dante had held his eyes constantly fixed on her, as we realize from the statement that he lowered his "gaze" (*viso*) as soon as she ended ("she," and not "they," as the second of the two plurals mentioned above would literally mean). With his head bent down, the poet remains absorbed for such a long time in his broodings and musings that Vergil asks him what he is thinking about, not in order to get an answer, but merely to rouse Dante from his mood:

> Quand' io intesi quell' anime offense,
> china' il viso, e tanto il tenni basso,
> fin che 'l poeta mi disse: 'Che pense?'

Dante is so engrossed in his thoughts that he fails to take notice of Vergil's words, and still remains speechless and motionless. When he finally decides to break the spell, he speaks not to reply to his master, but to unburden himself of the sorrowful reflections still agitating his soul. The language and rhythm seem to express the effort by which Dante breaks away from his mood, and the difficulty which he feels in articulating his words, the first of which will be only the sad exclamation "alas":

> Quando rispuosi, cominciai: 'Oh lasso,
> quanti dolci pensier, quanto disio
> menò costoro al doloroso passo!'

Dante's words sound like a melancholy acknowledgement of the decisive role which both imagination and instinct must have played in the moral crisis, the outcome of which was for the two lovers adultery and death: this is what the poet means by "sweet thoughts" (*dolci pensieri*), or suggestive and self-indulgent visions of love, and by "desire" (*disio*), or the seductive power of a yearning still unconfessed to its object, and perhaps unavowed by the subject itself. By referring to Paolo and Francesca as *costoro*, "those ones," "those two," the poet clearly shows that he still is looking down while uttering those words, which are thus addressed only to himself. But as soon as he wishes to speak to the two lovers, he lifts his eyes up, and gazes intently at them, while slowly unfolding his thoughts:

> Poi mi rivolsi a loro e parla' io,
> e cominciai:

Dante emphasizes that it is now his turn to speak. Here again the plural "to them" (*a loro*) notwithstanding, it is only to Francesca that he addresses himself. Dante, who up to now has spoken as a tactful courtier, becomes again the moralist who wants to know the how and why of man's fall. Thus now he wants to learn how two noble hearts like those could be brought to commit a sin made even more heinous by the betrayal of a brotherly bond. Hence the pilgrim does not hesitate to ask straightforwardly the question that has troubled his mind during his silent spell. He realizes that what he is doing is like probing an open wound, so he speaks with great delicacy, and softens, as much as possible, his touch. He begins by stating his compassionate feelings for what he calls all too kindly Francesca's "tortures" (*martiri*), as if her torments were excessive, even unjust, or at least such as to deserve the tears they are stirring within his heart:

> 'Francesca, i tuoi martiri
> a lacrimar mi fanno tristo e pio' . . .

Yet, without lingering further, boldly using an adversative particle and a concise imperative form, he enjoins her to tell when and how her criminal love began. He attenuates the crudity of his question by using the elegant and sophisticated language already used by Francesca, and by referring, like her, to Love as if it were a supernatural power or a superhuman being. Yet, although equally abstract, Dante's personification is less forceful: he attributes less responsibility to Love, whom he treats not as a despotic ruler, but as a gentle lord, who does not constrain, but rather unbinds. Thus Dante asks Francesca how Love made it not necessary, but possible, for Paolo and her to realize that the longing troubling their souls was but the temptation of sin:

> 'Ma dimmi: al tempo de' dolci sospiri,
> a che e come concedette amore
> che conosceste i dubbiosi desiri?'

The parallel words closing the first and the last line of the terzina, sealing their similarities and differences in the ringing echo of the rhyme, reveal how distant and near to each other are the innocent beginnings of love and its sinful consummation, first in thought, and then in deed. Dante knows how fatally and easily "sweet thoughts" (*dolci sospiri*) may be replaced by what he calls "doubtful wishes" (*dubbiosi desiri*), and with this marvellous expression fully reveals his genius as a searcher of the human soul. The adjective *dubbiosi* is certainly used in its etymological sense, meaning "ambiguous": and modern psychology would translate it with such terms as "subconscious," or "half-conscious." The very use of such an epithet shows that Dante needs to know everything about Francesca's fall: and such a need is dictated not by a vicarious or morbid curiosity, but by a deep urge for psychological and ethical knowledge. Dante the poet, through the simple and full answer which Francesca is about to give, will satisfy this urge, which affects the reader as well. To understand the meaning and value of all this it may suffice to recall that even one of the greatest literary and moral figures of modern culture, Leo Tolstoy, did not dare to look so fearlessly into the obscure depths of temptation and sin. In *Anna Karenina* we have a complete report of what happened to the heroine before and after her fall: but, as for the fall itself, the writer passed it over, as if to say: "the rest is silence." Tolstoy avoids telling us about the when and the how of Vronsky's and Anna's sin, and replaces with a series of suspension points the omitted tale of the climax of the story, of the novel's crucial event.[2] By doing so, the great Russian master showed his reverence for the mysteries of the human soul: but Dante showed the same reverence in the opposite way, by probing that mystery, and by laying it bare in front of us. Tolstoy refused to describe in detail Anna's fall to avoid either one of two alternatives. The first was to evoke that fall pathetically, or more simply, romantically: but this would have involved an attitude of indulgent forgiveness, and so destroyed the stern morality of the tale. The other was to represent Anna's fall realistically, in all its brutal ugliness, in the crudity of its naturalistic details: but this would have prevented both author and reader from feeling for the heroine all the sympathy she seems to deserve. Alessandro Manzoni was faced with the same dilemma, and, like Tolstoy, he solved it by omission and silence. Thus, in *The Betrothed*, he finally refused to include the pages he had already written about the psychological crisis which ends with the fall of the nun Gertrude, replacing them with only three words,

---

2. These significant suspension points separate the end of Ch. x from the beginning of Ch. xi in Pt. II of Tolstoy's novel, and immediately precede the sudden revelation that Anna has already become the mistress of Vronsky.

summing up all her future sins and crimes with the mere statement that she failed to reject the first, apparently innocent, advances of her would-be seducer: *la sventurata rispose* ("the unlucky woman replied").[3] Dante, no less of a moralist than Manzoni or Tolstoy, accepted the challenge implied in their dilemma, and as a poet succeeded in giving us a direct and total report of Francesca's fall which avoided the pitfalls of moralism and sentimentalism. This he did dramatically by letting Francesca tell in her own words how and why she became an adulteress.

Thus Dante the character asks his fatal questions without any qualm, and Francesca answers with great candor, and without shame. That question has stirred in her soul a feeling of overwhelming self-pity, and that feeling alone: since, as she says, there is no greater sorrow than remembering a happy past in a time of wretchedness. The sorrow is made even greater in her case by the realization that her past happiness and her present misery are equally irrevocable. Francesca implies that Dante may be unable to understand such truth, which, however, is well known to his teacher. Like the spirits who have been damned for their sins, Dante's companion will always long, if not for the happiness he may have once enjoyed on earth, at least for that eternal bliss which God's grace has denied him. Francesca has already recognized Vergil, although she has not remarked upon his presence. Here she corrects her previous oversight, thus indirectly conveying to him her interest in his person, and her sympathy for his plight:

> E quella a me: 'Nessun maggior dolore
> che ricordarsi del tempo felice
> nella miseria, a ciò sa il tuo dottore.'

The entire terzina must be read at a rapid pace, almost without stopping at the end of the line. By the feverish agitation of her words Francesca indicates that she is uttering a truth directly experienced, and not merely a gnomic sentence;[4] or better, a general truth which she personalizes both within and without herself, extending it to that Vergil who is Dante's teacher, and who has learned that lesson as sadly as she has. After this Francesca states her willingness, despite the pain it will cost her, to gratify the visitor's wish. So, she says, if you are so eager to know *la prima radice del nostro male*, "the first root of our ill" (where the last word, as always in Italian, means not only "ill," but "evil" too), I will comply with your request. But she warns him that by doing so she will speak and weep at the same time:

---

3. *I Promessi Sposi*, Ch. x.
4. Francesca's words are a gnomic sentence only in the sense that they paraphrase a famous passage in Boethius' *De Consolatione Philosophiae* (II, 4): "In omni adversitate fortunae infelicissimum est genus infortunii fuisse felicem."

'Ma s' a conoscer la prima radice
del nostro mal tu hai cotanto affetto,
farò come colui che piange e dice.'

The first two lines of the terzina are an obvious reminiscence from the *Aeneid* (II.10–13), and seem to be meant as another courteous allusion, or flattering tribute, to the great poet who was once Vergil. This charming trait, which could be defined as a compliment by quotation, indicates that Francesca never loses her feminine sophistication even under emotional stress. In a calm and quiet tone, before unveiling her most deeply buried memory, she announces the tears she may shed during her speech, but which we shall never see.

VII

Francesca tells her story as if she were reminiscing aloud. One day, Paolo and she were reading together, for their own entertainment, the romance of Lancelot du Lac, and particularly that section of the romance describing how the protagonist was overpowered by his passion for the fair Guinevere. Francesca alludes to all this very succinctly, through the single phrase: "how love seized him" (*come amor lo strinse*), where she uses again a violent verb, *stringere*, "to grasp" or "to squeeze," to indicate the violence of the passion mastering the knight's soul. We imagine the two sitting beside each other: one listening, the other, probably Francesca, reading aloud. But the only thing we are told by Francesca is that they were alone, without the company of even the fear of their weakness, or the suspicion of their own selves. It would be impossible to state more concisely the perfidy of temptation, lying in wait to assail two unprepared and defencelesss human hearts. The malice of sin threatens and ruins our souls when they yield to self-oblivion, when they abandon themselves, deceitfully, to their own innocence:

'Noi leggiavamo un giorno per diletto
di Lancialotto come amor lo strinse:
soli eravamo e sanza alcun sospetto.'

Francesca's memory rehearses all the unforgettable instants of that fatal moment. They were looking down at the pages of their book, when the suggestive power of the story suddenly raised their gazes toward each other; or, as Francesca says, "that reading made us lift our eyes." This happened more than once: and Francesca seems to lengthen the duration of each of those instants by the dieresis on the word *fïate*, "times." At every turn, each recognized the same paleness on the other's face. Yet the reading would have perhaps failed to seduce them into sin, if the climax of the tale had not finally broken down all restraints and overcome their resistance:

'Per piú fiate li occhi ci sospinse
quella lettura, e scolorocci il viso;
ma solo un punto fu quel che ci vinse.'

The crucial point, the passage by which they were vanquished, is
that famous scene in the romance where the noble Gallehaut begs
Guinevere to reward the gentle knight Lancelot for loving her so loy-
ally and faithfully, and the Queen complies and kisses Lancelot on
his lips. The scene, and the electric effect of its reading, are recalled
by Francesca with some of the loveliest lines of the canto:

'Quando leggemmo il disiato riso
esser baciato da cotanto amante,
questi, che mai da me non fia diviso,

la bocca mi baciò tutto tremante.'

The transition from a vicarious to a genuine consummation, from
the first kiss of Lancelot and Guinevere, which belongs to the realm
of imagination, to the first kiss of Paolo and Francesca, which took
place in the realm of experience, is beautifully conveyed not only by
the change of rhythmical pace, but also by the sudden transforma-
tion of Francesca's mode of expression, by the metamorphosis of her
language. The lips of Guinevere, the heroine of the romance, are at
first marvellously metaphorized into a *disïato riso*, or "longed-for
smile." These words are made even more insistently caressing by the
dieresis lengthening the adjective and intensifying the radiance of
the image. The select choice of words and sounds, as well as the
trope itself, by which the curved lips of the loved and loving Queen
lose all physical reality, becoming as light and incorporeal as their
inviting and wordless smile, tend to give a spiritualized and idealized
vision of that imaginary embrace. While the Queen's inviting gesture
is re-experienced from the viewpoint of the knight, dazzled by the
sight of her seductive smile, the kiss by which Lancelot seals her lips
is instead re-evoked from the standpoint of Guinevere, as shown by
the passive form of the verb "being kissed" (*esser baciato*), which sug-
gests a feeling of feminine abandon, a gesture of self-offering. As for
the complement agreeing with that passive form, "by so great a lover"
(*da cotanto amante*), it reveals Francesca's awareness of the personal
merits of her partner in passion and sin, and tends to equate his
qualities with Lancelot's aristocratic and chivalric virtues. All this im-
plies a process of self-identification: if Francesca sees in her lover the
peer of such a worthy as Lancelot, she may also see in herself the
equal of his Queen; and she may even think that she had a right to
betray Gianciotto, if Guinevere betrayed King Arthur himself. But
here the parallelism, and double impersonation, suddenly end. Up to

now Francesca has evoked a vision of romantic love through both empathy and sympathy, through the alluring mirror of both sentiment and art. As soon as she deals, not with the fleshless kiss of two fictitious creatures, but with the real one of two living beings, she immediately realizes that she was no Guinevere, and that Paolo was no Lancelot. This realization is evident in the line where she alludes, simply and directly, to her lover. Now she does not refer to him with the usual *costui*, "that one," but with *questi*, "this one," so as to indicate his physical and moral nearness to her. The relative clause following this pronoun (*questi, che mai da me non fia diviso*, "this one who will be never divided from me"), is a cry of possession, where pride mingles with despair. That pronoun and that cry presuppose either a fleeting turn of her eyes, or merely a blind gesture of her hand, as if to assure herself, as well as the two visitors, that her lover still is, and will forever remain, at her side. All this takes but a line, which separates, as a curtain or a barrier, the kiss she once read about from the kiss still alive in the memory of her flesh. Only after having raised such a barrier will she be able to re-evoke, in its loneliness and singularity, their own kiss: which she however catches only in Paolo's gesture. Paolo is described as she saw him at that moment, moving toward her full of trembling and fear. The vision reveals him to us as a weaker and more human vessel than even the timid Lancelot. And we, the readers, see Francesca receiving that kiss not on curved, but on closed and unsmiling lips, to which she refers by using a cruder, singular word. This is what we meant by the transformation of Francesca's language: and such a falling off from the spiritual to the physiological, from the "smile" (*riso*) of Guinevere to the "mouth" (*bocca*) of Francesca, is but the shift or descent from literature to life, from fiction to reality, from romanticism to realism; or more simply, from sentimental fancy to moral truth. Lust and adultery replace for a moment passion and love: a cry of nature breaks forever the mirror of illusion and the veil of self-deceit.

VIII

The proof of this is evident in the two statements by which Francesca concludes her tale, each being enclosed in a single line. The first is but an exclamation, ambiguous and significant at the same time. Its clear purport is the acknowledgment, on Francesca's part, of the role which the reading of that famous medieval romance played in their life, as well as the recognition that that role was identical with the one played by Gallehaut in the story they read not too wisely but too well. The ambiguity lies in the mixed tone of the phrase, conveying a double sense of regret for all the bliss and evil of which that hour was the seed: "Galeotto fu il libro e chi lo scrisse . . ."

By equating the effect of that reading with the action performed by Gallehaut, by identifying the unknown author of the romance with Gallehaut himself, who still preserves a graceful dignity despite the vileness of his services, Francesca treats the book and its author as if she would like to accuse and to absolve them at the same time. She cannot forget the beauty of the story and the glamor of the characters, since that beauty and that glamor still reflect a kind of redeeming light on the sin they committed at the example of Lancelot and Guinevere. While on one side Francesca tries to emphasize in her story all the aspects that may ennoble her experience, she has still too much sense of responsibility to lay more than part of their guilt on others than Paolo and herself. She knows that she has been more sinning than sinned against; hence she dares not call the romance and its writer by the ugly name of panderers. The reader feels nothing more need be added, yet Francesca has something more to say. Strangely enough, she feels it necessary to allude to what happened after the reading had aroused and bared to them their own "dubious desires." To be sure, the allusion is merely negative in character, and takes the form of another reference to the book which they forgot and discarded, as soon as it had led them to their first kiss: 'Quel giorno piú non vi leggemmo avante.'

At first sight, the final words of Francesca (since these are her final words) seem to be superfluous, and even to lack propriety: they may sound impudent, or at least too complacent, even more than merely unnecessary. What is Francesca's purpose in telling Dante that they did not read in that book any further? Why unveil so deviously, as well as so brutally, those intimate secrets which even a lost woman prefers to keep hidden? Only a harlot, devoid of the last shred not only of modesty, but even of self-respect, would go so far as to speak of her fall in such cynical terms. There is a difference between unchastity and impurity: a woman may be candid without being shameless. In all her behavior Francesca has consistently shown not only great delicacy of feeling, but also tactfulness and good taste. She has given proof of intellectual and moral courage by facing truth in all its nakedness, yet she has constantly avoided the pitfalls of vulgarity and coarseness. If such is the case, we are forced to conclude that her final words must mean something less plain and obvious than what they seem to suggest. I am unwilling to follow the example of some interpreters, who take those words at their face value. The clue we need is perhaps to be found in the very turn of the phrases by which Francesca opens and closes the story of her fall. The first and the last line of that story begin with almost identical words: "one day," "that day" (un giorno, quel giorno). In the second case the temporal reference appears to be hardly useful or necessary. It would have been sufficient to say, "and then we read no further." Yet Francesca feels the need to emphasize that they did not read any further "that day." These two small words cannot be explained away as a mere pleonasm, as syllables that are there solely to fill the line. They become pertinent and relevant, and as such, necessary, only if they are supposed to hint or imply that Paolo and Francesca took up again, on other occasions, the reading of the book which had been "the first root" of their sin. Why does Francesca wish to suggest these successive readings, after the one which was interrupted by their first kiss, on the first day of their love? Such a question may not be answered, yet it must be asked. The only thing we need to realize is that Francesca wants us to know that the two lovers returned on other days to the book which once for all has acted as their go-between. The reason for this, as for Francesca's indirect reference to such a fact, may be seen in a wish not so much to recapture the wild happiness of the first, fatal moment, as to recover, if only for an instant, the idealizing and sublimating illusions which literature creates around the realities of sex and lust. It was the worship of passion, the ideology of love, its idolatry and cult, which had hidden from their consciences the danger of damnation and the ugliness of sin; it was the written word, both harmless and harmful, that had spelled their doom. Yet they tasted the intoxicating sweetness of that worship or cult not only before, but even after knowing the bitterness of sin.

Now that Francesca has ended her story, the canto goes rapidly toward its end. At this point, Dante has very little to tell us. He merely observes that while Francesca had been talking, Paolo had been unashamedly weeping, and implies that his tears did not stop even after she had ceased to speak. From Dante's manner of speaking, rather than from what he says, we realize that he must never have taken his eyes from Francesca's face all the while she had been talking to him: and this is perhaps the first time he has been able to look into the tearful countenance of her lover. The echoes of Francesca's words, which still fill and rend his heart, or perhaps, even more, the pitiful spectacle of Paolo's grief, are too much for Dante, who breaks down under the stress. The poet suddenly swoons, and falls down like a dead man:

> Mentre che l' uno spirito questo disse,
> l'altro piangea, sí che di pietade
> io venni men cosí com'io morisse;
>
> e caddi come corpo morto cade.

Dante loses his senses out of compassion, while Paolo and Francesca lost their senses out of passion alone: yet, although caused by sentimental participation rather than by moral complicity, his fall parallels their fall. The almost perfect iambic beat of the line seems to reproduce the thud of his body, which for a while will lie on the earth as a lifeless object, as a soulless thing.

* * *

* * * The love story which Dante retells in his own way (which coincides, although only in part, with Francesca's way), is "romantic" in the old-fashioned meaning of that term: a meaning fully preserved in the French adjective *romanesque*, but partly surviving even in the epithet "romantic," to which modern usage has given such a broad semantic range. Medieval culture was full of trends which may be defined as "romantic" in the traditional sense; and it expressed those trends in literary forms which, being essentially anticlassical and new, took for their name the word from which both "romantic" and *romanesque* were to derive, that is, "romance."

* * *

* * * But Dante dares probe the innermost secrets of both passion and lust: and this is why, instead of contemplating "romantic love" from without, he dares to reconstruct the sinful story of Paolo and Francesca from inside, within the framework of the "romance" itself. Yet, as we shall see later, that framework is used not to re-evoke romantic love, but to exorcise it.

* * * The most relevant document which Dante left imbedded in the canto itself: namely, Francesca's manner of speaking, the language and diction she employs in telling her story of passion and death. The heroine makes abundant use of the medieval casuistry of love, and her discourse, far from being spontaneous, is rather deliberately constructed. Her words are, and are meant to be, highly conventional, even rhetorical, in character. This conventionalism is so intentional, and so intense, that we cannot certainly apply to her, and to her speech, the definition that Dante gives elsewhere (*Purgatorio*, xxiv.52–45) of himself, and of his own poetry of love:

> 'io mi son un che quando
> amore spira noto, ed a quel modo,
> che ditta dentro vo significando.'

By these words Dante means that when a genuine feeling of love truly inspires a poet's heart, it immediately determines the forms of expression best suited to itself. To do so, that feeling must have some purity and innocence, that love must be a matter of the soul, rather than of the senses. The feeling dictating Francesca's fashionable diction is of a very different sort; at any rate, the love of which she speaks in conventional terms is not necessarily identical with the love which bursts forth through the shell of that diction and often breaks it. When she is less self-conscious, Francesca's passion overflows beyond the barriers of convention, and even of convenance; but generally she tries to keep within the limits of a studied elegance, of a stylized modulation of both thought and speech. And this amounts to saying that one of the outstanding critical hypotheses, the one maintaining that Francesca speaks according to the tenets of the *dolce stil nuovo*, is completely wrong. The point may be proved in many ways: for instance, by arguing that no woman was ever a member of Dante's "circle," or that no feminine character ever speaks in the first person in any of the poems written by the poets of that school. It is true that Francesca's speech is full of literary mannerisms, but it is easier to find among them a few peculiar Provençal traits, than any characteristic features of "the sweet new style." The most typical Provençalism to be found in Francesca's speech is *piacer*, nearer, even linguistically, to the original *plazer*, than its equivalent *piacenza*, normally used before Dante's time by the Italian imitators of the Troubadours. As a matter of fact, Francesca uses the term *piacer* or *plazer* in a novel way, by applying it to masculine, rather than feminine, beauty; and this reference to the good looks of her lover contributes to the almost womanly, or at least, unmanly, impression that Paolo seems to produce.

Even so we must still recognize that the first line of Francesca's confession sounds not merely as a reminiscence, but as a repetition of the main belief of "the sweet new style" school, according to which there is an affinity, nay, an identity, between love and a noble heart. That line, which reads: "Amor ch'al cor gentil ratto s'apprende," seems to be an echo, or rather a replica, of the opening words of the famous *canzone* by Guido Guinicelli: "Al cor gentil ripara sempre amore," which the young Dante had paraphrased in the beginning of a famous sonnet of the *Vita Nuova*: "Amore e il cor gentil sono una cosa."

Yet, if my reading of the episode is right, I feel that despite their verbal identities Francesca's statement and the passages just quoted have different, even opposite, meanings. As used by Francesca, *amore* and *cor gentile* signify an experience and a reality that cannot be compared, except in contrast, with the ideals and values those two formulae designate in the language of Guinicelli and Dante. When these two poets connect those two concepts, they intend to say that the spiritual power of love finds its natural abode in a heart made noble by its own merits and virtues. But when Francesca makes the same connection, she means instead that passional love is the calling and destiny of every heart which is noble in this word's literal sense, that is, made such by the gentility of its blood. This is the way Francesca feels, as is proved by the manner in which she speaks about herself and of her own passion and person, or alludes to Paolo, whom she implicitly defines *cotanto amante*, "so great a lover," by so defining Lancelot. One must not forget that the notary Guinicelli, and that Dante, who was officially a member of the medical guild, were respectively citizens of Bologna and Florence, of two free communes, of two democratic commonwealths. Their very conception of love, despite its aristocratic origins, reflects already the cultural awareness of the new burghers' class. The "sweet new style" reacts against the feudal ideology of the Troubadours and their disciples, who believed literally in the doctrine of courtly love, and considered it a privilege of the highly placed and the well born. But Francesca was the member of a family that tried to reduce the city of Ravenna into its own fief, and the pride of her birth and station induces her to prefer the Provençal view. That view had survived the decline of Provençal poetry and culture, and had found new expression in the prose fiction of Northern France, where an equally refined, but less spiritual, sort of love was still considered as the exclusive privilege of knights and dames, of men and women of great breeding and lineage. For Dante and his group love will always remain a matter of election and grace, based on the reciprocal sympathy of two lofty souls; and the poet rephrases this doctrine in a famous passage in the *Purgatorio* (xxii.10–12), through the following words attributed to Vergil:

'Amore,
acceso di virtú, sempre altro accese,
pur che la fiamma sua paresse fuore . . .'

It has been suggested that these lines are meant as a kind of retractation of the principle embodied in the line where Francesca speaks of the fatality of love, of its refusal to absolve any person being loved from loving in return (*amor ch' a nullo amato amar perdona*); but the hypothesis seems to be groundless. Through the words just quoted Dante qualifies in a higher ethical sense the doctrine of his youth, his own belief in the reciprocity of spiritual love. As for Francesca's statement, no palinode was required, exactly because its equivocal meaning is clarified by the moral lesson contained in the entire episode. No correction was in this case necessary since, despite all appearances, even when using the same verbal expressions, she does not speak the language of Dante, or of all the poets who, as he said in another canto of the *Purgatorio* (xxvi.99), "rime d'amor usar dolci e leggiadre."

Nor, despite the Provençal mannerisms of her speech, have we any right to deduce that Francesca's manner of speaking is an echo of the diction of the Troubadours. Only Dante himself may help us to find the literary models and the stylistic examples after which he patterned Francesca's discourse. He offers such a help in another part of the canto just mentioned, where he affirms that Arnaut Daniel was the best craftsman of the vernacular word (*Purgatorio*, xxvi.117–119), and surpassed all his rivals in both "versi d'amore e prose di romanzi."

With this simple line, Dante sums up all the main forms of the literature in the vulgar tongue, as it had developed at that time in Tuscany and in Italy, as well as in Provence and France. He obviously considers only the forms endowed with formal dignity, addressed to a literate and nonpopular audience, dealing in different ways with the same great medieval theme, which, for the intellectual as well as for the social élite, was the theme of love. There is no doubt that Francesca's speech must be patterned on either one of these two main forms. It is true that Francesca's language is highly literary in character, and has very little to do with popular speech: its very sophistication and complexity stand out against the background of the simple style used by Dante in the narrative parts of the canto, and in the whole of his poem. Yet this does not mean that Francesca's manner of speaking is necessarily poetic, especially in the lyrical sense. We have already stated that that language differs from the style which Dante himself called both "sweet" and "new"; and one may add, not too paradoxically, that, although Dante shapes her words and thoughts into the rhythmical and metrical structure of the *Commedia*, she speaks not in verse but in prose. Thus, by making use of the line quoted above, one could say that her forms of expression derive not from the tradition of the poetry of love (*versi d'amore*), either in the *lingua del sí* or the *langue d'hoc*, but from the tradition of love fiction (*prose di romanzi*) in the *langue d'oïl*. After all, the name "Francesca" means nothing else but "French." Dante's heroine translates into her own terms the idiom she has learned from such French literary sources as the romance of Lancelot,[5] hence the formal conventionality, the rhetorical stylization, of her speech. Almost dialectically, that conventionality and that stylization transform themselves into their very opposites, becoming thus the aptest instrument, the most natural vehicle of which Francesca could avail herself not only to relate her story, but even to idealize and sublimate it.

This general imitation of the tone of the romantic narratives she used to admire so much does not mean that Francesca imitates in any special way the particular language of the romance of Lancelot, nor that, while re-evoking the effect provoked by the reading of that

---

5. There is no doubt that Dante read the French medieval romances in the original language. As for Paolo and Francesca, they must have read their *libro galeotto* in the same tongue: for, "if an Italian translation of *Tristan* was already extant from the Thirteenth Century, there is no proof that Lancelot had been granted the same fortune: moreover, and this is

romance, the poet patterned the story of its two readers after the most important episode of the romance itself. Immoral literature may influence life, but not in such a way as to pattern life after itself. When she establishes an apparently perfect parallel between the two "first" kisses, the one exchanged between Lancelot and Guinevere, and the one exchanged between Paolo and herself, Francesca gives the impression of remembering the one as fully as the other: yet Dante knows that she is wrong. The parallelism she implies is partial or relative; and one could say that she unconsciously reshapes the literary kiss to make it better agree with the real one. In other terms, she recollects what she did experience far better than what she did read. Her words mislead the reader (if not the poet) into believing that Lancelot and Guinevere too were "alone and without any suspicion" (*soli e senza alcun sospetto*), while, in

---

what matters most . . . French . . . was then the courtly language par excellence in the Italian North," according to Pio Rajna's statement in his article "Dante e i romanzi della Tavola Rotonda," *Nuova Antologia*, 1157 (1 June 1920). The same problem had been studied before Rajna by Paget Toynbee, in his essay "Dante and the Lancelot Romance," *Fifth Annual Report of the Dante Society of America*, Cambridge, Mass. (1886), and, more fully, in his *Ricerche e Note Dantesche* (Bologna, 1904); after Rajna, by Nicola Zingarelli, in his article "Le reminiscenze dal 'Lancelot'," in *Studi Danteschi*, I, 82–90.

All these studies deal in detail not only with the relevant lines in this canto, but also with another famous passage of the *Commedia* connected with the Lancelot romance, to which I have already referred in the present essay. This passage is to be found in *Paradiso*, xvi.13–15, and reads thus:

> onde Beatrice, ch'era un poco scevra,
> ridendo, parve quella che tossío
> al primo fallo scritto di Ginevra.

Here Dante alludes to the same chapter of the Lancelot romance to which Francesca refers in *Inferno*, v; but now he recalls merely a minor incident, preceding the climax of the chapter, which is the kiss exchanged between Lancelot and Guinevere. The one "who coughed" is the Dame de Malehaut, who is also in the grove, during the nightly meeting of the Knight and the Queen. The Dame is still in love with Lancelot, who was once her prisoner, although he pretends to have forgotten it. Pio Rajna (op. cit.) explains the reference, and its connection with the present situation, in the following way: "By coughing, and thus recalling back to herself the attention of Lancelot, the Dame de Malehaut warns him that she is nearby, and makes him understand that the secret he has been so jealously keeping (i.e., his love for the Queen) is no longer a secret for her. Likewise Beatrice, after having withdrawn a little aside, as feeling estranged from the worldly conversation between Cacciaguida and his descendant, with her laughter recalls Dante to the awareness of her presence, so that he may watch himself; and at the same time warns him that the reason of that proud *voi* had not escaped her." (Dante, who at first addresses his ancestor with "tu," shifts to the more respectful "voi" as soon as he learns Cacciaguida had been knighted before his death.)

I have discussed this passage in detail only to have the opportunity of commenting on the highly interesting closing line of the terzina, "al primo fallo scritto di Ginevra." These words are clearly a definition of the crucial chapter of the Lancelot romance; i.e., of the scene ending with the first kiss of the two lovers. The presence of the adjective *primo* may, in our context, throw some light on one of the most famous lines of *Inferno*, v, which is precisely "quel giorno piú non vi leggemmo avante": and make perhaps more valid my interpretation of that line. Even more significant is Dante's description of the romance itself as a *fallo scritto*, as a "sin written down," exactly because such a description sounds like an explicit replica of the moral judgment about romantic literature which this canto states implicitly, and which Francesca herself sums up in the words: "Galeotto fu il libro e chi lo scrisse."

their meeting in the grove at night, they were not only accompanied by Gallehaut, but also attended by the Queen's ladies in waiting, who were lingering nearby. What is even more important is that in the book it is the woman, and not the man, who kisses first. As a matter of fact, while the romance fails to mention that the Knight returned the Queen's kiss, Francesca does the same in regard to her response to Paolo's embrace. The parallel is partly one also of contrast, and the implication of this is so obviously suggestive that we do not need to dwell upon it. These details may however point out that Dante cared more for the spirit than for the letter of his text; and this scorn for literalness must be certainly taken into account also in regard to what we have said about his decision to let Francesca speak according to the diction of the love romances.

The very fact that the poet does not adopt the same diction himself, and fails to use it fully in those passages where the character speaking in the first person is not Francesca, but the protagonist of his own poem, clearly shows that even Dante the character avoids involving his own views and values in the language employed by his heroine. The man writing this canto is no longer the young literary enthusiast who once liked so much the French romances so dear to all the Paolos and the Francescas as to define them *Arthuri regis ambages pulcherrimae*, as he did in a famous passage of *De Vulgari Eloquio*, where however the word *ambages* is rather equivocal, and may mean "fancies," as well as "adventures."[6] Here Dante uses the language of the romances almost critically, or rather, as a dramatic device, through which he projects the psychology of Francesca, and within which he encloses her personality as within a shell. Francesco de Sanctis recognized the magnificent total result of Dante's vision and perspective, while ignoring the process or the method by which that result was achieved. In other words, he paid attention to the natural effects, rather than to the artificial components, of Francesca's speech. It is perhaps for this reason that he was led to interpret the canto in tragic, rather than in *romanesque* terms. Yet this was at least in part a happy mistake, because it saved him from the far more serious error of reading Francesca's words in lyrical key. With his profound insight, the great critic felt that, despite all appearances, Francesca speaks not only outside the frame of reference of "the new sweet style," but in opposition to it. This is what he means when he says that Francesca, "this first-born daughter of Dante," is also "the first truly living woman to appear on the poetic horizon of

---

6. The passage quoted from *De Vulgari Eloquio* may be found in I, x, 2. The double meaning of *ambages* is discussed by Pio Rajna, who prefers interpreting that word in its figurative, rather than in its literal sense. This term's equivocal significance seems to anticipate Petrarch's pun on *erranti* ("wandering" and "erring").

the modern age." Although readily admitting that such a figure
could be created only after "a long elaboration of the feminine ideal
in the poetry of the Troubadours and in the very lyrics of Dante," he
ends by saying that Francesca is the opposite of Beatrice. Within the
poetic tradition from which the latter derives, "man fills the stage
with himself; it is he who acts, and speaks, and dreams; while
woman remains in the background, named and not represented, like
Selvaggia and Mandetta; she stays there as man's shadow, as a thing
he owns, as an object he has wrought, as the being issued from his
rib, devoid of a separate personality of her own."[7]

XII

The last clue is a negative one: Paolo's silence, and the significance
of that silence. Paolo has no existence of his own. He speaks no
word during the entire episode; and even when Francesca refers to
her lover, the poet pays no attention to him. Dante seems to notice
his presence only at the end, and does so only to remark that Paolo
must have been weeping for a long time. It was natural for the poet
to place Francesca in the foreground of the episode, and Paolo in its
background; yet this fails to explain the poet's almost absolute indif-
ference to the lesser of these two protagonists. Such an indifference
is not casual, but deliberate. Dante's scorn is not directed toward
Paolo as a separate person, but toward what he stands for; and as
such it involves all men who like him are the slaves, rather than the
masters, of love. The passionate man, hardly ever as interesting or
suggestive as the passionate woman, is never called hero, while
many a woman in love is a heroine. It is said that love exalts the
lowly, and humbles the lofty ones; but this is true only in the sense
that the first is the feminine, and the second the masculine alterna-
tive. Especially in love is "the female of the species more deadly
than the male." For man, even more than for woman, love is almost
always a *liaison dangereuse*. Either one of the two actors or victims
of a love story will look pathetic to the eyes of mankind, but while
pathos may enhance a woman's personality, it lessens man's stature.
A pathetic hero is a contradiction in terms, since he is made to look
not only unheroic, but even unmanly. This Dante understood well:

---

7. This passage is quoted from the most important of all Francesco de Sanctis' Dante essays,
   and is given as translated by me. De Sanctis originally published that essay in 1869, under
   the title *Francesca da Rimini secondo i critici e secondo l'arte*. The essay was later included
   in the collection of his *Saggi Critici*. The text used here is the one reprinted in the 1952
   Laterza edition of *Saggi Critici* (VII, 240–256). Though disagreeing with de Sanctis' view,
   I still feel that his critique of the Paolo and Francesca episode is a masterpiece. Anything
   the great critic had to say about the *Commedia*, even beyond the famous pages in his *Storia
   della Letteratura Italiana*, is worth rereading. Such a task can now be easily done, since the
   Einaudi edition of the *Opere di Francesco de Sanctis*, made under the direction of Carlo
   Muscetta, has just devoted its 5th volume (Turin, 1955) to the *Lezioni e Saggi su Dante*.

so, while raising Francesca to prominence, he reduced Paolo almost to nought. De Sanctis recognized this very well: "Who is Paolo? He is not the man, or the manly type, such as to form an antithesis, to establish a dualism. Francesca fills the stage wholly with herself. Paolo is the mute expression of Francesca; the string trembling at what she says, the gesture accompanying her voice. The one speaks while the other weeps; the tears of the one are the words of the other."

This statement, a perfect aesthetic justification of Dante's conception, implies that the main character of the episode absorbs the lesser one; that its protagonist is this couple of lovers, even more than Francesca herself; that the two lovers form a single personality though such a personality is shaped by its feminine component, rather than by its masculine one. In this very conception Dante shows outstanding originality. No poet went as far as Dante in this reduction to a cipher of the masculine partner of a great passion. Considered alone, Paolo, a bleak pale creature whose only action is weeping, pales nearly to a vanishing point. Love changes man into woman's shadow, and this is true of Paolo not only as the ghost he now is, but as the man he once was. Francesca projects the memory of herself even before the time of her fatal affair, but evokes her lover only during the moment of their sin. And, unconsciously, she fixes him forever in a vision of passive pusillanimity. At least in appearance she describes him in the very moment he acted like a man: when he took the initiative, as he was supposed to do, and kissed her on her mouth. Yet Francesca finds it fit to remember that even in that instant of daring he was trembling in every fiber of his body, like a leaf. Commenting upon the simple and terrible words, *tutto tremante*, by which Francesca recalls the emotions of her lover in that moment of anguish and bliss, Francesco de Sanctis is led to observe that "certainly Paolo's flesh did not tremble out of fright." I am not so sure: I may even be ready to maintain exactly the opposite. Paolo perhaps trembled because he was afraid: of woman and love, or of death and of sin; or simply of the unknown, even of his own fear itself. In this passivity and pusillanimity Paolo strangely resembles the hero to whom Francesca and the poet liken him. In the second of the two romances of which he is the protagonist, *Le Chevalier de la Charrette*, Lancelot is described as willing to look like a coward, and even to risk infamy, merely to pursue his love object; while in *Lancelot du Lac* the Queen kisses him first, as soon as she realizes that he does not dare to do so himself; and, as the text states with comical naïveté, she gives herself the illusion of being the receiver rather than the giver, by taking the knight by his chin: "Et la roine voit bien que li chevaliers n'en ose plus fere; si le prent pour let menton et le base" (xxxi).

All this may suffice to prove not only that Francesca towers above Paolo, but that the poet towers above both. As I have frequently hinted, this cannot be said of Dante the character, whom the author, with great humility and charity, equates with the lesser part of his double creation. This happens at the very ending of the episode, when the reader witnesses at the same time, in two different men, almost the same heartbreak. It is at this point that we suddenly realize that Paolo had been unashamedly sobbing for the entire duration of Francesca's speech; and immediately after this, we learn that Dante has fainted as soon as Francesca has uttered her last word. For a while, at the close of the canto, Dante the character becomes thus the equal of Paolo, and even of Lancelot, who for a while seems to swoon himself, while talking with the Queen of his still unrewarded love. In this brief moment, Dante himself is but a creature of pathos, a victim of pity and self-pity, like Paolo and Lancelot. Dante the poet stops short of the ridiculous, but it is only the timely fall of the curtain which saves the final scene of the episode from an unexpected caricatural effect.

XIII

All this amounts to saying that love cannot ever be the tragic passion par excellence. Tolstoy acknowledged as much when he attributed the following words to Konstantin Levin, the masculine protagonist of *Anna Karenina:* "To my mind, love . . . both sorts of love, which you remember Plato defines in his *Banquet*, serve as the test of men. Some men only understand one sort, and some only the other. And those who only know the non-platonic love have no need to talk of tragedy. . . . In platonic love there can be no sort of tragedy . . . because in that love all is clear and pure because. . . . But perhaps you are right. Very likely . . . I don't know. I don't know."[8]

Unlike Tolstoy and his hero, Dante was one of those few human beings equally able to understand both kinds of love; and he understood them both as a man and as a poet. He was able to understand the kind of love which stops at the "sweet sighs," and which is generally expressed in lyric form, as well as the kind that experiences the "dubious desires," and manifests itself in romantic fiction. In the same way he understood that neither kind can be tragic. Dante is a moral realist, always subordinating pathos to ethos. So it is improper to interpret the episode of Paolo and Francesca in the light of the romantic view of poetry and life, as de Sanctis did, or according to the decadent view as did Gabriele D'Annunzio in his *Francesca da*

8. Pt. I, Ch. xi (as translated by Constance Garnett).

Rimini. The latter is not a tragedy, but merely a "poem of blood and lust" (*poema di sangue e di lussuria*), as the author himself so aptly said.[9] In the same way, while using continuously, and almost exclusively, the criterion of tragedy, Francesco de Sanctis gave us an interpretation of the Paolo and Francesca episode far more pathetic than tragic. "Sin is the highest pathos of tragedy, since this contradiction (between the sense of sin and the erotic impulse) is placed not without, but within the two lovers' souls," says the critic, thus reducing the situation to a psychological crisis, even more than to a moral conflict. It is in "the sweet thoughts," even more than in "the dubious desires," that de Sanctis sees "the tragic core of the story, the divine tragedy left unsaid on Francesca's lips, and which only Dante's reverie, so movingly imagined, calls forth and re-enacts," thus showing that he conceives the fall and the ruin of the two lovers in sentimental terms. De Sanctis concludes his analysis by affirming that "pity is the muse of this tragedy, which the poet unfolds only in its main lines, filling the rest with silence and mystery. . . ." But tragedy is made not only of pathos and pity, but also of ethos and terror. A full study of de Sanctis' essay reveals that the critic is reading their episode not in the light of tragedy, but in the light of romantic drama: as a story of love and death, stirring our emotions and feelings rather than our moral sense, as an effusion of sentiment, so pure as to need no catharsis. There is no doubt that this canto is based on an interplay of passion and compassion: yet neither one nor the other, not even their synthesis, can be taken at its face value.

I have already stated that Dante wrote the episode in the key of the love romances, but even this needs qualification, and cannot be taken for granted. In what he did, Dante went beyond not only the form he chose, but also beyond the sentiment which normally inspires or dictates that form. The love romance is primarily, but not exclusively, a medieval genre, so that it recurs even in modern literature, where it changes its style, replacing the convention of fancy with the conventions of realism, and taking the name and the shape of the novel, or of other types of fiction. Yet the new product will remain a love romance if it still expresses sentiment without judging it. This is certainly not the case with such a work as *Anna Karenina*, where the writer condemns his heroine at least by implication, by referring her judgment to the tribunal of God. Such is the sense of the scriptural epigraph that Tolstoy placed at the head of his novel: "Vengeance is mine; I will repay, saith the Lord" (Romans XII.19). Yet the same epigraph would be at least partly improper if placed at the head of this canto, since it would reflect solely the standpoint of

9. In the "Commiato," or "Farewell Song," which precedes the play.

Dante the character. In this episode, as in the entire *Commedia*,
God has already taken his vengeance, and Dante is a witness of this.
Paolo and Francesca have been condemned to everlasting death, to
the damnation of their souls: when faced with such a revelation, the
best man can do is silently to bow his head. Yet Dante is not to be
satisfied with this, and gives to God's verdict the assent of his own
conscience, even if he does so without words. Though verbally un-
stated, Dante's judgment is framed in literary terms; his moral mes-
sage is implicit in the situation and the structure of the story, so that
no further intervention on the poet's part is required to make it
meaningful to us.

Dante achieves this result by a dialectical treatment of the ro-
mance form—by what one might call a double mirror trick. There is
no doubt that the poet derived the idea that the reading of the
Lancelot romance had been "the first root" of the passion and ruin
of the two lovers, not on the authority of any external tradition, but
solely on the inner urgings of his own imagination. If the "how" and
"why" of Francesca's fall is an invention of Dante's, then its sup-
posed occasion becomes highly suggestive and significant. The real
kiss of Paolo and Francesca follows the imaginary kiss of Lancelot
and Guinevere, as an image reflecting its object in a perspective
similar and different at the same time. In brief, the seduction scene
fulfills within the entire episode the function of a play within a play:
more properly, of a romance within a romance. This creates an ef-
fect of parody, or, if we prefer to use a less negative term, something
akin to what in modern times has been called "romantic irony,"
which in this case operates in an antiromantic sense. This means
that the two romances, one of which may be likened to a frame, and
the other, to the picture enclosed therein, react reciprocally in such
a way as to annihilate each other. In his analysis of *Madame Bovary*,
starting from the presupposition that the modern novel is but an
offspring of the ancient romance, and that originally the former was
but a love story like the latter (as proved by the fact that in French
both are still called by the same name), Albert Thibaudet ends by
saying that Flaubert's masterpiece is in reality a *contre-roman*.[1] In
the same way, the "romance" of Paolo and Francesca becomes in
Dante's hands an "antiromance," or rather, both things at once. As
such, it is able to express and to judge romantic love at the same
time. While Dante the character manifests his sorrowful regret
through the mute eloquence of his bewilderment, and later of his
swoon, so Dante the poet expresses his judgment without uttering a
word, without even a gesture or a sign of reproof or reproach. Dante

1. In his *Réflections sur le Roman*, passim.

does not preach or plead, nor does he need to superimpose an edifying sermon on the structure of his story. His ethical message may be easily read not in the spirit, but in the very letter of his tale. It is Francesca herself that he entrusts with the literary moral of his fable. This moral is very simple, and could be summed up in the statement that writing and reading romantic fiction is almost as bad as yielding to romantic love. This obvious and almost naïve truth is all contained in the famous line, "Galeotto fu il libro e chi lo scrisse," by which, as Francesco D'Ovidio says, the poet confesses his horrified feeling at the thought that he too "could become a Gallehaut to somebody else."[2] But there is no reason for such a fear, since that line helps to destroy the very suggestion on which it is built. It is with traits like this that the poet created this masterpiece, based on the avoidance of tragedy,[3] as well as on the moral sublimation of the romance form.

GIUSEPPE MAZZOTTA

A Pattern of Order:
Inferno VII and *Paradiso* VII[†]

In his recent monograph, F. P. Pickering maintains that there are two distinctive and contradictory models for medieval historiography, respectively inspired by St. Augustine and Boethius.[1] Whereas the Augustinian model deals with the transcendent and linear order of universal history, from Creation through the Fall and Redemption to the Apocalypse, the Boethian model focuses on the contingent and concrete events of secular history-writing (lives of individuals, dynastic histories, shifting fortunes of people, etc.).

The difference between these two possible schemes of history would seem to depend on the opposed value that Augustine and Boethius assign to Fortune. St. Augustine's *heilsgeschichte* has no place for a goddess *Fortuna*, the voluble and blind deity of the pa-

---

2. *Nuovi Studii Danteschi*, II (Milan, 1907), 531.
3. This concept was first used by Erich Heller, in his article "Goethe on the Avoidance of Tragedy" in *The Disinherited Mind: Essays in Modern German Literature* (Philadelphia, 1952).
† From *Dante, Poet of the Desert*. Copyright © 1979 by Princeton University Press. Reprinted by permission of the author.
1. F. P. Pickering, *Augustinus oder Boethius? Geschichtsschreibung und epische Dichtung im Mittelalter-und in der Neuzeit*, Part I (Berlin: Erich Schmidt Verlag, 1967). See also F. P. Pickering, *Literature and Art in the Middle Ages* (Coral Gables: University of Miami Press, 1970), esp. pp. 168–96.

gans. Accordingly, the paradigm of history that he elaborates in his *De Civitate Dei*, for instance, is overtly regulated by a providential order.[2] Boethius, on the contrary, has a view of the role of Fortune which accounts for the mutability and vicissitudes of real experiences, not *sub specie aeternitatis* as St. Augustine would, but as *res gestae* in time and place. In the Boethian hierarchy of the universe, to be sure, Fortune mediates between God and his Providence on the one hand, and man and his fate and free will on the other. Yet Fortune is still a capricious and erratic entity forever playing her game and delighting in it.[3]

One doubts that these Augustinian and Boethian models can be envisioned, as they are by Pickering, as being rigidly juxtaposed. At any rate, it can be shown that Dante cuts through these categories in his *Divine Comedy*, and even combines the main lines of the insights of Boethius and Augustine in his representation of Fortune in the famous digression of *Inferno* VII.[4]

The canto opens with a reference to the unintelligible and threatening language of Plutus, the "wealthy one," according to a standard etymology of the name.[5] Plutus' two traits, unintelligibility and wealth, are the conceptual coordinates around which the doctrine of Fortune is largely plotted. If in *Convivio* Dante questions the justice in Fortune's distribution of wealth,[6] here in *Inferno* VII he alters that conception. We are told now that Fortune does not hold the things of this world in her clutches: she is an angelic intelligence, a "general ministra e duce" (l. 78), appointed by God to preside over the "splendor mondani" (l. 77), the wealth and power that lie in the

2. St. Augustine's attack against Fortune is contained in *De Civitate Dei*, IV, 18 and 19, respectively dealing with the myth of the good and bad Fortune, and *Fortuna Muliebris*. Cf. also the remark, "Non enim eas causas, quae dicuntur fortuitae, unde etiam Fortuna nomen accepit, non esse dicimus nullas, sed latentes: easque tribuimus . . . veri Dei . . . voluntati, . . ." (*De Civitate Dei*, V, 9, in CCSL XLVII).

3. Boethius links Providence, Fortune and Fate most explicitly in book IV, pros. 6 of *De Consolatione Philosophiae*; at the same time, he writes earlier in the text: "The pride of fickle fortune spareth none, / And, like the floods of swift Euripus borne, / Oft casteth mighty princes from their throne, / . . . She cares not for the wretch's tears and moan, / And the sad groans, which she hath caused, doth scorn. / Thus doth she play, to make her power more known, / Showing her slaves a marvel, when man's state / Is in one hour both downcast and fortunate" (*The Consolation of Philosophy*, English trans. rev. H. F. Stewart (Cambridge, Mass.: Harvard University Press, 1968), II, m. 1, pp. 177–9. See also *De Consolatione*, II, pros. 2 and m. 2, 1–8. For a general view, cf. Howard R. Patch, *The Goddess Fortuna in Mediaeval Literature* (Cambridge, Mass.: Harvard University Press, 1927). See also the important remarks by Vincenzo Cilento, *Medio evo monastico e scolastico* (Milan and Naples: Ricciardi, 1961), pp. 41–73.

4. A recent reading of the canto is by Gianluigi Toja, "Canto VII dell'*Inferno*," *Convivium*, 35 (1967), pp. 129–54. See also V. Cioffari, *The Conception of Fortune and Fate in the Works of Dante* (Cambridge, Mass.: Dante Society, 1940). Cf. Howard R. Patch, *The Tradition of Boethius* (New York: Oxford University Press, 1935).

5. Cicero, *De Natura Deorum*, II, xxvi, 66.

6. "Dico che la loro imperfezione delle ricchezze primamente si può notare ne la indiscrezione del loro avvenimento, nel quale nulla distributiva giustizia risplende, ma tutta iniquitade quasi sempre, la quale iniquitade è proprio effetto d'imperfezione" (*Convivio*, IV, xi, 6 ff.).

sublunary world of change and corruption. From this point of view it is significant that Dante should link Fortune to wealth and represent her in the area where avaricious and prodigals are punished: their contrary sins—the hoarding or dissipation or riches—disrupt the economy of the world governed by Fortune, and violate the principle, implicit in the wheel of Fortune, of exchange and circulation of common goods. In what clearly is a deliberate counterpoint to the circular motion of the wheel, the sinners are shown to move in half-circles, doomed, ironically, to exchange insults (ll. 28–33).

This irony has a dramatic value in the unfolding of the canto, for it is a sign of the reversals which Fortune enacts and, at the same time, it is a detail by which Dante points to Fortune's mockery of human attempts at mastery and control over the things of the world. The perpetual shifts of Fortune, who blindfolded changes "vain wealth" from race to race, follow a providential but inscrutable design, which teases man's efforts and sanctions the limitations of his reason. Since Fortune transcends human understanding, Vergil's rational exposition on her workings only heightens the sense that reason is precariously poised between the unintelligible bestiality of Plutus and the hidden purposes of this "ministra," who, in openly Boethian phraseology, appears as the distant spectator laughing at her own games in the world.

The distance between man and Fortune is suggested by her description as an entity contained in a self-enclosed circularity:

> ma ella s'è beata e ciò non ode:
> con l'altre prime creature lieta
> volve sua spera e beata si gode.
> ll. 94–6

The tercet, by the emphasis on the steady rotation of the wheel; the self-reflexiveness in two verbs ("s'è beata" . . . "si gode"), the stylistic stratagem of repeating (and reversing the order of) the same phrase ("s'è beata" turns into "e beata si gode"), mimes the movement of Fortune, from a human standpoint, as a circular and self-enclosed totality.

This Boethian view of the cyclical turns of man's fortunes seems, on the face of it, to be remarkably at odds with Dante's conception of history (derived from St. Augustine) with its beginning in the Creation of the angels and its consummation in the Apocalypse. However, the contradiction is only apparent, for Dante, in effect, harmonizes the conception of Boethius and Augustine. Fortune, the text states, came into being with the other primal angelic intelligences at the time of Creation (*Inferno* VII, ll. 73–6); in addition, Vergil quiets Plutus by referring to the war in Heaven, the epic battle between Michael and Satan, whose "superbo strupo" (l. 12) is the primal Fall which has rent the order of the cosmos. Finally, the canto also contains a direct allusion to the resurrection, when these sinners shall rise from their grave, "colpugno chiuso, e questi coi crin mozzi" (l. 57).

The Augustinian focus in Dante's representation of Fortune is further implied by the context of pride within which she is evoked in *Inferno* VII as well as in other glaring instances. *Paradiso* XVI, which in a way is the poetic counterpart of the Florentine chronicles, such as Villani's, tells the decline of the great Florentine families.[7] While their "dynastic history" is viewed as part of the ceaseless turning of Fortune's wheel (ll. 79–141), the sin of pride introduces their decline to reinforce the suggestion that Fortune rules over the world of the Fall.[8] In the representation of Fortune, in other words, Dante shares the Augustinian view of the providentiality of events. Like Augustine, he rejects as illusory the classical belief in chance: ultimately, the faith in the arbitrariness of chance is untenable because it completely abolishes the possibility of moral choice and the making of history.

By coupling Boethius' language with the fundamental elements of Augustinian historiography, Dante preserves the ambiguity which is the distinctive feature of Fortune's deceptiveness. It is only a commonplace to remark that for Boethius, Fortune first allures man with enticements of simulated bliss, only to cast him later into grief; for Alanus, she embodies all possible oxymora: reliably unreliable, blind seer, constant in fickleness, etc. For Dante, however, Fortune is deceptive only for those who abide in the darkling world of the Fall: in the instability of the fallen world, the more one attempts to hold on to the goods of Fortune, the more one plunges down to the bottom of the wheel. Fortune can be conquered by the exercise of poverty: by giving up the very material elements that she controls, and acknowledging its inherent providentiality. In this sense, the wheel of Fortune is a basic metaphor in Dante's vision of history, for it discloses the order that lies under the confusions and impermanence of temporal life.

This view of order underlying the darkness of the world of Fortune finds a direct extension in *Paradiso* VII, where Dante probes the question of the fall and redemption of man within the economy of Creation. In *Paradiso* VI, Justinian refers to two "vengeances" occurring within the plan of salvation history: the crucifixion of Christ was a

---

7. It is well known that the picture of serene life of the Florence of old that Cacciaguida evokes in *Paradiso* XV (ll. 97 ff.) bears a striking resemblance to the account in Giovanni Villani, *Cronica*, ed. F. Gherardi Dragomanni, 4 vols. (Florence: S. Coen, 1844–45), I, bk. VI, 69. In *Paradiso* XVI, for instance, the feud between the house of the Amidei and the Buondelmonti's (ll. 136–54) parallels the account by Villani's *Cronica*, I, V, 38. For further bibliography, see Giovanni Aquilecchia, "Dante and the Florentine Chroniclers," *Bulletin of the John Rylands Library*, 48 (1965), pp. 30–55, now rep. in *Schede di italianistica* (Turin: Einaudi, 1976), pp. 45–72.

8. "'Oh quali io vidi quei che son disfatti / per lor superbia! e le palle de l'oro / fiorian Fiorenza in tutt' i suoi gran fatti'" (*Paradiso* XVI, ll. 109–11). It might also be pointed out that Fortune is linked to the fall of Troy and its traditional pride: "E quando la fortuna volse in basso / l'altezza de' Troian che tutto ardiva, . . ." (*Inferno* XXX, ll. 13–14).

"vendetta" for Adam's sin, while Titus' destruction of Jerusalem was the just revenge for the crucifixion (ll. 88–93). From one point of view, these two events dramatize the centrality of the Roman Empire in the providential structure of history. At the same time, the pilgrim perceives them as a moral paradox, which Beatrice untangles in *Paradiso* VII in terms of the divine and human natures of Christ. Since Christ is the nodal center of both history and the cosmos, her explanation turns, in effect, into a complex rationale which discloses the justice and order in God's scheme of things.

The whole of creation, Beatrice states, is shaped by God's boundless love and goodness. There are some elements in creation which have been touched directly by the hand of our maker and which, therefore, will never perish. But God has also acted through the agency of vicarious Nature: this is the so-called secondary creation, which comprises the four elements, their mixtures and compounds, and which is subject to the penalty of corruptibility and death (*Paradiso* VII, ll. 124–8). The primary creation, on the other hand, which consists of brute matter, the heavens, the angels and the soul, includes also the human flesh, which shares in God's immortality and will be resurrected at the end of time (ll. 130–48). However, man can conquer death only because of Christ's atonement and sacrifice, the only way, actually, by which man's redemption could take place. Man was originally fashioned by God in his image and likeness, but the Fall disfigured him, banished him from Paradise and stripped him of his dignities (ll. 36–9 and 79–87). His inability to reach salvation "ne termini suoi" (l. 97) was such that the crucifixion was needed to "riparar l'omo a sua intera vita" (l. 104) and rescue him from the burden of sin.

This brief summary was necessary to show the several links, forged both in terms of conceptual frame and detail, which exist between *Inferno* VII and *Paradiso* VII. In *Inferno* VII Fortune is introduced by an allusion to the cosmic disruption caused by the pride of the fallen angels, and Fortune herself is an angelic intelligence which came into being at the time of creation. In *Paradiso* VII the burden of Beatrice's exposition is creation, the pride and disobedience of man and the restoring of harmony in the universe. If Fortune in *Inferno* VII is depicted as the governess of the world, in *Paradiso* VII Dante explores how God governs the world through Nature. The two cantos, actually, enact the interdependence that is conventionally posited between Fortune's outward goods and Nature's works and gifts.[9]

More cogently, in *Inferno* VII Fortune is cast in Boethian language; in *Paradiso* VII, the description of the universe created by

---

9. *De Consolatione Philosophiae*, bk. II, pros. 5, tells the distinction between Fortune and Nature. Cf. Alanus de Insulis, *Anticlaudianus*, ed. R. Bossuat (Paris: J. Vrin, 1955), VIII, ll. 45–146. Cf. also H. R. Patch, *The Goddess Fortuna in Mediaeval Literature*, pp. 65–75.

God's goodness, "La divina bontà, che da sé sperne / ogne livore, ar-
dendo in sé, sfavilla / sì che dispiega le bellezze etterne" (ll. 64–6),
translates a passage from *De Consolatione Philosophiae*, in which
Boethius addresses the Creator who made his work from chaotic
matter, not impelled by external causes, but by virtue of the highest
good existing within him without envy.[1]

There are other minor correspondences between the two cantos,[2]
but an important common feature is that just as in *Inferno* VII Dante
placed Boethius' view of Fortune within the Augustinian focus of the
Fall, in *Paradiso* VII the allusion to Boethius' text is placed within a
rigorous theological perspective. The famous ninth hymn of the
third book of *De Consolatione*, to be sure, recapitulates the great
themes of Plato's *Timaeus* and, along with the *Timaeus*, was the ob-
ject of persistent and controversial exegeses, especially at the School
of Chartres.[3] That the language of *Paradiso* VII is punctuated with a
number of textual recalls from Chalcidius' version of the *Timaeus*
has been pointed out ever since the early commentators of the
poem.[4] It has been suggested that Dante is aware of Guillaume de
Conches' controversial speculations over the *Timaeus* and the hymn,
"O qui perpetua mundum. . . ." I would suggest, however, that in
Paradiso VII Dante argues against the naturalistic thrust of Guil-
laume's position from the standpoint of Anselm's theology of the In-
carnation.[5]

For if the impulse behind the work of Guillaume is a faith in the
natural world, in the ability of reason to grasp the structure of the

1. "O qui perpetua mundum ratione gubernas / Terrarum caelique sator qui tempus ab aeuo
  / Ire iubes stabilisque manens das cuncta moueri, / Quem non externae pepulerunt fin-
  gere causae / Materiae fluitantis opus, uerum insita summi / Forma boni liuore
  carens, . . ." *De Consolatione Philosophiae*, III, m. 9. The hymn is also quoted in *Con-
  vivio*, III, ii, 17. It must be mentioned, however, that G. Fraccaroli, "Dante e il Timeo," an
  appendix to *Il Timeo*, trans. G. Fraccaroli (Turin: Bocca, 1906), pp. 391–424, believes
  that *Paradiso* VII, ll. 64–6, echoes Plato's *Timaeus* directly.
2. Gian Roberto Sarolli, *Prolegomena alla* Divina Commedia (Florence: Olschki editore,
  1971), p. 290, points out the "antithethical parallelism" between Plutus' "voce chioccia"
  in his "Pape Satàn, pape Satàn aleppe." (*Inferno* VII, ll. 1–2), and the "cantare" of "Os-
  anna, sanctus Deus sabaòth," of *Paradiso* VII, ll. 1–5. Another link is possibly to be found
  in the fact that the two cantos follow two parallel political cantos, thus stressing the point
  that a providential order lies under the chaos of history.
3. An account of the debate can be found in J. M. Parent, *La Doctrine de la création dans l'é-
  cole de Chartres* (Paris: J. Vrin, 1938), pp. 29–112. See also Pierre Courcelle, "Étude cri-
  tique sur les commentaires de la Consolation de Boèce," *Archives d'histoire doctrinale et
  littéraire du moyen âge*, 12 (1939), pp. 5–140; Tullio Gregory, *Platonismo medievale: studi
  e ricerche* (Rome: Istituto storico italiano per il Medio Evo, 1958); Winthrop Wetherbee,
  Platonism and Poetry in the Twelfth Century (Princeton: Princeton University Press,
  1972), pp. 19–36.
4. Pietro di Dante mentions Boethius' ninth hymn of the third book; Francesco da Buti sug-
  gests that both Boethius and Plato's myth of creation are echoed by Dante. See Biagi, ed.,
  Paradiso, pp. 166–7.
5. Tullio Gregory, *Anima Mundi: la filosofia di Guglielmo di Conches e la scuola di Chartres*
  (Florence: Sansoni, 1955), pp. 100 ff. suggests Dante's place in the ideological debate
  around Guillaume's doctrines. For the naturalistic elements in the doctrines, see R. W.
  Southern, *Medieval Humanism and Other Studies* (New York and Evanston: Harper and

universe, Anselm gave Dante the perspective from which he can question the basic optimism and, in one word, the humanism of Guillaume. Anselm's *Cur Deus Homo* is the perception of the radical evil that perverts man's will to the extent that redemption itself is not a natural desire, but a desire that comes from God.[6] The goodness of the natural order, the "naturalis iustitia" of Guillaume's glosses on the *Timaeus*, for Anselm had been shattered by the original sin, and his own argument, condensed in the now classical formula "faith seeking understanding," bears witness to the limitations of reason. In *Inferno* VII Dante explicitly warns against the presumption of reason to grasp the mystery of Fortune; in *Paradiso* VII the universe follows a pattern of order and rationality which is given to man by the grace of God.

It is of some significance, finally, that this doctrine of order in the cosmos should take place in the seventh cantos of *Inferno* and *Paradiso*. Seven is the symbolic number of creation and its harmonious perfection,[7] which, as has been shown, is central to the theme of the two cantos. The symmetrical correspondences between these two cantos, or the other numerous parallelisms of the poem for that matter, are not to be construed merely as an exercise which maps out the formal mechanisms of the text. For Dante they exemplify, rather, the design and order of history, in which the haphazard and chance are of necessity excluded. The poet's own symbolic construction mimes the plan of the Divine Architect who has fashioned creation, as the Book of Wisdom has it, "in measure, and number and weight" (11:21). This is the world of order which the poet constantly evokes for the benefit of man who dwells in the shadows of time, buffeted by shifting desires and banished from Paradise into the land of exile.[8]

Row, Publishers, 1970), pp. 29–85. For a more tempered view, see M.-D. Chenù, *Nature, Man and Society in the Twelfth Century*, trans. Jerome Taylor and Lester K. Little (Chicago and London: University of Chicago Press, 1968), pp. 1–48. See also Wetherbee, *Platonism and Poetry*, pp. 74–125. The presence of St. Anselm in *Paradiso* VII has been documented by A. Agresti, *Dante e S. Anselmo* (Naples: Tipografia Luigi De Bonis, 1887), pp. 25–32. Cf. also Hermann Gmelin, *Die Göttliche Komödie: Das Paradies* (Stuttgart: E. Klett Verlag, 1957), III, pp. 139–44.

6. Dante's sense of the Incarnation is partly inspired by Thomas Aquinas, *Summa Theologiae*, IIIa, q. 31, a. 1, resp. For a more radical view of Redemption, see *Cur Deus Homo*, I, 5, and II, 6 and *passim*. I am quoting from *Sancti Anselmi Liber Cur Deus Homo*, ed. F. S. Schmitt (Bonn: P. Hanstein, 1929). See also Karl Barth, *Anselm: Fides Quaerens Intellectum*, trans, Ian W. Robertson (Richmond: John Knox Press, 1960).

7. For the value of number seven, see *De Civitate Dei*, XI, 31–32, *CCSL* XLVIII. See also Macrobius, *Commentary on the Dream of Scipio*, trans. W. H. Stahl (New York: Columbia University Press, 1952), p. 71 and pp. 100–08. More generally, see Vincent F. Hopper, *Medieval Number Symbolism* (New York: Columbia University Press, 1968).

8. It ought to be pointed out that Adam's fall is described as a fall into exile: "'Or, figliuol mio, non il gustar del legno / fu per sé la cagion di tanto essilio, / ma solamente il trapassar del segno.'" (*Paradiso* XXVI, ll. 115–17).

JOHN FRECCERO

Medusa: The Letter and the Spirit[†]

Several times in the course of his poem Dante insists that his verses be read allegorically, but nowhere is his insistence more peremptory or more baffling than in Canto IX of the *Inferno,* after Virgil covers the pilgrim's eyes to protect him from the sight of the Medusa:

> O voi ch'avete li 'ntelletti sani,
> mirate la dottrina che s'asconde
> sotto 'l velame de li versi strani. (vv. 61–63)

These lines have always represented something of a scandal in the interpretation of Dante's allegory, primarily because they seem to fail in ther didactic intent: the *dottrina* referred to here remains as veiled to us as it was to the poet's contemporaries. More than that, however, the *dottrina,* whatever it is, seems scarcely worth the effort. The verses suggest a personification allegory—Medusa as moral abstraction— very different from the theological allegory that, since the work of Charles Singleton,[1] we have taken to be uniquely Dantesque. The allegory of the episode would seem to be no different from the "allegory of poets," described in the *Convivio* as a *menzogna* hiding a moral truth, so that we are tempted to conclude either that Dante's allegory, though obscure, is no different from that of other poets, or that this first explicit reference to it in the poem is somehow atypical.

My argument is that neither of these alternatives is correct and that this passage, when properly understood, can supply a model for understanding Dante's allegory throughout the poem. I hope to show that the allegory is essentially theological and, far from being of purely antiquarian interest as a bizarre exegetical theory irrelevant to poetic practice, it is actually indistinguishable from the poem's narrative structure. Christian allegory, I will argue, is identical with the phenomenology of confession, for both involve a comprehension of the self in history within a retrospective literary structure.

Perhaps the principal difficulty with the address to the reader in the episode of the Medusa has arisen from our tendency to read it as though it were dramatically unrelated to its context, a generic recall to a moral code exterior to the text. In fact, however, this passage, like all of the addresses to the reader, is exterior to the fiction, but

---

† From *Dante: The Poetics of Conversion.* Copyright © 1986. Reprinted by permission of the author.

1. Charles S. Singleton, *Dante Studies 1. Commedia, Elements of Structure* (Cambridge, Mass.: Harvard University Press, 1954); "Allegory." For general bibliography on Dante's allegory, see Robert Hollander, *Allegory in Dante's "Commedia"* (Princeton: Princeton University Press, 1996).

central to the text. The authorial voice is at once the creation of the journey and its creator, an *alter Dantes* who knows, but does not as yet exist, dialectically related to the pilgrim, who exists but does not as yet know. The addresses to the reader create the author as much as they create his audience; they compose the paradigm of the entire narrative, ensuring the presence of the goal at each step along the way. It is Dante's fiction that the author's existence precedes that of the poem, as though the experience had been concluded before the poem were begun. In reality, however, the experience of the pilgrim and the creation of the authorial voice take place at the same time, in the writing of the poem. The progress of the pilgrim and the addresses to the reader are dramatic representations of the dialectic that is the process of the poem. Journey's end, the vision of the Incarnation, is at the same time the incarnation of the story, when pilgrim and author, being and knowing, become one.

In precisely the same way that the pilgrim and the authorial voice are dialectically related to each other, the dramatic action involving the Medusa is related to the address to the reader immediately following it. This is suggested by a certain inverse symmetry: the *covering* of the pilgrim's eyes calls forth a command to *uncover* and see (*mirate*) the doctrine hidden beneath the verses, as if the command were consequent to the action rather than simply the interruption that it is usually taken to be. As readers of the poem, we ordinarily assume that the dramatic action is stopped from time to time for an authorial gloss, as if the poet were arbitrarily intruding upon a rerun of his own past in order to guide us in our interpretation. Here, however, the symmetry between the action and the gloss suggests a more intimate, even *necessary*, relationship. The antithetical actions (covering/uncovering) suggest that we look for antithetical objects (Medusa/*dottrina*) in two analogous or parallel realms: the progress of the pilgrim and the progress of the poem. The threat of the Medusa lends a certain moral force to the command to *see* beneath the strange verses, just as the address to the reader lends to the Medusa a certain hermeneutic resonance. It is *because* the pilgrim averted his eyes from the Medusa that there is a truth to be seen beneath the veil; because seeing it is a way of understanding a text, however, the implication seems to be that the Medusa is an interpretive as well as a moral threat. In other words, the aversion from the Medusa and the *conversion* to the text are related temporally, as the *before* and *after* of the same poetic event. Between those two moments, there extends the experience of the pilgrim, who has himself seen the *dottrina* and has returned as poet to reveal it to us.

A passage in the *Purgatorio* lends considerable weight to our suggestion that petrification is an interpretive as well as a moral threat and that the act of interpretation depends on a moral condition. At

the end of the second *cantica*, on the occasion of Dante's own reve-
lation, Beatrice chides him for his "pensier vani" and for the delight
he has taken in them:

> io veggio te ne lo 'ntelletto
> fatto di pietra e, impetrato, tinto,
> sì che t'abbaglia il lume del mio detto . . .
>   (XXXIII, 73–75)

If we apply this imagery to the episode of Canto IX, then it is clear
that petrification can mean the inability to see the light of truth in
an interpretive glance. Thus, the threat of the Medusa may in a
sense be a danger to be averted by the reader as well as the pilgrim:
an "intelletto sano," as Dante tells us in the *Convivio,* is a mind that
is not obscured by ignorance or *malizia,* a mind that is not petrified.[2]

The dialectic of blindness and vision, aversion and conversion in
the interpretation of the text, is central to biblical hermeneutics and
is discussed by St. Paul with the figure of the veil. The use of the
word "velame" in Dante's verses would seem to be an allusion to the
Pauline tradition. To speak of a truth hidden beneath a veil was of
course a banality in Dante's day, as it is in ours, but its familiarity de-
rived from its biblical origin, where the veil was literally a covering
for the radiant face of Moses and figuratively the relationship of the
Old Testament to the New. Paul, in II Corinthians, extends his dis-
cussion of the "letter that kills" and of the "spirit that gives life" by
blending the words of Jeremiah about God writing his law in the
hearts of his people with those of Ezekiel about the people of God
having hearts of flesh instead of hearts of stone.[3] In St. Paul's New
Testament perspective, the hearts of stone become the inscribed
tablets of the law of Moses, contrasted with the inscribed hearts of
the faithful. He then discusses the meaning of the veil:

> Having therefore such hope, we show great boldness. We do not
> act as Moses did, who used to put a veil over his face that the Is-
> raelites might not observe the glory of his countenance, which
> was to pass away. But their minds were darkened (*obtusi sunt
> sensus eorum*); for to this day, when the Old Testament is read
> to them, the selfsame veil remains, not being lifted (*non revela-
> tum*) to disclose the Christ in whom it is made void. Yes, down
> to this very day, when Moses is read, the veil covers their hearts;
> but when they turn in repentance to God, the veil shall be taken
> away (*Cum autem conversus fuerit ad Dominum, auferetur vela-
> men*). (II Cor. 3:12–16)

---

2. *Convivio* IV, xv, II. Cf. II, I, 4.
3. See R. P. C. Hanson, *II Corinthians* (London, 1954), p. 39, commenting on II Cor. 3
   and 4.

Paul here contrasts the letter of the Old Testament, written on tablets of stone, with the spirit of the New, who is Christ, the "unveiling" or *re-velation*. The significance of the letter is in its final term, Christ, who was present all along, but revealed as the spirit only at the end, the conversion of the Old Testament to the New. Understanding the truth is not then a question of critical intelligence applied here and there, but rather of a retrospective illumination by faith from the standpoint of the ending, a conversion. In the original Greek, the term used to describe the darkening of the minds of the Jews, *pōrōsis*, petrification,[4] is rendered in the Vulgate as *obtusio*, but the sense of hardness remains alive in the exegetical tradition, where the condition is glossed as *duritia cordis*.[5]

After the Revelation, the inability to see beneath the veil is attributable to the "God of this world," who strikes the unbeliever senseless. It is this God, which later tradition was to identify with the devil, that provides a generic biblical meaning for the Medusa:

> But if our gospel also is veiled, it is veiled only to those who are perishing. In their case, the God of this world has blinded their unbelieving minds, that they should not see the light . . . while we look not at the things that are seen, but at the things that are not seen. For the things that are seen are temporal, but the things that are not seen are eternal. (II Cor. 4:3 ff.)

The familiar dialectic of blindness and vision, as old as Sophocles, assumes a special poignancy in the life of Paul, who was at successive moments blind: first to the truth of Christ and then, on the road to Damascus, to the things of this world. Conversion is for him, much as it was for Plato, a turning away from the false light of temporal things, seen with the eyes of the body, to the light of eternity, seen with the eyes of the soul. Above all, blindness and vision are in the Pauline text metaphors for interpretation, the obtuse reading of faithless literalists transformed, by unveiling, into a reading of the same text in a new light.

I should like to propose that the episode of the Medusa is an application of this dialectic to both the pilgrim and the reader. The "before" and the "after" of the conversion experience are rendered sequentially and dramatically by the threat to the pilgrim, on one hand, and the authorial voice on the other. Between the aversion from a temporal threat and the conversion to the Christian truth, the *dottrina*, there is the Christ event in the experience of the pilgrim, the moment that marks the coming together of pilgrim and poet. From that ideal moment, Dante fulfills the role of a Virgil to the

---

4. On the word and its history, see J. A. Robinson, *St. Paul's Epistle to the Ephesians* (London, 1914), pp. 264–274.
5. *Glossa Ordinaria; Patrologia Latina*, 114, 55.

reader, sufficient to the task of averting his pupil's glance from the
"God of this world," the temptation of *temporalia,* yet not sufficient
for the task of *re-velation.* The threat to the pilgrim, petrification, seems
to correspond to the various conditions of unbelief suggested by the
Pauline text: blindness, hardness of heart, darkening of the mind,
senselessness; while vision (presumably accomplished by the pil-
grim/author and now proffered to the reader) corresponds to the
eternity of "things that are not seen." Literalists are blind to spiritual
truth precisely because they see temporal things, while the things of
this world are invisible to those who see the spirit within. The Christ
event in history, as described by St. Paul, is applied to the *now* of the
pilgrim's journey in his meeting with Beatrice and is left as testament
to the reader, who is exhorted to follow in his own way. En route,
however, both must avert their glance from the God of this world.

Whatever the merit of this dramatic outline, it still leaves us in
the realm of poetic fiction. Several difficulties immediately present
themselves, which can be resolved only by exploring more deeply the
relationship between the Pauline text and the verses of Canto IX. In
the first place, the Pauline dialectic is built upon the fundamental
opposition of two terms that are a unity in the Bible: the letter and
the spirit, figuratively translated into visual terms by the opposition
"veil"/"face of Moses" (Christ). Dante's use of the word "velame"
also suggests a translation into visual terms of the interpretive act
required of the reader at this point; what is not as yet clear is the
sense in which the threat of the Medusa is in Dante's text, as petri-
fication is in Paul's, the corresponding threat of the "letter that
kills." In other words, how is the face of Medusa the opposite of the
face of Moses? Secondly, once the opposition between the threat of
the Medusa and the *dottrina* is established, there remains the prob-
lem of their relationship, for letter and spirit, though opposed, are
still one, as the Old Testament, written on tablets of stone or en-
graved on the stony hearts of unbelievers, is still one with its New
Testament interpretation, written upon the "fleshly tablets of the
heart" (II Cor. 3:3). The same is true of the figure of the veil: it is
under the same veil, perceived by believers and unbelievers alike,
that the truth is hidden. Paul attributes interpretive blindness to the
"God of this world" but in Dante's text it is the diabolic threat that
must somehow lead beyond itself. In what sense might it be said that
the threat of the Medusa masks a *dottrina* that is nowhere to be
found on the printed page? The resolution of both difficulties will
become clear when we decide which, precisely, are the *versi strani*
referred to in the text.

Our solution must begin with some interpretive and historical re-
marks about the Medusa herself. Her story in antiquity seems a per-

fect counterpart to the story of the veiling of Moses' face. Dante was doubtless aware of the false etymology of her name concocted by the mythographers: *mē idōsan, quod videre non possit*.[6] To see her was death; to protect himself Perseus required the shield of Minerva, just as we, according to the allegorization of Albertus Magnus, require the shield of wisdom to protect us against *delectationes concupiscentiae*.[7] On the other hand, the face of Moses is a figure for the glory of Christ, *illuminatio Evangelii gloriae Christi* (II Cor. 4:4), requiring nothing less than a conversion in order to be unveiled (*revelatio*). It remained for Dante to associate the two stories, recasting the Pauline dialectic of blindness and vision into the figure of the Medusa (corresponding to St. Paul's "God of this world") and contrasting it with the admonition, immediately following, to gaze at the truth beneath the veil. The two stories serve as excellent dramatizations of the two moments of conversion: aversion from the self and the things of this world, conversion to God. Separating those two moments at that point extends the whole of the journey.

A closer look at the tradition surrounding the Medusa suggests a more than dramatic aptness in the choice of this figure for the representation of a diabolic threat. The most startling thing about traditional efforts to discuss this episode is that they have missed what to a modern reader is most obvious: whatever the horror the Medusa represents to the male imagination, it is in some sense a female horror. In mythology, the Medusa was said to be powerless against women, for it was her feminine *beauty* that constituted the mortal threat to her admirers. From the ancient *Physiologus* through the mythographers to Boccaccio, the Medusa represented a sensual fascination, a *pulchritudo* so excessive that it turned men to stone.[8] In Dante's text the theme of fascination survives; otherwise it would be difficult to imagine why Virgil does not trust the pilgrim's ability to shield his own eyes if the image were not an entrapment.

Fascination, in this context, suggests above all the sensual fascination celebrated in the literature of love. Whatever the significance of the Medusa motif to Freud and Ferenczi, we are dealing here

---

6. Fulgentius, *Mythologicon* I, 26, in A. Van Staveten, *Mythographi Laini* (Amsterdam, 1742), p. 657.

7. Quoted by Hermann Gmelin, *Kommentar: Die Göttliche Komödie* (Stuttgart: Klett, 1954), ad loc.

8. Among the encyclopedias, I have found W. H. Röscher, *Ausführliches Lexikon der griechishen und römischen Mythologie* (Munich, 1884–1937) to be most helpful on the subject of Medusa's beauty. Arnolf d'Orléans says of her: "illa autem mutabat homines in saxum quia pre amore illius obstupebant." Arnulfi Aurelianensis, *Glosule super Lucanum*, ed. Berthe M. Marti, Papers and Monographs, American Academy of Rome, 18 (1958), 470. CF. Boccaccio, *Genealogie* X, 9, ed. V. Romano (Bari: Latera, 1951), p. 496. See especially on the subject, A. A. Barb, "The Mermaid and the Devil's Grandmother," *Journal of the Warburg and Courtauld Institutes*, 29 (1966), and "Diva Matrix," in the same journal, 16 (1953).

with a highly self-conscious poetry and a kind of love poetry at that. An explicit reference in the text helps to identify the subject matter as specifically erotic and literary, rather than abstractly moral. When the Furies scream out for the Medusa, they recall the assault of Theseus: "Mal non vengiammo in Tesëo l'assalto" (IX, 54). This would seem to be an allusion to Theseus' descent into the underworld with his friend Pirithoüs, a disastrous enterprise from which he, unlike his hapless companion, was rescued by Hercules, but the point is that the descent had for its objective the abduction of Persephone; it was therefore an erotic, not to say sexual, assault.

The presence of the theme here is not merely anecdotal; Dante is himself in a sense searching for a prelapsarian Persephone, an erotic innocence which he recaptures, at one remove, in his encounter with Matelda at the top of the Mountain of Purgatory:

> Tu mi fai rimembrar dove e qual era
> Proserpina nel tempo che perdette
> la madre lei, ed ella primavera.
> (*Purg.*, XXVIII, 49–51)

These two references to Persephone in the poem, the first implied and the second clearly stated, suggest that the figure of the Medusa is somehow coordinate to that of Matelda. Whatever else she may represent, the pastoral landscape and the erotic feelings of the pilgrim would indicate the recapture, or near recapture, of a pastoral (and therefore *poetic*) innocence, a return to Eden after a long *askesis*. For the moment, it might be argued that the Medusa represents precisely the impediment to such a recapture: her association with Persephone goes back to the *Odyssey*, where Odysseus in the underworld fears that Persephone will send the gorgon to prevent him from leaving.[9] Whatever Dante's sources for making the same association,[1] the point is that, short of Eden, there is no erotic—or *poetic*—innocence.

A generation later, Geoffrey Chaucer was to use the Furies in a way that is quite consistent with my hypothesis about the passage in Canto IX. The invocation of *Troilus and Criseyde,* that bookish tale of woe, addresses the Furies, rather than the Muses, as the proper inspirers of the dark passion that is the subject of the romance. Indeed, the insistence on the Furies foreshadows the "anti-romance" quality of Chaucer's poem, a deliberate undercutting of a genre that had been the poet's own. The *Troilus* is in many ways a palinodic auto-critique: the language with which it begins, with its address to "Thesiphone . . . cruwel Furie sorynge," may even be an allusion to

9. *Odyssey* XI, ll. 634 ff.
1. See the possibly interpolated passage in *Aeneid* VI, 289, ed. J. W. Mackail (Oxford: Clarendon, 1930), p. 233n.

the passage under discussion here, as well as to Statius.[2] At any rate, it would seem to support our hypothesis: the threat of the Medusa proffered by the Furies represents, in the pilgrim's askesis, a sensual fascination and potential entrapment precluding all further progress.

Of all the texts that might support the hypothesis, one seems to me to give to the Medusa a specificity that is lacking in most moralizing interpretations: the *Roman de la Rose*. A passage from that work will establish the sense in which Dante's Medusa exists as a dark counter-statement to the celebration of a poetic eros for which the *Roman* was the quintessential type. It offers us a precise, if inverted, parallel of the action of Canto IX, an illusion, in Dante's view, of which the Medusa is the disillusioning reality. At the ending of Jean de Meun's poem, as the lover is about to besiege the castle, an image is presented to him from a tower, a sculptured image far surpassing in beauty the image of Pygmalion, fired by Venus' arrow. Of interest to us is that in some versions of the poem that might have been available to Dante, the image is contrasted for some fifty lines with the image of the Medusa:

> Tel ymage n'ot mais en tour;
> Plus avienent miracle entour
> Qu'onc n'avint entour Medusa . . .
> Mais l'ymage dont ci vous conte
> Les vertux Medusa seurmonte,
> Qu'el ne sert pas de genz tuer,
> Ne d'eus faire en roche muet.[3]

The passage goes on to draw an extraordinary parallel to the drama of Canto IX, an ironically optimistic view of the power of eros, of which Dante's Medusa seems the dark and reversed counter-image. The presence of mock-epic machinery in this erotomachia is matched by the pointedly non-Christian fortifications of Dante's infernal city. The Medusa does not appear in the *Roman,* any more than she does in the *Inferno,* but exists only as an antitype to Venus' idol. Dante's Medusa, on the other hand, *is* Venus' idol, stripped of its charm and seen, or almost seen, under the aspect of death. Recent study suggests that, as a youth, Dante had written a poetic paraphrase of the *Roman*; hence this episode constitutes his final judgment on the dark eros celebrated in that work.

The figure of the Medusa is a perfect vehicle for conveying this kind of retrospective judgment because it is inherently diachronic, stressing historicity and change: before and after, then and now, the

2. *Troilus and Creseyde* I, 6–11, and note, in F. N. Robinson (ed.), *The Works of Geoffry Chaucer* (Boston: Houghton Mifflin, 1961).
3. *Roman de la Rose*, ed. Ernest Langlois (Paris: Firmin-Didot, 1914), V, 107. The Interpolation occurs at vv. 20810–11. (Translation is by Matilda Bruckner.)

beauty of the lady changed to ugliness, fascination turned to horror. In ancient mythology she was said to be a kind of siren,[4] and in this temporal respect she resembles Dante's siren, the stinking hag of the *Purgatorio* whom the pilgrim, under the influence of song, takes to be a ravishing beauty.

A simple abstraction of personification allegory is least able to account for this temporal dimension of meaning, for the temporality is derived not from the gap that separates the poetic statement from some abstract moral code, but rather from the temporality of the beholder.[5] I should like to suggest that the temporality we sense in the threat of the Medusa is a representation of the temporality of retrospection, of a danger narrowly averted, of a former illusion seen for what it is. Such a temporality is the essence of the descent into hell, the past seen under the aspect of death. The traditional threat on all such journeys is the threat of nostalgia, a retrospective glance that evades the imperative to accept an authentically temporal destiny. Moreover, the threat is not merely a petrification, but also a *no return:* "Nulla sarebbe del tornar mai suso." The Gospel of Luke (17:32) warns of such a danger with an Old Testament figure that seems peculiarly appropriate here: "Remember Lot's wife."

The threat of the past faces St. Augustine just before his conversion, when his former mistresses seem to appear behind him, tempting him to turn and look at them, *respicere*, as they pluck at his "fleshly garment."[6] In the medieval allegorization of the journey of Orpheus to the underworld, a similar significance is given to the irreparable loss of Eurydice. According to Guillaume de Conches, Orpheus' descent represents the sage's effort to find himself, his Eurydice, and he is defeated by his nostalgia for his own former sin.[7] At this point in his descent, the pilgrim faces a similar temptation: the Furies, a traditional representation of guilt and remorse, urge him to confront what is, in effect, his own past as poet. Dante did not have to read the *Roman de la Rose* in order to learn of a lady who turned her lovers to stone, for he had in fact celebrated such a lady in his *Rime Petrose,* the stony rhymes, written for the mysterious *Donna Pietra.*

The *Rime Petrose,* the dazzling virtuoso pieces of Dante's youth, celebrate a violent passion for the "Stony Lady" whose hardness turns the poet, her lover, into a man of stone. In the survey of the progress of Dante's love and of his poetry from the *Vita Nuova* to the *Comme-*

---

4. A. A. Barb, "Mermaid," p. 9.
5. For the temporality of allegory, see Paul de Man, "The Rhetoric of Temporality," in *Interpretation: Theory and Practice*, ed. Charles S. Singleton (Baltimore: The Johns Hopkins University Press, 1969), pp. 190–191.
6. *Confessions* VIII, xi.
7. John B. Friedman, *Orpheus in the Middle Ages* (Cambridge, Mass.; Harvard University Press, 1970), pp. 104–109.

dia, the *Rime Petrose* constitute a surd element, radically fragmentary,
Contini has called them,[8] finding no clearly identifiable place in the
poet's development. At one point in the *Purgatorio* when Beatrice cas-
tigates the pilgrim for his infidelity, she accuses him of a love for "van-
ità," a "pargoletta," or little girl, using precisely the same word that the
poet had used somewhat disparagingly of his *Donna Pietra* in one of
the *rime.* The recall in the *Purgatorio* of this word has given rise to
endless speculation about the identity of the woman whom Dante de-
noted with the code name of "Donna Pietra." Critics have been right,
I think, to wish to see biography in the poem, but they have been in-
correct to imagine that the words of the poem were simply vehicles
for communicating true confessions. We have learned from Contini
that the biography of a poet, as poet, is his poetry,[9] and it is in a
quite literal sense that the *Rime Petrose* are present and relevant
here. In the same poem that has given rise to speculation about the
"pargoletta," there appear some verses of potentially greater signifi-
cance. They paint a wintry scene described by a despairing lover. They
should be compared with the *versi strani* of Canto IX:

Versan le vene le fummifere
    acque
per li vapor che la terra ha nel
    ventre,
che d'abisso li tira suso in *alto*;
    onde cammino al bel giorno
    mi piacque
che ora è fatto rivo, e sarà
    mentre
che durerà del verno il grande
    assalto;
    la terra fa un suol che par di
    smalto,
e l'acqua morta si converte in
    vetro. (*Rime* 43c, 53–60)

Con l'unghie si fendea ciascuna
    il petto;
    battiensi a palme e gridavan
    sì *alto*,
    ch'i' mi strinsi al poeta per
    sospetto.
"Vegna Medusa: sì 'l farem di
    smalto,"
    dicevan tutte riguardando in
    giuso;
"mal non vengiammo in
    Tesëo l'*assalto*."
          (*Inf*. IX, 49–54)

The description of a world without love, matching the poet's winter
of the soul, contains exactly the rhyme words from Dante's descrip-
tion of the Medusa, sibilants that might qualify as *versi strani* in the
address to the reader. Thus a passage that threatens petrification re-
calls, in a reified, concrete way, precisely the poem that described
such a reification at the hands of a kind of Medusa. The words
themselves reflect each other in such a way that they constitute a

---

8. "Introduction to Dante's *Rime*" (trans. Yvonne Freccero) in *Dante: A Collection of Criti-
   cal Essays,* ed. J. Freccero (Englewood Cliffs, N.J.: Prentice-Hall, 1965), p. 36.
9. Gianfranco Contini, "Dante come personaggio-poeta della *Commedia,*" in *Approdo,* N.S.
   4, no. I (1958), 19, rept. in *Varianti e altra linguistica* (Turin: Einaudi, 1970).

short-circuit across the temporal distance that separates the two moments of poetic history, a block that threatens to make further progress impossible. For the reader, the parallel threat is to refuse to see the allegory through the letter, to ignore the double focus of the *versi strani*. The echo of the *Rime Petrose* is an invitation to the reader to measure the distance that separates the *now* of the poet from the *then* of his *persona;* in the fiction of the poem, the Medusa is, like the lady of stone, no historic character at all, but the poet's own creation. Its threat is the threat of idolatry. In terms of mythological *exempla,* petrification by the Medusa is the real consequence of Pygmalion's folly.

The point is worth stressing. Ever since Augustine, the Middle Ages insisted upon the link between eros and language, between the reaching out in desire for what mortals can never possess and the reaching out of language toward the significance of silence. To refuse to see in human desire an incompleteness that urges the soul on to transcendence is to remain within the realm of creatures, worshipping them as only the Creator was to be worshipped. Similarly, to refuse to see language and poetry as continual *askesis,* pointing beyond themselves, is to remain within the letter, treating it as an absolute devoid of the spirit which gives meaning to human discourse. The subject matter of love poetry is *poetry,* as much as it is love, and the reification of love is at the same time a reification of the words that celebrate it.

The search for the self which is the quest of the poet can only be accomplished through the mediation of the imagination, the Narcissus image which is at once an image of the self and all that the self is not.[1] For a medieval poet steeped in the Augustinian tradition, the search for the self in the mirror of creatures, the beloved, ends with a false image of the self which is either rejected in favor of God, the light which casts the reflection, or accepted as a true image, an image which is totally other. Seeing the self in otherness and accepting the vision as true reduces the spirit to something alienated from itself, like a rock or a tree, deprived of consciousness. Like language itself, the image can only represent by pointing beyond itself, by beckoning the beholder to pierce through it to its ultimate significance. Idolatry in this context is a refusal to go beyond, a self-petrification.

Virgil is the mediator between Dante's former dark passion and verbal virtuosity on one hand and the restless striving of the pilgrim on the other, at least until his guidance gives way to the guidance of Beatrice. It may seem strange to think of Virgil at all in the context

---

1. For the adaptation of Augustinian theology to the medieval love lyric, see Frederick Goldin, *The Mirror of Narcissus in the Courtly Love Lyric* (Ithaca: Cornell University Press, 1967), pp. 207 ff.

of love poetry, except insofar as every poet is a poet of desire. Yet Virgil's portrait of Aeneas was a portrait of passion overcome. At the opening of the fifth book, as Aeneas sails away from Carthage, he looks back at its burning walls and leaves Dido forever behind him. The chaotic force of *folle amore*—mad passion—was epitomized for Dante by the figure of Dido and of Cupid, who sat in her lap. Further, it is under the sign of Dido that Paolo and Francesca bewail their adulterous love in hell. In the struggle between individual desire and providential destiny, Virgil's Aeneas is the man who renounces self in the name of his mission. It is for this reason that he helps the pilgrim avert his glance, until Beatrice shows the way to a reconciliation of human love with the divine plan. Just as the historic Virgil, in Dante's reading, had pointed the way out of the erotic impasse toward *lo bello stilo,* so in the poem it is Virgil who helps him to avoid the pitfall facing all poets of love. It is perhaps in this sense, specifically, that his help was spurned by Guido Cavalcanti (*Inf*. X, 63). In any case, Dante's encounter with Beatrice is the moment at which the poem transcends the Virgilian view of human love. Dante marks his beloved's return with the words "conosco i segni dell'antica fiamma" (*Purg.* XXX, 48), echoing the despairing words of Dido, while the angels sing "*Manibus, oh, date lilia plenis*" (give lilies with full hands), echoing the funereal gesture of Anchises in the underworld, but transforming the purple lilies of mourning into the white lilies of the Resurrection. At that point Virgil definitively disappears, when death, before which even he and his Rome had to bow, gives way to transcendent love (*Canticum Cant.* VIII, 6).

There is some evidence that our suggested reading of the Medusa episode may have been anticipated by a near contemporary of the poet, or at least that the problematic was recognized and radically transformed by him. I refer of course to Petrarch, whose very name was for him an occasion for stony puns. In the course of his *Canzoniere*, he provides us with a definitive gloss of Dante's Medusa. Like Pygmalion, Petrarch falls in love with his own creation and is in turn created by her: the pun *Lauro/Laura* points to this self-contained process which is the essence of his creation. He creates with his poetry the Lady Laura who in turn creates his reputation as poet laureate. She is therefore not a mediatrix, pointing beyond herself, but is rather enclosed within the confines of his own being as poet, which is to say, the poem. This is precisely what Petrarch acknowledges when he confesses in his final prayer to the sin of idolatry, adoration of the work of his own hands. Speaking of Laura no longer as the infinitely beloved, he calls her a Medusa: "Medusa e l'error mio m'han fatto un sasso." For all of his tears of repentance, however, there seems to be a consolation for a more secular age. Petrarch's enduring fame as the weeping lover suggests that if he was turned to stone because of idolatry, at least a stone lasts forever. If it is devoid of the spirit linking it to reality and to the life of the poet, it is nevertheless immune to the ravages of time, a monumental portrait of the artist. In the same poem, he sees the problem of reification and idolatry as inherent in all poetry, including that of his illustrious predecessor. This, I take it, is the point of his address to the Virgin as the only true mediatrix and "bringer-of-blessings"; *vera beatrice,* where the absence of capitalization drives the point home more forcefully. For Petrarch, precursor of Romanticism, there can be no middle ground, not even that occupied by Dante.

We are now in a position to answer some of the fundamental questions concerning Dante's allegory raised by the episode of the Medusa. Doubtless, the Pauline "God of this world" provides an appropriate and abstract moral meaning in the dramatization that might lead us to classify it as an example of the allegory of poets. At the same time, however, we have seen that the passage is charged with the temporality of the poet's own career, the Dante who is, looking back at the Dante who was, through the medium of words. This retrospective illumination is the very essence of biblical allegory, what Dante called the "allegory of theologians." The Christ event was the end term of an historical process, the "fullness of time," from the perspective of which the history of the world might be read and judged according to a meaning which perhaps even the participants in that history could not perceive. The "then" and "now," the Old Testament and the New, were at once the continuity and discontinuity of universal history, the letter and the spirit respectively of God's revelation. Christian autobiography is the application of this diachronicity to one's own life for the purpose of witness, "confession," of the continual unfolding of the Word.

Both confession and Christian allegory have their roots in the mystery of language. As language is unfolded along a syntagmatic axis, governed at each moment of its articulation by a paradigm present in the mind of the speaker and made manifest at the ending of the sentence, so the authorial voice in the text is the paradigm of the entire narrative, of which the evolution of the pilgrim is, as it were, the syntax. When this dialectic is translated into dramatic terms that purport to be autobiographical, we are presented with a narrative which seems to demand both continuity and discontinuity: an organic continuity, so that it may make a claim to authenticity, yet with the definitive detachment of the author who makes a claim to finality. For the pilgrim and the author to be one and the same requires nothing short of death and resurrection: death, so that the story may be definitive and final: resurrection, so that it may be told. This narrative translation of the dialectic of language may in turn be

translated into theological terms: conversion, the burial of the old
man and the birth of the new, the essence of Pauline allegory.
Christ, the ending of the story, is simply the manifestation of its
subject, paradoxically present as the paradigm, the Logos, from the
beginning. The final manifestation of the paradigm is the presence
of the Logos made flesh. Just as history required an Archimedean
point from which Christians could judge it to have been concluded,
so the literature of confession needs a point outside of itself from
which its truth can be measured, a point that is at once a beginning
and an end, an Alpha and an Omega. "Conversion" was the name
that Christians applied to such a moment in history and in the soul.
In this sense, biblical allegory, conversion, and narrative all share
the same linguistic nature.

When St. Paul refers to the relationship of the Old Testament to
the New, he is in fact applying this linguistic metaphor to the Christ
event, the spirit inseparable from the letter of the Bible whereby it
is made manifest. Without the letter, the spirit is the eternal Logos,
with no point of tangency to history; God's intentionality without
relation to man. Without the spirit, the letter is utterly devoid of
significance, as dead as the mute stones upon which it was written.
God's utterance to man is the Word incarnate.

Paul goes on to suggest that the Word of God interprets the
hearts of men, the stony tablets turning to stone the hearts of un-
believers, while the spirit writes upon the fleshly tablets of the
faithful. So too, in Dante's text, it is the power of the letter to en-
thrall the beholder that makes of it a Medusa, an expression of de-
sire that turns back to entrap its subject in an immobility which is
the very opposite of the dynamism of language and of desire.[2] To
see beyond it, however, is to see in the spiritual sense, to transform
the eros of the Medusa into the transcendent Eros of Caritas. This
is Dante's whole achievement as a love poet: a refusal of the poetics
of reification, sensual and verbal, for the poetics of "translation," as
scribe of the spirit which is written on "the fleshly tablets of the
heart":

> "I' mi son un che, quando
> Amor mi spira, noto, e a quel modo
> ch'e' ditta dentro vo significando."
> (*Purg.* XXIV, 52–54)

The book of memory has as its author God Himself. In this sense,
Dante's poem is neither a copy nor an imitation of the Bible. It *is* the
allegory of theologians in his own life.

---

2. See Jacques Lacan, *Ecrits* (Paris: Edtions du Seuil: 1966), p. 40, for a neo-Freudian re-
statement of the tyranny of the letter, or "signifier."

Nonetheless, the passage from the events of Dante's life to the words and images he uses to signify them is one that we cannot make. This is why it is impossible to guess at the identity of the *Donna Pietra,* just as it is impossible to see in the Medusa some event of the poet's life. We must be content with words on words, the double focus on a poetic expression, beyond which it would take an act of faith equal to Dante's to go; beyond which, indeed, there is no Dante we can ever know.

The address to the reader is thus not a stage direction, but an exhortation to conversion, a command to await the celestial messenger so that we, like the pilgrim, may "trapassare dentro."[3] Beneath the veil of Moses, we behold the light of the Gospel; beneath the veil of Dante's verses, the *dottrina* is derived from that, or it is nothing at all.

ROBERT M. DURLING

Canto X: Farinata and Cavalcante[†]

This canto has always been recognized as one of the summits of Dante's art. Full of human drama, it touches on Dante's exile and the fate of his friend Guido Cavalcanti; it is also, as recent scholarship demonstrates, theologically precise and rich in iconographic allusions. After the suspense-filled events of the two previous cantos—when Dante and Virgil are barred by "more than a thousand" (VIII, 82) devils from entering the city of Dis and are menaced by the Medusa, and after "Heaven's messenger" (IX, 85) has unlocked the gates with his "wand" (IX, 89)—the poets enter, to see no one, and nothing but a plain filled with sarcophagi that, Virgil explains, house the leaders of heresies and their followers. At the very end of Canto IX, the poets make an unusual turn to the right (in hell the poets turn always to the left, except here and in Canto XVII). This departure from tradition adds to the high pitch of anticipation with which we begin, and the canto's richness and drama amply reward us.

Canto X is part of a series of cantos of the *Inferno* that presents souls from Dante's native city and develops the closely related themes of the present corruption of Florence, as Dante views it, its

---

3. *Purg.* VIII. If as I have suggested, the arrival of the messenger is an *interpretive* descent, then the identification of that messenger with Mercury (from Statius, *Thebaid* II, 2; cf. Pietro di Dante) is peculiarly apt: the *Hermes* of a new Christian *hermeneutics.* The angel fulfills this and other roles of the classical messenger of the gods.

† From *Lectura Dantis: Inferno,* ed. Allen Mandelbaum, Anthony Oldcorn, Charles Ross. Copyright © 1998 by the University of California Press. Reprinted by permission of the University of California Press.

bitter history of faction and civil strife, and Dante's own involvement, which will lead to his permanent exile. The first of these cantos is *Inferno* VI, where we meet the glutton Ciacco, whom the pilgrim questions about the political future of Florence and the fate, in the afterlife, of prominent leaders. Ciacco's first answer predicts the temporary victory of the White party (to which Dante belonged) and the Black coup that followed it (an armed coup d'état by Charles of Valois and the Blacks in 1302), but Ciacco does not mention the repercussions this coup will have in Dante's life. Dante next inquires about five Florentines of the previous generation, all of whom, Ciacco replies, are even lower in hell. We meet the most important of them, Farinata degli Uberti, in this canto, and it is he who predicts Dante's exile.

The historical Manente degli Uberti, called Farinata (ca. 1205–1264), was from 1239 until his death the leader of the Florentine Ghibellines. In 1248 they drove out the Guelphs, only to be driven out, in turn, three years later. Farinata then led a Tuscan coalition of Ghibellines against the Florentine Guelphs, slaughtering them in a particularly bloody battle at Montaperti, near Siena, in 1260. A subsequent council in Empoli would have decided to raze Florence itself, if not for Farinata's singlehanded opposition. After another Ghibelline defeat at Benevento in 1266, a popular uprising in Florence drove the Ghibellines out of the city and destroyed a number of their houses (the Piazza della Signoria results from the destruction of the Uberti, Foraboschi, and other Ghibelline houses). Peace was established in 1280, from which Farinata's descendants were specifically excluded, as they were from later amnesties.

A minor problem presented by the canto concerns the charge for which Farinata and his wife were condemned in 1283 (when Dante was eighteen years old, and nineteen years after Farinata's death) by the Franciscan inquisitor for Florence, Fra Salomone da Lucca. The posthumous charge labeled them "Paterini," that is, adherents to the heresy of the Cathars, or Albigensians. Reconciling the charge in *Inferno* of epicureanism with Fra Salomone's claim is difficult, for the Cathars accepted the New Testament as inspired and held firmly to the immortality of the soul. Since the iconography of the canto involves the Eucharist, it is possible that the Cathars' rejection of the Lord's Supper (as a sacrament) is partly Dante's target. Or he may simply have decided to disregard the facts here, as in other parts of the poem.

We meet one other Florentine in this canto. Cavalcante dei Cavalcanti was also a member of the high nobility. He was a prominent Guelph, so prominent that in 1266, in one of the efforts to make peace in the city, his son Guido was betrothed to Farinata's daughter. That the two former political enemies share a single sarcophagus is a statement both about the intimacy of factional division within the walls of the city and about an essential identity of worldliness in the opposing leaders, who are now the prisoners of their shared pessimism. Cavalcante probably did not live beyond 1280, several years before the beginning of Dante's friendship with his son, dated by the *Vita nuova* as 1283.

In Farinata and Cavalcante, then, Dante encounters fathers: literally the father and father-in-law of his closest friend, but also fathers of his city, past leaders of Florence, where they were partly responsible for the heritage of civil strife that plagues it. Behind this encounter, as behind the meetings with his teacher Brunetto Latini (*Inf.* XV) and his ancestor Cacciaguida (*Par.* XV–XVII), lies the encounter in *Aeneid* VI of Aeneas and his father, Anchises. Anchises prophesies the difficult struggle Aeneas will undergo in Italy, shows him the spirits of his descendants (future heroes of Rome), and explains to him the workings of the universe, especially the cycles of incarnation and purification that immortal souls undergo. *Paradiso* XV–XVII correct and outdo this major model of eschatological poetry, and the encounter in *Inferno* X is in many ways its antitype. Farinata and Cavalcante are shown to lack Anchises' most striking traits, particularly his devotion to the gods and to his people. Also, both fathers here challenge or reproach Dante, rather than certify him for his mission, as Anchises encourages Aeneas and Cacciaguida certifies Dante.

As Dante and Virgil walk with the walls of Dis on their right and the tombs on their left, Dante asks if the inmates of the tombs can be seen, pointing out that "the lids—in fact—have all been lifted; / no guardian is watching over them" (8–9). This observation picks up and renews the original description of the tombs at the end of Canto IX: "The lid of every tomb was lifted up" (121). Exactly what position is imagined for the covers of the tombs is not stated clearly, but the question is probably resolved by lines 6–7, which imply that they are leaning against the sarcophagi. Expectation is further whetted by Virgil's assurance that the wish Dante has expressed to see the souls will be fulfilled, as well as the one he has not stated ("the longing you have hid from me" [18] is almost certainly a reference to Dante's desire to see Florentines). Virgil's identification of the Epicureans as those "who say (*fanno*) the soul dies with the body" (15) provides a provisional understanding of the *contrapasso* of this canto—these souls will be eternally buried with their bodies. The phrase includes a telling ambiguity. They *make* (*fanno,* 15) the soul die with the body. In so believing, these heretics literally *cause* their souls to die.

Within this context, then, the intense drama of the canto begins with the introduction of the main personage, Farinata, in stages carefully graded to set off the episode. First is the abrupt appearance in the text of Farinata's unannounced and unlocated words; only at their end are we told that the sound came "out of one sepulcher" (29). Dante is startled and frightened. Virgil explains that Farinata has stood and is visible "from the waist up" (33). There are several implicit stage-directions here. Since Farinata was not visible when the poets turned to the right, he was lying in his tomb. He has overheard the talk between Dante and Virgil, has identified Dante as a Florentine, and therefore has stood up to speak; since Dante must turn in order to see him, he is behind Dante and Virgil and to their left. Dante and Virgil still do not see Farinata directly, but his voice arrests them.

> "O Tuscan, you who pass alive across
> the fiery city with such seemly words,
> be kind enough to stay your journey here.
>   Your accent makes it clear that you belong
> among the natives of the noble city
> I may have dealt with too vindictively."
>   This sound had burst so unexpectedly
> out of one sepulcher that, trembling, I
> then drew a little closer to my guide.
>   But he told me: "Turn round! What are you doing?
> That's Farinata who has risen there—
> you will see all of him from the waist up."
>
> (22–33)

Finally we see Farinata directly through the pilgrim's eyes:

> My eyes already were intent on his;
> and up he rose—his forehead and his chest—
> as if he had tremendous scorn for Hell.
>
> (34–36)

All generations of readers have been struck by the indomitable pride and courage conveyed by Farinata's monumental figure, perhaps the most impressive in the entire *Inferno*. Especially the expression "up he rose" (*s'ergea*) conveys a sense of power and size. Later on Farinata is called "great-hearted" (*magnanimo* [73]), and, although in the last analysis Farinata is judged negatively (and as John A. Scott showed, the term *magnanimo* itself had both a positive sense and the negative sense of "ambitious, overweening"), still the initial impression is of a powerful personality, and we are forced to entertain, if only for the moment, the possibility of such a soul's actually being superior to the sufferings of hell. This accounts for the Romantic misreading of Farinata, from Francesco De Sanctis through Benedetto Croce and Erich Auerbach, which supposed that the theological "structure" of the poem was a kind of ex post facto encrustation, obscuring Dante's true subject, human individuality and force of character. Actually, Dante's emphasis on Farinata's breast is directly related to the fact that heresy sins against faith, wisdom, and love, all of which traditionally have their seat in the heart. But at this point the sense of respect inspired by Farinata's commanding figure is reinforced by the tone of Virgil's lines, his pushing of Dante toward Farinata, and his advice that Dante's words be *conte*, that is, "appropriate" (39), and possibly also "counted," "few."

The first part of the interview with Farinata is tense and hostile. The old nobility and family pride speak as Farinata asks, "Who were your ancestors?" (42), but it should be noted that Dante is not embarrassed by his own family's social status. Farinata identifies Dante's ancestors in a way that suggests they were of comparable social status with his own. He raises his eyebrows not in scorn at their social obscurity, but at their presumption in opposing him, his family, and his party. He is so caught up in the old strife that he clearly still takes satisfaction in having twice dispersed the Guelphs, and it is entirely characteristic that he speaks of the victories of his party and his armies as if they belonged to himself exclusively. Because the word for "occasion" (*fiata*) resembles that for "breath" (*fiato*)—Dante often associates them—Farinata's phrase *per due fiate* (48) conveys a suggestion that he dispersed his enemies with a mere breath each time.

The pilgrim has been instantly caught up in this confrontation of Guelph and Ghibelline, and he, too, acts out the old enmity, giving blow for blow and claiming that the ultimate victory belongs to his side. It is the pilgrim who introduces the terminology of art in connection with exile and return:

> "If they were driven out," I answered him,
> "they still returned, both times, from every quarter;
> but yours were never quick to learn that art."
>
> (X, 49–51)

Farinata had used the familiar *tu* form when scornfully inquiring of Dante's antecedents, but we find Dante answering him with the respectful *voi* form. (Only to three individual inhabitants of hell does Dante use the polite form: to Farinata and Cavalcante here and to his teacher Brunetto Latini in Canto XV; all are Florentines of the older generation.) It is a token of Dante's complexity of nuance that it is precisely in his assertion of Guelph superiority over the defeated Ghibelline that the respectful form occurs (as it does in line 63, a parallel context).

The exchange is interrupted now by another abrupt surprise, the appearance of the excited Cavalcante. He, too, has listened to Dante's voice while lying in the tomb; he has heard him identify his family. Now he appears as far as the chin; Dante infers that he is kneeling. Dante tells us in lines 64–65 that he also infers the identity of this new personage; he is evidently not able to recognize him. Thus Cavalcante's recognition of Dante as an intimate of Guido's seems to be a result of the strange foreknowledge of the damned, soon to be introduced as a major focus of the canto.

Everything about Cavalcante contrasts with Farinata. Farinata is heard before he is seen; we see Cavalcante look anxiously about before speaking. Farinata's erect bearing is the result of deliberate intention; Cavalcante rises only to his knees because he is so intent on seeing his son, and he stands erect only as a result of panic. Farinata speaks gravely and ceremoniously; Cavalcante speaks entirely without ceremony. Finally, Farinata must inquire into Dante's family, whereas Cavalcante knows Dante's connection with his son. Throughout, Cavalcante is excited, in motion, and without dignity; Farinata is calm, immobile, and self-contained.

The contrasts has iconographic significance. Dante with his fertile sense of analogy is establishing a parallel between Saint Paul's confrontation of two pagan philosophers (identified by Augustine as a Stoic and an Epicurean, philosophers of human self-sufficiency) in Acts 17:18, and the pilgrim's meeting with the two heretics, one subject to every wind of fleshly impulse, and thus particularly Epicurean, according to the traditional view, and the other utterly in command of himself and confident of his *virtus animi* and thus, in this respect, particularly Stoic.

Cavalcante's actions derive from a series of misunderstandings. His hope of seeing Guido springs from a misconception of the nature of Dante's journey, as he supposes Dante has undertaken it on his own, because of his natural gifts. If so, why hasn't his son accompanied him? He misinterprets Dante's reply, and finally he leaps to a mistaken conclusion about Dante's hesitation. The misunderstandings occur in rapid succession:

> He looked around me, just as if he longed
> to see if I had come with someone else;
> but then, his expectation spent, he said
>   in tears: "If it is your high intellect
> that lets you journey here, through this blind prison,
> where is my son? Why is he not with you?"
>
>   (55–60)

The first part of Dante's reply corrects Cavalcante's first misunderstanding. He is not led by his "high intellect," but by Virgil:

> I answered: "My own powers have not brought me;
> he who awaits me there, leads me through here."
>
>   (61–62)

Of course this beginning is already evasive. It does not explicitly state that his being led by Virgil (whom he does not identify) is the result of divine intervention, though the implication is perhaps clear enough. But the rest of the reply is so obscure as to have become the most famous crux in the entire poem, when Dante refers to "one your Guido did disdain" (*forse cui Guido vostro ebbe a disdegno* [64]). Cavalcante interprets *ebbe* (the ambiguous *passato remoto*) as meaning that Guido is dead:

> Then suddenly erect, he cried: "What's that:
> He 'did disdain'? [*dicesti 'elli ebbe'?*] He is not still alive?
> The sweet light does not strike against his eyes?"
> (67–69)

and when the puzzled Dante hesitates, Cavalcante despairs and falls backward into the tomb.

Cavalcante can be forgiven for misunderstanding Dante's reply; its obscurity has elicited much debate (see Chimenz and Mazzoni for accounts of the controversy up to 1972). The disagreements have focused on *cui* and *ebbe*. Does *cui* refer to Virgil, to Beatrice, or to God? Is the grammatical subject of *ebbe* Guido, or whoever is referred to by *cui*? If it is Guido (the usual view), what aspect of the verb is implied? Is it an aorist, denoting a definitive action? a perfect, denoting an action that has ceased (either because Guido is dead, as Cavalcante assumes, or for some other reason)? a present perfect, denoting an action that just now took place (like Cavalcante's own *dicesti* in line 68, as Charles Singleton pointed out)? Most critics have assumed that the line has a single, ascertainable meaning, and since the pilgrim's remark is not favorable to Guido they have assumed that when writing the *Comedy* Dante was willing to consign his friend to damnation.

But we simply do not know to what extent the two poets had become estranged. No doubt the *Vita nuova*, in spite of its dedication to Guido and signs of his influence throughout, is in part an elaborate refutation of the naturalistic and pessimistic view of love taken in Cavalcanti's great canzone "Donna mi prega," and it may have contributed to the cooling of their relations. There exists also a sonnet, addressed to Dante by name, in which Cavalcanti reproaches him with "low life" and wishing to please the many. A possible reading interprets the sonnet as condemning Dante's entrance into elective politics in the wake of the new Ordinamenti di Giustizia of 1295, which barred magnates like Guido, but not lesser nobles like Dante (Marti). After the outbreak of bloody rioting Dante, as a *priore* of the city, voted in June 1300 to banish the turbulent Guido along with other White and Black leaders. We have no direct evidence of the degree of conflict this decision evoked in Dante. A last piece of evidence from outside the *Comedy* is furnished by Dante's fifteenth-century biographer Leonardo Bruni, who relates that after the Black coup Dante was accused of having favored Guido's return to Florence (he was allowed to return because of the illness of which he died in August), and that Dante wrote an epistle, now lost, pointing out that by the time the decision was made, Dante was no longer a prior and had no voice in the matter. Again, the evidence is ambiguous.

Along with *Purgatorio* XI and *Paradiso* XIII, *Inferno* X gives much insight into Dante's attitude toward Guido. In Canto X Guido's fate is still a source of turbulence for Dante. The elder Cavalcante's anxiety about his son's death, with the pilgrim's ambiguous reply, is partly a projected version of Dante's own anxieties and ambivalences. They can be stated as a series of questions. To what extent was Dante responsible for causing or hastening Guido's death (by voting for his exile)? To what degree did he desire Guido's death? Did Guido die unrepentant, and if so, did his early death prevent his repentance? Most serious, to what extent did Dante take satisfaction from his friend's (or former friend's) early death and possible damnation? The presence of such questions in Dante's spirit, their burden of guilt and anxiety, has left its mark on all three canticles of the poem, in each case in or near the gateway cantos, the entry into the city of Dis, the entry into Purgatory proper, and the cantos of the Sun.

We see the intensity of Dante's anxiety in the dialogue with Cavalcante, which parallels God's questioning of Cain about Abel. Both feature the agonizing question: "Where is [he]?" (*Ubi est Abel frater tuus?* [Gen. 4:9] / *Mio figlio ov'è?* [61]), followed by an evasive reply, emphasizing custodianship: "Am I my brother's keeper?" (Gen. 4:9) / "He [Virgil] . . . leads me through here" (62)—Cain denies that he is a leader, Dante asserts that his own leader is another. There follows a further question, referring to the death of the brother / son: "What hast thou done? (*Quid fecisti?*) the voice of thy brother's blood crieth to me from the earth" (Genesis 4:11) / "What's that? (*Come dicesti?*) . . . He is not still alive?" (68). Finally, both passages predict the exile of the protagonist.

These striking parallels show that Dante was deeply troubled over his connection with Guido's death and possible damnation. They show that he felt he was in a sense answerable to Guido's father, though he evidently had not known him. The parallel with Cain, like the couching of the supposedly candid confession of poetic pride in *Purgatorio* XI in terms of a desire to exile Guido, shows that there was a fratricidal ingredient in Dante's rivalry with Guido. Thus both Dante's poetic and—a fortiori—his theological victories over Guido are charged with their degree of guilt. Currently the most widely held reading of line 63 is that offered by Pagliaro: "he who is waiting there is leading me to one (Beatrice) to whom your Guido disdained to be led." John Freccero suggested that Dante's *ebbe a disdegno* draws on Augustine's phrase *dedignantur ab eo discere* ("they disdain to learn from him" [*Confessions* VII, 21, 27]) and therefore contains an implicit reference to Christ. Dante's most severe criticism of Guido—or fear for him—would thus be that Guido's pride of intellect barred him from a true understanding of the Gospels and therefore from conversion.

But the search for a single unambiguous sense of the line not only disregards the pilgrim's hesitation and evasiveness (for example, in the context of the *Comedy* as a whole, Dante does represent himself as chosen for the journey because of his poetic genius, *per altezza d'ingegno*). It has also distracted attention from the deeper significance of Cavalcante's mistake, which springs from the Epicureans' systematic tendency to interpret the data of experience in a negative way, to see everything in terms of death. The text features the ambiguous *ebbe* and shows that it does not mean that Guido is dead; in the context of Dante's demonstration of the futility of negative misinterpretation, it seems clear that the text requires us to inquire into the possible positive meanings of Dante's *ebbe*.

Dante's "perhaps" is the key word in the line. It shows that he is unwilling to be definite. He dare not represent himself as certain of Guido's ultimate fate, but he is free to express his misgivings, which in themselves do him no discredit. His "perhaps" casts doubt on all definite meanings and requires the entire line to be spoken hesitatingly. Perhaps Guido's disdain bars him from this journey; on the other hand, perhaps there is hope for Guido. In fact when Dante later sends word to Cavalcante that his son "is still among the living ones" (III), he uses terms directly related, *per antithesin*, to heresy and its punishment. Heretics are not "among the living." They, unlike Guido, separate themselves from those alive in the faith.

Bruno Nardi was one of the few scholars who have been reluctant to believe that *Inferno* X damns Guido. He went so far as to suggest that the fictitious date of the journey, April 1300, was chosen partly, perhaps even mainly, in order to situate the journey before Dante's priorate and Guido's exile and death, so that Dante could avoid representing Guido's fate. Dante's famous *ebbe,* in any case, functions to keep open the possibility of Guido's salvation; Dante will give no unambiguous sign that he considers him damned. In a context filled with mystifying events, the pilgrim is contrasted sharply with the hasty Cavalcante. He is shown to be careful and accurate in his inferences (e.g., 64–66), and he inquires carefully into misunderstandings. Thus the poet's own refusal to draw a conclusion about Guido is part and parcel of his attack on the hasty pessimism of the Epicureans (cf., in a context closely related to *Inferno* X, Saint Thomas Aquinas's warnings against supposing one can know who is damned, who saved, *Par*. XIII, 112–142).

After Cavalcante has disappeared, attention reverts to Farinata, who has remained utterly immobile:

> But that great-hearted one, the other shade
> at whose request I'd stayed, did not change aspect
> or turn aside his head or lean or bend;
>   and taking up his words where he'd left off,
> "If they were slow," he said, "to learn that art,
> that is more torment to me than this bed."
>
>   (X, 73–78)

He has been pondering Dante's last words to him. They seem to
have brought him new knowledge of the fate of his descendants
(Gramsci suggested that his immobility results from his being trans-
fixed by his new knowledge), and he confesses that he is tortured by
it. This constitutes some softening of the rigidly hostile tone that
governed the earlier conversation. That the unhappiness of his
descendants "is more torment to me than this bed" rests, it would
seem, on the distinction between physical suffering, to which, as
great-hearted, he holds himself superior, and spiritual suffering, to
which he must now confess he is not immune. There is even some
shade of altruism in his concern for others.

> "And yet the Lady who is ruler here
> will not have her face kindled fifty times
> before you learn how heavy is that art."
>
>   (79–81)

Fifty months would take Dante to June 1304, a few weeks before
the abortive attempt of the Florentine Whites based at Arezzo to
force their way back into Florence, when Dante himself will have
learned how difficult it is to return from exile. This is the first and
the most explicit prediction of Dante's exile in the *Inferno*. The
pilgrim himself had introduced the metaphor of art, in his taunt at
line 51 ("Yours were never quick to learn that art"). There is a par-
ticular pathos and irony here, for not even Dante's poetic genius
will win him readmission to Florence. As Mario Sansone suggests,
Farinata seems in some sense to have accepted Dante as a fellow-
sufferer.

In his initial greeting to Dante, Farinata had said that "perhaps"
he had been too harmful to Florence (27). Now he reveals that he
does not understand at all why he is hated there. Why, he asks, do
the Florentines persecute his descendants? Dante explains that the
cause is their memory of Montaperti:

> To which I said: "The carnage, the great bloodshed
> that stained the waters of the Arbia red
> have led us to such prayers in our temple."
>   He sighed and shook his head, then said: "In that,
> I did not act alone, but certainly

>   I'd not have joined the others without cause.
>   But where I was alone was there where all
>   the rest would have annihilated Florence,
>   had I not interceded forcefully."
>
>   (85–93)

There is considerable complexity here. On the one hand, Dante wishes to pay a certain tribute to Farinata's saving of Florence and to suggest that the persecution of his descendants is excessive. On the other hand, if the Ghibellines had not attacked the city under Farinata's leadership, there would have been no opportunity to destroy it: Farinata should not be surprised that he is not regarded as a benefactor. His question shows a reluctance to condemn himself (27), which contrasts sharply with Dante's reluctance to judge Guido (63). Farinata's failure to understand is a further instance of the heretics' blindness.

That Farinata's impassivity may be crumbling points to one of the larger ironies that govern the canto. Dante's visit to the heretics contributes substantially to their sufferings by bringing knowledge of the fates of their descendants and their own reputations (secular versions of immortality). These human concerns are of course universal, so much so that, according to Cicero's widely read *Tusculan Disputations*, their universality is the most important single proof of the soul's immortality. In a whole range of matters, then—from their reliance on exclusively worldly values, to their mistaking the evidence in their own natures for the immortality of the soul, to Cavalcante's misparsing of Dante's *ebbe*—the Epicureans' pessimism betrays their systematic, willfully negative misinterpretation of experience.

A further important mistake of the heretics' comes into focus when Dante questions Farinata about the foreknowledge of the damned:

>   "Ah, as I hope your seed may yet find peace,"
>   I asked, "so may you help me to undo
>   the knot that here has snarled my course of thought.
>   It seems, if I hear right, that you can see
>   beforehand that which time is carrying,
>   but you're denied the sight of present things."
>   "We see, even as men who are farsighted [*c'ha mala luce*],
>   those things," he said, "that are remote from us;
>   the Highest Lord allots us that much light.
>   But when events draw near or are, our minds
>   are useless; were we not informed by others,
>   we should know nothing of your human state.
>   So you can understand how our awareness
>   will die completely at the moment when
>   the portal of the future has been shut."
>
>   (94–108)

Farinata's explanation involves an inversion of the natural pattern of memory (distant things are indistinct, closer ones clear). The metaphor of bad light (*mala luce,* 100), along with the reference to God as the intellectual sun, makes it clear that what Farinata is describing is like evening twilight, in which distant things, outlined against the bright horizon, are more easily visible than closer things, already enveloped in darkness. The metaphor of the end of time as like the closing of a door focuses a parallel with the future closing of the tombs. Until the Last Judgment, the damned will enjoy some vestige of the "good of the intellect," but afterwards hell will be as devoid of "light" as midnight. It has been debated whether the knowledge Farinata describes is shared by all the damned (more likely) or limited to the heretics; in either case the epistemological theme is central to this canto because those who denied the immortality of the soul necessarily mistook also the intellectual nature of the soul's supernatural goal (the Beatific Vision), implicit for Dante in the very gift of intellect.

That Dante's visit increases the punishment of Farinata and Cavalcante, as Sapegno observed, is one of the ways in which it prefigures the Last Judgment, when they will see Christ, their judge, face to face (cf. line 34: "My eyes already were intent on his," and Farinata's initial position to Dante's left). The canto is permeated with allusions to it, as we have in part already seen. Since the Epicureans denied the immortality of the soul, they denied the resurrection of the dead: "What doth it profit me, if the dead rise not again? *Let us eat and drink; for to morrow we shall die,*" wrote Saint Paul (I Corinthians 15:32), lines widely understood as referring to the Epicureans. As Augustine wrote, "Some Christians are Epicureans. What else are those one hears every day saying, 'Let us eat and drink, for tomorrow we die'? and that other saying, 'There is nothing after death, our life is the passage of a shadow'?" (*Sermo de scripturis* CL, 6). And so the Epicureans must act out an abortive resurrection, including its occasion in an act of hearing, for "the trumpet shall sound, and the dead shall rise again" (visual representations of the Last Judgment, like Dante's depiction of Farinata and Cavalcante, regularly show the dead as *harkening*). Their incomplete resurrection prefigures their final burial. And the denial of the general resurrection involves also the denial of the resurrection of Christ, to the iconography of which there are many allusions, such as the mention of the open tombs and the absence of guards in lines 8–9, and the fact that Dante's visit to a tomb recalls the visit of the Marys to Christ's (empty) tomb. In the *Convivio* (IV, xxii) Dante allegorized this visit as figuring the primacy of the contemplative life over the active life. Moreover, he identified epicureanism, stoicism, and Aristotelianism as "the three schools of the active life."

The impact of the allusions to Christ's death and resurrection (including Farinata's unintended echo in line 25—"Your accent makes it clear" [*La tua loquela ti fa manifesto*]—of those who accused Peter when he denied Christ for the third time, "For even thy speech [in the Vulgate, *loquela*] doth discover thee" [Matthew 26:73]) is intensified by the image of Farinata erect and visible from the waist up, an allusion to a particularly famous iconographic motif known as the *imago pietatis,* which represents the dead Christ from the waist up, with his head bent and his hands crossed in front of him. As numerous commentators have shown, most conclusively Ewald Vetter, this figure is a Eucharistic symbol; that is, it is a representation, not of the dead Christ at any particular historical moment (such as the descent from the Cross), but rather of the Body of Christ as it was believed to be present in the consecrated host of the Mass, the substance which, according to the doctrine of transubstantiation, is hidden under the appearance of the bread.

To deny Christ resurrected, then, is also to deny him in his Passion (as Peter denied him), to deny him in the Mass, and—in late medieval terms—to deny the Real Presence of the Body of Christ in the consecrated host. The doctrine of transubstantiation promulgated in 1215 and its somewhat later appendage, the Feast of Corpus Christi (dedicated to the consecrated host), were considered major weapons in the fight against heresy, since the heretic's proud adherence to his own errors sets him against the Eucharistic bond of love that unites the Church (see my article listed below). As Anthony Cassell notes also, with reference to the sacrament of baptism (the "portal of the faith that you embrace," Virgil calls it in *Inferno* IV, 36), the heretics' being visible to the waist alludes to the iconography of baptism, and their very tombs (*arche* [29]), allude to Noah's ark, the first great figure of baptism and of the Church.

The interview with Farinata ends with Farinata's revealing that his tomb contains more than a thousand souls, including the emperor Frederick II and Cardinal Ottaviano degli Ubaldini, another famous Ghibelline; we are not told the manner of Farinata's disappearance. Now it is Dante's turn to ponder what Farinata has said about his exile. Virgil admonishes him:

> And then that sage exhorted me: "Remember
> the words that have been spoken here against you.
> Now pay attention," and he raised his finger;
> "When you shall stand before the gentle splendor
> of one whose gracious eyes see everything,
> then you shall learn—from her—your lifetime's journey."
> (127–132)

Like Cavalcante, Dante has heard words he finds threatening; he is
to store them up in memory, assured that his doubts will be an-
swered. Virgil says that Beatrice will tell him of his future life, but in
fact it is Cacciaguida who will do so, and Dante will cite Farinata's
and Brunetto's prophecies when questioning him (*Par.* XVII). Thus
the pilgrim's carefulness in not jumping to conclusions but inquir-
ing until he has reached an accurate understanding, behavior that
so markedly contrasts with Cavalcante's, is shown to be a model of
what his attitude should be toward the central tragedy of his life, his
exile. He must have faith that at the appropriate moment its mean-
ing will be made clear.

In admonishing Dante, Virgil adopts a traditional and, for Dante,
very emphatic gesture: he raises his finger (129) in the timeless ges-
ture of instruction. This signal is the second of two references to
Virgil's hands in the canto. The first occurred when "my guide—his
hands encouraging and quick— / thrust me between the sepulchers
toward him" (37–38). Virgil's hands are "encouraging (*animose*) and
quick," it would seem, because he used them to write his poems,
thus to instruct and delight and to convey his spirit. (Allegorically,
this is one of the indications that Dante's reading of Virgil, perhaps
of *Aeneid* VI, had much to do with his interest in the Florentine
past.) All references to the body and its gestures in this canto—as
elsewhere in the poem—have turned out to be richly signifi-
cant. * * * It is striking, and doubtless intended to be noticed, espe-
cially in connection with the crossed, wounded hands of the *imago
pietatis,* that in the entire detailed representation of the gestures of
Farinata and Cavalcante there is not a single reference to either's
hands or arms. It would seem that in spite of their pride in intellect,
power, and worldly success, and in spite of their dedication to the
active life, in the last analysis they accomplished nothing.

BIBLIOGRAPHY

Bambeck, Manfred, *Göttliche Komödie und Exegese,* 1–59. Berlin,
1971.
Browe, Petrus. *Die Verehrung der Eucharistie im Mittelalter.* Mu-
nich, 1933.
———. *Textus antiqui de festo corporis Christi.* Münster, 1934.
Bruni, Leonardo. "Vita di Dante." In *Le vite di Dante, Petrarca, e
Boccaccio scritte fino al secolo decimosesto,* ed. Angelo Solerti. Mi-
lan, n.d.
Cassell, Anthony K. "Dante's Farinata and the Image of the Arca."
Yale Italian Studies 1 (1977): 335–370.
———. "Farinata." In *Dante's Fearful Art of Justice,* 15–31. Toronto,
1984.

Chimenz, Siro A. "Il 'disdegno' di Guido e i suoi interpreti." *Orientamenti culturali* 1 (1945): 179–188.

Contini, Gianfranco. "Cavalcanti in Dante." In *Un'idea di Dante: Saggi danteschi*, 143–157. Turin, 1976.

Croce, Benedetto. *La poesia di Dante*. Bari, 1920.

De Sanctis, Francesco. *De Sanctis on Dante: Essays*. Trans. and ed. Joseph Rossi and Alfred Galpin. Madison, Wis., 1957.

Durling, Robert M. "Farinata and the Body of Christ." *Stanford Italian Review* 2 (1981): 1–34.

Freccero, John. "Ironia e mimesi: il disdegno di Guido." In *Dante e la Bibbia*, ed. Giovanni Barblan, 41–54. Atti del Convegno Internazionale promosso da "Bibbia." Florence, 26–28 September 1986. Florence, 1988.

Frugoni, Arsenio. "Il canto x dell' *Inferno*." In *Nuove letture dantesche*, 1:261–283. Florence, 1966.

Marti, Mario. "Cavalcanti, Guido." *Enciclopedia dantesca*, 1:891–896. Rome, 1970.

Nardi, Bruno. "Dante e Guido Cavalcanti." In *Saggi e note di critica dantesca*, 190–219. Milan, 1966.

Ottokar, N. "La condanna postuma di Farinata degli Uberti." In *Studi comunali e fiorentini*, 115–123. Florence, 1948.

Pagliaro, Antonino. "Il disdegno di Guido." In *Saggi di critica semantica*, 359–380. Messina, 1953. Reprinted in *Ulisse: Ricerche semantiche sulla "Divina Commedia"* (Messina-Florence, 1967), 1: 198–210.

Paratore, Ettore, "Il Canto x dell' *Inferno*." *Letture classensi* 5 (1976): 215–255.

Sansone, Mario. "Cavalcanti, Cavalcante de'." *Enciclopedia dantesca*, 1:891. Rome, 1970.

———. "Farinata." *Enciclopedia dantesca*, 2:804–809. Rome, 1970.

Schiller, Gertrud. *Ikonographie der christlichen Kunst*. Vol. 3, *Die Auferstehung und Erhöhung Christi*. Gutersloh, 1971.

Scott, John A. *Dante magnanimo: Studi sulla "Commedia."* Florence, 1977.

Singleton, Charles S. "*Inferno* x: Guido's Disdain." *MLN* 77 (1962): 49–65.

Vetter, Ewald M. "Iconografia del *Varón de dolores*: Su significado y orígen." *Archivo español de arte* 36 (1963): 197–231.

MARC COGAN

The Poetic Application of the Structure of Hell[†]

The Contrapasso and the Relation between Poetic Details and Structure

The medieval Aristotelian psychological theory implicit in Virgil's description of the geography of Hell gave Dante only the skeleton of the *Inferno*. What we experience in the poem itself is that theory made concrete and vivid in the incidents and descriptions of the narrative. Many of the poetic details of the *Inferno* are intuitively comprehensible, but others are more obscure; and to the extent that we understand Dante's interpretation of Aristotle, we have a powerful clue both for illuminating his more obscure poetic choices and also for more fully understanding even the familiar ones. Nor does this process of illumination occur in one direction only. If our awareness of how Dante may have used Aristotle casts light on the incidents of the poem, it is equally the case that the incidents in their turn often suggest to us nuances of how Dante specifically understood the Aristotelian text he used as his philosophical source.

All of the poetic details are significant—location, geography, climate, physical appearance—all are surely intended to make concrete the abstract theory that determined the placement of a particular sin in a particular place in Hell. But foremost among the details, of course, are the punishments with which the damned are tormented. The punishments are the most compelling of the details. Physical descriptions of place appear from time to time in the *Inferno*, sometimes with more detail, sometimes less. But the punishments are always before our eyes, and it is the vividness with which Dante treats them that gives the *cantica* its force. We must be self-conscious and deliberate, then, in determining how best to interpret these most important narrative events in the context of Hell's structure and the structure of sin it embodies. Moreover, our decision with respect to the punishments will effectively determine what we will look for in the other poetic details as well. So, we must state our position with respect to what Dante once, and commentators many times, called the *contrapasso* that the damned endure.

My conviction is that we must distinguish the figurative principle of the punishments that we see the damned souls undergoing in Hell from that of the corrections we see souls undertaking in Purgatory.

† From *The Design in the Wax: The Structure of the Divine Comedy and Its Meaning.* Copyright © 1999 by the University of Notre Dame Press. Reprinted by permission of the University of Notre Dame Press. Notes have been renumbered.

What we see in the punishments of the damned are figurative replications of the actions or natures of the sins themselves. When, later, we see purgatorial corrections, what we see are figures that show actions opposite in nature to the vices being purged.[1] For Hell, the principle is enunciated by Bertram de Born, in the eighth circle of Hell:

> Io feci il padre e 'l figlio in sè ribelli:
>   Achitofèl non fè più d' Absalone
>   e di Davìd coi malvagi punzelli.
> Perch'io parti' così giunte persone,
>   partito porto il mio cerebro, lasso!
>   dal suo principio ch'è in questo troncone.
> Così s'osserva in me lo contrapasso.
>
> (*Inf.* xxviii, 136–42)[2] *counterpass*

Considering how important the notion of the *contrapasso*—presumably not any individual punishment itself, but the principle of justice that informs all of the punishments—is to the poem, it is strange to realize that this passage is the only time in the whole of the *Commedia* that Dante uses the term *contrapasso*. That being the case, given also how late in the *Inferno* it is before Dante deals with the principle explicitly, the location he chooses as the one in which to call attention to the principle is probably also significant. Bertram says that having divided others, he is now himself divided. He is punished among the sowers of discord, the *seminator di scandalo e di scisma* (*Inf.* xxviii, 35). Now, *seminator* is also a word that Dante only uses once in the entire *Commedia,* and given the nature of the principle Bertram enunciates, it is a noun pregnant with meaning. If Dante has waited until encountering these sowers of discord before making the notion of a *contrapasso* explicit, it is, I believe, so we can hear the echo of Paul in Galatians: "Quæ enim seminaverit homo, hæc et metet" (Gal. 6:7), Whatever a man sows, so shall he reap. And this is precisely what Bertram is undergoing. Having sown division, he has now reaped it. In his case, he now undergoes what he did; in other

1. Cf. John Freccero, "Infernal Irony: The Gates of Hell," in *Dante: The Poetics of Conversion,* pp. 106–7: "If the bodies in hell are really souls, then it follows that their physical attitudes, contortions and punishments are really *spiritual* attitudes and states of mind, sins made manifest in the form of physical punishment, It is therefore correct to say that the punishments *are* the sins." Cf. also Anthony K. Cassell, *Dante's Fearful Art of Justice* (Toronto: University of Toronto Press, 1984), p. 9: "[The punishment] is, in all cases, . . . a strict manifestation of the sin as guilt. . . . The images of the damned figure symbolically, iconographically, and theologically the very mystery and complexity of their sins." See also Silvio Pasquazi, *Enciclopedia dantesca,* article "*Contrapasso,*" 2:181–83, esp. p. 182, and Steno Vazzana, *Il Contrapasso nella Divina Commedia* (Roma: Ciranna, 1968). Also, Allan H. Gilbert, *Dante's Conception of Justice* (Durham: Duke University Press, 1975), p. 75.
2. Cf. Kenneth Gross, "Infernal Metamorphoses: An Interpretation of Dante's Counterpass," *MLN* 100 (1985): 42–69, esp. 48–49: "If nothing else, Bertran retains enough of his poetic insight to see that his punishment makes out of his sensible, corporeal form a symbol of the divisions he had formerly wrought within the body politic."

cases, we recognize that sinners continue to engage in the activity that was their sin (rather than to suffer its effects); but in whichever of these two patterns Dante chooses, the image we are given in the punishment, as we see in Bertram's case, is an image in which we can recognize the essential action of the sin that is being punished.

The principle of the corrections of Purgatory, as stated by Omberto Aldobrandesco, is exactly the opposite. Omberto recognizes that the correction imposed upon him among the proud consists in doing what he should have done, but did not do, while alive:

> E qui convien ch'io questo peso porti
> per lei, tanto che a Dio si sodisfaccia,
> poi ch'io nol fe' tra' vivi, qui tra' morti.
> (*Purg.* xi, 70–72)[3]

The purpose of Purgatory is the undoing of the vices that had afflicted the now repentant sinners while alive. Vices cannot be removed by a repetition of one's vicious actions: an Aristotelian would understand that such repetition would merely serve to confirm a vicious habit. Hence, it is altogether necessary as well as appropriate that the undoing of their sinful states be accomplished, and represented to us, by actions that are the opposites of the sins they had committed. It cannot at all be said of the sinners undergoing rehabilitation in Purgatory that they have reaped what they sowed.[4] Quite the contrary, whether we look at the corrections

---

3. Two *gironi* in Purgatory, and their corrections—of the wrathful, and of the lustful—seem to exhibit the actions of the vices, rather than their opposites. * * * Omberto's explanation of the *contrapasso* in Purgatory is unambiguous, and the new principle seems appropriate to Purgatory in both philosophical and poetic senses. In this context, it is perhaps worth considering that the dense and choking smoke of the third *girone* can represent the *extinguishing* of the flames of anger (flame being, in any case, a more common figure for anger than smoke), rather than the action of anger. With respect to the lustful, we should consider that lust would not be corrected by the absence or opposite of love, but by the presence of proper love. Both lust and love might reasonably be represented by fire. Here, as in the world, the two forms of love look confusingly similar. But the fires we see in the seventh *girone* are surely meant as refining fires of proper love. Cf. Gilbert, *Dante's Conception of Justice*, pp. 136–39 and 126–27, and Patrick Boyde, *Perception and Passion* (Cambridge: Cambridge University Press, 1993), p. 289.

4. Vandelli, as do many other editors, glosses the following verses from Guido del Duca in Purgatory with the citation from Galatians:

> Fu il sangue mio d'invidia sì rïarso,
> che se veduto avesse uom farsi lieto,
> visto m'avresti di livore sparso.
> Di mia semente cotal paglia mieto.
> (*Purg.* xiv, 82–85)

But the principle of Galatians is inappropriate here too. Having looked at others with envy, Guido now . . . cannot look at all. He does not continue to look with envy; he is not looked at with envy. He has reaped the opposite of his original action. I believe Trucchi is correct (*ad loc.*, DDP) in hearing, in Guido's statement, not the echo of Galatians but an echo from Proverbs: "Whoever sows iniquity shall reap vanity" (Prov. 22:8). Since Guido goes on to discuss the futility (one could say vanity) of desiring what cannot be possessed in common (*Purg.* xiv, 86–87), the echo of Proverbs would be appropriate.

they undertake or the ultimate result of those corrections. Having
sown a stiff neck, Omberto reaps its opposite, a bent one. Or, one
might say, having sown sin, Omberto will eventually reap, because
of his repentence, blessedness. Purgatory moves by opposition,
and the *contrapasso* in the *Purgatorio* must be recognized as de-
manding correction through action opposed to the sin that is to be
corrected. *Poetic mechanisms of purgatory*

In the *Inferno,* the descriptions Dante gives of the punishments are
meant to embody, make concrete, external, and visible, the intentions,
motives, and choices that inform the various sins.[5] In punishing the
damned through the actions of their own sins, these punishments
effectively become dramatizations of the underlying nature of each
sin, making manifest what may have been obscured or concealed in
the original act. In our world, sinful actions inevitably present them-
selves to us veiled by a cloud of circumstantial detail, detail that
makes it difficult to separate what is essentially sinful about the act
from the accidents amidst which we perceive it. In his striking de-
scriptions of their punishments, Dante is able to propose the
essences of the sins stripped of worldly circumstance, and ulti-
mately, if not immediately, more capable of being understood.[6] The
general nature of this poetic principle has long been the common
possession of readers of the *Inferno.* The parallelism of many of the
punishments to the sins they punish is almost intuitively apparent.
We see the lustful now driven by a whirlwind that is the image of the
passion that drove them while alive; the violent, moved by anger—a
"heating of the blood around the heart," as the Middle Ages would
express it[7]—find themselves eternally surrounded by boiling blood;
the traitors, so coldly calculating as to betray family, country, sover-
eign for gain, are set in ice.

While I believe that Dante is unwavering in his application of the
principle that the punishment mirrors the sin in the *Inferno,* there
has always been controversy regarding either the principle in general
or its applicability in particular cases. The likely source of ambiguity
on which disagreement could be based is Dante's practice of some-
times showing sinners re-enacting the specific actions of their sins

5. Gross, "Infernal Metamorphoses," speaks of punishments as "sins converted to torturing
   images by what Dante would persuade us is the allegorizing eye of eternal Justice" (p. 42).
   "The pains of the damned are more revelation than retribution; they compose difficult
   moral emblems which shadow forth sin's inward nature" (p. 47). Cf. Giorgio Padoan, "Il
   Canto degli Epicurei," *Convivium* n.s. 27 (1959): 13–39, esp. p. 14.
6. Cf. Vazzana, *Il Contrapasso,* p. 10: "In altri termini, la pena che Dante attribuisce ad ogni
   peccato è la faccia e la forma del peccato stesso, che ora Dio, col suo giudizio ha rivelato
   nella sua vera fisionomia. Quindi mai un rapporto di contrasto tra peccato e pena, ma di
   analogia. Anzi, più che di analogia, si tratta di identità: la pena è il peccato visto nella sua
   natura maligna, la sua figurazione; gli attributi della pena sono gli attributi del peccato;
   insomma ogni atteggiamento della pena è un giudizio del poeta su quel peccato."
7. See *ST,* 1a2æ 22, 2 ad 3. Cf. *de An.,* i, 1; 403b1–3, and John of Damascus, *de Fide ortho-
   doxa,* ii, xvi (*Burgundionis Versio,* c. 30, p. 122).

in their punishments, and other times undergoing the effects of those actions. His choice of active or passive representations is presumably dictated by poetic judgment. Sometimes the passive image may be more effective; in other cases, the active. But this practice can lead to a verbal equivocation, since in the case of passive representations, it is possible to say that the sinners are being punished by the "contrary" of their sin (since acting and undergoing are indeed contraries). Hence, some readers have fallen into the trap of saying, rather too casually, that these sinners are punished by the "opposite" of their sins.[8] But while it would be proper to say that the souls in Purgatory are being purged by the opposite of their sins, the sinners in Hell are not tormented by a sin's opposites, but by the sin itself. In the case of the schismatics, already noted, they are punished by undergoing what they once practiced. Their punishment in passive, relative to the action that was their sin, but they are nonetheless punished by the sin itself, and their passion provides an image of the sin, not its opposite.[9]

There is a powerful double sense of justice in punishing the damned by the re-enactment of their sins. First, these sins were actions freely chosen by the souls themselves during their lives. What could be more just than to allow them to continue to practice those illusory goods (now revealed as pains) which they had preferred to the one true good.[1] Second, justice demands that the damned be beyond change. Were they still capable of change, they could be capable of repentance, and then it would be unjust to continue their punishment

8. See, for example, Giovanni Busnelli, L'Etica nicomachea e l'ordinamento morale dell'"Inferno" di Dante (Bologna: Zanichelli, 1907), p. 152.

9. Even where the punishment seems unequivocally passive in respect of the action, Dante makes an effort to emphasize the sinners' recognition of and adherence to the action they now suffer. Richard Abrams, "Against the Contrapasso: Dante's Heretics, Schismatics, and Others," Italian Quarterly 27: 105 (1986): 5–19, points (p. 12) to an extraordinary instance of this in the same canto in which the term contrapasso itself appears for the only time in the Commedia. As Mohammed passes Dante, he shouts, "Or vedi com'io mi dilacco" (Inf. xxviii, 30), as if it were still he doing the dividing. See also Francesco d'Ovidio, "Il Canto XIX dell'Inferno," in Getto, Letture dantesche, pp. 345–76, esp. p. 352, on the passive representation of the sin of simony.

1. From this perspective one can scarcely speak of the damned as condemned to their punishments. They desired these actions while alive, and in a sense still do. Virgil explains that sinners rush to their punishment because their fear is turned to desire (Inf. iii, 126: "sì che la tema si volve in disio"), in regard to which Abrams, "Against the Contrapasso," p. 9, comments: "Each class of sinners embraces the divine judgment—fear turning to desire as the sinner fondly recognizes in his eternal fate, not an impersonal punishment, but a form of suffering reminiscent of his own inmost yearning." Cf. Karl Witte, "The Ethical Systems of the Inferno and the Purgatorio," in Essays on Dante, trans. C. M. Lawrence and P. H. Wicksteed (Boston: Houghton Mifflin, 1898), pp. 117–52, esp. p. 129. Also Vazzana, Il Contrapasso, p. 34: "Dio, che li ha giudicati in vita e che ha voluto che ciascuno da morto si avesse e fosse quello che volle e fu da vivo." From this perspective, Eleonore Stump, "Dante's Hell, Aquinas' Moral Theory, and the Love of God," Canadian Journal of Philosophy 16 (1986): 181–98, quite properly characterizes this as a manifestation not only of divine justice, but of God's love for the sinners (pp. 196–97). For a fuller discussion, see also Marc Cogan, "Delight, Punishment, and the Justice of God in the Divina Commedia," Dante Studies 111 (1993): 27–52.

eternally.[2] Unlike the souls of Purgatory, then, the damned must re-
main fixed in the damnable choices they made while alive.[3] And in-
deed, while undergoing their punishments, they undergo without cease
the experience of their same damnable activities. In doing so, they
thereby become ever more fixed in the characteristic actions that
damned them, since it is the repetition of a certain manner of acting
that, for an Aristotelian, renders a specific state of character more sta-
ble and durable. As they repeat these damnable actions, they repeat-
edly and justly incur the condemnation for these actions that has
doomed them to their places. They become, if one can say it, more per-
fectly damned with every iteration of the sin that is their punishment.[4]

(In Purgatory, by contrast, whose purpose is precisely change, and
where the allegorical goal of the narrative is to illuminate the virtues
that are the opposites of the seven capital vices, the corrections we
see in the literal narrative must, for a double reason, exhibit activi-
ties opposite to the vices.[5] They must do so, first, in order to be able
to serve as figures for their coordinate virtues. They do so as well be-
cause of the consistent Aristotelian theory of action that underlies
both the *Inferno* and the *Purgatorio*. If bad habits are inculcated and
made durable by repetition of bad actions, good habits must be
made durable by the repetition of proper activities.)

The *contrapasso* is first of all an ethical or theological principle.
Justice directs that the damned be punished by the very actions for
which they were damned; ethics instructs that the rehabilitation of
bad habits be by an opposing regimen. But it is the *poet's* application
of this theological principle that directs how we are to interpret the
poetic details of the poem in the light of the structure of Hell (and
later of Purgatory). The poet maintains faith with the principle of
justice and consistency with the structure of Hell by making the in-
dividual sin and its genus resemble that structure—whether we
mean that the punishment shows us the action of the sin or physical
details illuminate particular aspects of the sin. (In Purgatory, * * *
our strategy would call for the opposite conclusion. Details are con-
sistent with the structure of Purgatory when they reflect virtuous
conduct, the opposite of the vices under correction.)

As we read the *Inferno*, we are encouraged to consider the specific

---

2. *SCG*, iv, 93. Cf. 4 *Sent.*, 50, 1.
3. Abrams, "Against the *Contrapasso*," p. 9, provides a striking example of the fixity of
damned character. The despair Cavalcante Cavalcanti experiences in misinterpreting
Dante's remark about his son, Guido (*Inf.* x, 67–72), depends on his continuing to act as
if he believed that only life on earth mattered (as he had believed, insofar as an Epi-
curean, while alive), despite his now having the most vivid proof of a life beyond that one!
See also Francesco de Sanctis, "Il Canto V dell'*Inferno*," in Getto, *Letture dantesche*, pp.
73–90, esp. pp. 88 and 86: "Nell'Inferno il terrestre rimane eterno ed immutato; perché i
peccatori dell'Inferno dantesco servano le stesse passioni."
4. See also Stump, "Dante's Hell," pp. 196–97.
5. Cf. Gross, "Infernal Metamorphoses," p. 48.

actions engaged in by the damned, and the circumstances in which they engage in them, as furnishing clues to the nature of the sin whose punishment they are. These figurative representations of the sins are often simultaneously obscure and transparent: obscure, insofar as they often do not at first resemble their sins or the occasions of the sins; transparent, insofar as they ultimately provide a starker and therefore clearer picture of the real nature of the sin. What to our eyes makes the punishments initially seem dissimilar to their sins is that the sins, as we have noted, occur in this world surrounded by circumstances—including deceptions, self-deceptions, and rationalizations on the part of the sinners—which have all disappeared in Hell.[6] So these do not look like the sins as we know them. Yet, at the moment that we do recognize the sins in these punishments, we have made a breakthrough in recognizing the underlying action that was the real nature of the sin. We are invited by Dante to use the details of punishments to confirm familiar aspects of the sins, and also to suggest hitherto unacknowledged or obscure aspects of them.[7] Indeed, where we see punishments whose relation to their sins is not immediately apparent to us, we ought not imagine that Dante has suddenly employed a different principle, but, rather, that he is demanding that we consider the sin in an unexpected light, leading us thereby to a reinterpretation of its nature. Where we find sins "doubled," as it were—that is, where we find Dante punishing in two locations, as two sins, actions that we conventionally consider only one sin—we must make an effort to recognize what significant difference Dante may be attempting to exhibit by this diversity of embodiment and location.

As the details of punishments of the individual sins make visible and illuminate the natures of the sins, so grouping sins together in geographical regions of Hell objectifies what we would usually encounter as philosophical distinctions. Geographical proximity of punishments (and so of sins) must imply affinities in the natures of these sins. Distances between circles should reflect differences in nature.[8] Descriptions of geographical or geological separations or barriers between regions, then, are the figurative equivalent of philosophical distinctions between sins of substantially different natures. Where

---

6. Gross, "Infernal Metamorphoses," p. 50, states, "Only by dying into Eternity does the damned soul discover and become the emblematic form of its inward life." That is, while alive, that inward character is concealed by the circumstances of life. In death alone is the true nature of the action revealed, and only in the clarified posthumous state that Dante pictures does the action of the damned soul become didactic for us.

7. Cf. Vazzana, *Il Contrapasso*, p. 15.

8. Dante may even be going so far, with a sort of philosophic pun, as to indicate that he believed such sins share a common genus, in a strict philosophical sense of the term. For the physical connection of circles would have to be based on a common material substratum (figuratively, the continent beneath them in Hell), and it is the material cause that provides the genus of an entity.

no barriers or separations exist—where, that is, Dante and Virgil can simply walk between circles—their continuous movement should be the image of an essential continuity or kinship existing between discrete sins. (And when we look to this figurative strategy, we immediately recognize that Dante uses it to confirm Virgil's articulation of the structure of Hell in canto xi. Between each of the broad categories of sin Virgil describes there are geographical or geological barriers; between the individual sins within those groupings we find, on the other hand, a continuous, and usually unobstructed route for Dante and Virgil to follow.) Finally, to the punishments and their locations we should add for consideration details of climate and geology, the functionaries whom Dante posts to superintend locations, and the behaviors of the sinners Dante encounters.[9] All of these concrete imagistic details contribute content to the structure of sin embodied in the structure of Hell, at the same time that our understanding of their significance is guided by the principles according to which that structure was articulated.

One fundamental aspect of the poetic use of the structure of Hell bears repeating. The underlying philosophical structure of the *Inferno* is the architectonic principle of the narrative, establishing its order and directing the selection of appropriate figurative detail for the poem's incidents. But * * * the existence of this architectonic principle does not constrain Dante *poeta;* rather, it provides the opportunity for a real poetic liberation, freeing him from an otherwise impossible poetic task. Consider: if we had no theological or philosophical context in which to understand that, and why, certain sins in their nature were worse than others, Dante's descriptions of their punishment—by themselves—would have had to embody simultaneously both the essence of the sin and the degree of its gravity. Not only would the details of punishments have to be figures of the diverse sins, the punishments would themselves have to be ordered in such a way that each punishment would unequivocally appear worse to every reader, thus indicating the increasing seriousness of the sins encountered. Who could imagine it possible to do this? In the natural scheme of things, is it worse to be burned in a fiery tomb? Or to be hacked in half at every completed circuit of Hell? Is it worse to be up to one's neck in boiling blood or in excrement? In the *natural* scheme of things, it does not, of course, matter at all, and individual readers find different pun-

---

9. Cf. Gross, "Infernal Metamorphoses," p. 45: "The phenomenological totality which one might call the 'state' of each of the damned in Dante's Hell—a condition embracing body, mind, language, landscape, and weather—is a complex reflection of and on the sinful disorder of his soul." Also, Christopher Kleinhenz, "Eternal Guardians Revisited: 'Cerbero, il gran vermo' (*Inf.* vi, 22)," *Dante Studies* 93 (1975): 185–99, esp. 186–88. See also Vazzana, *Il Contrapasso*, p. 64, regarding the *bolge* that characterize the landscape of the eighth circle: "La stessa struttura a fossati del campo maligno rende due qualità della frode: lo star nascosta e l'insidia. La violenza è aperta, visibile."

ishments more horrific or disgusting for what will always be purely personal reasons. But the geographical location of the punishments gives an unequivocal measurement of their differing seriousnesses, so that we do not have to do so.

That the circles of Hell (and the sins represented in them) follow an ordered sequence that itself incorporates an explanation of the increasing seriousness of the sins frees Dante from having to undertake this impossible poetic feat. The primary geographic feature of Hell furnishes the initial and most straightforward of the poetic figures: the depth in Hell in which a sin is punished indicates its seriousness; downward is worse. Inasmuch as the regions of Hell are associated with the appetites that are the sources of all action, and inasmuch as the appetites are themselves ordered in terms of rationality or controllability by the reason (and, hence, culpability in the failure to control them), attribution of sins to the appropriate appetite locates the sin with respect to its seriousness, and therefore determines its physical location in the geography of Hell. Since we conclude from geography alone that to be punished lower in Hell is worse (whether or not the punishments for sins lower in Hell are ones we would personally consider more painful than for sins above them), Dante is freed to select punishments on the basis of how effectively they provide an image of the sins of which they are punishments.[1]

LEO SPITZER

Speech and Language in *Inferno* XIII[†]

The most recent commentary on this canto is that of Grandgent;[1] below are the lines in which he sums up the episode of Pier delle Vigne and treats of the language of the canto:

> The style of this canto abounds in curious conceits, such as the
>
> Cred'io ch'ei credette ch'io credesse
>
> of 1. 25, the "infiammati infiammar" of 1. 68, the double antithesis of 1. 69, and the involved paradoxes of the following tiercet. It would seem that meditation over Pier delle Vigne,

1. Cf. Vazzana, *Il Contrapasso*, p. 13.
† From *Italica* (19:3), 1942 Sept., 81–104. Copyright © 1942 by *Italica*. Reprinted by permission of *Italica*.
1. For the bibliography, as far as not specifically mentioned, v. Grandgent. I consulted also E. Auerbach, "Dante als Dichter der irdischen Welt"; K. Vossler, "Die göttliche Komödie," 2d ed. (Heidelberg 1925); Croce, "Dantes Dichtung" (translation of Schlosser). I am indebted for various suggestions to my pupils with whom I read the canto in class: A. Bianchini, E. Fenimore, F. J. Powers.

who dominates the canto, had filled our poet with the spirit of the older school, so that, either purposely or unconsciously, he imitated its artistic processes. Pier delle Vigne's epistolary style is highly artificial and flowery.

The suicide uses his freedom of bodily movement only to deprive himself of it, robbing himself, by his own act, of that which corporeally distinguishes him from a plant. Such a sinner, then, his wicked deed eternalized, may aptly be figured as a tree or bush. Dante's self-slaughterers form a thick, wild forest in the second ring of the seventh circle. There, upon hearing their sentence from Minos, they fall at random, in no predestined spot: they have put themselves outside of God's law, rebelling against his eternal plan. On the Day of Judgment they will return, with the rest, for their earthly remains; but, instead of putting on the flesh again, they will drag their corpses through Hell and hang them on their boughs, where the poor bodies will dangle forever, a torment to the souls that slew them. The pent-up agony of these spirits finds no means of expression until they are broken in leaf or branch; then the voice issues forth with tears of blood.

The like had been seen and heard by Aeneas in a Thracian grove, when, to deck an altar, he unwittingly plucked shrubs from the grave of Polydorus: blood trickled from the severed roots, and a voice came forth—not from the tree, as in Dante, but from the mound (*Aen.*, III, 39 ff.):—

> Gemitus lacrimabilis imo
> Auditur tumulo, et vox reddita fertur ad aures:
> Quid miserum Aenea, laceras? Jam parce sepulto,
> Parce pias scelerare manus. Non me tibi Troja
> Externum tulit. Haud cruor hic de stipite manat.

[From beneath the mound is heard a pitiful moan, and a voice from it is carried to my ears: "Alas, why do you tear me, Aeneas? Spare me now in my tomb, spare pollution to your pious hands. Troy bore me; I am not foreign to you, nor is this blood that oozes from the stem."]

In the suicides' wood, an outlet for the mournful voice is afforded by harpies, voracious, filthy birds with maidens' faces, which rend the foliage. They may well represent misgiving or fear of the hereafter—"triste annunzio di futuro danno."

Thus Grandgent (like other commentators, as we shall see) explains the particular devices of style in this canto as due to an association in the mind of Dante with the speech habits to be found in the writings of the historical character Pier delle Vigne. While not denying the existence of such an external association, I shall seek to establish a deeper motivation for Dante's choice of language.

First let us consider the treatment of the main motif: the fate of the suicides who are condemned to assume the shape of plants. As D'Ovidio points out, Dante has borrowed not only from Virgil but also from the author of the *Metamorphoses*: the *uomo-pianta* created by the Christian poet recalls Driope or Lotis or the Heliads (*Uomini fummo, ed or siam fatti sterpi*). This critic, however, points out the difference between an Ovidian and a Dantean metamorphosis, as regards the actual process itself through which metamorphosis is achieved: when, in Ovid, a living person "becomes" a plant (feet stiffening into roots, hair turning into foliage, etc.) there is a continuous identity between the person-as-a-whole and the plant into which he is transformed. But in the case of the suicides treated by Dante, there can, obviously, be no such continuity: it is not the person-as-a-whole, an indivisible unit of body and soul, that becomes a new kind of being; body and soul have been divorced by the act of self-murder and it is the soul alone that survives. These souls bereft of body go to be judged by Minos; wherever they have chanced to fall, there they put out new roots and grow themselves a new body—an ersatz body of meaner stuff to replace the human body from which they have been severed. Thus, in Dante, there is no "development," properly speaking: the soul itself continues to exist without change, while the life of the body is utterly destroyed— its possibility of growth, even into another form, cut off: the second body, the plant-like body, has no ties with the first, but is the product of a new birth that takes place only after death has severed the first body from the soul. Thus, because Dante is dealing here (as, indeed, throughout the *Inferno*) with the fate meted out to the souls of dead men, there can be none of that delicate tracing of transitory intermediate stages in which Ovid delighted, where it is possible to fix that certain moment of perplexity when the living person is no longer human and yet not quite plant or animal; the most famous of all such moments, commemorated by so many artists, is that of Daphne *becoming* a tree (cf. also, in the metamorphosis of Actaeon, the lines "Gemit ille, sonumque, / *Etsi non hominis, quem non tamen edere possit / Cervus* [He moaned in a way which was not human, nor was it the utterance of a deer]").

So much for the process of which the plant-man is the product: what of the product itself and its behavior? Here too Dante differs from Ovid: his *uomo-pianta*, in fact, is a composite of features drawn from both Ovid and Virgil: from the first, obviously, derives the concept of a person being transformed, though by a different process, into a plant (this is not Virgilian: Polydorus does not *be-*

come the myrtle tree);[2] from the second derives the incident in
which a plant is stripped of a branch, and a voice, though not that of
the tree, protests in pain: from Virgil Dante borrowed a segment of
epic activity.[3] These separate borrowings fuse (in an artistic meta-
morphosis) to give us something unknown either to Ovid or Virgil: a
plant that bleeds and speaks. This creature is "very man and very
plant": in its growth from a "seed" it has aped the birth and organic
growth of a plant; yet this plant not only bleeds (this in itself and
other similar phenomena may be found in Ovid), but reveals the an-
guished workings of a human mind and heart. It represents, then,
something quite different from the creations of Ovid, such as Dri-
ope and her like: with the latter we have to do only with a plant that
was once a human being; there is no painful insistence that this
creature, after its metamorphosis, is both plant and human. But the

2. And yet, although no actual metamorphosis is involved in the Polydorus incident, there is
   a trace of such an idea in the description of the conformation of the myrtle, "*densis
   hastilibus horrida myrtus* [A myrtle harsh with dense sticks]": this easily suggests a picture
   of the legendary Polydorus "shot through" with arrows; cf. *hic confixum ferrea texit telo-
   rum segetes et iaculis increvit acutis* [Here I am covered and pierced with a harvest of
   weapons that grow in sharp javelins].

3. D'Ovidio points out that, in addition to its exterior relationship with the Polydorus
   episode, this canto reveals an interior association: the guide Virgil, this Dantean charac-
   ter, is at the same time the historic Virgil, author of the *Aeneid,* and it is to his own epic
   poem that he is referring, when he speaks of *la mia rima*:

   > "S'egli avesse potuto creder prima"
   > Rispuose il savio mio, "anima lesa,
   > Ciò c'ha veduto pur con la mia rima,
   > Non averebbe in te la man distesa."

In these lines, which follow upon Dante's act of tearing off the twig, Virgil chides him for
his failure to take seriously to heart the account of Polydorus' fate, as found in the *Aeneid*:
if only Dante had believed, he would have been forewarned as to the consequences of mu-
tilating the bush. I should add that, in view of the strong medieval tradition concerning
the Christian potentialities of the *Aeneid,* we are justified in giving an even deeper mean-
ing to the "lack of faith" for which Virgil upbraids Dante: the latter has failed to realize
the implication of the Polydorus incident, that this prefigures the judgment visited upon
a sinner by the Christian God (Virgil himself seems, for a moment at least, to have been
astounded by the Christian replica of his Polydorus scene—this is the meaning I am
tempted to ascribe to the line . . . *la cosa incredibile mifece indurlo* . . . [the incredible
thing made me suggest it to him . . .]).

As to the relationship existing between the pilgrim Dante and his guide, I believe that
D'Ovidio puts a false emphasis on the personal vanity which Virgil the author betrays: this
is too modernistic an interpretation. Nor am I able to follow this commentator when he
would compare Virgil to a professor of medicine, who demonstrates to his pupil a "beau-
tiful clinical case," while maintaining a humorous aloofness from the suffering of the pa-
tient. Olschki (v. *infra*, Appendix) would emphasize the aloofness of Virgil with regard
both to Piero and Dante; these last two form a pair (a pair of politicians), according to
Olschki, and there takes place between them a "spiritual drama" from which Virgil disas-
sociates himself. I should object that it is rather Virgil and Dante who form a pair—a pair
of poets: it is thus that Piero sees them (*E se di voi alcun nel mondo riede, Conforti la
memoria mia* . . .). There is no evidence whatsoever that Virgil feels no interest in his
pupil—or that he feels no sympathy for Piero: he shows evident concern for the rehabili-
tation of Piero's reputation, which Dante shall undertake (thus whatever entente exists
between Piero and Dante has been encouraged by Virgil!). In the end, then, there is no
strict arrangement of two against one: Virgil, while more intimately connected with his
pupil, feels for Piero, and at the same time, would further the association of Piero and
Dante. Cf. the slightly divergent triangle of poets in the Brunetto Latini episode where
Virgil effaces himself lovingly, but never loses sight of his pupil.

plant-man Piero is described as a vegetal body which is capable of physiological manifestations and in which human consciousness survives unabated: this hybrid creation of Dante is more *monstrously* hybrid than anything to be encountered among the ancients.[4]

And this must needs be so, since to the medieval Christian poet the concept of hybridism is, in itself, repellent. The Christian system does not recognize "evolution of species": the species are neatly delimited according to a hierarchic order which purports to know the fixed and once-for-ever established *dignitates, proprietates* and *virtutes* of man, animal, plant, and mineral. Hybrid creation is outside of the natural plan of God; and, at the hands of Dante, it becomes, according to the law of the *contrappasso*, a symbol of sin and punishment—of punishment for the "anti-natural" sin of suicide by which the God-willed connection between body and soul has been broken. This plant-man, then, is no picture of a happy solidarity between natural man and animated nature but, on the contrary, of a tragic captivity of the soul (*anima incarcerata*) in a minor form of nature; by the creation (after the death of the body) of this monster which combines the human and the non-human, the poet succeeds in demonstrating the gulf that exists in nature between the human and the non-human. Thus the whole spirit of the Dantean metamorphosis is opposed to that of Ovid: the pagan poet with his pantheistic love for nature (of which man is a part), who could discover a nymph in every fountain, a dryad in every tree, was able to see in metamorphosis only the principle of the eternal change of forms in nature—animating this by the fiction of past human passion and grief, describing the whole "con copia e grazia tra boccaccesca e ariostea [with a fullness and grace somewhere between that of Boccaccio and that of Ariosto]" (D'Ovidio). It could be said that in Ovid the (gradual) transformation of a human into a vegetal being seems to take place almost *naturally*; but with Dante the link between nature and man has been broken by a tragic-minded Christianity; where Ovid offers to our view the richness of organic nature, Dante shows the inorganic, the hybrid, the perverted, the sinful, the damned. A

---

4. It is quite true that ancient literature offers examples of creatures that are just as *unequivocally* hybrid as are Dante's plant-men—viz. the Centaurs, half men and half beasts. But the blend of animal and human is in itself less repugnant than that of plant and human: indeed the ancients, who did not reject hybridism *in se*, could represent the Centaurs as essentially noble beings (even Dante, who in canto xi, has them, with their "bestial" form, symbolize the sin of bestiality, must speak respectfully of *il gran Chirone, il quale nudrì Achille*).

The undoubted loathsomeness of those bird-women, the Harpies, is hardly a case in point: the horror with which these were regarded by the Greeks was due, not to the fact itself of their hybridism, but to the blend of the beautiful (*virginei facies*) with the hideous which they offered. To Dante, on the other hand, they probably represented perversions, *qua* blends: he does not insist on the disturbing beauty of their faces, replacing *virginei* by *umani*: to him the main significance of these creatures lay precisely in their blend of the animal and the *human*.

metamorphosis at the hands of Dante must be, not graceful, in the way of Boccaccio and Ariosto, but tragic—in the way of Dante.

But while an Ovidian metamorphosis is presented as "natural," it is perhaps less "real" than that of Dante. Ovid is dealing with legendary lore which he retells *as if* he believed; his fabulations play in a remote past and they have the patina of a legend. But the two subjects of Dante's metamorphosis, Pier delle Vigne and the anonymous suicide, were near-contemporaries of the poet: they appear in his poem as belonging to the eternally present and as illustrating the judgment of God that is universally true—"de te fabula narratur." And the fate of these two in the other world is presented by Dante not as legend but as reality: the real judgment that God has in store for the soul of the sinner *in statu animarum post mortem* [In the state of the souls after death]; it is described in terms more graphic and more convincing than those of the ancient tales. De Sanctis has emphasized the directness of Dante's narration: he eschews the elegant impressionism of Virgilian devices which serve to anticipate, and thus to soften, the impact of events (*Mihi frigidus horror membra quatit / Eloquar an sileam?* [My limbs tremble with icy horror / Shall I speak or remain silent?]); instead the details as sensed by Dante are put squarely before the reader in a manner "che il naturale messo avanti renda irresistibile l'impressione del fantastico." The whole paradox of the *Divine Comedy* rests in the procedure of describing as real, and of conceiving as describable with the same precision that might be applied to an object of the outer world, that which, to our secularized imagination today, would seem to be the product of a gratuitous play of phantasy. Indeed, it is when the events are the most "fantastic" that they are presented most realistically: the fate of the plant-man Piero *must* be believed by us because it is accepted so completely by the victim himself: we see how he has adapted himself to his new estate when, in proclaiming his loyalty to his chief, he swears, not as men do, by their heads, but as plant-men (apparently) must do—*per le nove radici d'esto legno* [by the new roots of this tree].[5]

And not less must we believe that the events that transpire were accepted as real by Dante the pilgrim: Dante the author has filled this canto with details that afford *sense-data* to this character who is the chief witness, details which offer, in particular, an appeal to the eye and the ear. When Dante first comes upon the scene he is told by Virgil to watch out for strange apparitions (*riguarda ben, sì vedrai . . .*); Dante's gaze is at first disappointed, for he sees (*vedea*) nothing but

5. Thus I must reject the translation of *nove* by "strange": that Piero could so simply "take over" and modify in accordance with his new status, the traditional manner of making oath, seems to me evidence that he has ceased to find his condition strange. *Nove* is best translated "new"; thus we are reminded of the genesis of his vegetal body which is the product, not of gradual evolution from the human, but of a "new" birth. Cf. the expression *forme novelle* used of the souls in *Purg.* XXV, 88.

rows of plants, but, in compensation his ears are assailed by the
sound of voices lamenting (*sentia . . . trarre guai*), that seem to come
from unseen sources; it is this conflict between the visual and the au-
ditory that accounts for Dante's initial confusion. But in the mani-
festations of the plant-man, Dante is privileged both to hear and to
see: as he tears off a leaf, the stump moans and then becomes black
with blood (*gridò . . . bruno*). And in the single phrase *usciva inseme
parole e sangue* the two sense-data are fused together: there gushes
forth a stream of "speech-endowed blood," of "bleeding screams"—a
hideous revelation of the hybrid, which we must accept as a unit-
manifestation, because of the singular verb *usciva*.[6]

And now we have arrived at the point where we may consider the
nature of the *"speech"* (I am using this term to mean, not "lan-
guage," but "the production of language") of the suicides. No com-
mentator, so far as I know, has attempted to analyze this
process—though Dante himself has taken pains to give us an elabo-
rate hint of it; compare the famous simile:

> Come d'un stizzo verde, che arso sia
>   da l'un de' capi, che da l'altro geme,
>   e cigola per vento che va via;
> sì de la scheggia rotta usciva inseme
>   parole e sangue . . .

Casini, who notes the effectiveness of such details as the "ensem-
ble" of drops of sap and sound of wind, comments on the graphic
quality of this description and cites Venturi who praises its verisimili-
tude ("verità d'imagine e perspicuità di forma [imagistic truth and per-
spicuity of form]"). But to consider this simile mainly as a device for
enlivening description (an attitude that is a survival of rhetorical aes-
thetics) is to overlook the explanation which it contains for us of the
"origin of language" as this is produced in the plant-men.[7] Obviously
the ensemble of sap and windy sound which Casini admired is
meant to offer a parallel with the ensemble of blood and words that
issues from the plants: in both the visual and the acoustic are dis-
tinguished and fused by the poet. We have to do with a poetic equa-
tion: blood=sap, words=wind, thus the language of the plant-men
is mere *flatus vocis*, wind-begotten speech. This is borne out clearly

---

6. Here we have to do with a kind of hendiadys, as in *farò come colui che piange e dice* in the
Francesca episode, or *Parlar e lagrimar vedrai insieme* (*Inf.* XXXIII, 9).
7. This fact is overlooked by all the commentators I have read on this passage: De Sanctis in-
terprets the simile to mean that Dante does not hear the words spoken by the plant (!);
that his soul is concentrated in his eye. This is surely not true: Dante is ear as well as eye.
Torraca's contribution is to point out parallel similes in Provençal poetry, in which the
"weeping" of a fire-log is compared to the weeping of a poet-lover; he overlooks the fact
that this particular simile is meant to throw light on weeping that is precisely *non*-
human.—He may compare the "dehumanized" weeping of the pope who *piangeva con la
zanca* in *Inf.* XIX, 45.

in the lines that introduce the last words of Piero, as he prepares to make answer to a question of Dante's:

> Allor soffiò il tronco forte,[8] e poi
> *si convertì quel vento in cotal voce.*

But apart from delimiting the windy nature of the speech of hybrid beings, the simile serves to assign it to a rank according to a hierarchy of values. The fact that Dante chose to describe a hissing, guttering fire-log by way of characterizing the genesis of speech in his *uomini-piante* shows that he conceived this as representing a purely physical process: the issue of blood and cries is on the same low "material" level as is the issue of sap and hissing sound from a fire-log. Indeed, the fact that we have to do with speech of a non-human order, with speech that is a matter of bodily discharges, was already suggested by the terrible line *usciva inseme parole e sangue*; and that this is speech which is conditioned by physical factors alone is revealed by the incident in which Dante tears off the twig from the plant, thereby providing the channel through which the stream of blood and words could pour forth: only by such a physical gesture could the plant be enabled to "speak"—only by being torn and wounded.

This truth is hammered into our ears again in the latter part of the canto, devoted to the second (anonymous) suicide:

> e menommi al cespuglio che piangea,
> per le rotture sanguinenti, invano.

—again blood and words are coupled, again there is a reference to the tearing of a channel (*per le rotture*) through which the two-fold utterance of suffering finds an outlet.[9] A few lines later, after this plant has begun to speak, Virgil refers to its condition in words that echo all the concepts just treated:

> . . . "Chi fosti che *per tante punte*
> *Soffi con sangue doloroso sermo?*"

But the most vivid reference to the terrible conditions upon which speech may be released in the plants is to be found in the lines describing the function of the Harpies:

---

8. D'Ovidio comments on this passage, but only to question the significance of *forte*: why did it blow so *hard*? He answers, correctly enough, that because of the lapse of time since the tearing off of the twig had first given issue to speech, a greater effort was needed for the plant to draw breath enough to last out his words. But D'Ovidio might better have emphasized *soffio* than *forte*—as well as the entire line *si convertì quel vento in cotal voce* which describes the transformation of wind into voice or words (both meanings are possible with *voce*).

9. In this case the mutilation is caused not by Dante but by Giacomo da Sant' Andrea, the spendthrift who hides behind the bush into which the suicide has been transformed; that he chose this particular hiding place may perhaps be explained by the fact that in life Giacomo, after squandering his fortune, had attempted to commit suicide.

l'Arpìe, pascendo poi de le sue foglie,
fanno dolore, e al dolor finestra.

What Dante did once and inadvertently to a particular bush the
Harpies do systematically, in aevum, to the whole group of plant-
men; by feeding on the leaves of the bushes they open wounds and
provide an outlet for the grief that they have caused: eternally there
must come forth *inseme parol e sangue.*[1]

And with this reference to the Harpies we may note that the prob-
lem concerning the "genesis of speech," so important to this particu-
lar canto, becomes one with the arch-problem of the whole edifice of
the *Inferno:* that of the *contrappasso.* That Dante has transformed the
loathsome harbinger-birds of Virgil into instruments of moral punish-
ment is obvious and has been generally recognized (De Sanctis, D'O-
vidio, Torraca, Vossler); it also seems clear to me that the eternal
laceration wrought by the Harpies upon the suicides, is meant to be
the punitive counterpart of their own act of self-laceration:[2] one may
note that the words with which the second suicide refers to the muti-
lation visited upon his plant body (*lo strazio disonesto / c'ha le mie
fronde sì da me* DISGIUNTE) echoes the *disvelta* that is to be found in
Piero's description of his act of suicide: *Quando si parte l'anima feroce
/ dal corpo ond'ella stessa s'è* DISVELTA. (Of course, this before-
mentioned bodily mutilation was executed not by the Harpies but by
Giacomo, who, like Dante with Piero, became unwittingly an accom-
plice of the Harpies.) But the function of the Harpies was not alone
that of renewing everlastingly the wounds of the suicides, as De Sanc-
tis and D'Ovidio note, but, as Dante himself specifically states, "to

---

1. It must have been noted that, in our attempt to describe the process by which language is
achieved for the plant-men, we have drawn from passages which deal with the fate of
Piero, of the anonymous suicide, and of the group as a whole. For, though the suicides are
individually doomed (*Ciascuno al prun de l'ombra sua molesta*), they share a common
fate—and each identifies himself with the whole: consider the plural used by Piero, *Uo-
mini fummo,* and the line *come l'altre* (!) *verrem per nostre spoglie.* The story, thrice told,
is yet the same story, made terribly explicit: "this is the doom of Piero, this is the doom of
any suicide, this is the doom of all." And Dante wants us not only to comprehend his
dread truth; he would have us hear the *sounds* of this doom made manifest: the cries ut-
tered by two blood-tinged voices, first that of Piero, finally that of the anonymous suicide,
emerge from a chorus to which the whole multitude of plant-voices contribute: *tante voci
uscisser tra quei bronchi;* this is the first sound we hear, and it reverberates throughout the
canto. But, lest our ears grow dull, through constant exposure to the unholy din, Dante
allows this chorus to be broken for a moment as the spendthrifts, pursued by hounds
(again the *contrappasso:* they are torn and destroyed by ravening beasts because in life
they greedily destroyed what should have remained whole), burst upon the center of the
stage: for a moment human screams dominate all others, rising above the chorus of the
plant-voices. By this sudden introduction of the normal (framed by the two episodes of
individual plant-men) the abnormal is made more frightful.
2. Torraca suggests another variety of *contrappasso:* he would explain the onslaughts of the
Harpies as due to the fact that in their life on earth the suicides "had not endured the on-
slaughts of affliction." Thus to him the great sin of these creatures would lie not so much
in the anti-natural act of suicide itself as in their lack of fortitude: somewhat similar is the
attitude of Vossler, who states that the suicides were punished because they had not
found in life "das lösende Wort."

cause grief and, by the same token, to provide an outlet for it": to make the suicides suffer, at the same time allowing them the cruel consolation of expressing their suffering through the medium of their own ghastly brand of speech.[3] Thus Dante, in drawing the logical consequences of the law of *contrappasso*, has created a semi-human plant-like speech for his hybrid plant-souls (just as the devils and Nembrotte are endowed with a speech of their own: *del cul fatto trombetta*, *Inf*. XXI, 139; XXXI, 67, *Rafel mai amech zabi almi*).

And all this lies implicitly contained in that simple phrase, that conventional arrangement of subject + predicate: *il suo tronco gridò!*[4]

Now let us turn to the *"language"* or style of the canto. It is obvious that in discussing this second problem it would not be proper to limit ourselves to the language of the suicides: though Dante has devised a peculiar method of speech for these hybrid beings, he could not do otherwise than to represent their actual words as belonging to normal, human language, on the same level as that of the other characters—or of the author himself. One distinctive feature of the style of this canto consists in the use, to an extent unparalleled elsewhere in the *Inferno*, of onomatopoetic terms: consider, for example, the following list of harsh-sounding, consonant-ridden words which (often occurring in the rhyme) appear scattered throughout the canto for the purpose of evoking the concepts "trunk, bush" and "cripple, mutilate, dismember":

nodosi	fronde sparte	rosta	aspri sterpi	bronchi
tronchi	'nvolti	sterchi con tosco	schiante	scerpi
sterpi	monchi	tronco	scheggia rotta	nocchi
disvelta	stizzo	cespuglio	strazio	triste cesto

3. This is a consolation doubly cruel in that the expression of their suffering seems only to renew their grief: the tyranny of the need for self-expression by language, the self-mutilating sadistic power of speech which while seeming to give consolation only aggravates the wound—this has never been more powerfully symbolized, nay more graphically been depicted, than in this macabre episode.

4. Later on we find the much more matter-of-fact verb *dire* used in the same connection: *Noi eravamo ancora al tronco attesi,* / *credendo c'altro ne volesse dire.*

Such bold sentences, which mold a subject and a predicate not "naturally" belonging together in a sentence which makes this coupling appear as natural, revives the original polar current which exists in any sentence with the two members: subject-predicate. According to H. Ammann, *Die Sprache* II, 103, a verbal sentence depicts a "Zu-Wort-Kommen" of a living process: an observation is made by showing us something living ("ein Lebendiges"), the subject, as displaying its natural activity ("Lebensvorgang") in the predicate; in any sentence there is an "Urrythmus" of tension and relaxation which betrays itself in the musical shadings with which the sentence is pronounced:

< >   < >   < >

the roses flourish, the brook rustles. In the case of *il suo tronco gridò* (*dice*), the mold of the sentence makes appear as natural a highly paradoxical statement; in the same manner, the oath *per este nove radici . . .* molds a counter-natural attitude into the frame of a traditional oath. Both cases reflect the hybridism of plant-speech.

As we pass in review this bristling array of words we have almost the impression of being faced with a new language that recalls little of the melody and fluidity of the Italian tongue; these words have much of the quality that is to be found in Provençal, with its tendency toward monosyllabism and its clusters of consonants. Compare, for example:[5]

> Al prim pres dels breus jorns braus
> Quand brand'als brueils l'aura brava,
> E ill branc e ill brondel son nut,
> Pel brun tems secs qu'el desnuda . . .

> Guillems Fabres nos fai *en brau lengage*
> Manz braus broncs bren bravan de brava guia
> E rocs e brocs que met en son cantage.

[At the first approach of the brief harsh day, when the harsh wind shakes the wood and the branch and bough are made bare by the arid dark weather which strips them . . .
Guillems Fabres composes for us in harsh language many harsh knots . . . in a clever way . . . and roads and thorns that he puts into his song.]

In the passage just above there is an interesting allusion to the "brau lengage": this must refer to the deliberate device on the part of Provençal poets to exploit the effect of harsh strength to which their word-material so easily lent itself. And it is only probable that Dante's procedure, as illustrated in the list above, harks back to this tradition, representing an Italian "softening" of the *brau lengage*.[6] But it must be observed that, at the hands of Dante, the use of this device is attended with greater refinement and artistic economy; it is only seldom, for instance, that he offers an accumulation of onomatopoetic words within a line (as he does in *stecchi con tosco . . . ch'ode le bestie e le frasche stormire*): for the most part such elements are scattered, so that the canto is throughout pervaded with sound symbolism. Moreover, while the Provençal poets were apt to resort to this procedure to excess, delighting in sound effects for their own sake,[7] Dante was careful to limit it to cases where it was

---

5. V. Diez, *Poesie der Troubadours*, p. 88. Cf. also Scheludko, *Arch. rom.* XV, 159.
6. The same *brau lengage* is alluded to in such lines as *Così nel mio parlar voglio esser aspro* [so I wish to be harsh in my speech] of the *Madonna Pietra* poem (*Rime* 103) and the first line of *Inf.* XXII: *S'io avessi le rime aspre e chiocce* [If I had harsh and clucking verses]. These echo the "harsh rhymes" of the *sirventes*-technique of the troubadours which, "strictly conventional and oratorical as they are" (Borgese, *Speculum* XIII, 190), were adapted by Dante to his poetry of wrath.
7. A more "sincere" stylistic device of the Provençal poets is to be met with in their *descorts*: poems made deliberately discordant by means of a medley of metrics and languages, in order to correspond to the "out of tune-ness" of the soul of the poet. This parallelism of form and content which may seem naïvely pedantic to us today is to be explained by the

suitable to the context, where it would serve best to give a graphic representation of the ideas of moral crippling and laceration: the visual and the aural pictures of moral disease are consonant in their disharmony. In this way Dante was illustrating the medieval (and ultimately ancient) ideas concerning the correspondence between meaning and sound (cf. his opinion, expressed in the *Vita Nuova*, about the "amorous" sound of the word *amore*).

The consistent procedure just noted of expressing disharmonious conceptions by means of harsh-sounding words has been passed over by commentators; all, however, have remarked the abundance of rhetorical artifices to be found in this canto. The use of such devices as antithesis, alliteration, repetition of words and word-stems, puns and etymologies,[8] belongs to a long rhetorical tradition, and, according to Alfredo Schiaffini ("Tradizione e poesia"), the combination of these with the overloaded harshness of sounds was itself a regular procedure of medieval writers (in the passages just cited from the poetry of Provençal troubadours we may note that the "harsh words" have been coupled with semi-etymological alliterations). But it is possible to trace the rhetorical devices used by Dante to a more specific source: the majority of them occur in the language of the first suicide Piero, and Novati has proved that they are simply echoes of the elegances of style with which the historical personage Pier delle Vigne was wont to embellish his prose writings. Thus it would appear that Dante's choice of these rhetorical artifices was due to a desire on his part for historical characterization; Auerbach has pointed out a consistent tendency in Dante to make the souls in the other world recognizable by having them retain certain distinctive traits of character and physical appearance; here, then, we should have to do with a "linguistic" portrayal, corresponding to the general dogmatic procedure of preserving in the Beyond the earthly features of the various characters. Novati's proof is convincing and his discovery is important in that it offers an objective explanation for the presence of the devices in question; after him, no commentator could resort to such a subjective interpretation as that

---

high appreciation which the Middle Ages felt for the symbolic act: it may be applied to anything, whether great or small: symbolism, as used by man, is a consequence of the symbolism everywhere so manifest to human eyes, which God has put into his creation.

8. It was a favorite procedure of the times to offer punning etymological interpretations of names. In this canto there is no pun that may compare, for example, with the *de Vinea . . . vinea* "vine-yard" found in the writings of a correspondant of Piero's (v. Schiaffini, p. 100), and yet the *ambo le chiavi*, uttered by Dante's Piero, reflects the same tendency to play on names: obviously this contains an historical allusion to the other Peter, guardian of the keys. Indeed, exactly the same allusion is to be found in the writing of the same punning correspondent: *imperii claviger, claudit et nemo aperit, aperit et nemo claudit* [Keeper of the keys of the empire, who closes so that none shall open, who opens so that none shall close] (Schiaffini, l. c.). D'Ovidio points to this line as a source of *ambo le chiavi*—but without mentioning the allusion involved in both cases. Cf. the underlying pun *Orsini—orsacchi* in *Inf.* XIX, 71.

earlier advanced by De Sanctis, to whom the rhetorical passages in
the speech of the suicide Piero were an indication of his (momen-
tary) lack of sincere feeling!

Unfortunately, however, the commentators who have followed
Novati have seized upon the "fact" of historical correspondence in
order to stress a supposed piece of ironical and malicious caricature
offered by Dante. It is remarkable how quick are professors of philol-
ogy to gloat over any seeming expression of malice, if this is coupled
with verbal skill. The most outspoken member of this guild is
Vossler:

> Diese grosstiligen oder heroischen Bürokraten, die wir
> Deutschen besser kennen als jedes andere Volk, können tiger-
> haft und auch sich selbst gegenüber unmenschlich werden.
> Stürtzt oder entlässt man sie, so töten sie sich oder verfallen
> der Lächerlichkeit. *Auch in ihrer privaten Ausdrucksweise*
> *erkennt man den amtlichen Stil.* . . . Schwer und hoffnungslos
> gekränkt, verschliesst er [Piero] sich und verholzt im buch-
> stäblichen Sinn des Wortes. . . . Ihre [der 'trotzigen und eitlen
> Gewaltmenschen'] Seele, die nicht gedeihlich wachsen und lei-
> den konnte, verknöchert zum Dorngestrüpp. . . .

> [These heroic bureaucrats in the grand style, which we Ger-
> mans know better than other nations, can become tiger-like
> and inhuman even with respect to themselves. According to
> whether one attempts to ruin them or leave them alone, they
> kill themselves or sink into absurdity. Even in private life one
> can recognize the official style. . . . Grieviously and hopelessly
> stricken, (Piero) becomes locked within himself and literally
> grows-wooden. . . . The souls (of the "sulky and empty men of
> authority") which cannot flourish or endure ossify and become
> underbrush. . . .]

It is not difficult to see how Vossler has been induced by a purely
German phobia and by the existence of a purely German word-
association ("ein verknöcherter Bürokrat") to superimpose a fantas-
tic analogy of his own upon the parallelism willed by Dante. Having
learned from Novati that the language of Dante's Piero is substan-
tially that of the historical Piero, and that this represented the
"chancelry" or "bureaucratic" style of the times, he proceeds to
identify the Capuan *dittatore* with the bureaucrats whom he has
known and despised in Germany; he even goes so far as to suggest
that, since in life Piero was an "ossified bureaucrat" it is only fitting
that he must become a crippled thornbush in the Beyond. Moreover
he assumes that Piero was one of those whose style, in spite of
themselves, betrays the bureaucrat even in daily life—a victim, as it
were, of a stylistic *tic!* And we are asked to believe that it is such a

trivial and comical creature that Dante has made the chief figure of this canto; Vossler's implications about the private nature of Piero (is the Beyond anything like "private life"?) are entirely without foundation, as is also his assumption that the style of his writings was not noble and elegant, but poor fustian, and matter for derision. We are surely warranted in rejecting the "caricature-theory" (as does D'Ovidio: "In questi vezzi di stile Dante non mise un' intenzione quasi di caricatura. [With this stylistic manner, Dante did not intend caricature.]").

Moreover, I believe that the desire to achieve a historical characterization was not the sole, or even the prime, artistic motive behind the use of these rhetorical devices. At Dante's hand these become filled with a larger significance; they offer a sort of linguistic, or onomatopoetic rendition of the ideas of torture, schism, estrangement, which dominate the canto (much as the harsh-sounding words served to suggest the ideas of "crippled" and "trunk"). Compare, for example, the involved and twisted lines below, which bear in themselves the stamp of self-torture and self-estrangement, and ultimately of infructuous paradoxy:

> L'animo mio, per disdegnoso gusto,
>   credendo col morir fuggir disdegno,
>   ingiusto fece me contra me giusto.

After this hopeless entanglement in a verbal thicket, the lines become simple and candid (in the limpid tone of Racine's *Le jour n'est pas plus pur que le fond de mon cœur*), evoking a clearing: one emerges into the bright open sunshine:

> vi giuro che già mai non ruppi fede
> al mio signor, che fu d'onor sì degno.

There is here a correspondence between involved sentence and involved feeling, between simple sentence and candid feeling—a shifting of the shape of the sentences according to the shape of mood. In the line *Ingiusto fece me contra me giusto* I hear sounding above the intricacies of préciosité, the note *contra*, symbol of the counter-natural: the repetitions of word-stems (*ingiusto—giusto*; *me contra me*) suggest the outrage wrought by one half of the human soul against the other; here we may note, to a certain extent, a parallelism with the "*moi dédoublé*" as this is suggested in the most effective line of the second suicide: "IO fei *giubbetto* A ME delle MIE *case*." Torture and destruction again form the motif in the lines of Piero that describe the flames of the passion of envy, steadily mounting until all is consumed and honor reduced to strife:

> infiammò contra me li animi tutti;
> e li 'nfiammati infiammar[9] sì Augusto,
> che i lieti onor tornaro in tristi lutti.

Again, in the powerfully charged sentence describing the two-fold activity of the Harpies, we have to do, not only with repetition but with zeugma: *Fanno dolore e al dolor finestra*. The very compression of this line is symbolical of a grief which, although given continual utterance, must endlessly repeat itself nor ever find release.[1] Finally we may consider the pattern, old as epic poetry, "*a* but not *b*," which occurs three times in as many lines at the beginning of the canto:

> Non frondi verdi, ma di color fosco;
> non rami schietti, ma nodosi e 'nvolti;
> non pomi v' eran, ma stecchi con tosco.

D'Ovidio comments on the effect produced by the repetition of the device: he sees therein a deliberate monotony of syntax which "imitates that sort of calm that great stupefaction is wont to produce." But he says nothing about the device itself. To me this negative pattern, with its insistent note of schism, suggests the στέρησις or *privatio* by which, in ancient as in medieval philosophy, the evil is clearly defined as something characterized by the absence of good; Dante would make us see that this forest is a "wicked" forest.

It must have been observed that the passages above represent not only the language of Piero, but also of the second suicide and of Dante himself. This would clearly invalidate the premise of those who see in the author's use of these rhetorical devices only a program of historical characterization—unless, forsooth, we are to believe that Dante has blundered as an artist and, forgetting his original purpose, has proceeded blindly out of what modern psychologists would call automatism.[2] But it is difficult to imagine such a lapsus on the part of the conscious artist that Dante was; I should say that Dante has not forgotten but rather transcended his original purpose: granted that this may have been the starting point and may explain the fact that his attention was called to the stylistic features of the civil servant Piero, still, once his poetic imagination had seized

---

9. This particular repetition, the repetition of a finite verb in the form of a past participle, is a device with a long past in Latin (and especially late Latin) poetry and prose writing, cf. Stolz-Schmalz-Leumann-Hofmann, *Lat. Gr.* p. 831: *Mars hanc videt visamque cupit politurque cupita* (Ovid); *Croesum cepit captumque . . . donavit* (Orosius).

1. Compare a similar procedure in the famous line *Galeotto fu il libro, e chi lo scrisse*, where the subject *Galeotto* represents first the title of a book, then a human agent. Again one feels, in such a zeugmatic condensation, an expression of painful, fateful coercion. Cf. also *Inf*. XIX, 72 *che su l'avere e qui me misi in borsa*.

2. This would indeed seem to be the attitude of Grandgent, if we may judge by his phrase, ". . . either purposely or unconsciously"; we are asked to believe that Dante, filled with reminiscences of the chancelry style of writing, allowed the speech habits characteristic of the *dittatore* to encroach upon his own.

upon the devices that characterized this style, they could adapt themselves to a larger design, to play their part in the evocation of that atmosphere of disharmony which pervades the whole canto.[3] From this point of view, the more practical question of historical identification sinks into insignificance; it is right that the second suicide, a crippled being in the image of Piero, should share the crippled style of Piero; or that the pilgrim Dante, so sensitive to the disharmonious atmosphere surrounding the plant-souls, should record his reactions in phrases evocative of this disharmony.

This he does, with most startling effect, in the line to which Grandgent gives especial emphasis and which has proved such a stumbling-block to commentators of the "historical characterization" school: *Cred'io ch'ei credette ch'io credesse*. . . . In my opinion this line is the most felicitous possible "psychological characterization," serving to suggest vividly Dante's state of mind at this stage of the narration: i.e. the disruption of his mental communication with his master, as a consequence of the *smarrimento* [bewilderment] indicated in the previous line, when Dante's attention is diverted in various directions (advised by Virgil to "look" out for things unheard of, he is able only to recognize sounds); the verse *cred'io* . . . is the "onomatopoetic" rendering of his mental state of estrangement and confusion. Valid in itself, this tortuous mode of expression is also effective in an anticipatory function: before the curtain rises on the main protagonists, before the awful implications of their fate are unfolded before us, the note is sharply struck which shall pervade the whole canto.[4]

The rhetorical device illustrated by this significant line is simply that of repetition; indeed this is involved in all the passages discussed above—though often in combination with other devices. That, in nearly every case, the effect achieved is fundamentally the same is due of course to a deliberate artistic intention; the mere repetition of words, no more than any other stylistic device, is not anything formulable in the abstract, but must always be felt and tested against the background of the particular psychic climate. In this canto Dante is mainly interested in evoking the one conception of moral disharmony, whereas, in the Francesca episode, for example, in the line *Amor che a nullo amato amar perdona*, he uses the compelling forcefulness of word-repetition in order to offer a verbal equivalent of the coercion

---

3. One may recall in this connection the scene in Canto XV where Dante, in his intimate conversation with Brunetto Latini, turns to a new and more profound use certain of the rules of *bienséance* once propounded by Brunetto himself (for quotations V. the Torraca ed. of Dante, ad XV, 43; V. also 121–123).

4. This same procedure may also be noted in Dante's use of onomatopoeia, as when Virgil, at the beginning of the canto, is made to use the epithet *monchi* (significantly occurring in the rhyme with *tronchi* and *bronchi*) in order to state the simple idea, "your suppositions of the moment will prove to be wrong": *Li pensier c'hai si faran tutti monchi* (here, "mutilated" is used of ideas!; in both cases, then, we are offered a shibboleth of mental aberration).

toward reciprocation that is inherent in real love. In *caddi come corpo morto cade*, this same device serves to reinforce the impression of an inertia imposed by physical laws; in Malherbe's *Rose, elle a vécu ce que vivent les roses* [Rose, she has lived as roses live] it is a symbol of a serene surrendering to the laws of Nature; in the Latin sentence which inspired Racine: *Titus reginam Berenicem aburbe dimisit invitus invitam* [Titus, against his will, sent Queen Berenice from the city, against her will] it suggests the united impulses of the lovers which were dominated by their act of renunciation. The motto of stylistics should be (not *tot capita tot sententiae* but) "so many sentences, so many meanings": if style must express a psychic content, it can do this only by adapting the given devices to the particular situation: repetition in itself is multivalent; its specific nuance is brought out in the specific situation through a kind of collaboration between the situation and the devices offered by language—through an "adhesion" of language to the psychic content.

In all the passages discussed, Dante has used a stylistic pattern that was familiar in a manner specifically adapted to a particular situation or character: the rhetorical device is never used for its own sake, "in order to use the well-known rhetorical device of . . . ," as philologists like to reason; Dante recreates the given stylistic patterns by restoring their original strength. The *Amor che a nullo amato amar perdona* of the Francesca episode, followed by two other lines with an anaphoric *amor,* inserts itself easily into a well-known medieval pattern used by all preachers and orators (cf. *Per me si va,* several times repeated, inscribed on the gate of Hell; v. Hatzfeld on "Anaphoric Hymnal Style"); it is nevertheless an eternal expression of the nature of love—so much so that the modern reader (even the medievalist when he happens to be "just" a reader) does not even sense the presence of an old pattern. Striking examples of that "originality *à partir du connu*" characteristic of the real genius, who rereads the palimpsest of language!

Appendix: *The Anonymous Suicide in* Inferno *XIII*

Ever since De Sanctis led the way in his appreciative study of the *"personaggi eroici"* who throng the cantos of the *Inferno,* the commentators, stirred by a delight in the strong personalities of "Renaissance" proportions (which the *Inferno* was better able to satisfy than the other two *cantiche*), have, in dealing with this episode, tended too much to concentrate their gaze on the figure of the man Piero; De Sanctis entitles his essay on this canto "Piero delle Vigne," D'Ovidio "Il canto di Piero delle Vigne," Olschki ex professo deals only with the problem "Dante and Peter de Vinea." By raising him into such high relief one has obscured the fact that Dante intended him to be subordinated to the "law of the circle"; for he is presented, not only as an individual with a story of his own, but as the spokesman of a group with which he shares a common fate (as he himself avows), and as the interpreter of a universal judgment—which, we may suppose, had no little importance for Dante (cf. note 10). Moreover, by the process of isolating this figure for purposes of analysis, one destroys the artistic unity of the canto itself[5] which, like any great work of art, must be judged from the point of view of its ensemble effect. One must surely question the temerity of Croce's procedure, whereby Dante's work is split into the two parts: "lyrical poetry" (in which are presented the "powerful individualities") and "theological novel."

A particular result of this general attitude, when applied to Canto XIII, is the glorification of Piero at the expense of the second and anonymous suicide. Those who bother to mention him consider him worthy of only a few cursory remarks, and these are usually derogatory: D'Ovidio (who prophesies that this will continue to be "the canto of Piero") decries the "tragicità patibolare e grossolana" of the "mot de la fin" (io fei giubbetto a me de le mie case) in which the anonymous suicide refers to an "impiccagione a domicilio"; Vossler echoes the Italian critic, declaring this figure to be a man of no "feiner Gemütsart." Such judgments are in my opinion erroneous; they are perhaps to be explained by the fact that the second suicide, overshadowed by the first, has not been considered sufficiently striking to warrant a more careful examination. To my mind he is exceedingly important: not as an individual (for it cannot be denied that, as a "personality," Piero is far more arresting), but as essential to the structure and the ultimate significance of the episode itself.

From the point of view of structure one may note two types of parallelism which indicate that the two figures must be considered together; we have already called attention to parallelisms of style, and to the examples cited above others may be added: "tristo cesto"—"la farà triste"; "al cespuglio che piangea . . . invano"—"que' cittadin . . . avrebber fatto lavorare indarno." ["sad tuft"—"will make it sad"; "the thicket which wept . . . in vain"—"those citizens would have worked in vain"]. The second parallelism concerns the "two gestures": it may be remembered that Dante, held spellbound by the awful revelations of the plant-souls, finds no words with which to address them (he speaks only to Virgil, who talks for him to the suicides); the only overt tokens of his association with the suicides are given when at the beginning of the episode he tears

---

5. —or, better, of the "episode": the episode of the plant-men is really brought to an end only in the opening lines of Canto XIV, where Dante complies with the request of the second suicide to gather together the leaves torn from his body: raünai le fronde sparte.

off the leaf from the plant-man Piero, and at the end, gathers up, in an Antigone-like movement, the fallen branches (torn off by Giacomo da Sant' Andrea) around the dismembered plant-body of the second suicide. If we had only the stylistic parallels, we might be justified in interpreting them as indicating that the episode of the anonymous suicide (though still essential artistically) is merely an echo, a faint reminder of the first and more elaborate episode dealing with Piero; but in the case of the two complementary gestures it is unquestionable that the second of them strikes a note of climax and finality: Dante atones for his unwitting act of opening wounds by this deliberate and compassionate act of restoration; the episode is finally rounded out by this gesture, which would set at rest the troubled condition which the other gesture had called forth.

The incident of the second suicide, then, is highly essential to the structure of the poem; it is no less true that this figure is itself important to the *theme* of the canto, which (it must never be forgotten) concerns the workings of divine justice. And this figure is important precisely because of its lack of "individuality": Piero is indeed a great individual (in size he is a *gran pruno*, whereas the other is represented as so small that Virgil must bend over to speak to him), but, by the same token, this Renaissance-like figure is *only* an individual. The second suicide, on the other hand, has a greater rôle: he is all the Florentines who have slain themselves; he is Florence herself, who is steadily committing suicide by giving herself up to intestine wars: though the Baptist has succeeded Mars as patron saint of Florence, still the former *sempre con l'arte sua la farà triste*. It is with the tragedy of his native city that the anonymous suicide is concerned—not, like Piero, with his personal fate, his personal reputation (*Conforti la memoria mia*). And if we think of him as the representative of Florence, his last line in the canto appears as a sublimely terrible evocation of the self-destruction of a city: *Io fei giubbetto a me de le mie case*.[6] Little wonder that Dante is moved by *la carità del natio loco* (XIV, 1); and as he gathers up

---

6. The implications of the word *case* were overlooked by D'Ovidio, who sees in this line only the trivial theme of an "impiccagione a domicilio." But in the age of the medieval walled-town, *case* inevitably must have suggested a "house among houses"; the use of this word places the anonymous suicide against the background of his city Florence.

D'Ovidio also points to the vulgarity of the word *giubbetto*. That this was in French a popular, indeed a vulgar, term is stated by Arpad Steiner (*MLN* 1942) who quotes the thirteenth-century William of Auvergne to the effect that it belonged to the "argotdes malfaiteurs." But the very "vulgarity" of this word succeeds in suggesting most graphically the depth of degradation to which the House of Florence had sunk. A vulgar term is not necessarily anti-poetic: did not Dante, in moments of high poetic exaltation, resort to such terms as *puttana, bordello,* in his poetry of wrath? (And significantly enough, does not his elegant *dittatore* Piero precisely refrain from using *puttana* of Envy and use *meretrice?*) Cf. also Torraca on *drappo, Inf.* XV, 112.

tenderly the dismembered and scattered leaves, he is paying devotion to his native city.

If we compare the relationship between Dante and the (anonymous) Florentine on the one hand, and Dante and the Capuan Piero on the other, a certain parallelism becomes apparent: in each case we have to do with a gesture and a mood. But in the scene with Piero both these manifestations are of lesser significance: indeed the gesture of breaking off the twig was directed, not toward Piero himself but toward what to Dante was still only a bush; thus it could reflect nothing of his attitude toward the suicide. His attitude is of course reflected in the word *pietà*: in *tanta pietà m'accora* he tells us that he is moved to pity by the sad story of Piero. But surely in Dante's as in Corneille's scale of values, the feeling of pity for the sufferings of an individual must be less noble than the more comprehensive emotion of patriotic devotion. Thus, by weighing the significance of these parallel manifestations (which offer the only *direct* evidence on which we may rely), one arrives at the conclusion that, of the two suicides it is with the anonymous figure, despised and rejected by critics, that Dante would identify himself—not with the "powerful individuality," Piero.[7]

It is quite another conclusion which Olschki has reached and which he presents in the article entitled "Dante and Peter de Vinea" (*Romanic Review* XXXI, 105–111). By omitting all reference to the anonymous suicide, by weighing only the evidence, direct and indirect, contained in the first episode and interpreting this in the light of biographical data, he has succeeded in making a case for the close identification of Dante and Piero: the *pietà* which Dante represents himself as experiencing is to Olschki an indication that the poet has identified his own fate with that of the civil servant Piero, and this sympathetic association explains the fact that Piero is presented as innocent of the crimes with which he had been charged and of which he had been found guilty—according to the only documents which survive today. The fact that Piero is allowed to vindicate himself is obviously proof that Dante was himself convinced of the other's innocence, and it would seem only reasonable to assume that Dante was possessed of other evidence than that which has come down to us. But, according to Olschki, the poet was led to present Piero as an innocent victim of *invidia* and calumny for no other reason than that he, Dante, once a high official like Piero, had suffered such a fate: to Olschki the self-justifying portrait of Piero is evidence that Dante the man has identified himself with the historical character of Piero:

7. Cf. a similar diptych (the councilman of Lucca—Ciampolo Navarrese) in Cantos XXI–XXII.

... his [Dante's] sentiment for Peter de Vinea as a fellow-sufferer is confirmed by the similarity of the actual happenings. Both of them ... were sentenced for malversation in public office and on like charges. Conscious of his own innocence, and convinced that it was easy, and customary, to have a political opponent convicted of malpractice in office in order to dispose of him. Dante transferred his own experience to the chancellor and regarded him as the defenseless victim, like himself, of envious malignity. Thus he rescued the chancellor, whom he revered as highest official of the Empire, as poet and rhetorician, from the ignominy that clouded his posthumous repute. The feeling of companionship in life-experience induced him, again, to pass a self-willed judgment, which might also clear his own self of the suspicions cast upon him by his fellow men. These personal motives gave rise to his conviction, and to the legend, that Peter de Vinea was, blameless, thrown into misery. . . .

The world-judge adjudicates not according to the public opinion of his day, but according to his own conscience and his political experiences.

What we are really asked to believe, then, is that Dante's favorable judgment of Piero is the result, not of inquiry and weighing of evidence, but of sheer supposition—a judgment motivated largely by his own grievance against an unjust society: he cleared Piero in order to clear himself. I cannot keep from feeling that such an interpretation must cast discredit on the integrity of Dante's reasoning; nor can I understand the practical psychology underlying such a manoeuvre on Dante's part: if his judgment were based on sympathetic intuition alone, if there were at hand in his day no reliable objective evidence of Piero's innocence, how could he expect to convince his readers of this innocence? And, unless they were so convinced, Dante could hope to gain little success in clearing his own name, by drawing a parallel between himself and a character so questionable. Moreover, even assuming that he had a fair chance of rehabilitating the reputation of Piero, still this could serve Dante's own aim of self-rehabilitation *only* if a parallel between the two men were clearly established in the poem—and this Dante fails to do. He has not always failed to do this: in the episodes devoted to Brunetto Latini, for example, it is expressly indicated that Dante is identifying his own experience with that of his teacher (since Brunetto prophesies the ingratitude of Florence toward Dante); how is one to explain a lack of any such indication in this case, when, if we accept Olschki's interpretation, so much hangs upon the clear establishment of a personal parallel?

In the absence of such an establishment, Olschki is forced to depend upon such hints as Piero's denunciation of *invidia* (from

which Dante too had suffered) and the reference to Dante's *pietà*
toward Piero (a feeling "which comes over him whenever [and
only when] he has before his eyes victims of passions or misfor-
tunes like his own"). If this last statement ("and only when") were
true it could only mean that Dante was incapable of distinguish-
ing between pity and self-pity; fortunately, however, it may be eas-
ily disproved by a glance at the dictionary of Blanc, s.v. *pietà*,
where we are referred to such lines, for example, as *lamenti . . . /
che di pietà ferrati avean gli strali; / ond'io li orecchi con le man
copersi* [lamentations . . . whose arrows were tipped with pity,
wherefore I covered my ears with my hands] (XXIX, 44) which de-
scribe Dante as pierced by the shafts of pity as he listens to the
lamentations of the falsifiers in torment; is Dante here identifying
himself as a falsifier? (Cf. also, in XX, 28, the *"pietà"* expressed for
sooth-sayers, and the rebuke of Virgil: *Qui vive la pietà quand' è ben
morta*). And as for the evidence supposedly offered by the reference
to *invidia* in the following passage:

> La meretrice [*invidia*] che mai da l'ospizio
> di Cesare non torse li occhi putti,
> morte comune, *de le corti vizio . . .*

it seems to me that Olschki is reversing the emphasis intended by
Dante, when he says:

> The events leading to his condemnation had the same source
> at the Imperial Court as in Republican Florence, because the
> "invidia" that decided the poet's fate was *not merely the vice pe-
> culiar to princely courts, but the universal undoing of mankind*:
> "Morte comune, de le corti vizio."

Surely the passage as a whole presents *invidia* as characteristic of the
court *in particular*; the last line, while conceding this to be a general
evil (*morte comune*), labels it, nonetheless, "the court vice" (we should
translate then: "not merely the . . . undoing of mankind, but [espe-
cially] the court vice"). Piero is here concerned with describing the
situation at the court of Sicily, where *invidia* played such a destruc-
tive rôle; if Dante had meant that this description was at the same
time and in the same degree applicable to democratic Florence, there
is no reason why Piero should not have proceeded to draw such an
analogy.

ALISON CORNISH

The Harvest of Reading: *Inferno* 20, 24, 26†

Celestial phenomena are almost totally muted in Dante's *Inferno,* because Hell affords no view of the sky. Yet Virgil, Dante's guide, continues to be aware of the movements of the planets and is able to track the passage of time with surprising accuracy from under the ground. This uncanny ability smacks of the supernatural or necromantic powers with which the Latin poet was often credited in the Middle Ages.[1] There is also, however, a much humbler sort of reader of the stars foregrounded in the *Inferno.* Deep in the regions of fraud, we find three farmers set in relation to the legible heavens and marked as symbolic alternatives to rash sailors, deluded soothsayers, and even a certain perplexed classical poet. Farming is comparable to reading in that it requires the interpretation of signs with the goal of bringing forth fruit. The agricultural use of astronomical knowledge might be said to lie behind Hugh of St. Victor's metaphor of one's studies as a "field of labor," which, "well cultivated by your plough, will bear you a manifold harvest."[2] The star-gazing farmers of Dante's Hell establish the status of the *Commedia*'s astronomy as fruitful reading material, even in the blind prison of the *Inferno,* where the sweet light no longer strikes our eyes.

Dante could find a literary model for useful scrutiny of the visible heavens in the *Georgics,* Virgil's poem about farming. The Roman agricultural song begins by announcing its intention to discuss "under what star to turn the earth." The "bright lights of the world" that "lead the year sliding through the sky" give "sure signs" to the experienced husbandman and to the competent navigator, as to when to plough and when to set sail.[3] Michael Putnam notes that in the *Georgics* the Zodiac "offers crucial stability" in the "sustained paral-

---

† From *Reading Dante's Stars.* Copyright © 2000 by Yale University Press. Reprinted by permission of Yale University Press.

1. John Webster Spargo, *Virgil the Necromancer* (Cambridge: Harvard University Press, 1934); Domenico Comparetti, *Vergil in the Middle Ages* (London: S. Sonnenschein, 1895).

2. "Hoc ergo, o lector, quod tibi proponimus: hic campus tui laboris vomere bene sulcatus, multiplicem tibi fructum referet." Hugh of St. Victor, *Didascalicon* 6.3, *Patrologia Latina* 176.801; cf. 808. English translation from Hugh of St. Victor, *Didascalicon,* trans. Jerome Taylor (New York: Columbia University Press, 1981), p. 138. Augustine also uses agricultural metaphor in his interpretation of the literal sense of Genesis, suggesting that to stick to the meaning of the author and never deviate from the rule of piety is to have fruit from one's reading. Augustine, *De Genesi* 1.21, *PL* 34.262: "Aliud est enim quid potissimum scriptor senserit non dignoscere, aliud autem a regula pietatis errare. Si utrumque vitetur, perfecte se habet fructus legentis."

3. Virgil, *Georgics* 1.1–2, 1.5–6, 1.204–207, 1.252–258, 1.302–304. Text and translation from Virgil, *Eclogues. Georgics. Aeneid, 1–6,* trans. H. R. Fairclough (Cambridge: Harvard University Press, 1916).

lel between the farmer and the seafarer."[4] These two professions are traditionally linked through their shared reliance on fundamental astronomical learning. Indeed, they provide examples of the honest uses of a discipline often suspect for its futility or fraud. Cassiodorus remarked that astronomy was not to be despised if from it we learn "the proper season for navigation, the time for ploughing, the date of the summer's heat and of the autumn's suspected rains."[5] Farmers and sailors are not only the original astronomers but also model readers of many other natural signs, upon which their lives depend.

Reading the stars is, of course, also the occupation of professional astrologers, with which Italy was well furnished in Dante's time. Despite some inconsistency in terminology, there was always an acknowledged distinction between the study of the stars' order and motion (*ratio stellarum*) and the science of the stars' significance (*significatio stellarum*). Dante uses the same word, *astrologia*, both for what we would call astronomy and for what is sometimes specified as "judicial" astrology, because it involves judging propitious or inauspicious occasions. There is no question that Dante, like most educated people of his time, believed that the stars influenced the earth, had various effects on the growth and decay of plant and animal life, and could even incline human temperaments one way or another.[6] Although human reason is, to be sure, above the stars, the success of much astrological prognostication can nevertheless be ex-

---

4. Michael Putnam, *Virgil's Poem of the Earth: Studies in the Georgics* (Princeton: Princeton University Press: 1979), p. 24.

5. Cassiodorus, *Institutiones* 2.4, ed. R. Mynors (Oxford: Clarendon Press, 1963), p. 156: "Est alia quoque de talibus non despicienda commoditas, si oportunitatem navigationis, si tempus arantium, si aestatis caniculam, si autumni suspectos imbres inde discamus." English translation adapted from Cassiodorus Senator, *An Introduction to Divine and Human Readings*, trans. L. W. Jones (New York: Columbia University Press, 1946), p. 156.

6. Dominicus Gundissalinus, in *De divisione philosophiae*, ed. L. Baur, in *Beiträge zur Geschichte der Philosophie des Mittelalters*, vol. 4 (Münster, Germany: Aschendorff, 1903), pp. 119–120, expressed the difference this way: "Alfarabius dicit, quod astronomia est sciencia de significacione stellarum, quid scilicet stelle significent de eo, quod futurum est, et de pluribus presentibus et de pluribus preteris." See Cesare Vasoli's commentary to *Convivio* 2.13.28, in Dante, *Opere minori*, vol. 1, part 2, ed. C. Vasoli and D. De Robertis (Milan: Ricciardi, 1985), p. 241. See also Richard Kay, "Astronomy and Astrology," in *The "Divine Comedy" and the Encyclopedia of Arts and Sciences*, ed. G. Di Scipio and A. Scaglione (Amsterdam: John Benjamins, 1988), pp. 147–162; Richard Kay, *Dante's Christian Astrology* (Philadelphia: University of Pennsylvania Press, 1994), esp. pp. 1–9; Richard Lemay, "The True Place of Astrology in Medieval Science and Philosophy: Towards a Definition," in *Astrology, Science, and Society*, ed. Patrick Curry (Woodbridge, England: Boydell, 1987); Bruno Nardi, "Dante e Pietro d'Abano," in *Saggi di filosofia dantesca* (Florence: La Nuova Italia, 1967), pp. 60–62; I. Capasso and G. Tabarroni, "Astrologia," in *ED*, vol. 1, pp. 427–431; J. D. North, "Celestial Influence—The Major Premiss of Astrology," in *"Astrologi hallucinati": Stars and the End of the World in Luther's Time*, ed. Paola Zambelli (Berlin: Walter de Gruyter, 1986); Edward Grant, "Medieval and Renaissance Scholastic Conceptions of the Influence of the Celestial Region on the Terrestrial," *Journal of Medieval and Renaissance Studies* 17.1 (Spring 1987): 1–23; Paola Zambelli, *The Speculum Astronomiae and Its Enigma: Astrology, Theology and Science in Albertus Magnus and His Contemporaries* (Dordrecht: Kluwer Academic, 1992).

plained by the fact that most people simply follow their passions, as Thomas Aquinas pointed out.[7]

In the *Convivio*, Dante blithely asserts that our life and every living thing here below is caused by heaven, and that nature's seemingly infinite variety is due to the constantly changing disposition of the constellations. He even goes so far as to say that our minds, inasmuch as they are grounded in our bodies, are differently disposed depending on the circulation of heaven.[8] The length of a human life can be compared to an arc, because the shape describes the path from rising to setting of the planets that influence the whole of it.[9] Love is undoubtedly aroused by the revolutions of the heaven of Venus, as the ancients rightly inferred—although the pagans mistook the planet for a deity.[1] So, too, Dante repeatedly implies, his own literary and intellectual talent derived from his being born under the constellation of Gemini (*gloriose stelle, o lume pregno / di gran virtú*), probably to be identified with the personal star (*tua stella*) that Brunetto Latini implies might lead him to literary glory, and with the good star (*stella bona*) that might aid his careful genius, as the poet himself implies in the canto of Ulysses.[2]

Moreover, Dante seems to have believed that major events involving large numbers of people would be brought about and also presaged by particular planetary conjunctions. Just as the perfect disposition of the heavens mirrored the optimal terrestrial government at the time of Christ's birth, so untoward planetary configura-

---

7. *Summa Theologiae* 1.115.4 ad 3, vol. 15 (New York: McGraw-Hill, 1970), p. 106: "Plures hominum sequuntur passiones, quae sunt motus sensitivi appetitus, ad quas cooperari possunt corpora caelestis." For an analysis of Aquinas' view on astrology, see Thomas Litt, *Les corps célestes dans l'univers de saint Thomas d'Aquin*, chaps. 6, 7, and 8 (Louvain: Publications Universitaires, 1963).

8. *Convivio* 4.2.7: "E così la nostra mente in quanto ella è fondata sopra la complessione del corpo, che [ha] a seguitare la circulazione del cielo, altrimenti è disposta in un tempo e altrimenti un altro"; 4.21.7: "E però che . . . la disposizione del Cielo a questo effetto puote essere buona, migliore e ottima (la quale si varia [per] le constellazioni, che continuamente si transmutano), incontra che dell'umano seme e di queste vertudi più pura [e men pura] anima si produce; e secondo la sua puritade, discende in essa la vertude intellettuale possible." In *Convivio* 2.14.16–17, he lists all the things that would not exist without the movement of the crystalline heaven.

9. *Convivio* 4.23.6: "Oride, con ciò sia cosa che la nostra vita, sì come detto è, ed ancora d'ogni vivente qua giù, sia causata dal cielo e lo cielo a tutti questi cotali effetti, non per cerchio compiuto ma per parte di quello a loro sì scuopra; e così conviene che 'l suo movimento sia sopra essi come uno arco quasi, [e] tutte le terrene vite (e dico terrene, sì delli [uomini] come delli altri viventi), montando e volgendo, convengono essere quasi ad imagine d'arco asimiglianti."

1. Such seems to be the sense of the opening lines of *Paradiso* 8: "Solea creder lo mondo in suo periclo / che la bella Ciprigna il folle amore / raggiasse, volta nel terzo epiciclo." That it is not an indictment of belief in celestial influence is easily proved by Cunizza's happily confessing that she was conquered by the light of this planet ("perché mi vinse il lume d'esta stella" [*Paradiso* 9.33]) and by a similar admission by the Provençal poet Folquet de Marseilles ("questo cielo / di me s'imprenta, com'io fe' di lui" [*Paradiso* 9.95–96]). Cf. *Convivio* 2.5.15: "E perché li antichi s'accorsero che quello cielo era qua giù cagione d'amore, dissero Amore essere figlio di Venere"; and 2.6.5: "L'operazione vostra, cioè la vostra circulazione, è quella che m'ha tratto nella presente condizione."

2. *Inferno* 15.55; *Inferno* 26.23–24; *Paradiso* 22.112–115.

tions are associated with the degradation of present-day customs.[3] In "Poscia ch'Amor," the poet laments that grace and courtesy have swerved away from the world because of the state of the heavens (*Ancor che ciel con cielo in punto sia*, / *che leggiadria* / *disvia cotanto*), and in "Tre donne intorno al cor mi son venute" the virtues have been reduced to begging because men have encountered the rays of such a sky (*che sono a' raggi di cotal ciel giunti*).[4] In his epistolary invectives, Dante forecast upcoming revolutions in store for the contemporary world, which he claimed to know through "truth-telling signs" (*signis veridicis*), because "through the movement of heaven, the human intellect is able to understand its mover and His will."[5] Many of Dante's early commentators were convinced that the prophetic utterances scattered through the *Commedia,* such as the cryptic *veltro* and the *cinquecento diece e cinque*, referred to an imminent great conjunction of Saturn and Jupiter—*già stelle propinque.*[6] In the *Purgatorio*, Dante exhorts the heavens to hasten the arrival of the mysterious individual who will chase off the ancient she-wolf:

> O ciel, nel cui girar, par che si creda
> le condizion di qua giù trasmutarsi,
> quando verrà per cui questa disceda?
> (*Purgatorio* 20.13–15)

[O heaven, through whose turning it appears to be believed that conditions down here are transformed, when will come the one before whom she will flee?]

---

3. *Convivio* 4.5.7: "Poi che esso cielo cominciò a girare, in migliore disposizione non fu che allora quando di là su discese Colui che l'ha fatto e che 'l governa: sì come ancora per virtù di loro arti li matematici possono ritrovare. Né 'l mondo mai non fu né sarà sì perfettamente disposto come allora."

4. "Poscia ch'Amor," lines 58–60; "Tre donne," lines 66–67.

5. *Epistole* 6.4: "Et si presaga mens mea non fallitur, sic signis veridicis sicut inexpugnabilibus argumentis instructa prenuntians;" *Epistole* 5.8: "Et si ex notioribus nobis innotiora; si simpliciter interest humane apprehensioni ut per motum celi Motorem intelligamus et eius velle; facile predestinatio hec etiam leviter intuentibus innotescet." In *Monarchia* 3.15, Dante also argued that only God, who had a full and total view of the disposition of heaven, on which the disposition of earth depends, could be qualified to elect a world governor: "Cumque dispositio mundi huius dispositionem inherentem celorum circulationi sequator, necesse est ad hoc ut utilia documenta libertatis et pacis commode locis et temporibus applicentur, de curatore isto dispensari ab Illo qui totalem celorum dispositionem presentialiter intuetur."

6. *Inferno* 1.100–102; *Purgatorio* 33.41–45. Francesco da Buti interpreted Virgil's prophecy of the *veltro* as referring to "una influenzia di corpi celesti, che in processo di tempo verrà secondo il movimento de' cieli, che tutto il mondo si disporrà a sapienzia, virtù e amore . . . e questo era noto all'autore secondo la ragione dell'astrologo, et in ciò si manifesta ch'elli fosse astrologo." *Commento di Francesco da Buti sopra la Divina comedia di Dante Alighieri*, ed. C. Giannini (Pisa: Nistri, 1858), p. 46. Pietro, the poet's son, in the earlier drafts of his own commentary, believed that his father predicted that the longed-for political change would come about in the great conjunction due to occur in 1345. See Kennerly M. Woody, "Dante and the Doctrine of the Great Conjunctions," *Dante Studies* 95 (1977): 119–134; Leo Olschki, *The Myth of Felt* (Berkeley: University of California Press, 1949); Bruno Nardi, "Influenze celesti sugli avvenimenti di storia umana," in *Saggi*, pp. 55–61; Lemay, "The True Place," p. 22.

Beatrice, moreover, encourages us to expect prodigious political vicissitudes to "rain down" from the supernal wheels:

> raggeran sì questi cerchi superni,
> che la fortuna che tanto s'aspetta,
> le poppe volgerà u' son le prore,
> sì che la classe correrà diretta;
> e vero frutto verrà dopo 'l fiore.
>
> (*Paradiso* 27.144–148)

[These supernal wheels will irradiate such that the fortune that is so long awaited will turn the sterns to where the prows are now, so that the fleet will run straight; and true fruit will follow upon the flower.]

Her mixed metaphor of ships and fruit-bearing flowers follows inevitably from the double role of the stars—as guides and as causes. Stars steer attentive sailors to port, but they also bring forth fruit from well-tended plants, as farmers well know.

The Farmer among the Soothsayers

Belief in the impact of the stars on human affairs cannot therefore be the criterion on which such astrologers as Michael Scot and Guido Bonatti are condemned to the fourth subcategory of fraud.[7] Their punishment seems instead to be motivated by their concerted, and usually well-paid, efforts to avert or avoid the predicted effects of planetary motion. To put it in the most general terms, the soothsayers are in Hell not for trying to read nature's signs, but rather for reading them perversely—in much the same way, perhaps, that Francesca's eternal predicament is caused not so much by the book that she curses in canto 5, but rather by her uncircumspect use of it. The whole canto of the soothsayers has recently come to be seen as a meditation on correct and incorrect ways of reading, particularly as regards classical literature.[8] Indeed, Dante's epic predecessors contribute four of the seers of antiquity named in the *bolgia*—Tiresias from Ovid's *Metamorphoses*, Amphiaraus from Statius' *Thebaid*, Arruns from Lucan's *Pharsalia*, and Manto from Virgil's *Aeneid*. Virgil's text comes under particular scrutiny, as he is made to recant at

---

7. Kay, "Astrology and Astronomy," p. 158; "The Spare Ribs of Michael Scot," *Dante Studies* 103 (1985): 1–14; and "Dante's Double Damnation of Manto," in *Res publica litterarum* 1 (1978): 113–128.
8. Teodolinda Barolini ("True and False See-ers in Inferno XX," *Lectura Dantis* 4 [1989]: 42–54) declares that this canto "deals with the validity and legitimacy of the acts of writing and reading" because "prophecy is in fact a textual issue . . . essentially a matter of correct and incorrect reading." Zygmunt Barański, "The Poetics of Meter: Terza Rima, 'Canto,' 'Canzon,' 'Cantica,'" in *Dante Now*, ed. Theodore Cachey (Notre Dame: University of Notre Dame Press, 1995), p. 17: "As is now widely recognized, the *canto* of the soothsayers stands as one of Dante's major statements on classical literature."

length the account of Mantua's origins he gave in his epic. Dante's conspicuous re-reading of the *Aeneid* in the context of supernatural divination not only serves to contrast Virgil's *alta tragedìa* with his own *comedìa*, but also to differentiate the Italian poet's prophetic role from Virgil's vocation as *vates*, or prophet.[9]

Among the various pagan prophets and diviners of note, Dante has Virgil point out the aged seer Arruns, who discerned terrifying omens of civil war at the start of Lucan's *Pharsalia*. In the Roman epic, Arruns' expertise is primarily in the Etruscan arts of extispicy (the inspection of animals' entrails), augury, and the interpretation of lightning bolts, leaving the "secrets of heaven" and astrological prediction to the learned Figulus:[1]

> So they decided to follow the ancient custom and summon
> Seers from Etruria: the eldest of these, named Arruns,
> Lived in the otherwise abandoned city of Luca.
> This was a man well schooled in interpretation of omens—
> Motions of thunderbolts and veins, still throbbing, of entrails,
> Also the warnings of birds by special flight or behavior.[2]

Whereas Lucan imagined Arruns holed up within the walls of a deserted Etruscan city, Dante depicts his dwelling as a cave in the mountains. The tight, dark ditch, or bolgia, around which the seer now trudges, with his head contorted over his rear end, contrasts with the magnificent panorama of sea and sky he once had from up there:

> Aronta è quel ch'al ventre li s'atterga,
>   che ne' monti di Luni, dove ronca
>   lo Carrarese che di sotto alberga,
> ebbe tra' bianchi marmi la spelonca
>   per sua dimora; onde a guardar le stelle
>   e'l mar non li era la veduta tronca.
>   (*Inferno* 20.46–51)

Omitting the examination of entrails, Dante prefers to characterize Arruns' divinatory activity as a prolonged gaze into the stars and over the sea. His topographical positioning of the seer's cave, high above

---

9. This is the argument of Robert Hollander, "The Tragedy of Divination in *Inferno* XX," in *Studies in Dante* (Ravenna, Italy: Longo, 1980), pp. 131–218.

1. Lucan, *Pharsalia* 1.639. Cicero provides the classical definitions of the various arts of divination in his *De Divinatione*. See "Divination" in *Oxford Classical Dictionary*, ed. N. Hammond and H. Scullard (Oxford: Clarendon Press, 1970), pp. 356–357.

2. Lucan, *Pharsalia* 2.584–587: "Haec propter placuit Tuscos de more vetusto / acciri vates. Quorum qui maximus aevo / Arruns incoluit desertae moenia Lucae, / fibrarum et monitus errantis in aere pinnae." Latin text of the *Pharsalia* from *Lucan* (Cambridge: Harvard University Press, 1957). Translation by P. F. Widdows, ed., *Lucan's "Civil War"* (Bloomington: Indiana University Press, 1988).

the fields, introduces the figure of a peasant, totally alien to Lucan's text, that serves to make a marked moral contrast. The simple peasant of Carrara is intent on working the earth (*ronca*) with the hope of making it bring forth fruit, while the famous augur has his attention fixed on the signs and portents visible in the sky and over the horizon.

This incidental farmer inserted into the canto of the soothsayers actually has a common analogue in various indictments of astrology and other arts of divination. In his discussion of the value of astronomy as a liberal art, Cassiodorus differentiated its advantageous uses for navigation, ploughing, planting, and harvesting from its investigation in order to know one's fate, which is contrary to faith. He recommended that passages treating astrological prediction not only should not be read, but should be ignored as if they had never been written.[3] On the same theme, John of Salisbury invokes a farmer's proverb taken from Horace, saying that "he who puts his faith in dreams and augury will never be free of worry," but goes on to vouch for the "authenticity and value of those signs which have been conceded by divine ordinance for the guidance of man."[4] These are signs learned not through books but through experience, and are to the help of working men rather than philosophers: "Consequently farmer and sailors, as the result of certain familiar experiences, infer what ought to be done at any particular time by conjecturing the state of the weather to come from that which has preceded."[5]

A common source for both Cassiodorus and John of Salisbury would have been Augustine's belittling assessment of astronomy in the *De doctrina christiana*, where the profit of this science in the reading of Scripture is reduced to calculating the phases of the moon in order to celebrate the Lord's Passion: "Although the course of the moon, which is relevant to the celebration of the anniversary of the Passion of Our Lord, is known to many, there are only a few who

---

3. Cassiodorus, *Institutiones* 2.7.4: "Est alia quoque de talibus non despicienda commoditas, si oportunitatem navigationis, si tempus arantium, si aestatis caniculam, si autumni suspectos imbres inde discamus. Dedit enim Dominus unicuique creaturae suae aliquam virtutem, [quam] tamen innoxie de propria qualitate [noscamus]. Cetera vero quae se ad cognitionem siderum coniungunt, id est ad notitiam fatorum, et fidei nostrae sine dubitatione contraria sunt, sic ignorari [debent], ut nec scripta esse videantur."

4. *Ioannis Saresberiensis episcopi Carnotensis Policratici* 2.1 and 2.2, ed. C. Webb (New York: Arno, 1979), pp. 65, 68: "Rusticanum et forte Offelli proverbium est: Qui sompniis et auguriis credit, numquam fore securum"; "Futuras itaque tempestates aut serenitates signa quaedam antecedentia praeloquuntur, ut homo, qui ad laborem natus est, ex his possit exercitia sua temperare. Hinc agricolae hinc nautae familiaribus quibusdam experimentis." Translation from John of Salisbury, *Frivolities of Courtiers and Footprints of Philosophers*, trans. Joseph B. Pike (Minneapolis: University of Minnesota Press, 1938), pp. 55–56.

5. Ibid.: "Ad laborem natus est, ex his possit exercitia sua temperare. Hinc agricolae hinc naturae familiaribus quibusdam experimentis quid quo tempore geri oporteat colligunt, qualitatem temporis futuri ex eo quod praeteriit metientes."

know well the rising or setting or other movements of the rest of the stars without error. Knowledge of this kind in itself, although it is not allied with any superstition, is of very little use in the treatment of Divine Scriptures and even impedes it through fruitless study [*infructuosa intentione*]; and since it is associated with the most pernicious error of vain prediction it is more appropriate and virtuous to condemn it."[6] * * * Augustine was at pains to defend the special coincidence of astronomical events in the commemoration of the Passion as significant parts of God's eloquence, while distancing himself from astrological prognostication in general. In his letter to Januarius, he explicitly differentiates the "fruitless study" of astronomy from its valuable use by husbandmen and navigators. "Who cannot perceive the difference," he asks, between the "useful observation of the heavenly bodies in connection with the weather, such as farmers or sailors make; or in order to mark the part of the world in which they are and the course which they should follow—and prying into the future?"[7] Dante's juxtaposition of Lucan's seer, Arruns, with the simple Carrarese peasant is therefore not wholly without precedent, as farmers are traditionally cited as fruitful readers of the stars in contrast with immoderate seekers of hidden things.

In terms that recall Hugh of St. Victor's agrarian metaphor cited at the beginning of this chapter (*o lector . . . tibi fructum referet*), Dante explicitly likens his reader's task in the canto of the soothsayers to the art of husbandry. He admonishes us to ponder for ourselves how, if God lets us "take harvest from our reading," he could have looked dry-eyed on such deformations of "our image":

> Se Dio ti lasci, lettor, *prender frutto*
> *di tua lezione,* or pensa per te stesso
> com' io potea tener lo viso asciutto,

---

6. Augustine, *De doctrina christiana* 2.46, *Patrologia Latina* 34.57: "Sicut autem plurimis notus est lunae cursus, qui etiam ad passionem Domini anniversarie celebrandam solemniter adhibetur; sic paucissimis caeterorum quoque siderum vel ortus, vel occasus, vel alia quaelibet momenta sine ullo sunt errore notissima. Que per seipsam cognitio, quanquam superstitione non alliget, non multum tamen ac prope nihil adjuvat tractationem divinarum Scripturarum, et infructuosa intentione plus impedit; et qui familiaris est perniciosissimo errori fatua fata cantantium, commodius honestiusque contemnitur." English translation from Augustine, *On Christian Doctrine*, trans. D. W. Robertson (New York: Liberal Arts, 1958), p. 65.

7. Augustine, Epistle 55.8.15; *Patrologia Latina* 33.211: "Sed quantum intersit inter siderum observationes ad aerias qualitates accomodatas, sicut agricolae vel nautae observant; aut ad notandas partes mundi cursumque aliquo et alicunde dirigendum, quod gubernatores navium faciunt, et ii qui per solitudines arenosas in interiora Austri nulla semita certa vel recta gradiuntur; aut cum ad aliquid in doctrina utili figurate significandum, fit nonnullorum siderum aliqua commemoratio; quantum ergo intersit inter has utilitates, et vanitates hominum ob hoc observantium sidera, ut nec aeris qualitates, nec regionum vias, nec solos temporum numeros, nec spiritualium similitudines, sed quasi fatalia rerum jam eventa perquirant, quis non intelligat?" On the skills of prognostication and prophecy necessary to peasants and herdsmen, see also Piero Camporesi, *The Anatomy of the Senses: Natural Symbols in Medieval and Early Modern Italy*, trans. Allan Cameron (Cambridge: Polity Press, 1994), pp. 186–196.

> quando la nostra imagine di presso
> vidi sì torta, che 'l pianto de li occhi
> le natiche bagnava per lo fesso.
> 　　　　　　　　*(Inferno* 20.19–24)

The punishment, or *contrapasso,* of the fourth bolgia consists in a severe form of infernal palsy that has turned the heads of the damned all the way around toward their backs. Looking ahead is now denied them because of their excessive desire to see into the future while alive:

> perché volse veder troppo davante
> di retro guarda e fa retroso calle.
> 　　　　　　　　*(Inferno* 20.38–39)

The sinners rotate eternally around their circular ditch with a monstrous retrograde motion, "backing up" against the belly of their neighbor (*quel ch'al ventre li s'atterga*), the way the concave celestial spheres fit closely one inside the other, or, as one early commentator remarked, the way one student of divination follows closely on the books of his predecessor.[8] Virgil's emphatic scorn in canto 20 for Dante's tears of pity at seeing the weeping of the horribly deformed soothsaying sinners wash down their buttocks (*Qui vive la pietà quand' è ben morta* [*Inferno* 20.87–93]) has been taken as a marked rejection of the popular medieval legends that had transformed the Roman poet into an occultist wiseman and sorcerer.[9]

An extirpation of supernatural ambitions also seems to be the purpose of his long digression, taking up more than a third of the canto, on the origin of his native city, Mantua, in which he directly contradicts the account given in his own "high tragedy." In the *Aeneid,* Ocnus, "son of prophesying Manto," is said to have founded Mantua, giving it walls and his mother's name. As Teodolinda Barolini reminds us, he appears as a hero coming to the aid of Aeneas in the war against Turnus, with the image of Mincius, the river god and son of Lake Benacus, on the prows of his ships.[1] The essential difference between this version of Mantua's founding and its emendation in *Inferno* 20, aside from the elimination of the prophetess' son, is the removal of all taint of the supernatural. Mincio is no longer a river god but simply a river, not born of Lake Garda but formed by its overflow. The city's founders gather together along the swamp where Tiresias' daughter had "left her empty body" and called it Mantua "without further augury" (*senz' altra sorte*).

8. Anonimo Fiorentino, *Commento alla Divina commedia,* vol. 1, ed. P. Fanfani (Bologna: Romagnoli, 1866), p. 446.
9. Francesco D'Ovidio, "Dante e la Magia," *Nuova antologia* (1892): 213f.; and "Esposizione del canto XX dell'*Inferno,*" in *Nuovo volume di studi danteschi* (Caserta, Italy: A. P. E., 1926); Comparetti, *Vergil in the Middle Ages.*
1. Barolini, "True and False See-ers," p. 50.

If the story of the city's founding by Manto's son in the *Aeneid* served to imbue Virgil's birthplace with a heritage of divination, prophecy, or *vaticinatio,* closely associated with his claim to poetic inspiration, as Robert Hollander has argued, here in Hell Dante has him give a purely naturalistic history of the place, consisting primarily of a description of the waterways that descend from Lago di Garda to form the Mantuan marsh. Indeed, the description of the lake they both call Benaco is perhaps derived from not from the heroic epic, but from the agricultural poem, the *Georgics.*[2] Virgil's digression in canto 20 is a lesson on geography as he traces the natural hydraulic system of northern *Italia bella* at the foot of the Alps, a system that feeds the lake from, Virgil thinks (*credo*), more than a thousand springs. He focuses on the variability of names as the water spills out from Lake Benaco to become the river that is called Mincio until it falls in with the Po. Mantua is located in a flat area not far down the river's course, where the water spreads out to form a marsh that smells bad in the summertime.[3]

The prolonged river-narrative is not only nonheroic; it borders on the unpleasant. It provides a demystified reading of the landscape in a canto that is all about reading. This becomes evident from Virgil's striking insistence on the truth of this account, which might otherwise seem unremarkable and even off the subject. With considerable irony, Dante has his teacher instruct him to reject a passage in the *Aeneid,* a poem that he knows by heart (*che la sai tutta quanta*), and which he may well have regarded as divinely inspired and even prophetic. Dante declares that all other stories of Mantua's founding (presumably also and especially the one in the *Aeneid*) will henceforth be for him reduced to "spent coals," not unlike the extinguished power of the sorceress in the revised story of Mantua's origins, who left of herself only her "empty body" by the swamp where the city subsequently rose.[4] Dante's obedience to Virgil in the canto

---

2. Hollander, "The Tragedy of Divination." Aristide Marigo ("Le 'Georgiche'di Virgilio fonte di Dante," *Giornale dantesco* 17 [1909]: 31–44) suggested *Georgics* 2.159 as a source: "Teque / Fluctibus et fremitu assurgens, Benace, marino." Edward Moore (*Studies in Dante,* 1st ser. [Oxford: Clarendon Press, 1896], p. 178) thought that Dante knew the *Georgics* only through passages found in florilegia, such as the episode of Orpheus' head rolling down the river and calling the name of Eurydice (*Georgics* 4.523). But Marigo notes that virtually all Virgilian codices, including those of the thirteenth and fourteenth centuries, contain the *Bucolics* and the *Georgics* in addition to the *Aeneid.*

3. *Inferno* 20.61–81: "Suso in Italia bella giace un laco, / a piè de l'Alpe che serra Lamagna / sovra Tiralli, c'ha nome Benaco. / Per mille fonti, credo, e piú si bagna / tra Garda e Val Camonica, Apennino / de l'acqua che nel detto laco stagna . . . / Ivi convien che tutto quanto caschi / ciò che 'n grembo a Benaco star non può, / e fassi fiume giú per verdi paschi. / Tosto che l'acqua a correr mette co, / non piú Benaco, ma Mencio si chiama / fino a Governol, dove cade in Po. / Non molto ha corso, ch'el trova unalama, / ne la qual si distende e la 'mpaluda; / e suol di state talor esser grama."

4. *Inferno* 20.97–102: "'Però t'assenno che, se tu mai odi / originar la mia terra altrimenti, / la verità nulla menzogna frodi.' / E io: 'Maestro, i tuoi ragionamenti / mi son sì certi e prendon sì mia fede, / che li altri mi sarien carboni spenti.'"

thus requires his repudiation of Virgil's own poem; his faith in what he says here in the fourth bolgia of fraud inside Dante's *comedìa* requires that he treats what he said in the *alta tragedìa* as a "lie that defrauds the truth." In this literary competition, if that is what it is, the focus on water in the ancient poet's amended etiology of his city may also be particularly significant because of the association of rivers and their sources with literary originality and eloquence.[5] By reducing the *Aeneid*'s mythologized and mantic personifications to indifferent topographical facts (a lake, a river, a marsh), Virgil's lengthy correction of his own text might be seen as a kind of antidote to the sin punished in this bolgia, which involves "reading too much into" natural phenomena.

If the relevance of Virgil's dull geographical digression to the sin of divination is that Dante wants to distance the Roman poet from his medieval reputation as supernaturally inspired *vates,* it is all the more striking that this canto in particular should close with one of his intuitive, and to that extent mantic, readings of the stars:

> Ma vienne omai, ché già tiene il confine
> d'ambedue gli emisferi e tocca l'onda
> sotto Sibilia Caino e le spine;
> e già iernotte fu la luna tonda . . .
>
> (*Inferno* 20.124–127)

This is a time-reference of the infernal sort; it uses the moon instead of the sun, and moreover implies sunrise by speaking of moonset. From the perspective of Jerusalem, which shares Hell's chronological standard, when the moon is full the sun rises just as the moon sets in the west (here indicated by Seville). In the days that follow, it sets steadily later in the morning. At this point in the journey the setting of the moon would indicate an hour of about half past seven in the morning.

Commentators have contrasted Virgil's popular, even superstitious anthropomorphization of the moon as Cain with Beatrice's scholastic disputation on the qualities of the same planet in *Paradiso* 2. Yet, because the temporal indication is accurate, according to the fictional astronomy of the journey Virgil speaks the truth about the stars even without seeing them, presumably by the light of reason alone. The moon itself, here said to have been of some help to Dante during the night of his solitary travails in the dark wood, might be associated with just the kind of limited, secular knowledge Virgil represents. Augustine linked the moon with knowledge, in contrast with the sun of

---

5. Hollander notes Dante's "watery" sense of Virgil in "Tragedy," p. 192. David Quint ("The Virgilian Source," in *Origin and Originality in Renaissance Literature* [New Haven: Yale University Press, 1983], pp. 32–42), has identified the episode at the end of Virgil's own *Georgics* involving a visit to the source of all rivers as an allegorical topos of poetic originality and inspiration, much copied in the Renaissance.

wisdom in a reformulation of Psalm 18 (*Caeli enarrant gloriam Dei*): "Shine ye over all the earth; and let the day enlightened by the sun utter unto day a speech of wisdom; and night, enlightened by the moon, show unto night a word of knowledge. The moon and stars shine in the night, yet doth not the night obscure them; seeing they give that light unto it, in its degree."[6] In Purgatory, in fact, Virgil will conspicuously defer to the guiding authority of the sun itself, which at the start of the *Inferno* was defined as leading people aright by every path (*che mena diritto altrui per ogni calle* [*Inferno* 1.18]):

> 'O dolce lume a cui fidanza i' entro
>   per lo novo cammin, tu ne conduci'
>   dicea 'come condur si vuol quinc'entro.
> Tu scaldi il mondo, tu sovr'esso luci:
>   s'altra ragione in contrario non ponta,
>   esser dien sempre li tuoi raggi duci . . .'
>   (*Purgatorio* 13.16–21)

["O sweet light, whom I trust as I enter on the new road, you guide us," he said, "as one ought to be guided through this place. You warm the world and give it light: if no other reason contradicts them, your rays should always be guides."]

In conclusion, the canto of the soothsayers contrasts straightforward and useful interpretations of visible phenomena with the sin of divination, or perverse reading of natural signs. Virgil is pivotal to this issue, as poet (of nature and agriculture as well as of history and myth), as renowned necromancer, and as sage. As always, Dante characterizes Virgil as an immensely knowledgeable but often limited reader. Just because he avoids being condemned to this very bolgia for his popularly supposed occult powers does not mean that in his observation of the world he did not make mistakes, or miss out on the big picture. This is the characterization of Virgil, and of the best of classical antiquity in general, that will develop over the course of the *Commedia*. In the *Inferno*, it is the unassisted gaze of the pagan mind that seems to be the target of its few astronomical references, to each of which is attached the figure of a farmer.

The Farmer in Winter

As in the canto of the soothsayers, Virgil himself also seems to be the specific target of the long rustic comparison at the start of *In-*

---

6. Augustine, *Confessions* 13.19: "Lucete supra omnen terram, et dies sole candens eructet diei verbum sapientiae, et nox, luna lucens, annuntiet nocti verbus scientiae. Luna et stellae nocti lucent, sed nox non obscurat eas, quoniam ipsae inluminant eam pro modulo eius." Text and translation from *St. Augustine's Confessions,* trans. William Watts (Cambridge: Harvard University Press, 1912). This observation was made by Albert E. Wingell, in "Dante, St. Augustine, and Astronomy," *Quaderni d'italianistica* 2, no. 2 (1981): 123–142.

ferno 24. The astronomical opening of this simile, which Robert Hollander has gone so far as to dub Dante's Georgic, takes inspiration from Virgil's advice to shepherds to feed their goats with leafy plants in midwinter, "at the time when the cold Waterbearer (Aquarius) is now setting, sprinkling the departing year" (*iam cadit extremoque inrorat Acquarius anno*).[7] Whereas for the Romans the sign of Aquarius marked the end of the agricultural calendar (*extremo . . . anno*), as Hollander points out, Dante turns it around to presage the approaching end of winter, a time when the sun "tempers its locks," in the early part of the liturgical year (*giovanetto anno*):

> In quella parte del giovanetto anno
> che 'l sole i crin sotto l'Aquario tempra
> e già le notti al mezzo dì sen vanno . . .
>   (*Inferno* 24.1–3)

Dante calls attention, moreover, to the lengthening of the days after the winter solstice as the nights "head south" and the sun wends its way back toward the north.[8]

The opening lines of Dante's simile cast the near dead of winter in hopeful language, altering not the season, but the way it is viewed. The rest of the simile that the astronomical periphrasis introduces goes on to stage a parallel reassessment of the hibernal landscape. In early February a shepherd who has no stock of hay is distressed to see the ground all white, as if it were covered with snow:

> quando la brina in su la terra assempra
> l'imagine di sua sorella bianca,
> ma poco dura a la sua penna tempra
> lo villanello a cui la roba manca,
> si leva, e guarda, e vede la campagna
> biancheggiar tutta; ond'ei si batte l'anca,
> ritorna in casa, e qua e là si lagna,
> come 'l tapin che non sa che si faccia.
>   (*Inferno* 24.4–11)

When the hoarfrost (which was only impersonating its white sister) soon melts and the world alters its appearance, the simile's agrarian protagonist then gathers back his hope and, taking up his staff, drives his sheep out to pasture:

7. Virgil, *Georgics* 3.304. Robert Hollander, "Dante's 'Georgic' (*Inferno* XXIV, 1–18)," *Dante Studies* 102 (1984): 111–121. He credits Pietro di Dante (1340) with having first pointed out this Virgilian echo. Also noting the presence of the *Georgics* is David Baker, "The Winter Simile in *Inferno* XXIV," *Dante Studies* 92 (1974): 77–91.
8. This line can be interpreted to mean either that the nights are headed toward becoming half the length of the days or that "night," as the point directly opposite the sun, is now headed toward the south (*mezzogiorno*) just as the sun is headed north.

poi riede, e la speranza ringavagna,
veggendo 'l mondo aver cangiata faccia
in poco d'ora, e prende suo vincastro
e fuor le pecorelle a pascer caccia.

(*Inferno* 24.12–15)

The passage narrates an extended parable of misreading, or double take, beginning with the winter constellation from Virgil's *Georgics* now being read as a sign of imminent spring. The peasant misinterprets not only the pattern in the sky, but the pattern on the ground—hoarfrost's counterfeit of snow—and then completely alters his mood, regarnering hope, when he sees that the world has "changed its face." Even the simile's use of equivocal rhyme, words that look the same but mean different things (*tempra, tempra; faccia, faccia*), is a formal reflection of the deceptive appearances central to the region of fraud.[9]

The explicit tenor of the simile is Dante's initial distress at seeing the perturbation of his master upon discovering in the last canto the duplicity of devils (*elli è bugiardo e padre di menzogna*). As Margherita Frankel has noted, the revelation that devils do not always mean what they say comes on the heels of Virgil's stunned amazement at the body of Caiaphas crucified on the ground. Caiaphas' verdict sealing Christ's fate, to let one man suffer for the sake of the people (*porre un uomo per lo popolo a' martiri*), is expressed in a clear echo of Virgil's own *Aeneid*, where Jupiter concedes to let just one Trojan die in place of many: *unum pro multis dabitur caput*. This shocking twist to what must have seemed in the context of the Roman epic a positive trade-off, followed by the apparently astonishing discovery that the devil is "the father of lies," upsets Virgil to the point that he stalks off.[1] This is the perturbation that occasions the agrarian simile of canto 24. It is a crisis provoked not just by fraud, but by Virgil's apparent inexperience with black cherubim and tricksters of the sort he encountered in the circle of barratry, and by his amazement that even his own words might have been deceptive, or at least subject to a radically different interpretation.

Dante's shepherd in the simile may not be a good reader of Virgil's *Georgics*, because he failed to stock up on leafy plants in winter and has a curious way of interpreting the constellations (why shouldn't a farmer expect snow in early February?). Nonetheless, he does not give up hope. Virgil, in contrast, as a virtuous pagan assigned to

9. Margherita Frankel ("Dante's Anti-Virgilian *Villanello*," *Dante Studies* 102 [1984]: 81–109) notes that the *rime equivoche* "raise the contrast of their dynamic differentiation" and participate in the whole issue of appearance versus reality. See also Richard Lansing, *From Image to Idea: A Study of the Simile in Dante's "Commedia"* (Ravenna, Italy: Longo, 1977), p. 75: "The equivocal rhymes point up the problem of perception."

1. *Inferno* 23.145–146: "Appresso il duca a gran passi sen gì, / turbato un poco d'ira nel sembiante."

Limbo, is defined as someone who lives "without hope" (*che sanza speme vivemo in disio*).[2] Because Dante's pastoral image, unlike Virgil's in the *Georgics*, is inevitably charged with the spiritual resonances of Christ's words to Peter ("feed my sheep") as well as with Abraham's unwavering trust that "the Lord will provide," it constitutes an implicit criticism of Virgil's pastoral abilities, following on his rather embarrassing incompetence in dealing with some mischievous devils.[3] The farmer is better, the simile would seem to imply, than the poet of farming; not because he is better equipped or skilled or more experienced, but because he reads the signs of nature hopefully rather than astutely. It is a critique not of Virgil's know-how but of his attitude, which colors all he sees.

The Farmer in Summer

In the canto of the soothsayers, the sinister clairvoyance of an Etruscan magus is contrasted with the simple diligence of the Carrarese who works the land below. In canto 24, it is Virgil, the great sage, who is implicitly held up for comparison with a mere peasant. A third such contrast is apparent in canto 26, in the simile of the *villano* that introduces Dante's first glimpse of Ulysses.[4] In this passage, the two famous Greek heroes of the Trojan war now burning in the gullet of the eighth ditch are reduced to the status of bugs, or fireflies, seen from a great height by a farmer resting on a hillside:

> Quante il villan ch'al poggio si riposa,
>   nel tempo che colui che 'l mondo schiara
>   la faccia sua a noi tien meno ascosa,
> come la mosca cede a la zanzara,
>   vede lucciole giù per la vallea,
>   forse colà dov' e' vendemmia e ara:
> di tante fiamme tutta risplendea
>   l'ottava bolgia, sì com'io m'accorsi
>   tosto che fui là've 'l fondo parea.
>   (*Inferno* 26.25–33)

---

2. *Inferno* 4.42. Robert Durling and Ronald Martinez call attention to the affinities between this simile and the *rime petrose* and to its hopeful tendency, against those who would see it as a "paralyzed poetics." Robert M. Durling and Ronald L. Martinez, *Time and the Crystal* (Berkeley: University of California Press, 1990), p. 215.

3. See Frankel, "Dante's Anti-Virgilian *Villanello*," and Robert J. Ellrich, "Envy, Identity, and Creativity: *Inferno* XXIV–XXV," *Dante Studies* 102 (1984): 61–79, in which Ellrich notes the simile's christological meaning, as "caring for the flock" relates the scene to the image of Christ as Good Shepherd. See also Warren Ginsberg, "Dante, Ovid, and the Transformation of Metamorphosis," *Traditio* 46 (1991); Peter Hawkins, "Virtuosity and Virtue: Poetic Self-Reflection in the *Commedia*," *Dante Studies* 98 (1980): 1–18; Lawrence Baldassaro, "Metamorphosis as Punishment and Redemption in *Inferno* XXIV," *Dante Studies* 99 (1981): 89–112.

4. Durling and Martinez also link the summer pastoral simile of *Inferno* 26 to the hibernal one of two cantos earlier. *Time and the Crystal*, p. 217.

In this simile, the farmer's complete repose on a summer evening as he rests from his labors (the spring ploughing and the autumn harvest) could not be further removed from the damned sailor's impetuous rush across the ocean (*de' remi facemmo ali al folle volo*).[5] As commentators, beginning with the poet's son Pietro, have noticed, Ulysses' mad dash to the other side of the globe, resulting in the infernal torment of a tongue of fire, recalls the comparison, in the Epistle of James, of unrestrained speech to unguided ships and horses:

> If anyone does not offend in word, he is a perfect man, able also to lead round by a bridle the whole body. For if we put bits into horses' mouths that they may obey us, we control their whole body also. Behold, even the ships, great as they are, and driven by boisterous winds, are steered by a small rudder wherever the touch of the steersman pleases. So the tongue is also a little member, but it boasts mightily. Behold, how small a fire—how great a forest it kindles! And the tongue is a fire, the very world of iniquity. The tongue is placed among our members, defiling the whole body and setting on fire the course of our life, being itself set on fire from hell.[6]

Because Dante emphatically associates the virtue of hope with James's epistle when he meets the apostle in Paradise, its presence in *Inferno* 26 underscores Ulysses' presumption as a failure of hope.[7] The only portion of this New Testament text that was conventionally interpreted as indicative of hope is the image of the farmer's patience in the epistle's final exhortation, which Dante had translated in his *Convivio*: "Behold the farmer who awaits the precious fruit of the earth, patiently holding out until it has received both the early and the late" (*Onde dice santo Iacopo apostolo nella sua Pistola*: "*Ecco lo agricola aspetta lo prezioso frutto de la terra pazientemente sostenendo infino che riceva lo temporaneo e lo*

---

5. *Inferno* 26.125.
6. James 3:2–7: "Si quis in verbo non offendit hic perfectus est vir. Potens etiam freno circumducere totum corpus. Si autem equorum frenos in ora mittimus ad consentiendum nobis et omne corpus illorum circumferimus. Ecce et naves, cum magnae sint, et a ventis validis minentur, circumferuntur a modico gubernaculo ubi impetus dirigentis voluerit. Ita et lingua modicum quidem membrum est, et magna exaltat. Ecce quantus ignis quam magnam silvam incendit. Et lingua ignis est, universitas iniquitatis. Lingua constituitur in membris nostris, quae maculat totum corpus, et inflammat rotam nativitatis nostrae inflammata a gehenna." See Alison Cornish, "The Epistle of James in *Inferno* 26," *Traditio* 45 (1989–1990): 367–379; Richard Bates and Thomas Rendall, "Dante's Ulysses and the Epistle of James," *Dante Studies* 107 (1989): 33–44; and Maria Corti, "On the Metaphors of Sailing, Flight, and Tongues of Fire in the Episode of Ulysses (Inferno 26)," *Stanford Italian Review* 9, nos. 1–2 (1990): 33–47.
7. *Paradiso* 25.76–77: "Tu mi stillasti, con lo stillar suo, / ne la pistola poi; sì ch'io son pieno."

serotino").[8] Hence Dante's *villano,* awaiting the fruit of his land in the summertime between the early (spring ploughing) and the late (fall harvest) labors, is surely a figure of hope analogous to James's *agricola.* This agrarian figure who introduces the all-important encounter with Ulysses, tragic alter-ego of the poet, exemplifies that virtue of certain expectation (*attender certo*), as Dante defines hope to Saint James in *Paradiso* 25, that the presumptuous Ulysses totally lacks.[9]

The two figures are also opposed in the very different ways they are depicted as viewing the stars. While the farmer's existence is regulated by the seasons of the year, determined by the movements of the sun—the summer heat, the autumn harvest, the spring ploughing—the Greek sailor, despite his intention to circle the globe in pursuit of the sun (*dietro al sol*), marks time by the lunar phases:

> Cinque volte racceso e tante casso
> lo lume era di sotto dalla luna
> poi ch'entrati eravam nell'alto passo. . . .
> (*Inferno* 26.130–132)

Moreover, Ulysses makes the fatal navigational mistake of abandoning his pole star by crossing over into the southern hemisphere from which it can no longer be seen:

> Tutte le stelle già dell'altro polo
> vedea la notte e il nostro tanto basso
> che non surgea fuor del marin suolo.
> (*Inferno* 26.127–129)

The symbolic tenor of Ulysses' lost polar star is articulated in the exchange between a ship's governor and a failed leader in book 8 of Lucan's *Pharsalia.* In his nocturnal flight from the scene of the lost battle, Pompey distractedly consults the boat's helmsman on the navigational use of the stars. The pilot explains: "We do not follow those sliding stars that course over the starry heaven and that, be-

---

8. *Convivio* 4.2.10. James 5:7: "Ecce agricola expectat pretiosum fructum terrae, patienter ferens donec accipiat temporivum et serotinum." In his discussion of the fruits of the Virgin's womb in *Sermones de B. V. M.* 3.3, in *Opera omnia,* vol. 9 (Quaracchi, 1882–1902), p. 670, of the *fructus spei,* Bonaventure writes: "'Debet in spe qui arat arare; et qui triturat, in spefructus percipiendi' [Cor 9.10] Ista autem spes non permittit hominem fatigari, secundum illud Iacobi ultimo: 'Ecce, agricola . . . '" [James 5.7]. See Cornish, "The Epistle," pp. 378–379.

9. For the definition of hope as the sure expectation of the glory to come, see *Paradiso* 25.67–68: "'Spene,' diss'io, 'è uno attender certo / de la gloria futura.'" Teodolinda Barolini has reconciled the debate over Ulysses' fate, which has fueled a vast bibliography, by suggesting that the Greek hero so closely represents the poet's own ambitions that he is damned "for Dante's sins." Barolini, "Dante's Ulysses: Narrative and Transgression," in *Dante: Contemporary Perspectives,* ed. Amilcare Iannucci (Toronto: University of Toronto Press, 1997), p. 132.

cause of their continual motion, deceive poor sailors: but rather that pole that never sets and never submerges itself in the waves, illumined by the two Bears, is the one that guides our prows."[1] The sailor's nighttime disquisition on the stars is clearly less about astronomy or navigation than about governance. Unlike the sure pilot following his single pole, Pompey is wavering and indecisive, hovering, as in Lucan's description of the sun on that same evening, between two hemispheres "neither entirely in the region from whom he was hiding his light, nor in one to which he was showing it."[2] Dante's farmer, by contrast, is troubled by no such uncertain celestial displays, as he enjoys the sun at its maximum, even at dusk, in the season when it least "hides its face."

Dante's relaxed agrarian spectator may also owe something to the three humble witnesses to Icarus' ill-advised flight across the sky described in Ovid's *Metamorphoses*: "Some fisher, perhaps, plying his quivering rod, some shepherd leaning on his staff, or a peasant bent over his plough handle caught sight of them as they flew past and took stock still in astonishment, believing that these creatures who could fly through the air must be gods."[3] Like Ovid's fisherman, shepherd, or farmer, Dante's *villano* is an implicit observer, from a safe distance, of Ulysses' tragic fate, which, like Icarus' mad flight, also ends in flames. Ovid's observers look up in amazed admiration at creatures that resemble gods, whereas what Dante compares to the farmer's fireflies surveyed way down in the valley are in fact damned souls who in life were very close to gods. Explicitly compared with the eager pilgrim (*sì com'io*), the farmer's posture of illumined patience in fact contrasts with Dante's precipitous desire to see Ulysses inside the flame, and serves instead as a warning to the poet as he writes (to restrain the impetus of his genius so that it will not run where virtue does not guide it), as well as to the inevitably curious reader as he reads.[4]

All three of Dante's farmers encountered in the region of fraud in some way constitute a critique of the classical world. Yet the choice of an agrarian figure to counter the strained vision of the diviners, the shortcomings of Virgil as pastor, and the insane flight of Ulysses to the other side of the world might well derive inspiration from Vir-

1. Lucan, *Pharsalia* 8.172–176: "Signifero quaecumque fluunt labentia caelo, / numquam stante polo miseros fallentia nautas, / sidera non sequimur; sed qui non mergitur undis / axis inocciduus gemina clarissimus arcto, / ille regit puppes."
2. Lucan, *Pharsalia* 8.159–161: "Iam pelago medios Titan demissus ad ignes / nec quibus abscondit nec si quibus exerit orbem / totus erat."
3. Ovid, *Metamorphoses* 8.217–220: "Hos aliquis tremula dum captat harundine pisces, / aut pastor baculo stivave innixus arator / vidit et obstipuit, quique aethera carpere possent, / credidit esse deos."
4. *Inferno* 26.21–22: "E più lo 'ngegno affreno ch'i' non soglio, / perché non corra che virtù nol guidi."

gil's own poem on agriculture, which explicitly defines the restful life of the farmer as ignorant of fraud (*at secura quies et nescia fall-ere vita*).[5] In the *Georgics*, commonly cited as an authority in such astronomical handbooks as Sacrobosco's *Sphere* and Macrobius' commentary on Cicero's *Dream of Scipio*, the farmer is exalted to the status of someone whose knowledge of natural phenomena gives him power over nature. The ostensibly humble subject of the poem thereby becomes cognate with the poet's own aspirations, as Philip Hardie has observed. When, at the end of the second book, the poet declares blessed those who have "been able to win knowledge of the causes of things" and asks the "sweet Muses" to show him "heaven's pathways, the stars, the sun's many lapses, the moon's many labours," this request for information about celestial movement can also be read as a prayer to know not just the path *of* heaven, but the path *to* it.[6] All quests for knowledge translate into journeys; and some, like Ulysses', fail.

Like the canto of Ulysses, the first book of Virgil's agricultural poem also leads from a peaceful portrait of rural life into a violently contrasting image of headlong, precipitous disaster. From a discussion of "sure signs" given by the sun and stars for farming and navigation, the poet shifts to a recollection of the terrible portents announcing disastrous political events in recent Roman history. At Caesar's assassination, witnesses observed an eclipse of the sun, barking dogs, howling wolves, ominous birds, eruptions of volcanoes, bloated rivers, horrifying entrails, freakish lightning, and comets. Virgil magnificently juxtaposes the peace of rural life with the rage of these past wars by imagining a future time "when in those lands, as the farmer toils at the soil with crooked plough, he shall find javelins eaten up with rusty mould, or with his heavy hoes shall strike on empty helms, and marvel at the giant bones in the up-turned graves."[7] An appeal for an end to bloodshed concludes the book, depicting contemporary strife as a chariot run wild, not unlike Dante's image of Phaeton (*quando Fetòn abbandonò li freni*) or, for that matter, of Ulysses (*de' remi facemmo ali al folle volo*): "Impious Mars rages over the entire globe, just as when chariots burst from

5. Virgil, *Georgics* 2.467.
6. Virgil, *Georgics* 2.475–478, 575–579: "Me vero primum dulces ante omnia Musae, / quarum sacra fero ingenti percussus amore, / accipiant caelique vias et sidera monstrent, / defectus solis varios lunaeque labores;" lines 481–82 are repeated in *Aeneid* 1.745. Philip Hardie, *Virgil's "Aeneid": Cosmos and Imperium* (Oxford: Clarendon Press, 1986), p. 37: "On the surface this is an appeal for the communication of information on matters astronomical, but, given the underlying tendency in this whole passage to identify the landscape of the poet with that of his subject-matter, it is easy to read this as a request for directions on literal 'paths to the sky' (rather than 'the paths of heavenly bodies')."
7. Virgil, *Georgics* 1.493–497: "Scilicet et tempus veniet, cum finibus illis / agricola incurvo terram molitus aratro / exesa inveniet scabra robigine pila, / aut gravibus rastris galeas pulsabit inanis, / grandiaque effossis mirabitur ossa sepulcris."

the starting gates. They pick up speed and, uselessly holding the reins, the driver is carried along by his horses; the chariot does not respond to his commands."[8]

In Dante's *Inferno* astronomical knowledge is presented under the humblest possible aspect, exalting the farmer as a fruitful reader of the stars, of which Hell's damned have totally lost sight. A correct understanding of nature's signs, most vividly legible in the pattern of the heavens, was for Dante, as for Virgil, a powerful symbol of poetic aims. Virgil in his *Georgics* exhorts the Muses to give him the kind of knowledge of nature possessed by happy husbandmen, ignorant of their blessings but far from the clash of arms, bearing the last trace of Justice since she altogether left the earth.[9] But it is only as Dante's guide that he emerges temporarily from his permanent prison to see the stars again. In the *Inferno,* Dante's peasants, tied to the land but with a view of the heavens, provide a counterpoint to those whose excessive curiosity leads them to interrogate the stars and navigate uncharted seas, rather than to wait and hope. Ironically enough, the poet whose praise of rural life would have been a fundamental model for Dante's agrarian figures, is himself cut off from the celestial panorama and, from a Christian point of view, from the farmer's essential virtue: hope. The journey to the stars narrated in the *Commedia* is accomplished not by straining toward them, but by descending in the opposite direction, into the very earth.

PETER S. HAWKINS

Descendit ad Inferos[†]

Dante's *Inferno* seems at first glance to be largely a construct of classical poetry and Italian politics, a realm that lacks the *Commedia*'s overall rich allusiveness to Scripture. Not only are scriptural

---

8. Virgil, *Georgics* 1.511–513: "Saevit toto Mars impius orbe: / ut cum carceribus sese effudere quadrigae, / addunt in spatia, et frustra retinacula tendens / fertur equis auriga neque audit currus habenas." English translation from Gary B. Miles, *Virgil's "Georgics": A New Interpretation* (Berkeley: University of California Press, 1988), p. 108. On this passage in the *Georgics,* see Putnam, *Virgil's Poem of the Earth,* p. 79. See also David O. Ross, *Virgil's Elements: Physics and Poetry in the "Georgics"* (Princeton: Princeton University Press, 1987); and Giuseppe Mazzotta, *Worlds of Petrarch* (Durham, N.C.: Duke University Press, 1993), p. 276. Dante's depiction of Phaeton abandoning the reins is in *Inferno* 17.107.
9. Virgil, *Georgics* 2.458–460: "O fortunatos nimium, sua si bona norint, / agricolas! quibus ipsa, procul discordibus armis, / fundit humo facilem victum iustissima tellus"; 2.473–475: "Extrema per illos / Iustitia excedens terris vestigia fecit."
† From *Dante's Testaments: Essays in Scriptural Imagination.* Copyright © 1999 by the Board of Trustees of the Leland Stanford Jr. University. Reprinted by permission of Stanford University Press.

references comparatively scant, but the poet introduces no biblical paradigm such as we find at the outset of the other canticles—the Exodus in *Purgatorio* (2.46), the rapture of Paul to the third heaven in *Paradiso* (1.73–75). Instead, the *Inferno* is pervaded by Virgil's *Aeneid,* a poem Dante knows by heart, "tutta quanta" (*Inf.* 20.114), and that he identifies in his opening canto as the object of long study and great love. In particular, Aeneas's descent to the under-world serves as a model, not only for Dante Pilgrim—who, like "di Silvïo il parente, / corruttibile ancora, ad immortale / secolo andò, e fu sensibilmente" ("the father of Silvius went, while still mortal, to the immortal world, and was there in his bodily senses," *Inf.* 2.13–15)— but also for Dante the poet, who carefully traces the path of Virgil's deep and savage way in his own vernacular.

Yet it is also true that Dante's descent "to the immortal world" is inscribed within another journey to Hades: the descent of Christ into hell, his three-day sojourn among the dead, and his "harrowing" of all those who in ages past had longed for his coming. Virgil specif-ically refers to this event on several occasions in the first canticle: *Inferno* 4.52–63, 8.124–26, and 12.37–45. But it is recalled more indirectly whenever our attention is drawn to the ruined state of hell's "infrastructure," to its unhinged doorways, crumbled walls, and fallen bridges. Nor is it only the silent witness of architecture that brings Christ's descent to mind. For even in the year 1300, the demons are still haunted by the memory of a divine breaking and entering that took place centuries earlier. "Yesterday," recalls a devil in the Malebolgia, "più oltre cinqu' ore che quest' otta, / mille dugento con sessanta sei / anni compié che qui la via fu rotta" ("five hours later than now, completed one thousand two hundred sixty-six years since the road was broken here," 21.112–14). From clues like this one, delivered offhand but nonetheless lodged deep within in-fernal memory, we realize that Dante's own descent into hell extends from Good Friday afternoon to just before the dawn of Easter. Thus, he follows the underworld footsteps of Christ as well as Aeneas.

The trauma that *Inferno*'s demons cannot forget is the same event that the church began to confess around the mid–fourth century. Less than 100 years later, the clause "descendit ad inferos" was en-tered into the final version of the Apostles' Creed.[1] Yet, unlike the other articles of faith that pertain to the life of Christ ("he was con-ceived by the Holy Spirit, born of the Virgin Mary, suffered under Pontius Pilate, was crucified, died, and was buried"), the descent to hell lacks a narrative warrant in the Gospels, or any developed expo-sition elsewhere in the canon. Indeed, it is probably more accurate

---

1. For the history of the clause *descendit ad inferos*, see Kelly, pp. 378–83; also Schaff, *Creeds of Christendom,* 2: 46.

to speak of it as "scriptural" than as Scripture. Although hinted at by a number of New Testament texts, the harrowing itself is a theological fiction—a composite story constructed out of roughly twenty passages scattered throughout the Old Testament as well as the New.[2]

The Bible, therefore, provided the necessary elements for a narrative that it actually never told. It offered a cry in the darkness, a shattering of brass and iron, a triumphant Lord who freed those who were imprisoned in the shadow of death—but no harrowing. What the canon did not say outright, however, was supplied by a number of apocryphal texts.[3] The most important of these is undoubtedly the Gospel of Nicodemus, dating in Greek from the second century and then in Latin translation from the end of the fifth.[4] Because of the appeal of its vivid narrative, subsequently made available in

2. Christ's statement in Matt. 12:40, for instance, was taken as a prophecy of his own stay in the underworld: "For as [Jonah] was in the whale's belly three days and three nights so shall the Son of Man be in the heart of the earth three days and three nights." Other New Testament texts fill in the picture more or less directly. St. Paul writes in Rom. 14:9 that Christ died "that he might be Lord both of the dead and of the living"; there is also the passage in Eph. 4:8–10 where the apostle argues that, if the savior ascended to heaven, it is "because he also descended first into the lower parts of the earth" (v. 9). What Christ accomplished during his sojourn in those lower depths was suggested by some cryptic verses in the First Epistle of Peter: "he preached to those spirits that were in prison . . . [and] for this cause was the gospel also preached to the dead: that they might be judged indeed according to men, in the flesh; but may live according to God, in the Spirit" (3:19, 4:6). Elsewhere, in Acts 2:24–31, Peter proclaims that God raised Jesus from the grave, "having loosed the sorrows of hell, as it was impossible that he should be holden by it" (v. 24). His proof text here (quoted at v. 27) is David's "prophecy" of Christ in Ps. 15 (16):10: "Because thou wilt not leave my soul in hell; nor wilt thou give thy holy one to see corruption" (a text quoted in Acts 2:27). Even more explicit in its "foretelling" is Ps. 106 (107): 13–16: "Then they cried to the Lord in their affliction: and he delivered them out of their distresses. And he brought them out of darkness and the shadow of death; and he broke their bonds in sunder. Let the mercies of the Lord give glory to him, and his wonderful works to the children of men. Because he hath broken gates of brass, and burst iron bars."

  The roughly twenty biblical "sources" for the story of the descent are given by MacCulloch, pp. 45–66. See also Miller, pp. 25–55, esp. pp. 27–29; Chaine, esp. cols. 410–20; J. D. Quinn, "Descent of Christ into Hell," in NCE, 4: 788–89. Miller, pp. 31–34, describes the Reformation's "demythologizing" of the descent, when it was taken variously as a harmless element of folk religion (by Luther), as a way simply of affirming that Christ had truly died (by Zwingli), and as a "fable" (by Calvin). According to Reformed Christianity's Heidelberg Catechism, the descent served as a metaphor for Christ's "unspeakable distress, agony, and horror, which He suffered in His soul, and previously."

3. The earliest of these accounts is probably the Odes of Solomon, dating from the end of the first century. Miller lists other sources: "the Gospel of Peter, the Epistles of the Apostles, the Ascent of Isaiah, the Testament of the Twelve Patriarchs, the Sibylline Graces, the Acts of Thaddeus, and the Acts of Thomas, not to mention the later Anaphora of Pilate and Questions of Saint Bartholomew . . . [and] the Gospel of Nicodemus" (p. 26). For a fuller account of these apocryphal sources, see MacCulloch, pp. 131–73, and Chaine, cols. 395–410.

4. For the various versions of the descent narrative in the Gospel of Nicodemus (Greek, Latin A, Latin B), see Apocryphal NT, pp. 185–204. Unless otherwise noted, I will be citing the earliest (Greek) version of the text. For background on the Gospel of Nicodemus, in addition to the introduction offered by Apocryphal NT, pp. 164–69, see Barnstone, pp. 359–61; and Monnier, pp. 91–107.

many different vernacular versions, this "apocryphon" was soon ab-
sorbed into the church's biblical imagination. If never formally a
canonical Scripture, its account of the harrowing virtually became
gospel. And for good reason: it "discovered" for the faithful what was
otherwise a missing moment in the sequence of Holy Week events
stretching between the Passion and the Resurrection. It told a story
that needed to be told.[5]

This extraordinarily theatrical narrative eventually became drama,
first in the form of the quasi-liturgical *lauda* or *devozione* of Dante's
day and then as an episode in the cycles of the more secular mystery
plays.[6] But sacred theater was not the only means by which the de-
scent of Christ was publicized in medieval culture. Visual representa-
tions of the harrowing abounded—in sculpture, carving, manuscript

5. In the Gospel of Nicodemus the harrowing is recounted by two brothers, sons of the
priest Simeon (Luke 2:22–35), who together with their father were among those im-
prisoned in Hades "with all who have died since the beginning of the world" (in *Apoc-
ryphal NT*, p. 186). The tale they tell, therefore, is the account of their own rescue
from death, firsthand testimony of events that took place after the crucifixion, when,
according to the Gospel of Matthew, "the earth quaked, and the rocks were rent. And
the graves were opened: and many bodies of the saints that had slept arose" (Matt.
27:51–52). In the apocryphon the brothers recall that at "the hour of midnight there
rose upon the darkness there something like the light of the sun, and it shone and lit
us all, and we saw one another" (in *Apocryphal NT*, p. 186). One by one these Old Tes-
tament figures interpret this light by reference to the foretelling in Hebrew Scripture.
Thus Abraham rejoices to see the fulfillment of the promise long ago made to him in
Gen. 12:3, while David and Isaiah are filled with joy to have confirmation of what they
"foresaw by the Holy Spirit." Suddenly a voice like thunder proclaims the words of Ps.
23 [24]:7, "Lift up your heads, O ye princes, and be lifted up, O eternal gates, and the
King of Glory shall enter in." This prospect throws the forces of darkness into panic:
Hades and Satan bicker between themselves, and a swarm of demons rushes to secure
the massive doors of their city. But the gates of hell cannot prevail against the divine in-
truder: "the gates of brass were broken in pieces and the bars of iron were crushed and
all the dead who were bound were loosed from their chains, and we with them. And the
King of Glory entered as a man, and all the dark places of Hades were illuminated" (p.
188). After his spectacular entrance, Christ banishes Satan to hell's lowest region.
Then, starting with the very first human being, he delivers the saints of the Old Testa-
ment to their reward: "the King of Glory stretched out his right hand, and took hold of
our forefather Adam and raised him up. Then he turned to the rest and said, 'Come
with me, all you who have died through the tree which this man touched. For behold, I
raise you all up again through the tree of the cross'" (p. 189). All whom Christ delivered
are raised up with him on the third day. Once baptized in the river Jordan, they are
given white robes and "carried up in the clouds." When the two brothers finish writing
their transcript for Caiaphas, Annas, and the other astonished leaders of the temple,
they too are "seen no more."
6. Monnier, p. 96, speaks of the Gospel of Nicodemus as "a veritable Mystery Play *avant la
lettre*, depicting what will later become the way of representing the Resurrection in the
Mystery Plays. It divides itself into perfectly resolved scenes. The characters appear with
their characteristic traits, their tirades, their replies. The literature of different Christian
peoples will adopt this scenario without changing anything essential." For the motif of the
harrowing in medieval Latin liturgical drama, see Young, pp. 149–77; in secular drama,
see Kolve, pp. 192–97. On the development of Italian theater, see D'Ancona; De
Bartholomaeis. Iannucci, "Limbo," esp. pp. 84–89, draws attention to a particular *de-
vozione*, "Hec Laus Sabbati Sancti," dating from Dante's time, which was based on the
Gospel of Nicodemus, and incorporated into their Holy Saturday liturgy by lay companies of
Disciplinati. His citation of this work comes from V. De Bartholomaeis, *Laude drammatiche
e rappresentazioni sacre* (Florence, 1943), 1: 243–58. See also Monnier, pp. 211–45.

illumination, mosaic, and painting.[7] Despite some variation in composition and detail, the core iconography of the harrowing reproduces essentially the same picture. For instance, in the twelfth-century mosaic on the west vault of Venice's San Marco, a monumental figure of Christ commands the scene, holding the cross of his victory high above the wreckage of shattered hardware and sprung locks. Underfoot are the ruined gates of hell and the vanquished figure of Satan, who is shown splayed against the background darkness of a cavern or tomb. What primarily captures the viewer's attention, however, is the gesture on which the whole composition is centered. With a dramatic twist of his body, Christ grabs hold of Adam with a hand that still shows the imprint of his crucifixion, and pulls him up out of the grave and into his own glory. In vain, Satan clutches at Adam's foot, helpless against the redeemer in this tug-of-war. Eve and the other surrounding figures, who are in no way threatened by Satan's grasp, raise their hands toward Christ in what Otto Demus has called a "massed personification of entreaty."[8] Like Adam, they are hopeful that the redeemer will take them up.

By means of this single image, Christian iconographers were able to represent the theological complexity of Christ's redemption. Death and resurrection, defeat and victory, the intimate relationship of the New Adam to the Old, the incorporation of Israel into the New Dispensation, and the believer's own hope for deliverance—all these themes were brought together in a portrait of the savior doing the triumphant work of redemption.

What Dante made of the *descensus Christi* can best be seen against the background of theological traditions he was both working within and, in some instances, departing from. I say "traditions" because despite the fact that the medieval church accepted the harrowing as gospel—"Who, therefore, except an infidel, will deny that Christ was in hell?"[9]—there were different ways to understand what the event signified.[1] Both Clement of Alexandria and Origen, for instance, took the mysterious words in 1 Peter about Christ's preaching "to those spirits that were in prison" (4:1) to mean that the redeemer

---

7. Brief considerations of the iconographic tradition are offered by Monnier, pp. 193–209; H. Quillet, "Descente de Jésus aux enfers," cols. 610–11; and P. Verdier, in *NCE*, 4: 789–93. For a book-length study of the motif, albeit one limited to the Byzantine tradition, see Kartsonis, esp. pp. 227–36.

8. Demus, p. 72.

9. Augustine, letter no. 164, "To my lord Evodius," in *SL*, 1st ser., 1: 516, trans. J. G. Cunningham.

1. In addition to Quillet, "Descente de Jésus aux enfers," cols. 597–605, see Monnier, pp. 69–192; and Kelly, pp. 378–83; also, app. 5, "Descent into Hell," in vol. 54 of the Blackfriars *ST* (*Summa Theologiae*) R. Turner provides an excellent discussion of Dante's "position" within this tradition.

descended to hell in order to evangelize all of the dead—the Jews first, certainly, but also the Gentiles. As a result, the harrowing entirely emptied hell of human souls. Augustine, on the other hand, held that the purpose of Christ's descent was neither to preach to the dead nor to give anyone a second chance for belief, but rather to conquer Satan and deprive him of his captives. Although Augustine thought it presumptuous to define precisely who these souls were, on the whole he did not hesitate to say. The redeemed were the faithful of Israel, who did not worship idols or give themselves over to "the empty pride of human praise and glory," or neglect to hope in a redeemer.[2] Therefore, redemption was only for the descendants of Abraham, who, as the Epistle to the Hebrews puts it, "died according to faith, not having received the promises, but beholding them afar off, and saluting them, and confessing that they are pilgrims and strangers on the earth" (11:13).

Yet Augustine understood the appeal of a more universal deliverance that might take into account the fact of pagan genius as well as pagan virtue:

> Especially will men rejoice for the sake of some who are intimately known to us by their literary labours, whose eloquence and talent we admire—not only the poets and orators who in many parts of their writings have held up to contempt and ridicule these same false gods of the nations, and have even occasionally confessed the one true God . . . but also those who have uttered the same, not in poetry or rhetoric, but as philosophers.[3]

Still, even if it made compelling emotional sense to imagine such Gentiles among those whom Christ redeemed from hell, Augustine could not condone such wishful thinking. For here "the verdict of human feeling [is] different from that of the justice of God." To follow human feeling, in this case, would lead to heresy.[4]

Although Augustine's position in these matters by and large became the orthodoxy of the Western church, the descent of Christ to the dead remained subject to discussion throughout the Middle Ages.[5] Thomas Aquinas sorts through the entire tradition with his characteristic rigor in *Summa Theologiae* III, 52, 1–8, and offers a theological compendium against which we can judge both the ortho-

---

2. Augustine, letter to Evodius (no. 164), in SL (*A Select Library of the Nicene and Post-Nicene Fathers of the Christian* Church), 1st ser., 1: 516, trans. J. G. Cunningham.

3. Ibid.

4. Augustine, *De Haeresibus*, para. 79, p. 115: "Another heresy believes that upon Christ's descent into hell the unbelievers believed and all were liberated from hell [incredulos et omnes exinde existimat liberatos]." See also Kelly, p. 381.

5. In addition to R. Turner, see S. Harrent, in *DTC*, vol. 7, pt. 2, cols. 1748–49.

doxy and the novelty of Dante's presentation in the *Commedia*.[6]
Aquinas begins by rehearsing the many reasons why Christ visited
hell after his death: to deliver the faithful of Israel from the conse-
quences of original sin, to overthrow Satan, to rescue the ancient He-
brews, and to demonstrate within the underworld the power he had
previously shown on earth. He then goes on to distinguish between
one kind of hell and another. In upper hell—variously spoken of as
the "Limbo of the Fathers" and "Abraham's bosom"[7]—he places those
whom the redeemer came to save: those who believed in the coming
of a future savior, and who were faithful in their observation of Is-
rael's law and "sacraments." Since he understands the religion of the
Old Testament to be Christianity in the making, Aquinas character-
izes the patriarchs and prophets as souls who in some profound sense
were already believers in Christ: they were "joined to Christ's passion
in faith vivified by love, which takes away sin" (III, 52, 6, resp.).

In contrast to this group, other souls were gathered in an adjacent
but lower hell. Christ's descent meant nothing to them, except a re-
newed sense of their eternal desolation. For the redeemer de-
scended to these dead (and here Aquinas quotes John Damascene)
"not that he might convert the unbelieving or make believers out of
them, but in order to put their incredulity to shame" (III, 52, 2 resp.
ad 3). But who were these unbelievers? Aquinas distinguishes two
sorts who lived before the age of grace. There are those who had no
faith in Christ's passion; and those who, if they had faith, "had no
likeness in charity to the suffering Christ" (3, 52, 6 resp.). In the
first case, he seems to be referring to pagans who lived completely
outside the world of the Old Testament law and prophets; in the
other, to Jews who refused the faith of their ancestors and in so do-
ing rejected the love of Christ. Therefore, while Jews might have
been in one hell or the other, it would not have been so for the Gen-
tiles. Their fate was to remain forever in the hell of the lost, with "no
deliverance from the guilt of hell's punishment" (3, 52, 6 resp.).

Although in this treatment in the *Summa Theologiae* Aquinas in-
sists on a stark contrast between the saved of Israel and the Gentile
lost, elsewhere in his writings the status of the pagans appears in a
more ambiguous and hopeful light. In one of his *Quaestiones dispu-
tatae*, the *De veritate*, for instance, he asks whether it is necessary to
believe explicitly in Christ in order to be saved (quest. 14, art. 11).

---

6. *Summa Theologiae*, vol. 54, app. 5, pp. 214–15, provides a succinct summary of
Thomas's various considerations of the descent. A brief version of his theology is found in
a sermon he preached on the Apostles Creed during Lent 1273, close to the end of his
life; it is found in Thomas Aquinas, *Sermon Conferences*, pp. 78–85.

7. Aquinas discusses the Bosom of Abraham in STIII, 52, 2, resp. ad 4, and distinguishes
between the *limbus patrum* and the *limbus puerorum* in STIII, supp., 69, 5–6. See also
Fausto Montanari, "Limbo," in *ED*, 3: 651–54; P. J. Hill, "Limbo," in *NCE*, 8: 762–65;
and, perhaps most useful of all, Foster, *Two Dantes*, pp. 169–74.

Although his answer turns out to be a qualified Yes, among the first "difficulties" he contends with is Dionysius's assertion that "many Gentiles were saved before the coming of Christ." Aquinas does not dispute the reliability of Dionysius on this point, but he worries about the implications. Is the explicit belief in the redeemer, made possible for Israel by the law and the prophets, not necessary for those who lived in another religious world altogether?

To answer this question, Aquinas distinguishes between different kinds of people—between leaders and common folk—and then identifies specific kinds of belief required of each group in successive historical ages. From the time of the Fall until the coming of Christ, the period at stake for those in hell at the time of the descent, it was necessary for the "leaders" of Israel to have explicit faith in the redeemer. Ordinary Israelites, however, needed to believe only implicitly: they could trust either in the faith of their spiritual leaders or in divine providence. But what about Gentiles before the coming of Christ, who for all their worldly wisdom had no "teachers of divine faith"—neither a law to interpret nor prophets to heed? His solution to this ancient dilemma was to regard all pagans, no matter how spiritually eminent they may have been, as "ordinary people." Therefore, at least until the advent of the age of grace, it was enough for the Gentiles to have only implicit trust in a redeemer that was simply a part of their belief in divine providence. Furthermore, he says, "it is likely that the mystery of our redemption was revealed to many Gentiles before Christ's coming, as is clear from the Sibylline prophecies" (14, 11, resp. ad 5).[8]

Many Gentiles? Aquinas does not name names, nor does he anywhere actually state that the "evacuees" from the Limbo of the Fathers included anyone other than Old Testament figures. Nonetheless, he leaves a door open to mystery, grants the possibility that among those distinguished ancients whom Augustine could not accept as the elect—not only the virtuous but those who are "intimately known to us by their literary labours, whose talents and eloquence we admire"— there might also have been some whom Christ rescued from hell.

The Aquinas of *De veritate* was not alone in this largesse, despite the degree to which Augustine's negative verdict on the matter pre-

8. For a similar discussion of these issues, see STII-II, 2, 7 resp.: "Revelation about Christ was in fact given to many of the pagans, as is clear from their own prophecies. In Job we read, 'I know that my redeemer liveth'; and, as Augustine says, the Sibyl foretold certain truths about Christ. Moreover, it is recorded in the history of the Romans that, in the reign of Constantine Augustus and his mother Irene, a tomb was discovered in which there lay a man with a gold medallion on his chest, inscribed thus, Christ will be born of a virgin and I believe in him. 'O sun, you shall see me again in the reign of Irene and Constantine.' However, had any been saved who had received no revelation, they were not saved without faith in the mediator. The reason: even if they did not have an explicit faith in Christ, they did have an implicit faith in God's providence, believing that God is man's deliverer in ways of his own choosing, as the Spirit would reveal this to those who know the truth, according to the text of Job, 'Who teaches us more than the beasts of the earth.'"

dominated in the Western church. There were positive statements about the "faithfulness" of some pagans in Gregory the Great, Albertus Magnus, Bonaventure, and the early-fourteenth-century Florentine preacher Giordano da Pisa.[9] Peter Abelard went so far as to argue that in their exercise of reason, the great pagan philosophers had some foreknowledge of the Christian God. He maintained there was evidence of the Trinity, for example, in the writings of Plato, Cicero, and Macrobius, as well as in the oracles of the Sibyl.[1] Even Augustine, who otherwise took a hard line in such matters, was confident that at least the Sibyl was to be counted a member incorporate in the City of God. He also entertained the possibility that Plato was acquainted with the Bible, not only because of a concord between some of the philosopher's statements and those of Moses, but because it "seemed likely" that when Plato made his journey to Egypt he listened personally to the prophet Jeremiah (*City of God* 8.11).

Of all the Gentile candidates for sanctity, however, the foremost was Virgil, whose oracular Fourth Eclogue alone guaranteed him a stature comparable to that of the prophets of Israel:

> Ultima Cumaei venit iam carminis aetas;
> magnus ab integro saeclorum nascitur ordo.
> iam redit et Virgo, redeunt Saturnia regna;
> iam nova progenies caelo demittitur alto.
>
> (*Eclogue* IV, vv. 4–7)

(Now is come the last age of the song of Cumae; the great line of the centuries begins anew. Now the Virgin returns, the reign of Saturn returns; now a new generation descends from heaven on high.)

According to Eusebius, Constantine first gave these lines the theological interpretation that shortly became commonplace: the virgin who returns is Mary; the child sent from the sky, Jesus.[2] The emperor held that Virgil had full knowledge of all these allegorical meanings, but given the pagan world he lived in chose to express himself only covertly. Most, however, believed that the poet spoke beyond his own understanding—spoke true words, but in ignorance of their meaning. This is the position Dante assumes in *Purgatorio* 21–22, where Statius describes how he was in part saved by the truth of the gospel as it "sounded" in the Eclogue's mysterious open-

---

9. In addition to R. Turner's review of these various positions, esp. pp. 173–91, see the overview offered by Padoan in his excellent 1969 essay, "Il limbo Dantesco," in his *Il pio Eneo*, pp. 103–24, esp. pp. 108–10. Also see Durling's note 16, "Christ in Hell," in his edition of *Divine Comedy*, pp. 580–83.

1. Peter Abelard, *Theologia Christiana* 1.5, and *Patrologia Latina*, vol. 178, cols. 1140–66. For a good summary of Abelard's thought and its influence on later theologians (including Vivès and Zwingli), see Harrent, cols. 1748–52.

2. Comparetti, pp. 96–118, esp. pp. 99–103.

ing lines. Yet as the larger context of the *Commedia* proclaims, this consonance between Virgil and the New Testament could only be recognized by one who had already encountered the Christian message. The author of the Eclogue, on the other hand, was himself deaf to the good news hidden in his own text. Therefore Statius likens him to someone who carries a lantern in the darkness, but who holds it behind him, to show the way to those who come after: "che porta il lume dietro e sé non giova" (*Purg.* 22.68). Virgil's words were a lamp to other feet, a light to someone else's path. But to himself, they were as fugitive and obscure as messages spelled from the Sibyl's leaves: "horrendas canit ambages antroque remugit, / obscuris vera involens" ("dread enigmas and echoes from the cavern, wrapping truth in darkness," *Aeneid* 6.99–100).[3]

Dante's decision in the *Commedia* to put Virgil in upper hell, in Limbo, placed him at odds with all the theologians of his day. For everyone else, this shadowy realm of the afterlife—at least since the harrowing of hell—was the exclusive abode of souls innocent of every sin except the original one, that is, of infants who had died without baptism.[4] According to Aquinas, these newborn souls dwelled forever in a kind of oblivion, unaware of their loss of the beatific vision; according to Bonaventure, they lived in a state neither sad nor happy, yet were dimly aware of the bliss they were denied.[5] Apart from these subtle distinctions, however, there was common agreement on an essential point: after Christ's descent to hell,

---

3. Dante alludes to this passage in *Par.* 17.31–33, where he contrasts Cacciaguida's "chiare parole e . . . preciso latin" ("clear words and . . . precise discourse," v. 34) with the Sibyl's baffling message: "per ambage, in che la gente folle / già s'inviscava pria che fosse anciso / l'Agnel di Dio che le peccata tolle" ("dark sayings, such as those in which the foolish folk of old once ensnared themselves before the Lamb of God who takes away sins was slain"). See Schnapp's discussion of these lines, *Transfiguration of History*, pp. 140–41. Also, for a larger treatment of Virgil and the Sibyl, see Hollander, *Il Virgilio Dantesco*, esp. pp. 138, 145–51; and Allevi.

4. Padoan, *Il pio Enea*, p. 105, argues that Dante opposed himself "drastically to the entire theological tradition of his time (as well as those coming afterward) by saying that in Limbo there are to be found not only children who died at a most tender age but also adults. The innovation is enormous, indeed extraordinary." A similar assessment is made by Paparelli (pp. 147–48) with regard to Dante's particular departure from Aquinas. The predicament of the unbaptized is treated indirectly in *Par.* 32.49–84, where St. Bernard details the different ways an infant could be saved, depending on the historical era in which he or she lived: "In the early ages, their parents' faith alone, with their own innocence, sufficed for their salvation. After those first ages were complete [i.e., after the covenant with Abraham], it was needful for males, through circumcision, to acquire power for their innocent wings; but after the time of grace had come, without perfect baptism inChrist such innocence was held there below [i.e., in Limbo]" (vv. 76–84). For a discussion of the theological traditions behind this doctrine of the three ages, as well as Dante's singular position on the unequal distribution of grace among unbaptized infants, see Botterill, both "Doctrine, Doubt, and Certainty" and *Dante and the Mystical Tradition*, pp. 96–101.

5. In his extensive commentary on *Inferno* 4, Manzoni contrasts the positions of Aquinas and Bonaventure, and establishes Dante's particular reliance on Bonaventure with regard to the Limbo dwellers' melancholy awareness of living "in hope without desire" (pp. 85–93)—what Paparelli refers to as Limbo's "atmosfera tutta virgiliana" (p. 148).

Limbo was the exclusive realm of infantile ignorance and innocence.

It should come as a surprise, therefore, that in *Inferno* 4 Dante shows no particular interest in these unbaptized babies. Rather, he draws our attention to one of the most extraordinary inventions of his poem: a population of mature, sophisticated pagan worthies who lived their lives before the coming of Christianity and therefore "non adorar debitamente a Dio" ("did not worship God aright," *Inf*. 4.38).[6] Virgil freely acknowledges the defect of faith, both in himself and in his companions. Because none of them ever crossed through the waters of baptism, the unique "porta de la fede" ("the portal of the faith," v. 36), they are all barred from salvation. But aside from this lack of faith, Virgil admits no other moral defect:

> Per tai difetti, non per altro rio,
> semo perduti, e sol di tanto offesi
> che sanza speme vivemo in disio.
> (*Inf*. 4.40–42)[7]

(Because of these shortcomings, and for no other fault, we are lost, and only so far afflicted that without hope we live in longing.)

In all of this, Dante presents his contemporary readers with one theological impossibility after another—not only a Limbo thronged with illustrious adults, but also the notion that such adults might be stained only by original sin and not by any other *peccatum*.[8] These the-

---

6. In addition to the many pre-Christian figures in Limbo, Dante includes three Moslems who were themselves "medievals": Avicenna (d. 1037), Averroes (d. 1198), and the Saladin (d. 1193). The first two are there, no doubt, because of their work on Aristotle; the last, because of his reputation for magnanimity.

7. Foster, *Two Dantes*, pp. 174–253, offers the most sustained theological sorting out of "Virgil and the Limbo-Dwellers" in light of the varied expositions given in the first two canticles, i.e., in *Inf*. 1.124–26 and 4.33–42; and in *Purg*. 3.34–45, 7.7–8, and 7.25–36. See also Hollander, *Il Virgilio Dantesco*, pp. 125–28; and Iannucci, "Limbo," pp. 74–81. Both Foster (*Two Dantes*, pp. 250–53) and Hollander (pp. 126–27) grapple with Virgil's confession that he was "ribellante" against God's law (*Inf*. 1.125), which stands in striking contrast to his other protestations of innocence. According to Iannucci, "In Limbo Dante is not so much interested in the idea that God endows man with a free will potentially capable of securing salvation, an idea expressed by Aquinas and upheld by Dante in the rest of the *Commedia*, as in the mystery of elective grace and predestination" (p. 81).

8. Aquinas, for example, could not be more clear on this matter in *De veritate*: "It is not possible for an adult without grace to be only in original sin, because as soon as he has attained the use of free choice, if he has prepared himself for grace, he will have grace; otherwise his very negligence will be imputed to him as a mortal sin" (*Truth* 24, 12, ad 2). Likewise, in 28, 3, ad 4: "The opinion that an adult may have original sin without any actual sin is held by some [e.g., Albertus Magnus] to be an impossible position. For when he begins to be an adult, if he does what he can, there will be given to him the grace by which he will be free of original sin; but if he does not do what he can, he will be guilty of a sin of omission. Since everyone is obliged to avoid sin and he cannot do this without setting his aim upon the due end, as soon as anyone is in the possession of his faculties he is obliged to turn to God and make Him his end. By so doing he is disposed for grace. Furthermore, Augustine says that the concupiscence deriving from original sin makes infants disposed to experience concupiscence, and adults actually to do so; for it is unlikely that one who is infected with original sin will not submit to the concupiscence of sin by a consent to a sin."

ological anomalies were noted by contemporary readers of the *Commedia* and came up whenever the poet's orthodoxy was discussed.[9]

In *Inferno* 4, Dante does not shrink from the surprise element of his theological invention; in fact, he underscores it by having his own namesake within the poem be astonished at what he finds in Limbo—so many "gente di molto valore" ("people of great worth," v. 44) in a place where only unbaptized infants were supposed to be. Therefore, he presses Virgil about Christ's descent to hell: why were some of the dead taken up and others left behind? And might there be any currently dwelling in Limbo who one day would come to know salvation? He asks, "uscicci mai alcuno, o per suo merto / o per altrui, che poi fosse beato?" ("did ever anyone go forth from here, either by his own or another's merit, who afterwards was blessed?" vv. 49–50). By way of response, Virgil offers his personal memory of the *descensus Christi*:

> rispuose: "Io era nuovo in questo stato,
> quando ci vidi venire un possente,
> con segno di vittoria coronato.
> Trasseci l'ombra del primo parente,
> d'Abèl suo figlio e quella di Noè,
> di Moïsè legista e ubidente;
> Abraàm patrïarca e Davìd re,
> Israèl con lo padre e co' suoi nati
> e con Rachele, per cui tanto fé,
> e altri molti, e feceli beati.
> E vo' che sappi che, dinanzi ad essi,
> spiriti umani non eran salvati."
> *(Inf.* 4.52–63)

([he] replied: "I was new in this condition when I saw a Mighty One come here, crowned with a sign of victory. He took hence the shade of our first parent, Abel his son, and Noah, and Moses, obedient giver of laws, Abraham the patriarch and David the king, Israel with his father and his children and with Rachel, for whom he did so much, and many others; and He made them blessed. And I would have you know that before these no human souls were saved.")

Given all that might have been said, Virgil's answer here is oddly disappointing. He gives only the fully expected Old Testament names, divulges a piece of information that Dante would already have

---

9. Padoan argues (*Il pio Enea*, pp. 113–15) that the poet's contemporaries were outraged by his "shattering" ("rottura") of theological tradition in *Inf.* 4: "tradizione qui non è infranta: è volutamente ignorata, distrutta, annullata" ("here tradition is not broken: it is willfully ignored, destroyed, annulled") (p. 113). He goes on to cite the fulminations of St. Antonino, bishop of Florence in the late fourteenth century, who dismissed the entirety of Dante's vision as "nothing but poetry" (p. 114). See also Mésoniat, pp. 81–83.

known—namely, that before the harrowing "no human souls were saved"—and sidesteps the vexed issue of whether any virtuous Gentiles were also taken up into glory.[1] Nor does he describe any of the harrowing's most dramatic moments, so richly savored in the Gospel of Nicodemus and subsequent theatrical representations: the shattering of the gates of hell, the demons' confusion, the wild joy of the patriarchs at their release. Instead, Virgil gives a bare account of the one moment in salvation history to which he was ever made privy. The only surprise is that, contrary to what we find in the Gospel of Nicodemus, the harrowing is described by someone who was *not* liberated by Christ. Virgil speaks as one left behind when others were taken up. He addresses himself to Christian history from the far shore of the abyss that separates the damned from those who are at rest in God: "between us and you, there is fixed a great chaos: so that they who would come from hence to you, cannot, nor from thence come hither" (Luke 16:26).

Joining "us and you" is Adam, whom Virgil rightly claims as "our first parent," and therefore as the common forefather of humanity. But from this common ancestry he and his companions inherit only original sin. Otherwise, they have no spiritual kinship with the people of Hebrew Scripture; they do not share the circumcision given to Abraham, or the covenant handed down to Moses, or the messianic expectation made known in the preaching of the prophets. Virgil can recite the essential Old Testament names and offer the appropriate epithets—"Moses, obedient giver of laws, Abraham the patriarch and David the king." In so doing, he can also point to the six ages of world history, as Augustine had calculated it, stretching from Adam in the beginning to Christ "in the fullness of time."[2] But neither this roster of biblical figures nor the time line on which they are arranged is rel-

---

1. This might well have been the place to mention Cato, who would have been "old" in Limbo's condition at the moment of Christ's descent, and who must have been among the "many others" Christ made blessed on that occasion. In the opening canto of *Purgatorio*, in fact, Virgil recognizes that Cato "at the last day" will be resurrected in a glorified body and therefore be among the blessed: "la vesta ch'al gran dì sarà sì chiara" (v. 75). What Virgil does not understand is that neither Cato's Roman antiquity nor his former residency in Limbo make a lasting bond between him and any of the pagans who remain there, not even his former wife, Marcia. Of her Cato tells Virgil, "Or che di là dal mal fiume dimora, / più muover non mi può, per quella legge / che fatta fu quando me n'usci' fora" ("Now that she dwells beyond the evil stream no more may she move me, by the law which was made when I came forth from there," vv. 88–90).

2. The commentary tradition has long noted that Virgil's listing of Old Testament exempla follows Augustine's division of world history into six ages, found in his explication of Ps. 92:1: "For the first period as the first day, was from Adam until Noah: the second, as the second day, from Noah unto Abraham: the third, as the third day, from Abraham unto David: the fourth, as the fourth day, from David unto the removal to Babylon: the fifth period, as the fifth day, from the removal to Babylon unto the preaching of John. The sixth day beginneth from the preaching of John, and lasteth unto the end: and after the end of the sixth day, we shall reach our rest. The sixth day, therefore, is even now passing." *Exposition on the Book of the Psalms*, in *SL*, 1st ser., 8: 457, trans. A. Cleveland Coxe.

evant to his pagan circle. Nor are the Old Testament souls he names here anywhere to be found on Limbo's "enameled green." In contrast to Homer, Horace, Socrates, and Plato—the spirits seen walking decorously, speaking seldom but with great authority—none of the biblical figures Virgil mentions are any longer in hell. His scriptural roll call only serves to draw attention to their current absence.

Everything in this brief recollection heightens the poignancy of Virgil as a figure who stands outside looking in, like Moses on the edge of a Promised Land he would never enter. As a result, instead of the sense of jubilation, almost of comic relief, that so frequently characterizes the harrowing of hell in Christian tradition, Virgil's spare narrative of the event is suffused with a quiet sense of tragedy.[3] In the very place where patriarchs once rejoiced to behold their salvation, we find the bewildered sadness of someone who lived and died just before the "fullness of time."

Virgil's marginality—and the limits of his understanding of the harrowing—are again made apparent in *Inferno* 12.31–45. Standing above a river of blood filled with souls who in life "took to blood and plunder" ("che dier nel sangue e ne l'aver di piglio," v. 105), he catches sight of some rocky debris where once had stood a solid wall. Then he reflects on the event that effectively divides hell's sense of time into a before and an after:

> Or vo' che sappi che l'altra fïata
>   ch'i' discesi qua giù nel basso inferno,
>   questa roccia non era ancor cascata.
> Ma certo poco pria, se ben discerno,
>   che venisse colui che la gran preda
>   levò a Dite del cerchio superno,
> da tutte parti l'alta valle feda
>   tremò sì ch'i' pensai che l'universo
>   sentisse amor, per lo qual è chi creda
> più volte il mondo in caòsso converso;
>   e in quel punto questa vecchia roccia,
>   qui e altrove, tal fece riverso.
>   (*Inf.* 12.34–45)

Here Virgil reveals what the crucifixion's earthquake felt like inside hell, when all the foundations shook within the "deep foul valley." It was a moment when "the universe felt love" ("l'universo /

3. This reversal is central to Iannucci's reading of *Inf.* 4: "The structure of medieval depictions of Limbo is comic. So profoundly entrenched was the association between the redemption and the harrowing in the mind of medieval man that it was well nigh impossible to conceive of Limbo in any other terms. Only a man like Dante, who possessed a sense of tragedy as well as comedy, a humanistic sympathy for pagan culture, and, most of all, a broad vision of history which set the sacred and profane side by side, could overturn this structure." "Limbo," pp. 104–5.

sentisse amor," vv. 41–42).[4] But again his comprehension of this truth is only partial, and owes everything to Empedocles' philosophy rather than to any Christian notion of a universe governed by love. The "amor" he speaks of is part of an Empedoclean cycle of love and hate, order and chaos that occurs endlessly at random and to no particular purpose. Within such a scheme, birth and death have no inherent theological value, no "reason." All is simply, as Aquinas noted, a matter of chance: "[Empedocles] said nothing more than that it was naturally disposed to be so" ("nisi quia sic aptum natum est esse").[5] True, Virgil is not entirely identified with this position; it is only "as some believe" ("per lo qual è chi creda," v. 42). Nonetheless, his appeal to Empedocles' undirected ebb and flow suggests the limits of his understanding of the Christ event.[6] Virgil is able to entertain the possibility that in one moment the universe was shaken by love, but he does not see reality as grounded in that mystery, or know the Incarnation of Christ as the unique turning point in history. He felt hell tremble, and saw a "Mighty One" despoil the inferno of its booty; he still does not, however, comprehend what actually happened "in quel punto" (v. 44).

Virgil's personal reminiscences of the harrowing in *Inferno* 4 and 12 are occasions when he remembers how once he stood on the threshold of Christian revelation but could not cross over—the unique moment when he *almost* entered another spiritual world. But it is not only through these personal recollections that Dante brings the descent of Christ into the *Inferno* or uses the "comedy" of the harrowing to heighten our sense of Virgil's tragic loss. Toward these same ends the harrowing is also reenacted within the narrative, more or less subtly refigured. For instance, as Amilcare Iannucci has argued, Dante forges both a temporal and spatial correspondence between the *descensus Christi* and Beatrice's Good Friday descent to Limbo,

---

4. See Schnapp's discussion of this passage, *Transfiguration of History*, pp. 22–23, as well as the wider consideration offered by his chapter "History in the Grip of Mars," pp. 14–35.
5. In his note to *Inf.* 12.42, Singleton suggests that Dante is following Thomas Aquinas in his exposition of Aristotle's *Metaphysics* (*Exp. Metaphys.*, bk. 3, lect. 2, n. 478): "For Empedocles said that there exists in the world a certain alternation of hate and friendship, in such a way that at one time love unites all things and afterward hate separates them. But as to the reason why this alternation takes place, so that at one time hate predominates and at another time love, he said nothing more than that it was naturally disposed to be so [*ut quodam tempore dominaretur odium, et alio tempore amor, nullam aliam dicebat, nisi quia sic aptum natum est esse*]." See Giorgio Stabile, "Empedocle," in *ED*, 2: 666–67.
6. In *Purg.* 3.34–45, Virgil contrasts the condition of those who have faith in the Trinity and in the Incarnation of Christ (i.e., in "the infinite course taken by One Substance in Three Persons," the need for "Mary to give birth"), with those who desire fruitlessly, and in that way experience eternal grief. He says that he is speaking of "Aristotle and of Plato and of many others," no doubt including himself in that latter group of "molt' altri."

the event that initiates Dante's liberation from the spiritual hold of the "selva oscura" and ultimately brings him to the City of God.[7] Each canticle offers, in fact, a reprise of her visitation to the underworld: it is mentioned by Virgil in the flashback of *Inferno* 2.52–120; by Beatrice in her reproof to Dante in *Purgatorio* 30.136–45; and then by Dante himself in the very last words he addresses to her, recalling how concern for his salvation impelled his lady momentarily to exchange heaven for hell:

> O donna in cui la mia speranza vige,
> e che soffristi per la mia salute
> in inferno lasciar le tue vestige . . .
> (*Par.* 31.79–81)

(O lady, in whom my hope is strong, and who for my salvation did endure to leave in Hell your footprints . . .)

By "harrowing" Dante, Beatrice also liberates Virgil, enabling him to travel away from Limbo as far as the Garden of Eden atop Mount Purgatory. But for Virgil, the exit is only temporary, his deliverance but a matter of a few days in eternity. After this respite he must once again return to a place "non tristo di martìri, / ma di tenebre solo, ove i lamenti / non suonan come guai, ma son sospiri" ("not sad with torments, but with darkness only, where the lamentations sound not as wailings, but as sighs," *Purg.* 7.28–30). In the end, the gates of hell prevail against him.

* * *

BIBLIOGRAPHY

Allevi, F. *Con Dante e la Sibilla ed altri dagl'antichi al volgare*. Milan: Edizioni Scientifico-Letteraire, 1965.

Botterill, Steven. *Dante and the Mystical Tradition: St. Bernard of Clairvaux in the "Commedia"*. Cambridge: Cambridge University Press, 1994.

Chaine, J. "Descente du Christ aux enfers." In *Dictionnaire de la Bible, Supplement*. Ed. F. Vigouroux, vol. 2, cols. 395–431. Paris: Letouzey, 1934.

Comparetti, Domenico. *Vergil in the Middle Ages*. Trans. E. F. M. Benecke. Princeton: Princeton University Press, 1997.

D'Ancona, Alessandro. *Origini del teatro italiano*. 2 vols. Turin: Loescher, 1891.

---

7. Iannucci makes a careful correlation between Christ's descent into hell and that of Beatrice, first in "Limbo," pp. 95–97 (esp. p. 95 n. 45), and then in a related essay, "La discesa di Beatrice," in *Forma*, pp. 53–81.

Demus, Otto. *The Mosaic Decoration of San Marco in Venice*, ed. Herbert L. Kessler. Chicago: University of Chicago Press, 1988.

Durling, Robert M., ed. *The "Divine Comedy" of Dante Alighieri*. Trans. R. Durling; ann. Ronald L. Martinez. Oxford: Oxford University Press, 1996.

Foster, Kenlem. *The Two Dantes*. Berkeley: University of California Press, 1977.

Harrent, S. "Infidèles (salut de)." In *Dictionnaire de théologie catholique*. Ed. A. Vacart, E. Mangerot, and E. Amann; 15 vols. in 20. Paris: Letouzey, 1908–50.

Hollander, Robert. *Il Virgilio Dantisco: Tragedia della "Commedia."* Florence: Olschki, 1983.

Iannucci, Amilcare. "Limbo: The Emptiness of Time." *Studi Danteschi* 52 (1979–80): 69–128.

Kartsonis, Anna D. *Anastasis: The Making of an Image*. Princeton: Princeton University Press, 1986.

Kelly, Henry A. *Tragedy and Comedy from Dante to Pseudo-Dante*. Berkeley: University of California Press, 1993.

Kolve, V. A. *The Play Called "Corpus Christi."* Stanford: Stanford University Press, 1966.

Mac Culloch, J. A. *The Harrowing of Hell*. Edinburgh: T. and T. Clark, 1920.

Manzoni, Francesco. "Suggio di un nuovo commento alle *Commedia*: Il canto IV dell' *Inferno*." *Studi Danteschi* 42 (1965): 29–206.

Mésoniat, C. *Poetica Theologia: La "Lucula noctis" di G. Dominici e le dispute letterarie tra '300 e '400*. Rome: Edizione di Storia e Letteratura, 1984.

Miller, David L. *Hells and Holy Ghosts: A Theopoetics of Christian Belief*. Nashville: Abingdon, 1989.

Monnier, Jean. *La descente aux enfers: Étude de pensée religeuse d'art et de la littérature*. Paris: Librairie Fischbacher, 1904.

Montanari, Fausto. "Limbo." In *Enciclopedia dantesca*. Ed. Giorgio Petrocchi, 5 vols. Rome: Enciclopedia italiana, 1970–.

Padsan, Giorgio. *Il pio Ema e l'empio Ulisse*. Ravenna: Longo: 1977.

Paparelli, Gioacchino. *Ideologia e poesia di Dante*. Florence: Olschki, 1975.

Quinn, J. D. "Descent of Christ into Hell." In New Catholic Encyclopedia, vol. 4, 788–89.

Schaff, Philip. *The Creeds of Christendom, with a History and Critical Notes*. 6th ed., 3 vols. Grand Rapids, MI: Baker Book House, 1983.

Schnapp, Jeffrey. *The Transfiguration of History at the Center of Dante's "Paradise."* Princeton: Princeton University Press, 1986.

Singleton, Charles S. *The Divine Comedy*. Trans. and comm. Charles Singleton. Princeton: Princeton University Press, 1970–75.

Turner, Ralph V. "Descendit ad inferos: Medieval views on Christ's
Descent into Hell and The Salvation of the Ancient Just." *Journal
of The History of Ideas* 27 (1966): 173–94.

Young, Karl. *The Drama of the Medieval Church, vol. 1*. Oxford:
Clarendon, 1933.

TEODOLINDA BAROLINI

Transition: How Cantos Begin and End[†]

Canto beginnings are divided by Ettore Paratore into those where
the connection to the preceding canto is firm ("inizi di salda connes-
sione," of which he posits sixteen in the *Inferno*, ten in the *Purgato-
rio*, and eight in the *Paradiso*), and those where the connection is
looser ("di connessione più lassa").[1] Concentrating on the *Inferno*,
he subdivides beginnings that maintain a firm connection into two
types: (1) those in which the beginning marks the addition of some-
thing new; (2) those in which the previous ending is completed or
reiterated without the introduction of a new event. Although I did
not model my analysis on Paratore's, having preferred to categorize
canto endings rather than canto beginnings (closure seemed some-
what more palpable and quantifiable than incipience), his emphasis
on the introduction of the new coincides with my approach, and his
overall findings, with respect to the slackening of the *Commedia*'s
transitions as the poem proceeds, are fully endorsed by my own.

The difference between canticles is highlighted by such an exercise.
Once again, the *Inferno* is the "crowded" canticle, the one for which
the basic division I apply to canto endings—between transition and
lack of transition—is most useful but also most in need of complica-
tion and subdivision. With respect to the *Purgatorio* and *Paradiso*, my
findings are offered more for the sake of comparison than because I
find them entirely satisfactory. Here the distinction between transition
and nontransition is less workable, since the transitions of these can-
ticles are frequently so diffuse that it is difficult to pinpoint them with

---

† From *The Undivine Comedy*. Copyright © 1992 by Princeton University Press. Reprinted
by permission of Princeton University Press.
1. See the opening pages of "Analisi 'retorica' del canto di Pier della Vigna," *Studi dan-
teschi* 42 (1965): 281–336. Unfortunately, although Paratore writes of "quella nuova tec-
nica di connessione più lassa, a onda più lenta e più larga, che contraddistingue la
maggioranza dei canti del *Paradiso*" (282), he does not give us his data for *Purgatorio* and
Paradiso, so that we do not know, for instance, which are the *Purgatorio*'s ten "inizi di
salda connessione." Guglielmo Gorni discusses the sources of the *Commedia*'s incipits in
"La teoria del 'cominciamento,'" *Il nodo della lingua e il verbo d'amore* (Florence:
Olschki, 1981), 143–86, as well as offering an "Indice alfabetico dei capoversi dei canti
della *Commedia*."

any precision; as a result, my decisions to classify an ending as transitional or not may seem increasingly subjective and arbitrary.

This inquiry ultimately serves to address the concept of the canto, which it probes by investigating the canto's boundaries. What is a canto? How does it function? Why does Dante choose to invent the division into cantos, rather than divide his poem into long books of the sort Vergil uses in the *Aeneid*? Conceptually, I believe that the choice of the canto is connected to Dante's obsession with the new; the division into cantos renders the spiraling rhythm of new dawns and new dusks, the incessant new beginnings and endings that punctuate the line of becoming. Formally, I believe that the roots of the canto are to be sought in Dante's vernacular apprenticeship. A long canzone is roughly the length of a canto (Dante's longest canzone is "Doglia mi reca," which at 158 lines is longer than most cantos).[2]

In the *Inferno* we note how frequently canto endings coincide with changes of locale, with literal forward movement, and we note that such correspondence occurs less frequently as the poem proceeds (which is one of the reasons that it becomes progressively more difficult to assess whether a canto ending is transitional or not). As the canto's boundaries coincide less and less with clear-cut fictive and/or geographical boundaries, the question of precisely what a canto serves to delimit becomes, if anything, more intriguing. Indeed, the lack of coincidence between literal transition and textual transition causes us to wonder about the nature of transition itself. What features must be present for a transition to occur? What principles are at work in the *Paradiso*, where canto endings never coincide with literal movement, and where canto beginnings are so spectacularly rhetorical?[3] I have not undertaken to answer such questions (to which I was alerted by the surprising complexities of this little undertaking) but merely to put in front of the reader some data that might provide a useful starting point for further investigation.

A canto ending may, moreover, mark the ending of a narrative segment without registering a sense of an ending; in other words, we may know with hindsight that a canto ending corresponds to the

---

2. In *Dante's Poets: Textuality and Truth in the "Comedy"* (Princeton, N.J.: Princeton University Press, 1984), 107–8, I touch on canzone length in Dante, Arnaut, and Guittone, noting that the *Commedia* is "the equivalent of many canzoni stitched together." Gorni makes a similar point: "Non mi pare che . . . si sia mai guardato ai canti della *Commedia* come a un insieme di cento canzoni, fornite di altrettanti incipit" (164).

3. For the reader's information, literal forward (or upward) movement in the *Paradiso* occurs at the following points: transition to the moon in *Par.* 2.25; transition to Mercury in *Par.* 5.93; transition to Venus in *Par.* 8.13; transition to the sun in *Par.* 10.34; transition to Mars in *Par.* 14.83; transition to Jupiter in *Par.* 18.61; transition to Saturn in *Par.* 21.13; transition to the fixed stars in *Par.* 22.111; transition to the primum mobile in *Par.* 27.99; transition to the empyrean in *Par.* 30.38. These passages are in themselves worthy of study, for the ways in which their rhetoric both accomplishes and masks the necessary transition.

end of a geographical region, but not realize this as we read the canto ending itself. (Such unregistered transitions become frequent in the *Paradiso*, but there is a case in the *Inferno* as well.) In these instances I have classified the canto ending as nontransitional, since it is the explicit registering of transition in the closing verses, the active pressing into service of the formal delimiter, that I have taken as my guideline. Thus, as I indicate in the following tables, there are cantos that, according to Wilkins, "end with the ending of the account of a particular region,"[4] but whose endings I nonetheless consider nontransitional, because there is no way to tell as we read the canto ending that a transition is about to occur.

INFERNO ENDINGS

Transition

PURE FORWARD MOTION

Inf. 1. "Allor si mosse, e io li tenni dietro": the model of a pure forward motion ending.

Inf. 2. "intrai per lo cammino alto e silvestro": although "intrai" indicates entry into the new, this still seems categorizable as a "Pure Forward Motion" ending in that it does not really register the presence of the new.

Inf. 10. Transition begins in verse 133, "Appresso mosse a man sinistra il piede," concluding in the canto's final verse "che 'nfin là sù facea spiacer suo lezzo" (136); although, as Wilkins notes, the travelers do not leave the sixth circle, they certainly move forward.

Inf. 11. The transition is marked by Vergil (rather than by the narrator) in four verses, beginning "Ma seguimi oramai che 'l gir mi piace" (112) and concluding "e 'l balzo via là oltra si dismonta" (115).

Inf. 14. The transition is again marked by Vergil in four verses: "Omai è tempo da scostarsi / dal bosco; fa che di retro a me vegne: / li margini fan via, che non son arsi, / e sopra loro ogne vapor si spegne" (139–42).

Inf. 20. "Sì mi parlava, e andavamo introcque."

Inf. 21. Forward motion with the devils as escort, beginning "Per l'argine sinistro volta dienno" (136), and concluding "ed elli avea del cul fatto trombetta" (139).

Inf. 22. "E noi lasciammo lor così 'mpacciati."

Inf. 23. "ond'io da li 'ncarcati mi parti / dietro a le poste de le care piante."

---

4. See "Cantos, Regions and Transitions in the *Divine Comedy*," *The Invention of the Sonnet and Other Studies in Italian Literature* (Rome: Edizioni di Storia e Letteratura, 1959), 103–10.

ENTRY INTO THE NEW/TRANSITION ACCOMPLISHED

Inf. 4. "E vegno in parte ove non è che luca": the model for this category.

Inf. 6. The quasi-formulaic nature of these endings is well demonstrated by canto 6's four-verse finale, which is echoed in canto 7: "Noi aggirammo a tondo quella strada, / parlando più assai ch'i' non ridico; / venimmo al punto dove si digrada: / quivi trovammo Pluto, il gran nemico.

Inf. 7. Compare this ending to that of canto 6: "Così girammo de la lorda pozza / grand'arco, tra la ripa secca e 'l mézzo, / con li occhi vòlti a chi del fango ingozza. / Venimmo al piè d'una torre al da sezzo."

Inf. 9. "passammo tra i martìri e li alti spaldi": the last verse (133) concretizes the transition registered earlier ("e noi movemmo i piedi inver' la terra" [104]).

[*Inf.* 17. Entry into the new is accomplished in verse 133, "così ne puose al fondo Gerïone," but transition is delayed by Geryon's departure; see listings under "Transition Initiated" below.]

Inf. 19. "Indi un altro vallon mi fu scoperto."

Inf. 27. Transition begins in verse 133, "Noi passamm' oltre," concluding "a quei che scommettendo acquistan carco" (136).

[*Inf.* 31. Like *Inf.* 17: Entry into the new is accomplished, "Ma lievemente al fondo che divora / Lucifero con Giuda, ci sposò" (142–43), but delayed by the giant's departure; see "Transition Initiated" below.]

Inf. 34. "E quindi uscimmo a riveder le stelle."

TRANSITION INITIATED BUT DELAYED

1. Closure is signified (twice by the pilgrim's fall), but transition is delayed until the next canto.

Inf. 3. "e caddi come l'uom cui sonno piglia."

Inf. 5. "E caddi come corpo morto cade."

Inf. 18. "E quinci sian le nostre viste sazie": Vergil's concluding emphasis on satiety suggests the transition to come.

2. Withdrawal of a companion; transition is postponed until after the departure.

Inf. 12. "Poi si rivolse e ripassossi 'l guazzo": Nesso's retreat.

Inf. 15. Brunetto's departure begins "Poi si rivolse" in verse 121 (like Nesso's at the end of canto 12), and concludes "e parve di costoro / quelli che vince, non colui che perde" (123–24).

Inf. 17. "si dileguò come da corda cocca": Geryon departs after depositing the travelers in the eighth circle.

Inf. 31. "e come albero in nave si levò": Antaeus's departure is evoked in a simile, as is Geryon's.

No Transition

Inf. 8. "tal che per lui ne fia la terra aperta": the canto ends *in medias res*, with Vergil's words announcing the arrival of the *messo*, who does not appear until midway through canto 9.

Inf. 13. "Io fei gibetto a me de le mie case": the canto ends with the words of the Florentine suicide. Although transition occurs in the fourth verse of the next canto (same pattern as canto 6), there is no hint of it at the end of canto 13 (unless in a sense of closure conveyed by what is said; see canto 26 below).

Inf. 16. "che 'n sù si stende e da piè si rattrappa": the canto ends *in medias res*, with the arrival of Geryon, described in the following canto.

Inf. 24. "E detto l'ho perché doler ti debbia!": the canto ends with Vanni Fucci's prophecy; his story continues into the next canto.

Inf. 25. "l'altr'era quel che tu, Gaville, piagni": the canto ends with the narrator's identification of one of the thieves, without a clear transition.

Inf. 26. "infin che 'l mar fu sovra noi richiuso": the canto ends within Ulysses' narrative, without a clear transition, but with perhaps a sense of closure conveyed by the verse's content.

Inf. 28. "Così s'osserva in me lo contrapasso": the canto ends with the words of Bertran de Born.

Inf. 29. "com'io fui di natura buona scimia": the canto ends with the words of Capocchio.

Inf. 30. "ché voler ciò udire è bassa voglia": the canto ends with Vergil's rebuke.

Inf. 32. "se quella con ch'io parlo non si secca": the canto ends *in medias res*, with the pilgrim's query to Ugolino, whose story resumes in the following canto.

Inf. 33. "e in corpo par vivo ancor di sopra": the canto ends with the narrator's comment on what he has seen. Although, as Wilkins notes, this is a canto whose ending coincides with the ending of a geographical region, Dante offers no narrative signpost to this effect, thus anticipating a procedure that he will frequently adopt in the *Paradiso*.

In Sum

Twenty-three endings register transition of some kind or another; these transitions become more complex and less straightforward as the canticle progresses. Of the eleven canto endings that do not register clear transition, a concentration is found in the last third of the canticle.

The question of nontransitional endings would be further complicated if one were to take into account the sense conveyed by spoken discourse; thus, the final verse of canto 26, spoken by Ulysses, con-

‚s a sense of closure that is, for instance, less palpable in the final verse of canto 29, spoken by Capocchio. The same could be observed, perhaps, of the final verses of cantos 24 and 28, spoken by Vanni Fucci and Bertran de Born respectively, as compared to the final verse of canto 32, spoken by the pilgrim and dedicated to bridging the gap between cantos 32 and 33. I raise this matter in order to alert the reader to my inconsistency. * * *

GIUSEPPE MAZZOTTA

Canto XXVI—Ulysses:
Persuasion versus Prophecy†

Canto XXVI tells mainly the story of Ulysses' tragic shipwreck as the hero ventures beyond the pillars of Hercules into uncharted seas. It is also true, however, that, perhaps more than any other canto in the *Comedy,* Canto XXVI cannot really be read separately from the others. In fact, so fascinated are the pilgrim and the poet by their encounter with the Greek hero that it will play a pivotal role in the dramatic economy of the entire poem: at key points of the narrative—from Dante's initial hesitation and fear lest his own journey prove *folle* ("wild and empty" [II, 35] to his final survey, from the heaven of the fixed stars, of "Ulysses' mad course" (*Il varco / folle d'Ulisse* [*Paradiso* XXVII, 82–83; my emphasis])—Dante anticipates or recalls Ulysses' epic journey as the steady point of reference enabling the pilgrim to define the inner sense of his own quest.

Taken by itself, the story of Ulysses as told in *Inferno* XXVI is the focus of a number of Dante's intellectual and moral concerns, and it affords the poet a pretext to reflect on his own poetic strategies and poetic language. That Dante's imaginative stakes are high in this canto is exemplified by his own bold, radical revision of the essential structure of the classical version of the myth. He leaves no doubt that the mythic discourse of antiquity is to be read from a perspective that is alien to it.

According to the ancient tradition, which finds its crystallization in Homer's two epics, Ulysses is the supremely crafty hero who leaves his native Ithaca to fight for ten years in the Trojan war and, after the destruction of Troy, returns to Ithaca. Neoplatonic com-

---

† From *Lectura Dantis: Inferno*, trans. Allen Mandelbaum and Anthony Oldcorn, ed. Allen Mandelbaum, Anthony Oldcorn, and Charles Ross. Copyright © 1998 by the University of California Press. Reprinted by permission of University of California Press.

mentators interpreted Ulysses' journey away from Ithaca and back to Ithaca as a philosophical allegory of the *nostos*, the return of the soul to its place of origin after its descent into the dross of materiality and its subsequent laborious purification from it[1]

In *Inferno* XXVI Dante breaks with this neoplatonic tradition. In Dante's representation Ulysses is no longer a paradigm of the successful philosophical flight of the soul to its divine homeland. Quite to the contrary; although Dante shows Ulysses as he frees himself from the magic lures of Circe and is about to return to Ithaca, Ithaca will no longer be Ulysses' final destination. Neither love for his wife and his family nor duty to his country can conquer in him the desire to know in their full range the splendors and miseries of the human experience. By this insistence on the necessity of moving into an unfamiliar, unexplored world, Dante breaks open the closed circle of Greek philosophical thought, replacing it with the conviction that harmonious, rational closures are fictions. Accordingly, Dante shows Ulysses as a visionary who arrives home only to set out again on a mad quest (the operative word is *folle*, 125) into the unknown world, in the tracks of the sun and with a few loyal companions.

Dante's Ulysses moves within this large conceptual framework, but Dante's narrative reinterprets the central assumptions of the myth. There is no return home for Ulysses from his new quest, and his journey into the unknown is a heroic, but ultimately tragic, violation of all boundaries and limits. For all his admiration of Ulysses, Dante exposes the limits of Ulysses' heroic vision. Along with Diomedes, Ulysses is the only epic hero among the fraudulent sinners (on either side of Ulysses are the five contemporary Florentine thieves of Canto XXV and the mercenary *condeottiere* Guido da Montefeltro of Canto XXVII). Thus Dante establishes a dramatic contrast between the grandeur and singularity of the epic hero of antiquity and the petty, provincial, unheroic world of his own time. And yet, beyond the apparent differences of degree and achievement between them, all the sinners, Ulysses included, belong to the same moral area of fraud: Ulysses is really no better and no worse than a common Florentine thief.

Dante's ambivalent sense of the greatness and the limits of Ulysses (and of Greek philosophical discourse in general) is conveyed by a prodigious deployment of rhetorical machinery, at once complex and detailed. He unveils the covert strategies and subtle techniques of rhetorical persuasion, thereby uncovering also the hidden, murky basis of the seemingly luminous Greek *logos*. Rhetoric, in effect, af-

---

1. The neoplatonic interpretation of Ulysses is advanced by John Freccero, *Dante: The Poetics of Conversion* (Cambridge, Mass, 1986), 136–151. Another important perspective on Canto XXVI is that of Bruno Nardi, *Dante e la cultura medievale* (Bari, 1949), 153–164.

fords the context within which Dante represents Ulysses' great claims for himself. It also allows Dante to reflect on the pretensions and possibilities of language to produce or adequately represent reality. From this standpoint, Canto XXVI shows Dante interrogating stylistic levels of representation, and the relation between political rhetoric and prophecy, and the links between rhetoric and ethics. More important, it shows Dante as he comes to terms with his own poetic claims and poetic authority.

The rhetorical substance of the canto comes immediately to the fore. The story it tells is that of a mind-bewitching orator who moves men by the power of his speech to the pursuit of the good and the true. Human beings, Ulysses claims, are not made to live like brutes but to follow virtue and knowledge (118–120). In making this statement, Ulysses casts himself as the rhetorician who fashions moral life: an Orpheus or a civilizing agent who assuages the beast within and sees life as an educational process. Ulysses, in short, embodies the values of Ciceronian rhetoric that reached Dante primarily through a text of political rhetoric composed by one of his ideal teachers: Brunetto Latini's *Retorica*.[2]

For Brunetto, as for Cicero in his *De inventione*, rhetoric is the foundation of history, in the sense that the political order of the city is rooted in the gift of language. Within their humanistic visions, the orator's language is a cohesive force that persuades men to move away from their original bestiality. Both Cicero and Brunetto are aware, to be sure, of the damage eloquent men can cause the state unless they posses wisdom and are moved by ethical ends. There is no doubt that one thematic strain of Canto XXVI focuses precisely on the concerns both Cicero and Brunetto articulate regarding politics and rhetoric.

The canto enacts an extended reflection on the fates of secular cities: Florence, Prato, Thebes, Troy, Rome and the quest for a "new land" (137) constitute the historical points of reference within which rhetoric emerges as a discipline capable of fashioning history. More specifically, the canto's opening lines (1–12) feature Dante's prophecy that the city of Florence will soon reach its apocalyptic end; while in its closing lines (136–142) Ulysses' vision of a new land climaxes in a catastrophe. Dante's understanding of rhetoric shuttles between the promise of a new city and the prophetic announcement of the destruction of the old one.

Furthermore, Dante casts Ulysses—for all his craftiness—as the rhetorician who lacks the attributes of wisdom called for by Cicero

---

2. A more detailed account of the rhetorical substance of the canto is available in Giuseppe Mazzotta, *Dante, Poet of the Desert* (Princeton, 1979), 66–106. Cf. also Giorgio Padoan, "Ulisse *fandi fictor* e le vie della sapienza," *Studi danteschi* 37 (1960): 21–61, reprinted in *Il pio Enea, l'empio Ulisse* (Ravenna, 1977), 170–204.

and Brunetto. Ulysses is shown at Troy as he steals the Palladium (63), the icon of Minerva or the simulacrum of wisdom and, grasping at its *appearance*, undermines his extended claim (98–99) of experience with the world as well as the vices and worth of men. Dante even seems to place Ulysses' experience within an ethical context:

> "When
> I sailed away from Circe, who'd beguiled me
> to stay more than a year there, near Gaeta—
> before Aeneas gave that place a name—
> neither my fondness for my son nor pity
> for my old father nor the love I owed
> Penelope, which would have gladdened her,
> was able to defeat in me the longing
> I had to gain experience of the world
> and of the vices and the worth of men."
>   (90–99)

It has long been acknowledged that Ulysses dramatizes himself in this speech as another Aeneas. As he recounts his departure from Circe at Gaeta he explicitly mentions Aeneas: "before Aeneas gave that place a name" (93). The interpretive twist given by Ulysses to Aeneas's journey is remarkable. The hero's mission to be the carrier of tradition from Troy to Italy emerges as an activity of naming, his history-making a "poetic" mission as he names the island in memory of his dead nurse. Apparently, naming is the process by which man memorializes his world, marks his losses, as the world comes to be history, the place of man's nostalgic recollections. For Ulysses, however, to mention Aeneas's naming of places discloses a further irony: he disguises himself as Aeneas and identifies himself with the latter's *pietas*. Yet the priority he claims over the Trojan hero (*before* Aeneas, he says) reveals the illusoriness of the identification and underscores Ulysses' own failure to name. The canto, in general, exemplifies Ulysses' excessive rehearsal of geographic toponyms (103, 104, 110, 111), but as he comes closer to the unknown world, that world remains unknown to him, and his language collapses into merely temporal specifications.

But Ulysses' speech goes on to evoke the line of domestic affections that should have kept him at home but in which he cannot acquiesce. The lexicon is charged with ethical resonances—"fondness for my son" (94), "pity / for my old father" (94–95), "the love I owed / Penelope" (95–96)—that invoke public duty and private responsibilities in order to justify the supposedly higher moral imperatives of the journey. Yet Ulysses' journey is not an ethical quest nor is it a case of rhetoric joined to ethics. A sharper intimation of the divorce between rhetoric and ethics in the canto occurs when Ulysses defines the object of his quest as worth and knowledge (*virtute e canoscenza* [120]).

In effect, by having Ulysses equate virtue and knowledge as if they were the same thing, Dante retrieves the fundamental error of Socratic thought: the illusory belief that to know a virtue is tantamount to having that virtue. More than that, by making virtue the object of rhetoric Dante lays open the intrinsic error of rhetorical language: virtue is contained within the statement but its fulfillment lies outside that statement. In Canto XXVI Ulysses attempts to travel the distance that separates words from facts and to fill those words with reality.

The speech in which Ulysses narrates his experience forces on us Dante's sense of language. Ulysses evokes his journey between the shores of Spain and Africa, his trespassing beyond the pillars of Hercules, and then he recalls the "brief address" (*orazion picciola* [122]) he made to his companions:

> " 'Brothers,' I said, 'o you, who having crossed
> a hundred thousand dangers, reach the west,
> to this brief waking-time that still is left
>   unto your senses, you must not deny
> experience of that which lies beyond
> the sun, and of the world that is unpeopled.
>   Consider well the seed that gave you birth:
> you were not made to live your lives as brutes,
> but to be followers of worth and knowledge.'
>   I spurred my comrades with this brief address
> to meet the journey with such eagerness
> that I could hardly, then, have held them back;
>   and having turned our stern toward morning, we
> made wings out of our oars in a wild flight
> and always gained upon our left-hand side.
>   At night I now could see the other pole
> and all its stars; the star of ours had fallen
> and never rose above the plain of the ocean.
>   Five times the light beneath the moon had been
> rekindled, and, as many times, was spent,
> since that hard passage faced our first attempt,
>   when there before us rose a mountain, dark
> because of distance, and it seemed to me
> the highest mountain I had ever seen.
>   And we were glad, but this soon turned to sorrow,
> for out of that new land a whirlwind rose
> and hammered at our ship, against her bow."
>
> (112–138)

Ulysses' brief address is set within the imagined area beyond the known world, an open and unbounded region. The strategy of isolating language in a spatial vacuum discloses its peculiar feature. There is no necessary correspondence between *res* and *signa*, between things and their signs, nor is a sign the receptacle of a reality. Tragedy creeps into Ulysses' epic quest as he ventures from the known world to the forbidden land he approaches but never reaches. The vision of the mountain dark because of distance heralds a tragic denouement, couched in a stylized rhetorical definition of tragedy: "And we were glad, but this soon turned to sorrow." The line translates *verbatim* the formula "tragic song begins in joy and ends in grief."

The tragic reversal that shatters any illusion of a possible *return* of the hero is the truth underlying Ulysses' rhetorical seduction of his companions. The phrase "brief address" (*orazion picciola*) affects modesty; the apostrophe "Brothers" (*O frati*) draws Ulysses' companions into a state of complicity and flatters their worth by making them akin to the hero. The speech, moreover, is marked by hyperbole that throws into relief the grandeur of the quest and by a *captatio benevolentiae* that celebrates their common past achievements. The frequent and conspicuous enjambment (112–113; 114–115, etc.) and the cosmic dimensions of the directions (*giunti a l'occidente* ["reach the west"]; *di retro al sol, del mondo sanza gente* ["beyond the sun, and of the world that is unpeopled"]) stress the epic expansiveness of the experience. The recurrent sounds and alliterative modulations of the Italian text (*cento* [hundred, 112], *giunti* [reach, 113], *occidente* [west, 113], *sensi* [senses, 115], *rimanente* [lies beyond, 115], *esperïenza* [experience, 116], *mondo sanza gente* [world unpeopled, 117]—as well as *cento . . . occidente, sensi . . . sanza, rimanente . . . mondo*) create the persuasive harmonies of Ulysses' speech: the repetition of the same sound compels the rhythm to return on itself and creates an incantatory, suspended effect.

It is within this general belief of Ulysses that his language can bend the wills of his listeners and move them to action (as in fact it does) that we appreciate Dante's ironic stance regarding his hero's claims. One such irony is clearly visible in the choice of Virgil as the privileged interlocutor of Ulysses. Virgil provides the clue to the irony that will invest both himself and Ulysses when he insists that he—the author of "noble lines" (82), that is, Virgil's epic—should be speaking to Ulysses, the epic hero. The implication of the detail is clear: formal propriety ought to be observed, the epic poet is the proper interlocutor of the epic hero. Yet, in the canto that follows, Guido da Montefeltro's apostrophe, "O you to whom I turn my voice, / who only now were talking Lombard" (XXVII, 19–20), retrospectively undercuts the possibility of rigidly formalized levels of representation. In point of fact, Dante exemplifies and simultaneously abrogates the juxtaposition of the lofty language of the epic with the realities of the vernacular dialect. Separations of style, which classical rhetoric upholds in the conviction that to every subject matter corresponds a fixed level of style, is an empty fiction in Dante's Christian world.

The irony does not invest Ulysses alone: it also invests Virgil and his claim, made earlier in the poem, that he has written an *alta . . . tragedìa* (XX, 113). That claim, it may be remembered, was advanced in the context of the canto of the soothsayers, the sinners who perverted prophecy. The more immediate context was a debate on the origin of the name of Mantua, a city founded, as Virgil now affirms, by Manto, daughter of the Theban Tiresias. This statement contradicts the one Virgil himself made in the *Aeneid*. The privileged epic of Rome in other words contains errors that need correction, and by this token Virgil places in question his own authority.

For Dante, Ulysses' error far exceeds Virgil's. Whereas Virgil corrects himself, Ulysses is blind to the fact that he does not control language but is, to all intents and purposes, controlled by it. The detail of the tongues of fire that envelop and conceal the sinners and by means of which Ulysses tells his story (42, 48, 87 ff.) draws attention to Dante's ironic representation of the Greek hero. The tongue of fire in which Ulysses is enveloped is to be primarily construed as an instance of Dante's *contrapasso*. Ulysses had a fiery inward longing (*ardore* [97]), from which his desire to know originates. Now, ironically, he is *inside* the flame, trapped by it. There can be no doubt, however, that this tongue of fire has a number of other crucial resonances.

Commentators have traditionally stressed that the flames Dante sees in Canto XXVI are a pointed parody of the descent of the pentecostal tongues of fire upon Christ's disciples, and that Ulysses' sin of evil counseling is primarily a sin against the good counsel of the Holy Spirit. It might be added in this context that the production of sound through the metaphor of the wind (88) ironically recalls Acts 2:2 in which the descent of the Spirit is described as occurring in tongues of flames and to the sound of a mighty wind. The allusion to the inspirational *afflatus* prepares a sustained reflection on Ulysses' language and its relation to the prophetic word. It prepares, more important, a reflection on Dante's own poetic language, wavering as it does between prophecy and rhetoric.

The opposition between prophecy and rhetoric is underscored by the implied antithesis between Elijah and Ulysses obliquely announced at lines 34–39. As the pilgrim approaches the flame-wrapped sinners he recalls Elisha watching Elijah, the prophet who was borne up by a whirlwind in a chariot of fire. The terms of the comparison are such that Elijah is presented as the antitype of Ulysses, while Dante is like Elisha. These thematic contrasts are concerned with the contrast between spurious and genuine prophecy. This contrast is made more cogent by the fact that the tongue of fire is an image that describes both the gift of prophecy and the rhetorical craft. In Acts (2:30), for instance, the cloven tongues of fire designate the apostles' prophetic language. At the same time fire is the adornment of rhetoric in Alan of Lille's *Anticlaudianus*. In Canto XXVI the tongue of fire holds the rhetorician Ulysses as it did the prophet Elijah.

The double exegesis of the flame in terms of rhetorical and prophetic allusions dramatizes Dante's sense of the proximity of prophecy and rhetoric. It would seem that Ulysses' rhetoric, then, is the degradation of prophecy, or that prophecy is the norm from which Dante denounces the lies of rhetoric. Nonetheless, it is clear that Dante is also interested in showing the kinship between them, their dangerous sameness. Why would this be the case?

The opening lines of Canto XXVI feature Dante's own prophetic wrath against the city of Florence:

> Be joyous, Florence, you are great indeed,
> for over sea and land you beat your wings;
> through every part of Hell your name extends!
> Among the thieves I found five citizens
> of yours—and such, that shame has taken me;
> with them, you can ascend to no high honor.
> But if the dreams dreamt close to dawn are true,
> then little time will pass before you feel
> what Prato and the others crave for you.
>
> (1–9)

Dante's poetic outburst is followed (23 ff.) by a moment of self-reflexiveness on the part of the poet: threatened by the danger of his own poetic imagination, Dante is intent on bridling his creative powers: he will curb his talent (*'ngegno* in line 21 translates the Latin *ingenium*, the word for the poetic faculty) lest it run unguided by virtue. The willed curbing of his talent or *ingegno* betrays Dante's suspicion that his own poetic undertaking may bear a likeness to Ulysses' rhetorical venture. Once again, as in Canto II, Dante fears that he may be reenacting Ulysses' mad quest.

But Dante's self-reflexiveness and self-government also reflect the prophetic outburst he voices against the city of Florence. At stake in the act of curbing his *ingegno*, then, there is Dante's consciousness that his voice constantly balances the claim of speaking with fiery prophetic self-assurance and the awareness that his prophecy is a contrived rhetorical act. Doubt accompanies the poet throughout his journey and it is the sign of the authenticity of his claims.

We can understand, finally, why the figure of Ulysses exerts such

a singular fascination on Dante and why the memory of Ulysses
haunts the pilgrim long after he has moved beyond Canto XXVI. In
spite of his fascination, however, Dante draws a sharp distinction
between himself and Ulysses. Ulysses' journey ends in tragedy, and
his deception ends up being a self-deception, a way of succumbing
to the literalness of his language, of being trapped by his own
tongue, of himself believing in promises on which he cannot deliver.
Ironically, this craftsman of persuasion is spellbound by his own
song, the way he is caught within the tongue of fire, the way he was
spellbound by the song of the sirens (cf. *Purg.* XIX, 22).

Dante's posture in Canto XXVI is neither that of Ulysses nor that
of Elijah. He forces on us another term of comparison for himself
when he evokes the story of Elisha watching Elijah's ascent (34 ff.).
Like Elisha, the witness to the ascent of Elijah, Dante now comes
through as the fascinated spectator of mighty events and horrors.
But, as every reader of the *Divine Comedy* knows, this self-
contained spectatorial posture is not real. Unlike Ulysses and like
Elijah, Dante will ascend beyond the sun and will see God face to
face. And he will be gifted with the virtue the Greek hero lacked: the
hard virtue that will allow him to make his way back from the lofti-
est journey ever taken.

ROBERT HOLLANDER

Inferno XXXIII, 37–74: Ugolino's Importunity†

This brief treatment of Ugolino's sin against God and against his
own children assumes that the reader neither cares for nor requires
presentation of the ample catalogue of opinions that variously put
forward the nobility, humanity, and pathos conveyed by the an-
guished monologue of the traitorous count.[1] Since the classic state-
ment by Francesco De Sanctis, readers of the episode have been
mainly (and correctly) convinced that its central emotional experi-
ence involves what De Sanctis calls "the drama of paternity."[2] My
task here is not to debate the degree of sympathy that Dante ex-

---

† From *Speculum* 59 (1984): 549–55. Copyright © 1984 by *Speculum*. Reprinted by per-
mission of *Speculum*. Notes have been edited.

1. For such a review (with bibliography), see Umberto Bosco, "Il conte Ugolino nella 'Com-
media,'" in *Enciclopedia dantesca*, 5 (Rome, 1976), 799. See also the "Appendice bibli-
ografica" in *La divina commedia* [*Inf.* and *Purg.*], *con i commenti di T. Casini/S. A. Barbi
e di A. Momigliano*, Introduzione e aggiornamento bibliografico-critico di Francesco Maz-
zoni (Florence, 1972–73).
2. Francesco De Sanctis, "L'Ugolino di Dante," in his *Opere*, 5 (Turin, 1967), 681–704
(originally published in 1869).

pected his reader to feel for Ugolino, despite his palpable sins, but to demonstrate that the text demands from us a pivotal awareness of the literary resonance of the words which he speaks. Once we become aware of the source of his plangent narrative, which contains more words for sadness and weeping than any other in the *Commedia*,[3] we may begin to understand that the "drama" of Ugolino's paternity should enlist our sympathy less than our dispassionate analysis of his response to the pleas of his children, no matter how intensely moved we may be by their and their father's torment.

Ugolino's Displacement of Significance. As John Freccero puts the case, Ugolino's "tragedy is a failure of interpretation, as well as an inability to accept the suffering of his own children."[4] Opposing De Sanctis's sympathetic reading, Freccero continues in a similar vein: Ugolino "is condemned by Dante not only as a traitor but also for his inability to grasp the spiritual meaning in the letter of his children's words" (p. 58). While I would unhesitatingly align myself with the broad contours of Freccero's treatment of the "drama of interpretation" which we should allow ourselves to encounter in the pathetic scene, my own sense of its crucial particulars is quite different from his.[5] I would like to begin by noticing three brief passages in the first and introductory half of Ugolino's narrative (vv. 4–36).

(1) The sinner interrupts his eternal repast to address Dante with a reprise of Aeneas's words to Dido, "Infandum, regina, iubes renovare dolorem" (*Aeneid* 2.3): "Tu vuo' ch'io rinovelli / disperato dolor . . ." (*Inferno* XXXIII, 4–5).[6] The citation has become something of a commonplace in the commentaries (it was perhaps first advanced by Bernardino Daniello),[7] frequently accompanied by the observation that Dante had already cited the passage in Francesca's words to Paolo in *Inferno* V.[8] If many agree that Dante is citing the same Virgilian passage that he had previously borrowed to such

3. In *Inf.* XXXIII, 5–75, the words *piangere, lagrimare, doglia, dolere, dolore*, and *doloroso* occur a total of thirteen times. On this point see Robert Hollander, *Allegory in Dante's Commedia* (Princeton, 1969), p. 306. And see Vittorio Russo, "Il 'dolore' del conte Ugolino," in his *Sussidi di esegesi dantesca* (Naples, 1966), pp. 147–81, for an earlier appreciation of the large presence of *dolore* and its derivatives here.

4. John Freccero, "Bestial Sign and Bread of Angels (*Inferno* 32–33)," *Yale Italian Studies* 1 (1977), 53–66; quotation on p. 57.

5. Freccero's article is rich in suggestions. Since I will not discuss his several visitations of biblical text in his consideration of Ugolino's literalistic misinterpretation of the final events in his and his children's lives, I would like here to acknowledge my admiration for many of Freccero's insights.

6. The text of the *Commedia* reproduced here is that of Giorgio Petrocchi, *La commedia secondo l'antica vulgata* (Milan, 1966–67). The Vulgate is cited from *Biblia Sacra iuxta Vulgatam Clementinam*, ed. A. Colunga and L. Turrado, 4th ed. (Madrid, 1965); translations are supplied by the Authorized King James Version, ed. E. S. English and M. B. Bower (New York, 1948).

7. *Dante con l'espositione di M. Bernard[in]o Daniello da Lucca sopra la sua Comedia dell'Inferno, del Purgatorio & del Paradiso . . .* (Venice, 1568).

8. See *Inf.* V, 121–26. For my own treatment of the parallels between the opening of *Aeneid* 2 and this passage see *Allegory in Dante's Commedia*, pp. 108–11.

telling effect, it has apparently not occurred to any to wonder why he should have chosen to repeat the quotation. In my opinion it is a signal to us to read Ugolino's self-exculpating narrative just as we have gradually learned to read Francesca's similarly distorted and self-serving version of her history. For while both may give something like veridical accounts of events, neither gives anything like a valid rendering of the spiritual significance of their narratives. By having Ugolino begin by quoting the same Virgilian text which we have already heard from the lips of Francesca, Dante alerts us to the fact that we should distance ourselves from this last "sympathetic sinner" in Hell, just as we have had to do from all those who seek to capture our good will in their effort to achieve in the favoring pages of the poet what they had failed to do in God's "Book of Life."[9] Since Dante should probably be understood to repeat himself only with a purpose, I suggest that this second citation of *Aeneid* 2.3 serves to remind us that Ugolino, like Francesca, desires Dante's (and through him our) sympathy but in fact does not deserve to have it. We've heard that one before.

(2) Ugolino's description of his narrative purpose is as follows:

> però quel che non puoi avere inteso,
> cioè come la morte mia fu cruda,
> udirai, e saprai s'e' m'ha offeso.
>
> (19–21)

After he has finished his importuning of Dante's pity, we may observe that he has succeeded only insofar as the poet will condemn Pisa for putting Ugolino's sons to such punishment (85–87: "Che se 'l conte Ugolino aveva voce / d'aver tradita te de le castella / non dovei tu i figliuoi porre a tal croce"). Dante's reaction—feeling pity for the children—should remind us that what Ugolino seeks is pity for himself, a desire to which Dante at no point accedes. The first-person pronominal adjective and pronoun in this passage are crucially revelatory of Ugolino's self-centered paternity; he is a Pisan Lear whose children are primarily important to him as extensions of himself; where Dante will eventually have pity for the children, their father's pity is centered on himself.[1]

(3) Ugolino's interpretation of his dream (vv. 25–36) is absolutely

---

9. See Hollander, *Allegory in Dante's Commedia*, pp. 301–7, for an earlier version of this understanding of the ironic distance which Dante either expected or hoped for in his reader. The phrase "Book of Life" here refers not to Apocalypse 20.12 but to Dante's gnomic references to his poem's resemblance to God's "history of the future" in *Par.* XIX, 112–14, and in *Inf.* XXIX, 57. The last passage is the subject of my study, "Dante's 'Book of the Dead': A Note on *Inferno* XXIX, 57," *Studi danteschi* 54 (1982), 31–51.

1. It is perhaps for such reasons that Dante, if he was aware (as he most likely was) of the relatively advanced ages of the two sons and of the fact that the two younger ones were in fact grandchildren, treats all four as though they were Ugolino's own young offspring.

accurate. In Macrobian terms the dream of the hunting hounds and the torn wolf and whelps has the characteristics both of a *visio* and of a *somnium*. That is, it is a clear revealing of events to come, while it also requires a kind of allegorical (or at least metonymic) substitution (*lupo* and *lupicini* = Ugolino and the children; *cagne* = Pisan followers of Ruggieri). Ugolino's interpretation is literally correct: Ruggieri and his allies will put him and his offspring to death. Yet, and as Marianne Shapiro has shown, the very words with which he describes the temporal power of the archbishop, "maestro e donno" (28), point to the need for a spiritual interpretation of the dream.[2] For in John 13.13 Christ speaks to his disciples in the following words: "Vos vocatis me Magister et Domine, et bene dicitis: sum etenim" ("Ye call me Master and Lord: and ye say well; for so I am"). The implicit point made by Ugolino's unconscious (and Dante's conscious) citation of Scripture is that Ugolino should have been aware of the significant distinction between the absolute and sinful temporal power seized by his enemy and the absolute and benevolent spiritual power that resides in the Lord.[3] Perhaps nothing is more disturbing in Ugolino's heart-breaking narrative of woe than the absence of any reference to the spiritual food which might have saved, if not the speaker, then at least his children.

Bread, Stone, and the Importunate Friend. Inferno XXXIII and XXXIV are well considered companion pieces. In the first we find Dante's portrait of an archetypal failed father gnawing on the nape of his enemy, in the last the archetypal rebellious son chewing on three kindred spirits who also rebelled against God. Even this inverse parallelism should have warned those who would read Ugolino in the sympathetic light so often and warmly proposed for him against such a response. Further, and to cite the words of Marianne Shapiro, "The problem of Scriptural language in *Inferno* XXXIII is one with which any interpretation of the *Comedy* must come to grips."[4] While my own sense of what biblical text is most centrally

2. "Addendum: Christological Language in *Inferno* XXXIII," *Dante Studies* 94 (1976), 142.
3. A precisely similar ironic displacement is to be found in Pier della Vigna's oath in *Inf.* XIII, 74–75: ". . . vi giuro che già mai non ruppi fede / al mio segnor. . . ." Whether one adheres to the interpretation that Pier is lying (see Anthony K. Cassell's chapter on Pier in his forthcoming *A Fearful Mode of Justice*) or that he possibly tells the truth about his temporal loyalties (see William A. Stephany, "Pier della Vigna's Self-Fulfilling Prophecies: The 'Eulogy' of Frederick II and 'Inferno' 13," *Traditio* 38 [1982], 193–212), the most important realization available to the reader is that by committing suicide, as a new Judas (a brilliant interpretation put forward by Cassell, expanding on a near-perception of Pietro di Dante, in *Petri Allegherii super Dantis ipsius genitoris Comoediam commentarium, nunc in primum in lucem editum* [written in 1340], ed. Vincenzo Nannucci [Florence, 1845]), he *has* broken faith with his true Lord.
4. "Addendum," p. 141. Bosco, "Il conte Ugolino," p. 799a, presents an excellent summary of the classical texts (Statius, Virgil, Ovid) that are apparent behind moments in the scene. However, while he states that "L'episodio è fitto di reminiscenze classiche e bibliche," he does not refer to any of the latter. See also Umberto Bosco and Giovanni Reggio, eds., *La divina commedia* (Florence, 1979), p. 487.

necessary to a keener understanding of the Ugolino episode is not the same as hers, I am in agreement with this statement of principle.

If John 13.13 offers us a text which affords a better interpretation of Ugolino's dream, Luke 11.11—if it has not heretofore been observed as doing so—probably more than any other text can help us to penetrate to the center of Ugolino's flawed paternity. Five years ago, in a class devoted to this canto, a Princeton undergraduate was reminded of the Gospel passage: "Quis autem ex vobis patrem petit panem, numquid lapidem dabit illi?" ("If a son shall ask bread of any of you that is a father, will he give him a stone?").[5]

That Scripture is a continuing source for Dante's poem has never been in doubt.[6] Not only is there more reference in the *Commedia* to the Bible than to any other text, but Dante's covert insistence on the kinship of his work to God's volume is now increasingly recognized as an essential strategy of his design for the *Commedia*.[7] In this instance the striking appositeness of a phrase from the New Testament should send us to that text in order to discover whether what we are dealing with is a gesture toward a significant field of meaning or a highly detailed reminiscence of a specific passage. While Matthew's version of the pertinent material sounds promising enough, it is only in Luke's account (11.5–13) that we find the parable of the importunate friend ("Parabola de amico importuno"):

> And he said unto them, Which of you shall have a friend, and shall go into him at midnight, and say unto him, Friend, lend me three loaves [*tres panes*];
>
> For a friend of mine in his journey is come to me, and I have nothing to set before him?
>
> And he from within shall answer and say, Trouble me not: the door [*ostium*] is now shut, and my children are with me in bed [*pueri mei mecum sunt in cubili*]; I cannot rise and give thee.

5. The student was Cristina Kraus (Princeton '80) in the autumn of 1979. Neither her remark nor the only printed reference which I know to the passage's relevance to *Inf.* XXXIII is specifically directed to Luke (rather than to Matthew 7.7–11). See James Nohrnberg, "The *Inferno*," in *Homer to Brecht: The European Epic and Dramatic Traditions*, ed. M. Seidel and E. Mendelson (New Haven, 1977), p. 99: ". . . the pitying father who nonetheless suffers the death of a son, like Abraham [see Freccero, "Bestial Sign," pp. 57–58]; or the father who will not give his son a stone when he is asked for bread, in the example of fatherly love offered by Jesus." I am indebted to Rachel Jacoff for reminding me of this passage.

6. On this subject Edward Moore, *Studies in Dante: First Series* (Oxford, 1969), originally published in 1896, remains an essential text. Vincent Truijen, "La Sacra Scrittura," in *Enciclopedia dantesca*, 5:94–99, offers more recent discussion and bibliography.

7. For my own * * * work on this topic see "Dante *Theologus-Poeta*," *Dante Studies* 94 (1976), 91–136, reprinted in my *Studies in Dante* (Ravenna, 1980), with bibliographical indications. And for my view of the counterbalanced hidden polemic against his classical sources, Virgil in particular, see *Il Virgilio dantesco: Tragedia nella "Commedia"* (Florence, 1983).

[And if the other shall persevere in his knocking,] I say unto you, Though he will not rise and give him, because he is his friend, yet because of his importunity he will rise and give him as many as he needeth.

And I say unto you, Ask, and it shall be given you; seek, and ye shall find; knock, and it shall be opened unto you.

For every one that asketh receiveth; and he that seeketh findeth; and to him that knocketh it shall be opened.

If a son shall ask bread of any of you that is a father, will he give him a stone? or if he ask a fish, will he for a fish give him a serpent?

Or if he shall ask an egg, will he offer him a scorpion?

If ye then, being evil, know how to give good gifts unto your children: how much more shall your heavenly Father give the Holy Spirit to them that ask him?

It seems beyond the needs of evidence to do more than set these verses next to the text of *Inferno* XXXIII, 37–74, in order to establish that no other text was more in Dante's mind as he composed this one.[8] The reversals of the parable are as telling as the verbal reminiscences. Jesus imagines a man who, being a baker, is uniquely capable of making such provision. Selfishly, the baker, locked up in his house for the night with his children, at first refuses to grant his friend's request, but is finally won over by the importunate friend's continued knocking. In Dante's recasting of the parable, Ugolino's children are the importuners, seeking bread (v. 39: "dimandar del pane"); the friend who knocks at the door becomes the unseen but heard agents of Ruggieri, nailing shut the door of the tower; and Ugolino, importuned by his own children, remains throughout as stone-hearted as was the baker when his bread was first sought (v. 49: "sì dentro impetrai").[9] In such ways, then, do Ugolino and the children play out the roles of importuned and importuner. But Ugolino, unlike even that evil man in the parable who eventually relents and provides, offers his own children only his stony silence. At the same time, as teller of this disastrous and eventually self-incriminating narrative, it is *he* who importunes Dante. The man who would not weep

8. Other passages in Luke's eleventh chapter have long been recognized behind Dante's words: 11.17 in *De monarchia* 1.5.8; 11.27 in *Inf.* VIII, 45. See Moore, *Studies*, p. 330. The same sources are also listed by Truijen, "La Sacra Scrittura," p. 97.

9. For Ugolino's petrifaction Niccolò Tommaseo. *La divina commedia con le note di Niccolò Tommaseo e introduzione di Umberto Cosmo*, reprint of 2nd (definitive) edition of 1865 (Turin, 1927–34), followed by G. B. Giuliani, "Dante spiegato con Dante: L'episodio del Conte Ugolino," *Jahrbuch der Deutschen Dante-Gesellschaft* 4 (1877), 239–71, cites 1 Samuel 25.37: ". . . et emortuum est cor eius intrinsecus, et factus est quasi lapis" ("his heart died within him, and he became as a stone"; the heart is Nabal's, reacting to Abigail's news of the might of David). While Dante's words may indeed reflect these words, I would argue that he had superadded them to those concerning the stone that he knew from Luke.

with and for his children (vv. 49, 52) is now angered because Dante
will not weep for him (vv. 40–42).[1] Powerless to give the children
the bread which they crave, he did have the ability to offer them the
spiritual bread which satisfies a more significant hunger. Therein
lies his failure as a father.[2]

In the Boethian prison house, Ugolino fails to acknowledge the
only antidote to his and his children's spiritual malaise held out to
him by Scripture. He could have, for instance, told the children that
he was grieved to have been the unwilling cause of their torment (he
rather pointedly does not do so). He also could have urged them to
believe that their suffering would be only momentary, that they
should hope for a better end, one that might be achieved if only they
would pray. All that would have been necessary would have been that
they speak the words of the Lord's Prayer together. Indeed, chapter
11 of Luke's gospel begins with the account of Jesus's gift, when he
was asked by one of the disciples to teach them how to pray, of that
prayer ("oratio dominica" is the rubric for verses 1–4 in the Vulgate),
the text of which Dante will reproduce in his own vernacular version
at *Purgatorio* XI, 13–24.[3] Thus does the entire context of Luke 11 fit
Ugolino's narrative, imposing a suppressed marginal commentary
upon utterance which might otherwise seem more noble than self-
serving and wrongly aimed.

The week of Ugolino's suffering, as Guido da Pisa (1327) was the
first to point out, reminds us that Macrobius, in the *Somnium*, had
said that man could live only seven days without food.[4] Ugolino's

1. While post-romantic readings, like Momigliano's (*La divina commedia commentata da At-
tilio Momigliano* [Florence, 1946–51]), confer a tragic dignity on Ugolino's failure to speak
a word (vv. 48, 52, 64, 65; we hear only the voices of the children, importuning: vv. 39, 51,
61–63, 69; he cries out for them only *after* they are dead: v. 74), it is more reasonable to be-
lieve that his silence is the result of his misplaced Stoic reserve, itself, in a Christian con-
text, the very sign of despair. For Chaucer's apparently similar view, see below, n. 4.
2. For a similar view see Stefano Ignudi, *La divina commedia, commento del P. Stefano
Ignudi dei frati minori conventuali* (Padua, 1948–59), on verse 72: ". . . non una parola
da padre cristiano che pensa all'anima sua e dei figliuoli, per perdonare e consegnarsi in
pace nelle mani di Dio!"
3. I am indebted to an anonymous reviewer for *Speculum* for this suggestion.
4. Alessandro Vellutello, *La commedia di Dante Alighieri con la nova espositione di Alessan-
dro Vellutello* (Venice, 1544), objects that one can live eight, not seven, days without
nourishment. In either case Ugolino may be understood to have died after a week. The
detail both helps to confirm the debated textual variant "due di" (in place of the "tre di"
found in some manuscripts; see discussion in Petrocchi) and to undercut the infrequent
but spectacular belief that he ate the children. As a number of commentators have ob-
served, he has promised to tell us the manner of his death (v. 20) and thus recounts, one
day at a time, the five days of his children's *digiuno* and then the final two days of his
own. For an earlier and similar appreciation see F. Betti, *Comento della Divina comme-
dia di Ippioflauto Tediscen* [pseudonym of F. Betti], *pubblicato per cura dei suoi amici F.
Barotta e F. S. Cianci* (Vasto, 1873[–78]): "parmi di aver decisa la cosa . . . che il Conte
Ugolino avea promesso di narrare, come egli era morto; . . . per cui rimarrebbe una in-
soffribile ed imperdonabile lacuna, se avendo raccontata la morte de' proprii figli, lasci-
asse indecisa la sua. . . ." Thus the text requires that we understand that his narrative
concludes with his death by starvation. Cf. the paraphrase of verse 75 in Mazzoni: "Fi-
nalmente mi venne dal lento esaurimento per digiuno . . . quella liberazione che il do-

seven days in the unmaking parallel God's seven days of creation. Like the importuned and eventual provider in Christ's parable, he lies behind a locked door with his children. Unlike him, he will not be moved by entreaty. His posthumous importuning of Dante did not move our poet, at least not on his behalf. As has so often been the case with regard to other great figures of the *Inferno*, it has been all too successful with the poet's enthusiastic admirers. Luke's words may help to restore the moral ground upon which Ugolino's drama is played out.

---

lore, per atroce che fosse, non riusciva a darmi" (*La comedia di Dante Alighieri annotata nelle sue bellezze e compendiata nel racconto dell'intero poema da Guido Mazzoni* [Florence, 1924]). Or consider Geoffrey Chaucer's still more pithy epitome (Monk's Tale, 2455): "Hymself, despeired, eek for hunger starf." The history of this *crux interpretum* is presented in my "Ugolino's Supposed Cannibalism: A Bibliographical Note" (*Quaderni d'Italianistica*, 1985), one burden of which is to demonstrate the force of the fact that the first five hundred years of response of the verse either ignored or rejected the singular "cannibalistic" interpretation (that of Jacopo della Lana) found in the early commentators—which is currentlyl enjoying a "renaissance" on both sides of the Atlantic.

Dante Alighieri: A Chronology

1265	Dante is born under the sign of Gemini (middle of May—middle of June).
1283	Dante becomes of age.
1284	Marries Gemma Donati, who bears him three children (Jacopo, Pietro, and Antonia), and perhaps a fourth (Giovanni).
1289	June 11, the Battle of Campaldino fought between Arezzo and Florence, in which Dante takes part.
1290	June 8, the death of Beatrice. Dante begins his philosophical studies.
1290–93	The *Vita Nova* is written.
1294	Spring, Dante meets Charles Martel in Florence.
1295	Dante enters political life.
1300	Jubilee year proclaimed by Boniface VIII. Easter of this year is the fictive date of the journey in the poem. Dante is prior for two months (June 15–August 15).
1301	The approach of Charles of Valois. Dante sent on an embassy to Boniface VIII.
1302	January 27, the first sentence of exile against Dante reaches him in Siena. He is sentenced to death March 10. Birth of Francesco Petrarca.
1305	Clement is the new pope. Papacy moves to Avignon.
1304–7	*De vulgari eloquentia* and the *Convivio* are written.
1308	Henry of Luxembourg crowned emperor.
1310	The descent of Henry VII into Italy. Dante's epistle to him. Starts to write *De monarchia*.
1313	Death of Henry VII near Siena. Birth of Giovanni Boccaccio.
1314	The *Inferno* is completed. Dante writes letter to Italian cardinals.
1315	Florence offers to repeal his sentence on condition that he acknowledge his error, but Dante refuses. He moves to the household of Cangrande della Scala in Verona.
1319	Dante is in Ravenna. *Purgatorio* is completed. Correspondence with the Humanist Giovanni del Virgilio.

1320   Dante lectures in Ravenna on *De Quaestio de aqua et terra*.

1321   *Paradiso* is completed. September 13 or 14, death of Dante in Ravenna.

Selected Bibliography

• indicates works included or excerpted in this Norton Critical Edition

Auerbach, Eric. *Dante: Poet of the Secular World*, trans. Ralph Manheim. Chicago: The University of Chicago Press, 1961.

Barbi, Michele. *Life of Dante*. Trans. and ed. Paul G. Ruggiers. Berkeley: University of California Press, 1954.

• Barolini, Teodolinda. *The Undivine Comedy*. Princeton: Princeton University Press, 1992.

Bergin, Thomas G. *From Time to Eternity: Essays on Dante's "Divine Comedy."* New Haven and London: Yale University Press, 1967.

Boyde, Patrick. *Perception and Passion in Dante's Comedy*. Cambridge: Cambridge University Press, 1993.

Cachey, Theodore J. Jr. *Dante Now; Current Trends in Dante Studies*. Notre Dame: University of Notre Dame Press, 1995.

Charity, A. C. *Events and Their Afterlife: The Dialectics of Christian Typology in the Bible and Dante*. Cambridge: Cambridge University Press, 1966.

• Cogan, Marc. *Design in the Wax: The Structure of the Divine Comedy and Its Meaning*. South Bend: The University of Notre Dame Press, 1999.

• Cornish, Alison. *Reading Dante's Stars*. New Haven: Yale University Press, 2000.

D'Entreves, Alessandro Passerin. *Dante as Political Thinker*. Oxford: Clarendon Press, 1955.

• Durling, Robert M. "Canto X: Farinata and Cavalcante." In *Lectura Dantis: Inferno*, ed. Allen Mandelbaum, Anthony Oldcorn, and Charles Ross. Berkeley: The University of California Press, 1998.

• Freccero, John. "Dante's Prologue Scene." In *Dante Studies* 84 (1966): 1–25.

• ———. *Dante: The Poetics of Conversion*. Ed. Rachel Jacoff. Cambridge, Mass.: Harvard University Press, 1986.

Gilson, Etienne. *Dante the Philosopher*. Trans. David Moore. London © 1948, 1978 by the Pontifical Institute of Mediaeval Studies, Toronto.

Halpern, Daniel, ed. *Dante's Inferno: Translations by 20 Contemporary Poets*. Hopewell, NJ: Ecco Press, 1993.

• Hawkins, Peter S. *Dante's Testaments: Essays in Scriptural Imagination*. Palo Alto: Stanford University Press, 1999.

Hollander, Robert. *Dante: A Life in Works*. New Haven: Yale University Press, 2001.

• ———. "Inferno XXXIII, 37–74: Ugolino's Importunity." *Speculum* 59 (1984): 549–55.

Jacoff, Rachel, ed. *The Cambridge Companion to Dante*. Cambridge: Cambridge University Press, 1993.

Keen, Maurice. *A History of Medieval Europe*. London: Routledge & Kegan Paul, 1968.

Kleiner, John. *Mapping the Underworld; Daring and Error in Dante's 'Comedy'*. Stanford: Stanford University Press, 1994.

• Mazzotta, Giuseppe. *Dante, Poet of the Desert*. Princeton: Princeton University Press, 1979.

• ———. "Canto XXVI: Ulysses: Persuasion Versus Prophecy." In *Lectura Dantis: Inferno*, trans. Allen Mandelbaum and Anthony Oldcorn, ed. Allen Mandelbaum, Anthony Oldcorn, and Charles Ross. Berkeley: The University of California Press, 1998.

• Poggioli, Renato. "Tragedy or Romance? A Reading of the Paolo and Francesca Episode in Dante's *Inferno*." *PMLA* (1957): 313–58.

Raffa, Guy P. *Divine Dialectic: Dante's Incarnational Poetry*. Toronto: University of Toronto Press, 2000.

Reade, W. H. V. *The Moral System of Dante's Hell*. Oxford: Clarendon Press, 1909.

• Spitzer, Leo. "Speech and Language in Inferno XIII." *Italica* 19.3 (Sept. 1942): 81–104.

Toynbee, Paget. *A Dictionary of Proper Names and Notable Matters in the Works of Dante*. Oxford: Clarendon Press, 1898.